Highland Swordsmanship
Techniques of the Scottish Swordmasters

Edited By
Mark Rector

Chivalry Bookshelf

HIGHLAND SWORDSMANSHIP
Techniques of the Scottish Swordmasters

being a COMPENDIUM of
the redoubtable SOLDIER, fencing master, and prize fighter
Donald McBane's

"Expert Sword-Man's Companion"

AND

Late Deputy-Governour of Edinburgh Castle & celebrated SWORD-MAN
Sir William Hope's

"New Method of Fencing"

& to the both of which is added the fine ESSAY
"Gaelic Swordsmanship"
by Mr. Paul Wagner

Including PREFATORY remarks by

Maestro Paul Macdonald, IMAF, BFHS, &c., Edinburgh

Mr. Milo Thurston, Linacre School of Defence, Oxford

& the Editor, Mr. Mark Rector, Chicago Swordplay Guild

HIGHLAND SWORDSMANSHIP
Techniques of the Scottish Swordmasters

Published by

Chivalry Bookshelf

http://www.chivalrybookshelf.com
(866)-268-1495

© 2001 Mark Rector; Contributions copy right
original authors: Paul Wagner, Paul Macdonald,
Milo Thurston

Design by Brian R. Price

Printed in the United States of America

Publisher: Chivalry Bookshelf, Union City, CA.

ISBN: 1-891-448-15-3

SUBJECTS
Fencing | Martial Arts | History--Scotland

Hope, Sir William (1660 - 1724)
McBane, Donald (1664 - c.1728)
    Rector, Mark, ed. (1961 -)

CONTRIBUTORS
    Wagner, Paul (1967 -)
    Macdonald, Paul (1972 -)
    Thurston, Milo (1971 -)

Table of Contents

Acknowledgements

The editor wishes to thank the following people, for their assistance in the production of this book:

Nicole Allen, J. Christoph Amberger, Ashley Bishop, Richard Brown, Diarmid Campbell, Michael Carleton, the Chicago Swordplay Guild, James FitzGerald, Roman Guelfi-Gibbs, Steve Hick, Marty Higginbotham, Ophelia Julien, Nick King, Adrian Ko, Sue Lasser, Linacre School of Defence, Paul Macdonald, Marilyn Markle, Patrick McKee, Greg Mele, Tim Olivas, David Peck, Brian R. Price, Stuart Pyhrr (Curator, Arms and Armor, Metropolitan Museum of Art), Allen Reed, Dale Seago, Bjorn Skaptason, Jill Sultz, Milo Thurston, Paul Wagner, Adam Williams.

Photo Credits (McBane smallsword, spadroon & pistol duel)
Photography by Marty Higginbotham. The fencers are Ashley Bishop and Mark Rector. Costumes provided by Nicole Allen; smallsword provided by W. Kevin Dougherty; pistol provided by Allen Reed; and spadroons provided by Adam Williams and Popinjay's Armory.

Additional Photo Credits (McBane broad- or backsword)
Photography by Brian R. Price. Fencers are Dale Seago, Patrick McKee & Roman Guelfi-Gibbs of Bunjinkan San Francisco; Richard Brown & Diarmid Campbell of the Highland Mercenaries, a performance group based in Northern California. Weapons provided by Adrian Ko of Sword Forum International (SFI), the Highland Mercenaries, Dale Seago and Brian R. Price.

Illustration Credits (Gaelic Swordsmanship)
Special thanks to Paul Wagner for providing a surfeit of illustrations drawn from unavailable manuscripts used in his article, in McBane and in Hope. Paul's enthusiasm for this project in the final hours helped to give it shape and additional substance.

Contributors

Mark Rector, this book's editor and visionary, is an actor, playwright, stage combatant and fight choreographer, as well as a student and practitioner of historical swordplay. He is the translator and editor of *Medieval Combat* (Greenhill, 2000), Hans Talhoffer's *Fechtbüch* ("Fight Book") of 1467. Mr. Rector is a founder of the Chicago Swordplay Guild and an Associate Director of the Swordplay Symposium International, the most influential international organization supporting the study of historical swordsmanship.

Paul Wagner is a founding member of the Stoccata School of Defence in Sydney, Australia, where he holds the rank of Provost and teaches courses in single sword according to George Silver, sword-and-buckler according to I.33, English quarterstaff, and English longsword. Coming from a background in re-enactment, Paul was President of the Macquarie University Dark Ages Society for five years while studying for a Ph.D., and has several books due for release in the near future, including "Pictish Warrior AD 297 – 841" for Osprey Publishing and "Master of Defence: The Works of George Silver" for Paladin Press.

Paul Macdonald was born in the West Highland village of Glenuig, Moidart, Scotland. With a keen interest in historical swordsmanship, he founded the Dawn Duellists Society in 1994 and became a fencing instructor at Napier University. After extensive study and training in sword making, Maestro Macdonald established *Macdonald Armoury* in 1998. His work as a swordsmith is well regarded for its high level of quality and historical accuracy. Maestro Macdonald is a founder and Director of the British Federation for Historical Swordplay, a member of the Association for Historical Fencing, a founder of the International Master of Arms Federation, a recognized Master-at-Arms by the Federazione Italiana Scherma Antica e Storica, and a member of the Advisory Council of Swordplay Symposium International.

Milo Thurston is the founder of the Linacre School of Defence. The LSD is located in Oxford, England, and provides instruction in the methods of Sir William Hope and other masters whose philosophy and methods are compatible. His previous martial arts experience includes judo, sport and classical fencing. He is currently pursuing a research career in the biological sciences.

Performers
&
Portrayers

Editor Mark Rector (left)
& Ashley Bishop.

California Players (from left): Diarmid Campbell of the *Highland Mercenaries;* Roman Guelfi-Gibbs of Bunjin-kan San Francisco; Dale Seago, Lead Instructor for Bunjin-kan SF; Patrick McKee Bunjin-kan SF; Richard Brown, also of *Highland Mercenaries.*

Introduction

Mark Rector

Och hey! for the splendor of tartans!
And hey for the dirk and the targe!
The race that was as the Spartans
Shall return again to the charge![1]

Scotland! The name conjures images in our minds of kilted clansmen, Highland games, fine whiskey, the minstrelsy of Robert Burns, and lone pipers on misty moors. It is a land as complex as the pattern of a Highland tartan. Scotland has had many cultures overlaid one upon another, interwoven into a unique whole. Unknown and forgotten broch builders, mythologized Picts, Gaels, Britons, Norsemen, and Normans, all shed their blood in conquest and defense of the lands north of Hadrian's wall.

The Highland Scot has long been celebrated in story and song for his courage and fearsomeness in battle, and his skill as a swordsman in personal combat. History and literature ring with the blare of bagpipes and the wild, skirling "Highland Charge;" the romantic imaginings of Sir Walter Scott; Rob Roy MacGregor, whether cutthroat and cattle reiver or gallant hero; the Bonnie Dundee; Gillies MacBean defending the wall at Culloden; and the valiant Blue Bonnets of the '15 and the '45. Theirs is the story of broadswords and targes, wielded in bare-legged charges by men who knew neither doubt nor fear. The threat of an incursion of Scots was enough to throw the English countryside into a panic. Fighting beneath banners proclaiming *Veritas Vincit*, "Truth Prevails," Scots armies were able to overcome incredible odds to achieve one astonishing victory after another. Whether considered a dangerous and ignorant savage or nature's nobleman, the Highland Scot enjoys a proud tradition of excellence in the fighting arts.

The Lowland Scots have their own complex past, sometimes glorious, often tragic, embodied in memories of the Canmore Kings, the heroes of the ancient poem *Gododdin*, Robert the Bruce,

the battlefields of Stirling and Flodden, rampaging Border reivers, and the Stuart monarchy. Ruled by a nobility swinging between the influence of England and France, tied by blood to their fierce brethren, the Lowlanders walked a tenuous line between two worlds. Doomed to be "wild Scots" to the English, and effete townsmen or English lackeys to the Highlander, they were a blending of both lands into a singular people, required for their survival to achieve skill in arms.

It is no surprise then that two of the most important books on swordsmanship written in the early years of the 18th century should come out of Scotland. Nor that their character should combine Highland, English, and Continental methods. Donald McBane's *Expert Sword-Man's Companion* (1728), and Sir William Hope's *New, Short, and Easy Method of Fencing* (1707) are remarkable in so many ways. Paired together, they form a superb, complementary expression of swordsmanship north of the Solway Firth in the 1700's. Both were written by men with years of practical experience with the sword. Both attempt to bring together the various theories of swordplay into a unified method that may be applied to all weapons, edged or pointed. Each book wrestles with the technical and ethical realities of defending one's life and honor with a sword.

Sir William Hope, Baronet Balcomie and Deputy Governor of Edinburgh Castle, was closely related to the Highland clan Keith, and dedicated his book to their chief, his uncle, the Earl Marischal of Scotland.[2] He had thirty years of experience as a swords-

---

[1] *The Return*, by Pittendrigh MacGillivray. From the *Oxford Book of Scottish Verse*, Clarendon Press, Oxford, 1966.

[2] "Amongst the most romantic names in Scottish history is that of Keith, Marischal of Scotland, and a Celtic ancestry is claimed for the race." The Keiths were hereditary Marischals of Scotland since the reign of Malcolm IV (1153-1165). Innes of Learney, 153.

man and Fencing Master, and had written three other books on the subject before he sat down to pen his *New Method*. At the age of forty-seven, Hope had the courage to undertake a thorough revision of his previous work.

> "Being to establish the *Art of Defence*…upon quite another foot and Method than what it hath been formerly; security and safety being my only aim. The reader must not be surprised if in place of a neat and graceful posture…and genteel method of play…he meet only with a good, secure, and homely posture, and a firm and solid defence and pursuit flowing from it."[3]

He was dismayed by the niceties of contemporary "school-play," influenced as it was by the French fencing theory then sweeping across Europe, which he considered difficult to learn, dangerously insufficient on the field of honor, and worthless in battle. Arising out of a need to find a smallsword counter to the heavy blows of the broadsword, and in order to simplify fencing to its most fundamental essentials, Hope sought a "universal method" for use with the smallsword, spadroon (a light weight "cut-and-thrust" sword), and broadsword. His solution was to discard the traditional French guards in favor of a single defense: the Hanging Guard in Seconde. This natural and all-purpose defense is a variant of the ancient "true guardant" ward,[4] and, along with the "downright blows" he taught should be made from it, links Hope's *New Method* to the long tradition of Highland broadsword and backsword fighting methods.

> "For without all doubt, the *Art of the Back Sword* is the Fountain and Source of all true defence, and that of the Small only a branch proceeding and separate from it."[5]

Hope provides a thorough explanation of his reasons for adopting this guard, answering objections to it and offering the advantages for it. He devotes the entirety of Chapter 4 to defining the fencing terms employed in the book. He gives practical advice on how to select a sword, and tells soldiers the basket-hilted broadsword is the best weapon they can choose for battle. He devotes a good deal of his text to the philosophy and ethics of swordsmanship. And, like McBane, he admonishes his reader to approach personal combat with the sword dispassionately and honorably, with "calmness, vigour, and judgment."

[3] Hope, William, *New, Short, and Easy Method of Fencing*, 1707, p. 101. [All reference for Hope & McBane refer to the present edition]

[4] See Silver, George, *Brief Instructions upon my Paradoxes of Defence*, c. 1605, ed. Matthey, Col. Cyril, 1898, p. 87.

[5] Hope, William, *New, Short, and Easy Method of Fencing*, 1707, p. 125.

Donald McBane could not possibly be more different . He came from a poor family in Inverness, and spent much of his adult life as a common soldier in the Highlands and on the Continent. He achieved a mastery of the sword out of sheer necessity, to preserve his life and livelihood in the rough-and-tumble garrisons of the armies of the time of Queen Anne.

McBane's book is in two parts: *General Directions* on fencing, and *The Remarkable Passages and Actions of the Life of the Author*. His directions on fencing are simple and pragmatic: "For all is fair play whil'st Swords are presented and you're disputing the victory." He learned to fight with a sword in the barracks hall and in the fencing schools of Dublin, but his expertise was refined in the crucible of the duel and while storming French fortresses "sword in hand." He provides easy-to-understand descriptions of the guards, defences, and attacks of the sword; and offers practical lessons and advice.

> "If you are engaged with a *Ruffin* [ruffian], or a stranger, be watchfull that he does not throw his hat, dust, or something else at your face which may blind you, upon which he will take the opportunity to make a home thrust…"[6]

But perhaps the most remarkable aspect of McBane's book is his candid and entertaining autobiography. It is a story that could have been ripped from the pages of Fielding or Defoe, and anticipates Fraser's "Flashman." It is full of humor, bawdry, and insights into the everyday life of a soldier in the service of the Duke of Marlborough.

McBane describes his humble beginnings and the events that led him to a lifetime of soldiering. As a new recruit, he found himself on the receiving end of two devastating Highland charges at the battles of Mulroy and Killiecrankie; served as an infantryman and gunner at Fort William in the Highlands; and fought for eleven hard years as a grenadier with the regiment of Royal Scots in the War of the Spanish Succession in "Holland, Germany, Flanders, and France." When not making war, McBane earned a handsome living as a Fencing Master, gambler, and pimp.

He endured countless wounds with sword, bayonet, and musket ball and was blown up by a grenade at the siege of Liége. In garrison, he was frequently forced to defend his gambling operations and string of prostitutes (his "mistresses") at the point of the sword. Bloodied, beaten, often given up for dead, he always survived.

[6] McBane, Donald, *Expert Sword-Man's Companion*, 1728, p. 59 [present edition].

McBane retired from military service at the age of forty-seven, only to take up the profession of prize fighting in London at a time when such fighting was done with sharp swords rather than bare fists. The diarist Samuel Pepys can take us there:

> "And here I came and saw the first prize I ever saw in my life; and it was between one Mathews, who did beat at all weapons, and one Westwick, who was soundly cut several times both in the head and legs, that he was all over bloody. And other deadly blows they did give and take in very good earnest, till Estwick [sic] was in a most sad pickle. They fought at eight weapons, three boutes at each weapon. It was very well worth seeing, because I did till this day think that it had only been a cheat; but this being upon a private quarrel, they did it in good earnest; and I felt one of their swords and find it to be very little, if at all, blunter on the edge then the common swords are."[7]

By his own account, McBane successfully fought thirty-seven of these contests. His last such fight was at Holyrood House in Edinburgh, when he was an astonishing sixty-two years old.

> *"With thy back to the wall and thy breast to the targe,*
> *Full flashed thy claymore in the face of their charge;*
> *The blood of their boldest that barren turf stain,*
> *But alas! thine is reddest there, Gillies MacBain!"*[8]

Hope and McBane were near contemporaries. Hope was born in 1660, the year of the Stuart restoration, McBane in 1664. The "Glorious Revolution" of 1688 brought the Protestant William III to the English throne, whose draconian rule of Scotland would lead to the massacre at Glencoe and the disastrous Darien trading venture. William and John Churchill, Duke of Marlborough, forged the "Grand Alliance" of European powers aligned against the dynastic ambitions of Louis XIV of France. During the reign of Queen Anne, the last Stuart monarch, the War of the Spanish Succession (1702-1713) would drag all of Europe into the most bloody and savage warfare the world had yet witnessed. In 1707, the year Hope's *New Method* was published, England and Scotland were unified, forming Great Britain. This, and the accession of the Elector of Hanover to the throne as George I, set the stage for the unsuccessful attempt to restore James Edward Stuart in 1715. McBane re-enlisted with the government forces in 1715, serving as a sergeant of dragoons at the battle of Preston. Hope's cousins, the Earl Marischal and the Earl of Kintore, fighting with the Jacobites, would be forced to flee Scotland after the Stuart defeat. The final unsuccessful attempt to restore the Stuart pretender in 1745 culminated in the devastating Jacobite defeat at Culloden.[9] The aftermath of Culloden would prove even more devestating, as, through enforced clearance of the Highlands, bans on the tartan and bagpipe, and fierce proscriptions on owning swords or training household troops, the English made a concerted attempt to destroy the Highland way of life.

The arrangement of *Highland Swordsmanship* is thematic, each element building on the one before it. Paul Wagner's excellent essay, *Gaelic Swordsmanship*, provides a glimpse at the medieval influences on the martial arts of the Highland warrior, and details some of the key sources for reconstructing their swordsmanship. Donald McBane, whose biography begins with his flight from a Highland charge, logically follows next. In the *Expert Sword-Man's Companion* we learn the military broadsword and spadroon method that ultimately supplanted the medieval style of the Highlanders, and receive instruction on fighting with and against the targe, the Lochaber axe, the staff, and the spear. From McBane, we also learn the basic theory and method of the smallsword, the ubiquitous dueling weapon of the 18th century. Finally, Sir William Hope's *New Method of Fencing*, written in reaction to the English, Scottish, and Continental forms of swordsmanship he encountered, unites the arts of the broadsword and smallsword into one "easy" method.

Here then are the fencing books of Sir William Hope and Donald McBane, flip sides of the same Scots coin: the gentleman and the rogue, the Deputy Governor and the common soldier, both of them ardent and devoted Masters of the Sword. Read in conjunction with each other, they provide sound instruction in the realities of practical swordsmanship.

---

[7] Pepys, June 1, 1663, v. 4, 167-8.

[8] Attributed to Byron. McIan, 82.

---

[9] A member of McBane's clan, Gillies MacBean, achieved immortality at Culloden. "Six feet four and a half inches in height, and armed with claymore and target, he was a formidable figure. When the Argyll militia broke down a wall on the right, which enabled the dragoons to attack the flank of the Highland army MacBean set himself at the gap, and cut down man after man as they came through. Thirteen in all, including Lord Robert Ker, had fallen under his strokes, and when the enraged enemy closed round him in numbers, he set his back to the wall and proceeded to sell his life as dearly as possible. An English officer, struck by his heroism, called to the soldiers to 'save that brave man,' but at that moment the heroic Major fell, his thigh bone broken, a dreadful sword cut on his head, and his body pierced with many bayonet wounds." Eyre-Todd, 220-21.

Och, then, for the bonnet and feather!
The Pipe and its vaunting clear:
Och, then, for the glens and the heather!
And all that the Gael holds dear.

The Return. See note 1.

Gaelic Swordsmanship

Paul Wagner

The Scottish Highlanders were one of Europe's last tribal societies, and inherited many customs and institutions virtually unchanged from the ancient Celtic tribes. The sword in particular held a special place in Highland culture, and they were one of history's few primarily sword-armed armies, amassing a remarkable series of victories over conventional troops throughout the 16th, 17th and 18th centuries. While a considerable amount of literature exists on the tactics used by the Gaels, such as the famous "Highland Charge,"[1] Gaelic swordsmanship itself has received little attention and is often dismissed as being "simple" or "crude." However, it could be argued that the secret of the Highlander's military success lay not in the tactics of the clan armies, but at the level of the individual swordsman.

Highland Weaponry

Before the disarming act of 1747, the Highland warrior was one of the most completely armed in Europe. A Highlander's weapons were an essential part of his character. They were worn as a normal part of his attire, and rarely did he venture forth without a range of arms upon his person. In the 18th century it was recorded that;

> "...it is well known that highlanders go about almost constantly armed, partly with a view of being always ready to defend themselves or to attack their enemies, and partly that being accustomed to the instruments of death they may be less apprehensive of them."[2]

The ownership of and proficiency with weapons were part of the duty of every clansman to his chief, and the Highlands could produce a formidably armoury - a roll taken by the Earl of Atholl in 1638 records that 523 men between them owned 448 swords, 3 two-handed swords, 112 guns, 11 pistols, 149 bows, 125 targes, 9 lochaber axes, 2 halberds, 11 breastplates, 8 "headpieces," 2 "steel bonnets," a pair of plate sleeves, and a coat of mail.[3] A number of the clansmen's weapons were unique to the Highlands, such as the all-steel Scottish pistol that made a useful club after it was discharged. Little can be said of the use of such unique arms, except that the techniques would have presumably been somewhat equivalent to those found in other Western European nations for broadly similar weapons.[4]

The dirk, for instance, was a thick-backed single-edged dagger often up to 18 inches long and sometimes held in the left hand in conjunction with the targe. Always held in an overhand grip, it was presumably wielded in much the same way as the long daggers of medieval masters such as Talhoffer and Fiore dei Liberi, taking advantage of the long blade to perform "locking" techniques.[5]

The "Lochaber axe" was another unique weapon, consisting of large cleaver-like blade, often backed by a hook, mounted on a long shaft and usually tipped with a butt spike. Although few existing examples survive on their original shafts, period depictions of the weapons indicate a pole of 8 to 9 feet long, suggesting a mode of use equivalent to that of the Welsh Hook, a similarly long, light polearm, as described by George Silver and Joseph

---

[1] See for example Hill, James Michael, *Celtic Warfare 1595-1763*, 1986, Reid, Stuart, *Highland Clansman 1689-1746*, 1997, and Stevenson, David *Highland Warrior: Alasdair MacColla and the Civil Wars*, 1985.

[2] Logan, James, *The Scottish Gael*, 1831 and Laffin, John, *Scotland the Brave*, 1974.

[3] Wallace, J., *Scottish Swords and Dirks: A reference guide to Scottish Edged Weapons*, 1970.

[4] It has been noted that even between radically different cultures such as Germany and Japan, similar weapons used for similar purposes "resulted in startling parallels in technique between the German and Japanese schools of swordsmanship," (p. 26) and "The differences in technique that do exist are readily explained by the characteristics of the weapon itself, such as the length of blade or the number of edges." (p.41), Galas, S. Matthew, "Kindred Spirits: The Art of the Sword in Germany and Japan", in *Journal of Asian Martial Arts*, vol. 6, #3, 1997.

[5] See Talhoffer, Hans, *Medieval Combat: A Fifteenth-Century Illustrated Manual of Swordfighting and Close-Quarter Combat*. Translated and Edited by Mark Rector. London, 2000.

Swetnam,[6] rather than the shorter, heavier pollaxes of continental Europe.

The distinctive Highland form of two-handed sword, colloquially (if incorrectly) known as a "claymore,"[7] is a particularly interesting weapon. The downswept quatrefoil-terminated quillons and long handle give the sword an immediately impressive look, but the broad, thin blade, optimised for cutting, was relatively short and light compared to other forms of two handed swords. With a remarkably consistent length of around 135cm, and a blade of only around 1m, these swords were significantly shorter than either European or Lowland Scottish two-handers, which both averaged about 170cm long. They were also light, averaging only 2.2kg, compared to the 3 - 3.5kg of continental European and Lowland Scottish two-handed swords. However, the weights and dimensions of the weapon match closely with that recommended by the Englishman George Silver. This suggests that English fencing sources, including the obscure Ledall (Additional MS. 39564) and Harleian MS. 3542 manuscripts, might be better models for interpreting their use than either the better documented German or Italian traditions.[8]

One of the most distinctive Highland armaments was the combination of "a very broad sword" and "a strong handsome target," which became the standard Highland weaponry during the Jacobite era. While "bucklairs" were widely used in the Highlands until at least the mid-16th century,[9] the target or "targe" had also been in use since at least the 14th century, and became the standard Highland shield. The Highland targe was a stout round shield constructed of dense, strong wood, either oak or Scots pine, with two layers of 1/4 inch planks glued together at right-angles,

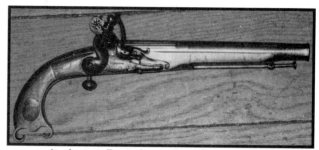

(Author's Collection): An all-steel Scottish pistol.

forming a strong cross-ply. The front was covered with tough cow-hide and further strengthened with brass studs and metal plates on the front and sides. The back was covered with cow, goat or deer skin, and stuffed to absorb blows, and fitted with an arm loop and iron or leather hand grip, allowing a dirk to be held in the left hand and wielded offensively. Some targes also had a 10 inch spike that could be screwed into the central boss.[10] Surviving targes are generally in the 18-21" range,[11] and were thus a unique form of shield, significantly smaller than the large round targets described by Renaissance fencing masters like di Grassi and Marozzo, but somewhat larger than the small bucklers used in medieval manuals such as Tower Manuscript I.33.

The basket-hilted broadsword or "claymore" is one of the most distinctive swords in the world, and it's origins have been hotly debated. Increasingly the evidence suggests that the basket-hilt was in fact originally developed by the Scottish Highlanders at a surprisingly early date. Simple asymmetrical half-guards of thin bars began to be constructed around simple cross-hilts in England around 1520, and by 1560 a classic, fully developed "Edinburgh" style hilt was recorded in a portrait of Lyttleton of Longford.[12] Both the English and Lowland Scots were of the opinion that this style of sword was of Highland origin, and by 1576 they were universally referred to as "heland hiltis" in Scotland or "Irishe hilts" in England[13] (who referred the Highland Gaels as "Irish"). The style and method of construction of the early Eng-

---

[6] Silver noted that "Of the lengths of the battle axe, halberd, or black bill, or such like weapons of weight, appertaining unto guard or battle…In any of these weapons there needs no just length, but commonly they are, or ought to be five or six foot long, & may not well be used much longer, because of their weights." (Ch.20), while "the perfect length of your short staff, or half pike, forest bill, partisan, or glaive, or such like weapons…will commonly fall out to be eight or nine foot long." (Ch.19) Silver, George, *Paradoxes of Defence*, 1598.

[7] See Wagner, Paul, and Thompson, Chris, "The words claymore and broadsword" in *SPADA*, Vol.2 (in press).

[8] Thanks to the Royal Museum of Scotland for the provision of data on their collection of two-handed swords. Silver noted that the two-handed sword should not be "too heavy for his strength that has it," and the blade must be of "convenient length agreeing with his stature that has it, which is according with the length of the measure of his single sword blade." (*Paradoxes of Defence*, 1598, Cap. 10.), a style of weapon that, according to the author's analysis, would also seem to be used in Ledall's Additional MS. 39564, and match the characteristics of the Highland longsword exactly.

[9] See p.58 Reid, Stuart, *Highland Clansman 1689-1746*, 1997.

[10] Wallace, J., *Scottish Swords and Dirks: A reference guide to Scottish Edged Weapons*, 1970.

[11] *Culloden: The Swords and the Sorrows*, National Trust for Scotland, 1996.

[12] Blair, Claude, "The Early Basket Hilt in Britain" in *Scottish Weapons and Fortifications 1100-1800* Ed. David Caldwell, 1981.

[13] Wallace, J., *Scottish Swords and Dirks: A reference guide to Scottish Edged Weapons*, 1970.

lish examples are directly derived from West Highland "snouted" or "beaked-nosed" guards, and even the large spherical pommels on early English basket-hilts are identical with much earlier Highland two-handed "claymore" pommels, pointing to a Highland origin.[14] It seems clear that the basket-hilted broadsword was a Highland invention, either inspired by English half-hilts and developed prior to about 1540, or developed prior to 1520, and the inspiration for the English hilts.

Highlanders had a preference for long (approx. one meter or 40 inches), broad, but thin cutting blades, which the German manufacturers called *Grosse Schotten* or "Broad Scots" blades.[15] Sabre blades imported from Europe were also popular, and were known as *turcael* or "Turkish," and there were even serrated blades similar to Landsknechte swords.[16] The Highlanders called the sword a *claidheamh mor* or "big sword," presumably to distinguish it from the Lowland smallsword and cut-and-thrust

A Highland-manufactured basket-hilted broadsword or 'claidheamh mor', late 16th/early 17th century (private collection).

"sheering sword,"[17] and of this weapon, at least, enough evidence exists to build up a fairly accurate picture of the style of swordsmanship practiced by the clan warriors.

The Highlander in Single Combat

Individual combat was the cornerstone of Celtic warrior society. Even in the 16th century it was standard practice for the leaders of Scottish or Irish warrior bands to challenge each other to single combat in the manner of their Iron Age ancestors - for example, when an Anglo-Irish force of Galloglas mercenaries under a Captain Merriman encountered some 500 Highland "Redshanks" in Ulster in 1586, the Scottish commander Alexander MacSomhairle issued such a challenge, which the English Captain was somewhat loathe to accept. Instead a "lusty Galloglasse" declared that *he* was the real leader of the English force and stepped forward, and in the ensuing fight was killed.[18]

It is clear that the only way the famously "undisciplined" Highlanders, whose primary tactic was to "run towards the enemy in a disorderly manner,"[19] could have prevailed so regularly over conventional soldiery was through a clear superiority at close-quarter combat. Accounts of the Highland Charge emphasise the mob-like nature of the clan warriors, whose only real ambition seemed to be to close with the enemy as soon as possible and engage in single-combat - for example, after the charge of the Jacobite right wing had triumphed at Sheriffmuir in 1715, an eyewitness described how they "arrived in such confusion that it was impossible to form them according to the line of battle projected...every one posted himself as he found ground."[20] However, there are numerous accounts of 17th and 18th century Highlanders in action indicating that as individual swordsmen they were superbly skilled.

For example, in 1655 Sir Ewen Cameron of Lochiel and 32 of his elite *luchd-tagh* (household troops) attacked and destroyed 138 English soldiers who had been sent to chop down some of the Cameron's woods, with a loss of only five of their own.[21] Rob Roy MacGregor had a reputation as the finest broadsword fighter in Scotland, and in his time he fought and won at least 22 duels,

[14] Blair, Claude, "The Early Basket Hilt in Britain" in *Scottish Weapons and Fortifications 1100-1800* ed David Caldwell, 1981.

[15] Wallace, J., *Scottish Swords and Dirks: A reference guide to Scottish Edged Weapons*, 1970.

[16] Reid, Stuart, *Highland Clansman 1689-1746*, 1997. The sword of the German *Landsknechte* soldier traditionally had heavily serrated blades. See *Wallace Collection Catalogues: European Arms and Armour: Volume II Arms*, London, 1962.

[17] See Wagner, Paul, and Thompson, Chris, "The words claymore and broadsword" in *SPADA*, Vol.2 (in press).

[18] Hayes-McCoy, G. A., *Scots Mercenary Forces in Ireland 1565-1603*, 1937.

[19] Quoted in Guest, Ken and Denise, *British Battles*, 1996, p.190.

[20] Quoted in Guest, Ken and Denise, *British Battles*, 1996, p.183.

[21] Jack, Thomas C., *History of the Highland Regiments, Highland Clans, etc, from Official and other Authentic Sources*, 1887.

as well as fighting in several pitched battles and numerous skirmishes, once attacking and killing a dozen Scottish soldiers who were trying to execute a young woman.[22] After the battle of Prestonpans, a young clansman was presented to Prince Charles after having cut down 14 English soldiers with his broadsword, and at Culloden Gilles MacBean famously killed 14 Campbells in his heroic attempt to hold the breach in the enclosure wall single-handed.[23] Sergeant Donald MacLeod was a famous Black Watch man who fought at Schellenberg, Blenheim and Ramillies, was wounded at Sherriffmuir and Fontenoy, and fought on at Louisberg and Quebec. The champion swordsman of the regiment, he defeated two French officers and a German, before being challenged by a giant of an Irishman named MacLean, who lost his arm for his effort.[24] Even the infamous pirate "Blackbeard," Edward Teach, had no answer to Highland swordsmanship when the Royal Navy's Lieutenant Maynard boarded his ship in November, 1718. Maynard wounded Blackbeard with a pistol shot, then engaged the cutlass-armed pirate with his smallsword;

> "Maynard and Teach themselves began the fight with their swords, Maynard making a thrust, the point of his sword went against Teach's cartridge box, and bended it to the hilt. Teach broke the guard off it, and wounded Maynard's fingers but did not disable him, whereupon he jumped back and threw away his sword and cut Teach's face pretty much; in the interim both companies engaged in Maynard's sloop, one of Maynard's men, being a Highlander, engaged Teach with his broad sword, who gave Teach a cut on the neck, Teach saying 'well done lad': the Highlander replied, 'If it be not well done, I'll do better'. With that he gave him a second stroke, which cut off his head, laying it flat on his shoulder."[25]

There are also numerous detailed descriptions of how the Highlanders dealt with British bayonet lines. By the time of the 1745 Rebellion the British Army had fully developed the concept of "defence in depth." This utilised firing by ranks in order to keep up continuous fire against the charging clansmen, and if the Highlanders even reached their target they would have great difficulty penetrating the hedge of bayonets presented by three close

ranks.[26] Although often accused of being slow to adapt to new military technology, in fact the Gaels quickly invented a counter to the ranked defence-in-depth;

> "When within reach of the enemies' bayonets, bending their left knee, they, by their attitude, cover their bodies with their targets, that receive the thrusts of the bayonets, which they contrive to parry, while, at the same time, they raise their sword arm and strike their adversary. Having once got within the bayonets, the fate of the battle is decided in an instant, and the carnage follows; the Highlanders bringing down two men at a time, one with their dirk in the left hand, and another with the sword."[27]

> "(They) stooped low below the charged bayonets, they tossed them upward by the target, dirking the front rank man with the left hand, while stabbing or hewing down the rear rank man with the right; thus, as usual in all Highland onsets, the whole body of soldiers was broken, trod underfoot, and dispersed in a moment."[28]

(Author's Collection)
Variations on the Gaelic open ward as depicted in period artwork; a) (greyed figure left) Charging highlander from military print of Culloden, Aberdeen University, c. 1746; b) A propoganda print of Jenny Cameron, 1745; c) From Blaeu's map of "Scotia Antiqua," 1643.

---

[22] Murray, W. H., *Rob Roy*, 1996.

[23] Mackay, William, *A brief account of some familiar Highland weapons*, 1970.

[24] Laffin, John, *Scotland the Brave*, 1974.

[25] Quoted in Konstam, Angus, *Pirates 1660-1730*, 1998, p.12.

[26] Hill, James Michael, *Celtic Warfare 1595-1763*, 1986.

[27] Johnstone, Chevalier de, *A Memoir of the 'Forty-Five*, 1858, p.68.

[28] Quoted in Harrington, Peter, *Culloden 1746: The Highland Clan's Last Charge*, 1991, p.40.

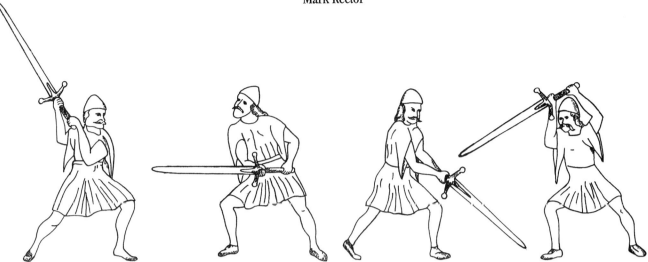

Wards for the two-handed sword from "The Book Of The Club Of True Highlanders" (1881), which correspond to the four basic guards of German swordsmanship (vom Tag – from the Roof, Pflug- the Plow, Alber- the fool and Ochs- the Ox)

The technique described above is extremely sophisticated and difficult to execute - approaching the bayonet line at a run, the swordsman must drop low with the left leg, deflect the front-ranked bayonet upwards with the targe, then pass forward with the right foot, striking the second-rank soldier to the right with the broadsword while simultaneously dirking the front-ranked man in the chest. This is an extremely impressive feat, and is indicative of the supreme skill of the Highland warrior.

The Highlander in Battle

Although the clan swordsmen were obviously highly skilled, there is no clear record of their fencing methods. Celtic culture was, by and large, a non literary one, and none of the Highland masters are known to have recorded their knowledge as the English, Germans or Italians did, while only two Scots who might be hoped to be familiar with Highland methods published manuals contemporary with the clan period, Sir William Hope and Donald McBane.

Hope devoted a surprising proportion of his books instructing his students how to deal with broadsword-armed opponents, and warned them not to lunge, thrust, or even "Stand not to an Ordinary Guard, for then he would Disable your Sword Arm,"[29] but by his own admission he did not fully understand broadsword when he wrote his first few books. His later *New Method* was heavily influenced by a Scottish broadsword master named Machrie, but sadly does not provide any real insights to the Highland fencing methods of the day. [By the time he came to write his *New Method of Fencing* in 1707, Hope obviously had extensive experience with Highland broadsword methods. While "new" in Hope's conception, his hanging guard, his appraisal of distance, his theory of defence, and his advocacy of "downright blows" with the broadsword may be seen in many older fencing treatises. Ed.]

Although not a clansman, McBane was born in the Highlands, and proudly boasted of it in his biography *"...at which my Highland blood warmed...."* [McBane certainly followed his clan as a young man at the battle of Mulroy. Ed.] He faced two Highland charges, and served for years in a Scottish regiment at Fort William, and thus might be most expected to be influenced by the clans. He does offer advice on how to deal with Highlanders armed with traditional weapons such as broadsword and targe, from which useful insights can be gleaned. Yet by his own admission, he knew nothing of swordsmanship until "I went...to a *Sergeant* who Taught Gentlemen the Art of the *Small Sword*, I desired the Favour of him to Teach me that Art of the Sword."[30] McBane remained true to his conventional training in smallsword, and rather that the limb-severing, head cleaving style of the Highlanders whose swords were wielded "circling in the air,"[31] his attacks with the broadsword were done by "throwing quick at the Inside and Outside of the Face,"[32] in conventional military style.

In contrast, eyewitness accounts of Highlanders in battle are clear that they retained a more medieval style of swordplay. Lowland Scottish and English troops were always horrified by the damage done by the Highland broadswords, such as at Killiekrankie in 1689;

---

[29] Hope, Sir William, *The Scots Fencing Master*, 1687, p.159.

[30] McBane, Donald, *The Expert Sword-Man's Companion*, 1728, p.81.

[31] Quoted in Guest, Ken and Denise, *British Battles*, 1996, p.200.

[32] McBane, Donald, *The Expert Sword-Man's Companion*, 1728, p.64.

"Many officers and soldiers were cut down through the scull and neck, to the very breasts; others had sculls cut off above the ears. Some had both their bodies and crossbelts cut through at one blow; pikes and small swords were cut like willows."[33]

…or the local newspaper account of the Battle of Prestonpans in 1745;

"...the field of battle presented an appalling spectacle rarely exhibited even in the most bloody conflicts. As almost all the slain were cut down by the broadsword and the scythe, the ground was strewn with heads, legs, arms, hands and mutilated bodies."[34]

The descriptions indicate that the primary attack delivered by Highland swordsmen was a descending cut onto the head. Accounts of Killiekrankie in 1689 talk of "heads lying cloven,"[35] and how "many…were cut down through the scull and neck, to the very breasts,"[36] while at Culloden Lord Robert Kerr died with "his head being cleft from crown to collar-bone."[37] At Clifton in 1745 the English (dismounted) dragoons sent out to harass the retreating Jacobites were issued with iron helmets to wear beneath their hats, and when charged by the Macphearson rearguard "the poor swords suffered much, as there were no less than fourteen broke on the dragoons skull caps…before it seems the better way was found of doing their business."[38] The "better way" meant the thrust, and despite the surprise of the English armour, the Highland swordsmen still inflicted 40 casualties with a loss of only five of their own.[39]

Pictures of Highland Warriors

Although we have no native Gaelic fencing manuals, iconographic evidence can provide a considerable amount of evidence of the style of fencing practiced by the native Highlanders prior to the Disarming. There are a number of contemporary illustrations and portraits of sword-armed clansmen, all of which confirm that they retained a style of fencing that had passed out of use elsewhere in Europe by around 1600.

The single most common stance depicted in contemporary artwork is a High or *Open Ward*,[40] held left-foot-forward, with the shield in front of the chest and the sword elevated above the head - Richard Watt's "Alastair Grant the Champion" is one of the better known, but many other contemporary pictures show the same general position. Such wards are shown or described in many medieval and early Renaissance *Fechtbücher* ("fencing books") from throughout Europe, including Tower Manuscript I.33 (c.1300), Talhoffer (1467), Durer (1520), Meyer (1570) and George Silver (1595).

The second most common ward is also held left-foot-forward, with the hilt low by the right hip and the blade roughly horizontally, pointing forward, shown alongside *Open Ward* in David Morier's famous painting "Episode from the Scotch Rebellion" (1747). Silver called this the *Passata* ward,[41] and it is again common in other medieval sources.

Laurie and Whittle's 1747 engraving "The Battle of Culloden" has a particularly interesting group of figures representing the charge of the Jacobite right wing, depicting a variety of wards that seem to represent the shift in stance as the clansmen approached the bayonet line. The 4th and 3rd men in the row are in a *Passata* and *Open Ward* respectively, with their shields flat on. The 2nd row figure has brought his shield forward and edge-on beside his sword-hand, in what can only be likened to the *Half-Shield* ward of MS. I.33, the oldest known European fencing

---

Figure above: Highlander with Lochaber axe from the "Penicuick Sketches." Note the length of the pole.

[33] Quoted in Guest, Ken and Denise, *British Battles*, 1996, p.179.

[34] Quoted in Maclean, Fitzroy, *Bonnie Prince Charlie*, 1988, p.91.

[35] McBane, Donald, *The Expert Sword-Man's Companion*, 1728, p.77.

[36] Quoted in Guest, Ken and Denise, *British Battles*, 1996, p.179.

[37] Quoted in Guest, Ken and Denise, *British Battles*, 1996, p.200.

[38] Quoted in Maclean, Fitzroy, *Bonnie Prince Charlie*, 1988, p.137.

[39] Ibid.

---

[40] The "Open Ward" is described in Silver, George, *Brief Instructions upon my Paradoxes of Defence* (C.1605), ed. Matthey, Col. Cyril, 1898, Cap. 3., Pt. 1. as; "Open fyght is to Carrye yo'r hand & hylt a loft above yo'r hed, eyther w' yo'r poynt upright, or point backwards w'ch is best."

[41] Silver, George, *Brief Instructions upon my Paradoxes of Defence* c.1605, ed. Matthey, Col. Cyril, 1898, Cap.3 Pt. 4; "Passata: is either to pass with the Stocata, or to carry your sword or rapier hilt by your right flank, with your point directly against your enemy's belly, with your left foot forward, extending forth your dagger forward as you do your sword, with narrow space between your sword & dagger blade, & so make your passage upon him."

[42] Forgeng, Jeffery L. (transl.) *Fechtbuch I.33* draft manuscript, unpublished, F3/p.4.

[43] For a practical explanation of this manoeuvre see "Talhoffer's sword and duelling shield as a model for reconstructing Early Medieval sword and shield techniques" by Stephen Hand and the author in *SPADA*, Vol. 1, 2002.

The wards of the Penicuick Sketches a) A Clan officer with single sword; b) "The Crook" Note how the hilt is held below eye level, a detail which distinguishes the I.33 ward from other "Hanging guards." For a functional explanation see "Footwork in *Fechtbücher I.33*" by the author in *SPADA*, Vol. 1, 2002; c) An Open ward--Note how the shield is held facing inwards; d) and e) "Walpurgis' Ward", another open ward variation; f) The same guard held sword-foot-forward; [Ed. This could be interpreted either way] g) Highlander in an "Iron Door"-like ward; h) A dramatic "Underarm."

manual (c.1300 AD).[42] The figure in the front row has raised his sword into *Open Ward*, and is receiving a bayonet in the body, while the figure to his left is slipping his targe over to his right side to deflect a bayonet aimed at his right armpit while bringing his sword down on the Redcoat's head.[43]

By far the best record of native Highland sword styles are the "Penicuick Sketches," which clearly demonstrate the commonality between the 18th century Highland style and the medieval form of European swordplay. These are a series of sketches drawn by an unknown artist in the Penicuick area of Scotland during the 1745 Jacobite Rebellion, and consist of around 50 figures, of which around a dozen are armed with sword and/or targe. The sketches show ample evidence of close observation of actual Highlanders, with their garb, arms and accoutrements all accurately drawn, and it is a fair assumption that the fighting postures illustrated are also an accurate representation of the actual use of Highland weapons.[44]

Like other contemporary illustrations, nearly all the Penicuick figures are standing sword-foot-back, in the "medieval" style stance, with weapons "charged" ready to deliver powerful cuts on-the-pass. The combatants are generally in a low crouch, their feet widely spaced, forming the typical L-shape with the front foot pointing at target, and the rear foot roughly a right angle to it. Interestingly, four of the fourteen figures are left-handed, which might be considered artistic licence intended to make the exotic Gaels appear more "sinister" except that they are known individuals, identified by name. [In *Witness to Rebellion*, the author suggests that these figures may have been meant for the engraver, and were thus drawn in reverse. However, the arrangement of the buttons on the coat of figure (c) on the preceding page does not conform to this notion, and so the editor is inclined to accept Mr. Wagner's theory that these gentlemen are indeed depicted as being left-handed. Ed.] Only one figure has

a sword alone. While the rest are all wielding targes, none have a dirk gripped in their shield hand as well.

The sword positions depicted in the Sketches are varied and particularly revealing, and their relationship to medieval swordplay is immediately obvious. *Open Ward* is shown once again, but the most common is a variation with the blade vertical and the sword hilt pulled back roughly level with the right shoulder. The only real analogue of this appears in I.33 as one of the Priest's "special wards," held by the enigmatic Walpurgis.[45]

Two figures are in the *Open Ward* and two are in what I.33 names *Underarm*, and another has adopted an outside hanging ward with low hilt, shown in both Silver and I.33.[46] One is in a *Low Ward* found in medieval longsword and Italian Renaissance sword and buckler treatises.[47] The right-foot-forward *Medium*, *Inside* and *Outside* guards typical of the later military style of Highland broadsword are notable by their absence.[48]

The targe positions shown in the "Penicuick Sketches" are more difficult to interpret than the sword wards. Some of the figures appear to have their targes held close to the left of their face, on at least a 45° angle if not flat-on. They would thus seem to be in danger of obscuring the swordsman's vision, despite McBane's warning that "a Man that does not understand the Targe is better without it that with it, as it blinds his own Eyes."[49] In other sketches, the targes are low and flat-on, protecting the body, or edge on, protecting the left side and closing the line to the sword-arm.

This variety of postures might be explained by the different conditions of use the Highland soldiers had to face. For example, against a bayonet line, the shield might be expected to be held low to guard the belly. When duelling a single-sword armed British officer the shield might be best separated from the sword,

Battle scene from the Penicuick Sketches. A group of clansmen meet a charge of dragoons. From left to right the wards depicted are Underarm, Walpurgis' Ward, and an Open Ward. The dead would appear to be Redcoats, with drum and infantry hats. Note how the leftmost body has had his bayonet sliced off the end of his musket.

Charging Highlanders from Laurie and Whittle's "The Battle of Culloden" (1747). From left to right they are in an Open Ward, Passata, Half-Shield, Open Ward again, and another Half-Shield. The right-most figure is slipping his targe to deflect the bayonet aimed under his sword-arm, a sophisticated movement that is used with both I.33's small buckler and Talhoffer's great duelling shields. This would seem to have been the Highlander's answer to Cumberland's much-vaunted orders to thrust bayonets at the underarm of the clansman to the right rather than the one directly ahead.

but when duelling another shield-armed clansman it might be kept closer to the line of attack,[50] while when coming under fire (one sketch shows the men facing a dragoon charge and being fired on by pistols) they would be held up to cover the face.

Apart from the aforementioned example of the dragoons, there is no indication which of these possibilities any of the Penicuick figures were engaged in or practicing for when sketched, except in one case. Here two clansmen are shown duelling with sword and shield in a very dramatic "action shot." The left-hand figure is shown with his shield edge-on by his side, launching an overhand thrust at the right-hand figure, who is lurching backwards and covering his head with his shield. This would seem to be an unlikely reaction to this thrust if that were all that was happening, and it would appear that the right-hand figure has struck first, and is lifting his targe to defend the expected counterattack to the head as he passes out; instead, however, the defender has passed forward with a thrust aimed at the breast, underneath the shield. Although little in the way of concrete technique can be gained from this sketch, it does illustrate the use of passing footwork, movement in-and-out of distance, and the use of thrusts, cuts and feints as part of Highland swordplay.

Conclusion

The Penicuick Sketches and other iconographic sources, although invaluable reference material, could not by any stretch be said to be enough to reconstruct the native fencing style of the Highland clansmen. They do, however, present several clues as to which sources would be most appropriate to work with. It is obvious the medieval style of swordsmanship was certainly the basis of Gaelic technique, even in the mid-18th century. Manuals such as Fiore, Durer and Talhoffer are certainly appropriate, but the Englishman George Silver is probably the most relevant model, simply because Silver wrote specifically for the basket-hilted sword.[51] The impressive similarity between the wards of the Penicuick Sketches and those shown for sword-and-buckler in Tower Manuscript I.33 would also suggest that this is an appropriate source for reconstructing the use of the targe, even if the larger shield necessitates some significant modification in I.33's technique.   --P.W.

[44] Brown, I.A., & Cheape, Hugh, *Witness to Rebellion; John Maclean's Journal of the Forty-Five and the Penicuick Drawings*, East Linton, 1996.

[45] Forgeng, Jeffery L. (transl.), "Fechtbuch I.33" draft manuscript, unpublished. "Walpurgis" is a female combatant who appears in the second half of the manuscript, and the reason for her inclusion, by name no less, is unclear.

[46] Silver, George, *Brief Instructions upon my Paradoxes of Defence* c.1605, ed. Matthey, Col. Cyril, 1898, & Forgeng, Jeffery L. (transl.), "Fechtbuch I.33" draft manuscript, unpublished.

[47] See Galas, S. Matthew, "The Flower of Battle: An Introduction to Fiore dei Liberi's Sword Techniques," in *Hammerterz Forum*, vol. 2, #3, 1996, and Galas, S. Matthew, "Kindred Spirits: The Art of the Sword in Germany and Japan," in *Journal of Asian Martial Arts*, vol. 6, #3, 1997.

[48] While it should be noted that there are also parallels between the depicted Highland wards and those for sword-and-buckler in some Renaissance Italian manuals, there are also significant differences. For a full explanation see Wagner, Paul "Highland Swordsmanship" in *SPADA*, Vol.1, 2002.

[49] McBane, Donald, *The Expert Sword-Man's Companion*, 1728, p.60.

[50] For a practical explanation of the use of the shield, see "Talhoffer's sword and duelling shield as a model for reconstructing Early Medieval sword and shield techniques" by Stephen Hand and Paul Wagner and "Footwork in I.33" by Paul Wagner in *SPADA*, Vol. 1, 2002.

[51] Silver esteemed the "single hilt" greatly for the protection it gives the hand as well as it's offensive capability, and it's usefulness in battle conditions; "And what a goodly defence is a strong single hilt, when men are clustering and hurling together…then their hilts (their handes being aloft) defendeth from the blowes, their handes, armes, heads, faces and bodies." (Silver, *Paradoxes of Defence*, 1598, Ch.23).

Bibliography

For a more detailed analysis of the Penicuick Sketches and other sources, please see "Highland Swordsmanship" by the author, in *SPADA*, Vol. 1 (2002).

Anonymous. MS I.33. South German sword and buckler manual held in the Royal Armouries at Leeds c.1300.

Blair, Claude, "The Early Basket Hilt in Britain" in *Scottish Weapons and Fortifications 1100-1800*, ed. David Caldwell, 1981.

Brown, I.A. and Cheape, H., *Witness to Rebellion; John Maclean's Journal of the Forty-Five and the Penicuick Drawings*, East Linton, 1996.

Culloden: The Swords and the Sorrows, National Trust for Scotland, Glasgow, 1996.

Chapman, R. W. (ed), *Johnson's Journey to the Western Isles of Scotland and Boswell's Journal of a Tour to the Hebrides with Samuel Johnson, LL.D*, London, 1924.

Di Grassi, Giacomo, *Ragione Di Adoprar Sicvramente L'Arme si da Offesa, Come da Difesa*, Venetia, 1570.
   His true Arte of Defence, Translated by I.G. Gentleman, London, 1594.

Dei Liberi, Fiore, *Flos Duellatorum*, Milan, 1409.

Durer, Albrecht, *Fechtbuch*, c.1520.

Elcho, David, Lord, *A Short Account of the Affairs of Scotland in the Years 1744, 1745, and 1746*, Edinburgh, 1907.

Forgeng, Jeffery L., (transl.), *Fechtbuch I.33* draft manuscript, unpublished, 1998.

Galas, S. Matthew, *The Flower of Battle: An Introduction to Fiore dei Liberi's Sword Techniques*, in *Hammerterz Forum*, Vol.2, No.3, 1996.
   Kindred Spirits: The Art of the Sword in Germany and Japan. in *The Journal of Asian Martial Arts*, Vol.6 No.3, 1997.

Guest, Ken and Denise, *British Battles*, London, 1996.

Hand, Stephen and Wagner, Paul, "Talhoffer's sword and duelling shield as a model for reconstructing Early Medieval sword and shield techniques", in *SPADA*, Vol.1, 2002.

Harleian MS. 3542 (British Museum, MS. 3542, ff 82-85), c.1450.

Harrington, Peter, *Culloden 1746: The Highland Clan's Last Charge*, Oxford, 1991.

Hayes-McCoy, G. A., *Scots Mercenary Forces in Ireland 1565-1603*, Dublin and London, 1937.

Hill, James Michael, *Celtic Warfare 1595-1763*, London, 1986.

Hope, Sir William, *The Scots Fencing Master*, 1687.

Jack, Thomas C., *History of the Highland Regiments, Highland Clans, etc., from Official and other Authentic Sources*, 1887.

Johnstone, the Chevalier de, *A Memoir of the 'Forty-Five*, London, 1858.

Konstam, Angus, *Pirates 1660-1730*, Oxford, 1998.

Laffin, John, *Scotland the Brave*, London, 1974.

Ledall, J. untitled, (British Museum, Additional MS. 39564), c.1520.

Logan, James, *The Scottish Gael*, London, 1831.

McBane, Donald, *The Expert Sword-Man's Companion*, Glasgow, 1728.

MacIan, R.R., *The Clans of the Scottish Highlands*, London, 1845.

McIntyre North, C.N., "*Clann man gaidheal an guaillibh a cheile*" ("The Book Of The Club Of True Highlanders"), vol. 1 and 2, 1881.

Mackay, William, *A brief account of some familiar Highland weapons*, 1970.

Maclean, Fitzroy, *Bonnie Prince Charlie*, London, 1988.

Marozzo, Achille, *Opera Nova*, 1536.

Meyer, Joachim, *Kunst des Fechten*, c. 1570.

Murray, W. H., *Rob Roy*, 1996.

Reid, Stuart, *Highland Clansman 1689-1746*, Oxford, 1997.

Silver, George, *Paradoxes of Defence*, London, 1599.

Silver, George, *Bref Instructions Upo my Pradoxes of Defence*, Unpublished MSS Sloane 376., British Library, c. 1605.
   Brief Instructions upon my Paradoxes of Defence, c.1605, ed. Matthey, Col. Cyril, London, 1898.

Stevenson, David, *Highland Warrior: Alasdair MacColla and the Civil Wars*, Edinburgh, 1984.

Stewart, David, of Garth, *Sketches of the Highlanders of Scotland*, Edinburgh, 1822.

Swetnam, Joseph, *The Schoole of the Noble and Worthy Science of Defence*, 1617.

Talhoffer, Hans, *Medieval Combat: A Fifteenth Century Illustrated Manual of Swordfighting and Close-Quarter Combat*. Translated and Edited by Mark Rector, London, 2000.

Wagner, Paul, *Footwork in I.33* by in *SPADA*, Vol.1, 2002.
   Highland Swordsmanship in *SPADA*, Vol.1, 2002.
   and Thompson, Chris, *The words claymore and broadsword* in *SPADA*, Vol.2 (in press).

Wallace, J., *Scottish Swords and Dirks: A reference guide to Scottish Edged Weapons*, 1970.

Wallace Collection Catalogues: European Arms and Armour: Volume II Arms, London, 1962.

Notes on the Text & Illustrations

A Note on the Text

Eighteenth century print can prove challenging for the modern reader. Spelling is often creative. Every other word seems to be either capitalized or put into italics, or both. Punctuation, in particular, can cloud otherwise cogent passages. Periods are reserved for the ends of paragraphs, while commas and semi-colons are sown broadcast throughout the text.

The editor has endeavored to make the act of reading the words of these remarkable authors a pleasant experience, rather than an exercise in cryptography. In the main body of the text, spelling has been unified, although some of the more interesting archaic spellings have been retained, to imbue the text with its original flavor. Capitalization and italics have been reduced and made more consistent. An effort has been made to allow the text to flow more easily, without materially altering it.

The reader will notice that the valedictory, introductory, and supplementary material remains essentially in its original form. It is the editor's hope that the contrast between these sections and the main body of the text will prove interesting and informative. It is his further hope that the aesthetic experience of reading the book as a whole will thereby be a pleasurable one.

A Note on the Illustrations

Donald McBane's *General Directions* were originally accompanied by twenty-two copper-plate illustrations. They were directly copied from the illustrations to Sir William Hope's *New Method*, already included in this edition. Therefore, we have determined to supplement McBane's *General Directions* with photographs of fencers using the appropriate weapons. We hope this will enhance McBane's work, and spare the reader much confusion.

In the original edition of Hope's *New Method of Fencing*, his *Scheme* and sixteen figures appeared on a single fold-out sheet, pasted into the back of the book. We have taken the liberty of separating the component pairs of figures and placing them throughout Hope's text.

A Note on the Arrangement of McBane's Book

In the original edition of McBane's book, the *General Directions* come first, followed by the *List of Regiments, Life of the Author, Art of Gunnerie*, and the essay *What is a Man?*

Introduction to Donald McBane's

Expert Swordman's Companion

Paul Macdonald

*T*he Expert Sword-Man's Companion is a true experience. It is a treatise of truly practical swordsmanship, borne from decades of necessary application, coupled with the incredible autobiographical account of the author, Donald McBane.

McBane was a Scotsman to whom adventure was no stranger. He was raised in the Highlands and lived during a memorable time in Scotland's history when the country was perhaps at its most turbulent. In a suffering nation where Clan stood against Clan, it could hardly be considered mercenary for a young Scot to join a Government Company, more a valid option.

Hence, McBane relates to us some forty years of personal experience as a soldier living by the sword, detailing his first live duel at the age of 28 (the only of which we hear him lose) right through to his last victorious encounter fought in Edinburgh at the age of 62.

McBane's ability in swordsmanship was renowned by both military and public as his reputation grew. He speaks of receiving lessons from several fencing Masters in the earlier years of his military career before setting himself up "for a Master my self," around 1699. There is no doubt that McBane sought and received academic fencing tuition, yet his own treatise on fencing is quite unlike any other.

What is presented is a condensed practical guide to the use of weapons as drawn from a wealth of living experience. McBane's honest tone is straightforward and takes us through not so much a complete system, but the best technical advice and general observations to be used when Life is at stake in swordsmanship. This is not a beginner's manual but, as the title states, a Companion for *Expert* Sword-Men.

The main weapons concerned are the small sword and sheering Sword or Spadroon, though a multitude of the other weapons and characteristic fencing styles are covered that one would be most likely to face in early 18th century Europe. All realistic dangers and possibilities are addressed including the throwing of dust in the face and other unwelcome objects, butting with the head, stabbing in the back, to name but a few. These are any-thing but fair play in the salle, but McBane more than intimates at the tried and tested nature of these very real actualities.

The human variables of the fight he addresses highlight similarities with the works of Sir William Hope. Where Hope speaks of "Artists" and "Ignorants," McBane recognises the same when facing "Skillfull" and "Unskillfull" persons, and also towards "Gentlemen" and "Ruffins."

McBane himself dealt with all levels of society in his long career as a professional soldier, fighter, and entrepreneur. His life story mixes the thrills of opportunistic Adventures with the stark realities and horrors of war.

McBane's second battlefield encounter was that of Killiecrankie, a now famous Scottish battle, recounted in legend and song, where on the 17th July 1689, Viscount Claverhouse and his Highlanders defeated General Mackay and his reinforcements in a violent and bloody affair.

On that day, a young Donald McBane, a Scot facing Scots, stood as one of General Mackay's men, and received the Highland charge. To this day, at the Pass of Killiecrankie is the famously marked "Soldier's Leap," where a brave soldier leapt eighteen feet over the raging water of the Pass. That soldier was Donald McBane.

His legend lives on in the country of his birth, and I hope that this new publication of McBane's work will further realise the name and spirit of a true champion in life and in fence to that of a wider audience.

Perhaps the most important lesson to be learned from McBane is that of his last, namely that he *"resolves never to Fight any more, but to Repent for my former Wickedness."*

To Live is to Learn, To Fence is to Live.

Maestro Paul Macdonald, I.M.A.F.
Director, British Federation for Historical Swordplay.

Edinburgh, Scotland
November 2001

THE
Expert *Sword-Man's*
Companion

Or the True Art of

SELF-DEFENCE.

With

An ACCOUNT of the Authors LIFE,
And his Transactions during the Wars
With France.

To which is Annexed,

THE *ART* OF *GUNNERIE*

By Donald McBane.

GLASGOW,

Printed by James Duncan, and are to be sold at his Shop in the *Salt-Market*,
near *Gibson's Wyne*.

M.DCC.XXVIII.

The
AUTHOR
to the
READER.

Thrice Sprightly *Reader*, it is *BANE* requires,
That this his Labours lighten your Desires,
To Martial Glory, While he hereby Wills
And Hopes you'll shun Appearances of Ills,
None better is than this, for *Self-Defence*,
When taken in a True and Genuine Sense.
Time was, the *Author* Travel'd far and near,
Under the Notion of a *Musquetier*;
And shortly after to a *Pike-man* rose,
Plac'd in the Fore-front to offend our Foes.
Soon after for the Space of Twenty Years,
Was I one of the *Royal Granadiers*:
Inroll'd in Lord *George Hamilton's*[1] Command,
The Hope and Honour of our Native Land.
　　　In Sixteen Battles Foughten, I have been,
And Fifty-two great Sieges I have seen.
Five-Score and Sixteen Times I did Advance,
In *Flanders*, *Holland*, *Germany* and *France*.
My Countries Cause, hot Skirmishes I join'd,
And Victory of my Enemies I obtain'd.
　　　My Fourth Course was a *Serjeant* of *Dragoons*,
Well known at *Preston*, and at other Towns.
And Lastly I'm *Fort Williams Cannonier*,
Thanks be to GOD, my En'mies I don't Fear;
Who was so oft embroil'd in Bloody Wars,
Indent as 'twere and Carv'd with Cuts and Scars;
Which Fortune seem'd to favour and o'er look,
That I might serve you with this *Little Book*.
Buy it, and try it, then upon my Word,
A good Tongue still will prove a Trusty Sword.
But where ther's no Evading of a Strife,
Here's what will serve you for to save your Life.
　　　So Count it not a Fault in me,
　　　If you'r the Father of a Plea.

---

[1] George Hamilton, first Earl of Orkney. Commander of the Royal Scots.

To the *Scotish Hero,*
or a
POEM.

Written to the *Heroick, Magnanimous* and Valiant Gentleman *Daniel*[2] *Bane*, Master of *Defence*; upon his Encountering and Defeating an *Irish Gladiator*, at the *Abby* of *Holy-Rood-House*[3] upon a Publick Stage; before great Numbers of Nobility, Gentry, Military, and Commons: Upon the *23d*, Day of *June*, 1726.

Some Write Amours, some treat of Rural Things
  Whil'st others treat of Scepters and of Kings.
Each have their Praise, but this Demands the Skill,
Of *Homer's* Vain, or *Varus'* lofty Quill.
The *Scotish* Hero *Daniel Bane* I Sing,
May *Helicon* to me assistance bring.
Draw nigh *Apollo*, and you Sacred *Nine*,
The Theam requires a higher Strain than mine.
His *Semitar*,[4] his *Stature* and his *Face*,
Points his Extract from no Ignoble Race:
But his inherent Merits are so Rare,
There be but Few who may with him Compare.
He of a Disposition meek and mild,
He to the Wars inclin'd even from a Child.
And when Abroad in *England, Holland, France,*
Did every where his Countries Fame Advance.
Ajax in *Greece*, or *Hector* brave in *Troy,*
Ne'er more were fear'd than this our *Scotish* Boy.
Whither in Private or in Publick Field,
He Victor was, and made his Foes to yield.
Grown Old at length, and spent with Warlike Toil,
He did Return unto his Native Soil.
Resolv'd no more to Fight, when lo he's told,
An *Irish* raw Bravado stout and bold;
Imperiously all *Scotish* did Defy,
He laid his former Resolution by,

And from great Distance came in haste to see,
Who was the Man, and what a Spark was he.
He took the *Challenge* up, and modestly
He set a Day, their Valour for to try.
When met, our *Hero* mov'd with generous Rage,
Beat at first time *O Bryan* off the Stage;
His Luck was good he fell, for had he stood,
He there had lost his Life and *Irish* Blood.
Fool hardy he Appear'd on *Stage* again,
But all his Bragadocia Threats were vain;
For Valiant *Bane* like *Lyon* void of Fear,
With furious Blows did this the Youngster tear.
Seven Bloody Wounds he gave, but none he got,
And thus the *Tague*[5] was Vanquish'd by the *Scot.*
Just so me thinks did poor *Thersites*[6] fly,
When Valiant *Ajax* unto him came nigh.
The Nobles Cry'd brave *Bane*, the Honour's ours,
The Shame's *O Bryans*, and the Praise is yours.
Hold on great Sir, the Cause you have begun,
And let your Fame be known from Sun to Sun.
Mean time Except this Paper Compliment,
Which unto you is by a *Poet* sent.
As I have Inclination, had I Wealth,
I'd to the *Scotish Hero* Drink a Health.

Nemo me Impune Lacesset.[7]

---

[2] "Daniel" and "Donald" appear to be used interchangeably to denominate McBane.

[3] Holyrood House is the Royal residence of Edinburgh.

[4] Scimitar. A curved cavalry sword.

[5] Taig, teague. n. British. A Roman Catholic. A derogatory term used by Protestants. The nickname used to denote an Irishman in general and derives from an English rendering of the Gaelic proper name *Tadhg*. (It is sometimes further anglicized to tyke.) *Bloomsbury Dictionary of Contemporary Slang*, 1997.

[6] An ugly, abusive Greek soldier killed by Achilles in the Trojan War. *The American Heritage Dictionary of the English Language*, 1978.
"AJAX: Thou bitch-wolf's son, canst thou not hear? [Beating him] Feel, then. THERSITES: The plague of Greece upon thee, thou mongrel beef-witted lord! AJAX: Speak then, thou vinewedst leaven, speak: I will beat thee into handsomeness… thou cur!" *Troilus & Cressida*, Act II, Scene 1, by William Shakespeare.

[7] "No one provokes me with impunity." Motto of the Crown of Scotland and of all Scottish regiments. *The Oxford Dictionary of Quotations*, 1999.

Donaldi Bani famigerati ad *Andreæ O Bryan*, chartam provocatoriam Responsum.

Ipse ego Donaldus Banus, *ferma albus & altus,*
None huic Andreæ *thrasoni occurrere decro;*
Huic ego, cumque Deo, philopatrius obvius ibo,
Arte rudis qui me ad pugnam provocat audæo:
Non obstant phrast, Thrasone, & temopre curto
Quando iniit pugnam Galli *cum paupere Pullo,*
Spectatum admissi fortes nos forte videbunt
Quod pugit O Bryan *non est tam, credo, Magister*
Præsidii felix; tutelæ sive patronus,
Quin hunc ignavum faciunt mea plectra caponem.

Ad DONALDUM BANUM CARMEN.

Olim Donaldi *vixerunt hic duo* Bani,
Regni prædo unus, reus alter Seditionis.
Dilut has meculas, nunc extat tertius unus
Mistrum priscorum decus & tutemen Jernum.

Here Liv'd of Old, two[8] Monster *Donald Banes*,
Mark'd with Seditious and Usurping Stains,
Lo, now a Third wipes off this foul Disgrace,
The Shield and Glory of our Antient Race.

THE
Beginning and *End* of MAN.

ord! What is *Man*? Originally *Dust*; Ingendered in Sin, brought forth with Sorrow; Helpless in his Infancy, Extravagantly Wild in his Youth; Mad in his Manhood, Decripped in his old Age: His first Voice moves Pity, his last Commands Grief. Nature Cloaths the Beasts with Hair, the Birds with Feathers, the fishes with Scales, but *Man* is Born Naked; his Hands cannot handle, his Feet cannot Walk; his Tongue cannot Speak, nor his Eyes see aright; Simple is his Thoughts, Vain is his Desire; Toys is his Delight; he no sooner puts on his distinguishing Character *Reason*, but he Burns it with Wild-fire *Passion*; Paints it with abominable Pride, Tears it with insatiable Revenge, Dirts it with Avarice, and Stains it with Debauchery: his next State is full of Misery, Fears Torment him, Hopes intoxicate him; Cares perplex him, Enemies assault him; Friends Betray him, Thieves Rob him; Wrongs oppress him, and Dangers way-lay him; His last Sense is Deplorable; His Eyes dim, his Hands feeble; Feet Lame, Sinews shrunk, Bones dry; His Days are full of Sorrow, his Nights full of Pain; His Life Miserable, his Death Terrible: His Infancy full of Folly, Youth of disorder and Toil; Age of Infirmity: *Lord! What is Man?* A dunghill blanch'd with Snow; a May-game of Fortune, a Mark for Malice; a Butt for Envy: If Poor he is despised, if Rich he is Flattered; if Prudent he is mistrusted, if Simple he is derided: His Beauty is a Flower, his Strength is Grass; his Wit a Flash, his Wisdom is Folly; his Judgement weak, his Art Imperfection; his Glory a Blaze, his Time a Span; himself a Bubble, he is Born Crying; Lives Laughing, and Dies Groaning.

---

[8] Possibly the Scots kings Macbeth and Donald Ban, both claimed by clan MacBean. Eyre-Todd, 218. *Macbeth* (c. 1005 - 1057) King of Scots (1040-57). Son of Finlaech, mormaer (earl) of Moray, and probably a grandson of Malcolm II, Macbeth asserted his claim to the throne against Duncan I, whom he killed near Elgin. In 1045 he killed Crinan, Duncan's father, in battle, but in 1057 he was himself killed by Duncan's son, Malcolm Canmor. Both Macbeth and his wife, Gruoch, gave generously to the church, and in 1050 he made a pilgrimage to Rome. *Donald, III, Bane* (c. 1031 - 1100). King of Scots (1093-94, 1094-97), after seizing the throne on the death of his brother Malcolm III. His sobriquet Bane means 'fair'. He was dethroned by Malcolm's son, Duncan II, in 1094. He soon regained power but was defeated and captured by another of Malcolm's sons, Edgar, who had him blinded and imprisoned until his death. Both Duncan and Edgar were supported by the English against Donald. *Market House Books Dictionary of British History*, 1987.

THE
Remarkable *Passages* and *Actions*
of the
LIFE of the *AUTHOR.*

*M*y father lived two miles from Inverness. He kept a farm and a public house. I was always wild and would not wait on the schools (which I find is to my great loss this day). I was full for any thing but work. At length my father took thought to put me to a trade, and then I was bound to a tobacco spinner[9] in Inverness. When I was some time at it, my mistress began to lessen my dish, which I could not endure. I, being a raw young fellow, would have eaten two days meat in one day. So I went and [en]listed myself a soldier in Captain McKenzie's Company. This was in the year 1687, at which time I was twenty-three years of age. A little after I listed, we marched from Inverness to join the Laird of McIntosh against Cappoch Mcdonald,[10] who would take a piece of land from McIntosh, notwithstanding it was declared by law to belong to McIntosh. The two Clans was both on foot, and our Company was still with McIntosh, who marched towards Mcdonald and his Clan until we came in fight of them (which made me wish I had been spinning tobacco). McIntosh sent one of his friends to Mcdonald to treat with him and see if he would come into any reasonable terms. Mcdonald directly denied, but would fight it, be the event as it would. Then both parties ordered their men to march up the hill, our Company being in the front. We drew up in a line of battle as we could, our Company being on the right. We were no sooner in order but there appears double our number of the Mcdonalds, which made us then to fear the worst, at least for my part. I repeated my former wish (I never having seen the like). The Mcdonalds came down the hill upon us without either shoe, stocking, or bonnet on their head. They gave a shout and then the fire began on both sides and continued a hot dispute for an hour. Then they broke in upon us with their sword and target and Lochaber axes,[11] which obliged us to give way. Seeing my Captain sore wounded and a great many more with heads lying cloven on every side, I was sadly affrighted, never having seen the like before. A Highland-man attacked me with sword and targe and cut my wooden-handled bayonet out of the muzzle of my gun.[12] I then clubbed my gun and give him a stroke with it, which made the butt-end to fly off. Seeing the Highland-men to come fast upon me, I took my heels and run thirty miles before I looked behind me. Every person I saw or met, I took him for my enemy. At length I came to the garrison of Inverness. What was left of our Company came up some time after. We remained there until the next year, '88, when King William[13] came over and our Company was broke.

I was then obliged to list in King William's service in Grant's Regiment. We lay at Inverness for near two years, in which time

---

[9] Tobacco was shipped from the American colonies to Scotland for re-export to the Continent. "Big fortunes were made by the swaggering, red-cloaked *tobacco lords*…" Maclean, 189.

[10] Clan MacBean has been associated with the Clan Chattan, and hence Clan Mackintosh, since the days of King Robert the Bruce. In 1667 clan leader Paul MacBean undertook to follow Mackintosh "as his chief, with all his men, tenants, family, and followers of the Clan Vean, against all men except only the King, Lord Huntly, and the Laird of Calder." Eyre-Todd, 219-220. In 1688 Mackintosh raised his clansmen, friends, and a company of Regulars under MacKenzie of Suddie, to settle a territorial feud with the Macdonnels by "fire and sword." They attacked the Macdonells of Keppoch at Mulroy and were routed. Innes, 213. For his part, "Macdonnell of Keppoch was nothing more than a highway robber…he had no regard for his word or the law." Petrie, 259.

[11] Traditional Highland weapons. The sword would be a basket-hilted broadsword or backsword (the former having two edges, the latter one edge), often called a "claymore." The target or targe is a large, round, hide-covered shield, with brass studs. The fearsome Lochaber axe is a pole arm, similar to a halberd.

[12] "It must be admitted that Mackay's troops were singularly ill-equipped for this type of warfare, for their bayonets were of the old type, that is to say they were screwed into the barrels of the muskets." Petrie, 97. Churchill credits Mackay with the innovation of the ring-bayonet (which allows the musket to be fired while it is attached), as a result of the Battle of Killiecrankie. Churchill, v. 3, 108.

[13] William III of Orange, Stadholder of the United Provinces (the free Netherlands), and husband to Mary, the daughter of King James II and VII of England and Scotland. In the winter of 1688 the Protestant William landed on the English coast with 11,000 troops to dispute with the unpopular Catholic King James for the throne. The commander of the British army, Lord John Churchill (later the Duke of Marlborough), deserted the King and joined William. One month later, as the desertions mounted, James fled England for France, never to return. In April of 1689, William and Mary were crowned King and Queen of England. After a bloodless coup, the "Glorious Revolution" was complete, and the Protestant succession was secured for the time being. Durant, 288-311.

Clavers[14] began to raise an army for King James,[15] in opposition to King William, Clavers having got the most part of the Highland Clans to join him. General Mckay,[16] commanding under King William, having but a few men, there was a draught drawn out of Colonel Grant's regiment to reinforce Mckay, of whom I was one. After we joined the General, we were commanded to march to the Blair of Athol, where we got a certain account of our enemy. Hearing of their number and nearness to us, we drew up at the house of Runrawrie, then passed the pass of Killicrankie,[17] having a great water in the rear and another on the right of our line. We left our baggage in the rear at the smith's house and drew up in battle order and stood for some time. At length our enemy made their appearance on the top of a hill. We then gave a shout, daring them, as it were, to advance, which they quickly did to our great loss. When they advanced, we played our cannon for an hour upon them. The sun going down caused the Highlandmen to advance on us like mad men, without shoe or stocking, covering themselves from our fire with their targes. At last they cast away their muskets, drew their Broad Swords and advanced furiously upon us, and were in the middle of us before we could fire three shots apiece, broke us and obliged us to retreat.[18] Some fled to the water and some another way (we were for the most part new men). I fled to the baggage and took a horse in order to ride the water. There follows me a Highland man with sword and targe in order to take the horse and kill my self. You'd laugh to see how he and I scampered about. I kept always

the horse betwixt him and me. At length he drew his pistol and I fled. He fired after me. I went above the pass where I met with another water very deep. It was about eighteen foot over betwixt two rocks. I resolved to jump it, so I laid down my gun and hat and jumped and lost one of my shoes in the jump. Many of our men was lost in that water and at the pass. The enemy pursuing hard, I made the best of my way to Dunkel, where I stayed until what of our men was left came up. Then every one went to his respective regiment (this battle was foughten in the year '89).

In the year '90, General Mckay commanding the army, we encamped at Inverlochie in Lochaber, at which time we began to build Fort William.[19] It was the King's pleasure to break three regiments in order to make one strong regiment under the command of Colonel John Hill. The names of the regiments that were broke was Glencairn, Grant, and Kenmuire's.

General Mckay and his army marched off and left Colonel Hill's regiment in the Fort, and him Governor of the same. I remained there and served in one Colonel Forbes' Company. At that time I had little skill how to manage my pay, so there was an Old Soldier ordered to take care of me and to manage my pay as he pleased. He gave me nothing but what he thought fit. When I asked him for money he would for ordinary give me a blow. I resented it several times but I came off second best. I complained to my officer, but found it in vain, for at that time if any difference fell out betwixt two soldiers, they were obliged to decide it with their swords. I was afraid to venture on my Governour, he being a bold Old Soldier. Being a sort of a Gentleman, [he] was allowed to wear a sword. I had nothing but a wooden-handled bayonet and did not know how I should be upsides with him. By chance I got some money from my friend, so I went directly to a Sergeant who taught Gentlemen the art of the Small Sword. I desired the favor of him to teach me that *Art of the Sword*. He answered he could not because my pay would not satisfy him. I desired but fourteen days teaching and gave him a crown[20] in hand, which he embraced. I was taught privately so that none

[14] John Graham of Claverhouse, Viscount Dundee (b. ca. 1650). He is the "Bonnie Dundee" of song and story. "There are hills beyond Pentland and lands beyond Forth,/Be there Lords i' the south, there are Chiefs I' the north!/There are brave Dunniewassels, three thousand times three/Will cry 'Hey!' for the bonnets o' Bonnie Dundee." Traditional.

[15] James II of England and VII of Scotland, the last Stuart king.

[16] General Hugh Mackay of Scourie. Commander of the Scots Brigade in Holland and Commander-in-Chief in Scotland under King William. Grimble, 162. Killed at the Battle of Steinkirk in the Netherlands in 1692. Churchill, v. 2, 112.

[17] "When William was proclaimed King, Graham of Claverhouse, now Viscount Dundee, rode north to raise the loyal clans for King James who had himself now landed in Ireland. A body of troops under General Hugh Mackay was sent by William to put down the Highland Jacobites. At sundown on 27 July 1689, at the head of the narrow gorge of Killiecrankie in Perthshire, the Highlanders fell upon William's soldiers 'like madmen' and almost annihilated them. But Dundee himself was killed in the battle and his troops were left without a leader." After their subsequent defeat at Dunkeld, the Highland resistance faded away. James' defeat at the Battle of the Boyne in Ireland ended the attempt to restore him to the throne. Maclean, 139-142.

[18] This is a classic example of the famed and feared "Highland charge," in which the Highlanders rush upon their enemy, fire a volley, throw away their muskets, and charge with broadsword and targe. This embodiment of Highland valor would achieve its apotheosis on the field of Culloden in 1745.

[19] The British Government used three forts, stretching across Scotland from the Firth of Forth to the Moray Firth, to control and subdue the Highlands: Fort William near Inverlochy; Fort Kilchumin at the southern end of Loch Ness, built in 1716, and later renamed "Augustus" after the Duke of Cumberland; and Fort George on the Moray Firth. Begun as a timber palisade by the Cromwellian General Monck in 1654, in 1690 the fort was strengthened with twenty-foot high stone walls, fifteen cannon, and barracks for a thousand soldiers. Maclean, 142, 166-7.

[20] Readers always wants to know, "how much is that worth today?" This is a very difficult question to answer. Authorities contradict each other (naturally enough, given the subjective nature of the exercise). I am therefore reluctant to step upon this slippery slope. However, Will and Ariel Durant state, in their wonderful book on the Age of Louis XIV, that a crown in 1779 was *possibly* worth $12.50 in 1962. It is *possibly* equivalent to ten times as much today, in 2001, and we will leave it at that. Durant, ix..

might know of it. Then I took some spirits to me, and would live no longer as I had done, but would fight the old fellow. I got a sword of one of my neighbors and went privately with it under my coat unto the canteen where the Old Gentleman was. I demanded the remainder of my pay. His answer was, "You saucy rogue, if you ask any money of me, I'll beat you back and side. When I think fit I'll give you money." I replied, "Sir, that will not do. Either give me money or give me Gentlemen's satisfaction immediately." Says he, "Sirrah, with you it's not worth my while." I urged him so that he and I went to the back of the garrison in the dusk of the evening, least any person should see us. We drew on each other. I had a Small Sword, he had a Broad. After two turns, he beat my sword out of my hand. I took my heels. He, running after me, overtook me and gave me a blow with the flat side of the sword, obliging me to submit to him. He carried away my sword and pawned it in the canteen for two gallons of ale. My neighbor, seeing his sword go for ale, was very displeased with me, but there was no help for what was past.

Dale Seago caught in a bad position from student Patrick McKee.

Next morning I went to my old Master, and gave him some more money, and asked him what guard I should keep with a Small Sword against a Broad. He shewed me to keep a low guard, and slip from his blow, and push[21] above his sword when it goes to the ground, and make a half-thrust to his sword arm, and to save my Small Sword from his. Next day being pay day, he [the

Old Soldier] took up my money as he had done formerly. I went and demanded my pay from him. He answered, I got meat and drink, and "What occasion have you for money?" I told him I would have it whether he would or not. Whereupon he gave me a blow with his sword and scabbard, which I took very ill, and went to see for a sword but could get none. I was at last obliged to take one of my comrades' sword, whether he would or not, and put it under my coat. I came where the Old Gentleman was. He being in company, I called him to the door and desired the remainder of my money without any further delay. Otherways, walk to the place we formerly were at, which he immediately did. In our way, he was always saying I should not come off so well as I did before, for he would cut a leg or arm off me. I was resolute and no way afraid. We came to the place where we fought before. He put off his coat. I would not, thinking it would save his sword from cutting me. We looked about to see if any person were in view, then we drew, and after two or three turns, he making a great stroke at my leg, I slipped him, and thrust him through the body before he could recover himself. Finding he was wounded, he struck furiously, and giving way, he fell forward. I, seeing that, pushed him in the leg, least he should run after me as before. I then commanded him to give me his sword, which he did. I put the sword into the scabbard, and went into the garrison to the drawer that sold the drink, and gave the Gentleman's sword to him, desiring him to give me my sword and keep that sword until he saw the owner of it. The swords I had taken, I laid them down where I got them. By this time he was carried into the garrison by some cow-drivers. A surgeon was called to dress his wounds. His officer came and asked how he came by that misfortune. He refused to tell, being a high spirited man. I then became master of my own pay, and his likeways, time about, for it was half a year before he fully recovered of his wounds. I then began to think something of myself and purchased a sword. This was my first adventure with the sword, in the year 1692.

After this I lived peaceably for some time, and continued learning at the fencing school publicly for two months. I had several bouts with the Scholars. I came off still Master.

In the latter end of the year there was a draught out of our regiment to reinforce our regiments in Flanders. Twenty men of a company were drawn. They were all disarmed, and with a guard marched as prisoners to Lieth. I was one of the guard. When they were shipped, I went on board to drink with my old comrades. I fell asleep. The wind blew. When I awakened, the ship was past the Bass. I then desired the Captain to set me on shore. He said it was such good lusty lads as I they wanted in Flanders, and the first shore I should be on should be in Holland, where I would be very much made of, "Because you are a volunteer of your own accord." We landed at Haversluce [Hardersluis?] in

---

[21] Fencing terms are defined in the Glossary, in McBane's *General Directions*, and in Chapter 4 of Hope's *New Method*.

Holland, from which we marched to Mastrick [Maastricht], where we stayed two days to refresh ourselves. We marched from that to Brussels, where our army was in camp, where the officers of the sundry regiments came and drew for us. It was my good fortune to fall into Lord Orkney's Royal Regiment.[22] A little after, we laid siege to Namuir [Namur], where we had a very hot siege. In order to divert our siege and raise it, the French bombarded Brussels, notwithstanding our Flying Army was on the other side of the town. Before they left it, they burnt a great deal of it. We continued a close siege at Namuire [Namur] for a long time, with great loss of men on both sides. I was in six storms against the city, five of which I came off pretty safe. The sixth time I was sorely wounded: three times shot, six times stabbed with a bayonet. In this attack, the French and we went through one another in taking the palisades. All our wounded men were carried to Brussels to an hospital there, where the surgeons came and dressed our wounds. I keeping a good heart, I soon recovered. This was in the year 1695.

Next year our Grand Army encamped at Rotterdam, where my former Captain came from Fort William to view the camp. Seeing me there, he was not well pleased at my coming to Holland, contrary to orders. He spake to my Captain and promised him two men for me the next year if he would let me go over to my former regiment. The Gentleman immediately complied, and my Captain and I came over again to Fort William, where I continued until the Peace of Rejwick [Ryswick],[23] which was concluded

September 20th, 1697. In a few months afterwards we were relieved by Brigadier Maitland. We were broken [discharged] in the Fort, every one being obliged to make his best shift.

I came home to my parents at Inverness. My father being dead, I stayed with my mother some time. She, being in no extraordinary circumstance to maintain an idle man, desired me to go work for my bread or go to my old trade again. I desired her to provide me some money and I would go and seek my fortune. My mother gave me twenty shillings,[24] and a suit of new clothes, and her blessing.

I took leave of all friends and came off for Perth, where I listed in the Earl of Angus' Regiment. I served there as a pike-man for some time. One day, being on guard, I happened to be absent from my duty. The Corporal being angry, upon my appearing he obliged me to stand four hours sentry, and beat me for my absence, at which my Highland blood warmed. I resolved to be revenged on him when the guard was relieved next morning. I told the Corporal he had affronted me on the guard, for which I would have satisfaction, which he was very willing to give. He desired me to go to the South-Inch (which is very near to the town of Perth) and he would follow me quickly. When he came, he asked if I was for death or life. I told him I was for any thing that happened. We drew on each other. After some turns, he received a thrust on the breast bone. He, falling backward, cried, "You rogue! Run, for I am killed!" I said I wished it were otherways. I took him by the hand, desiring him to rise, but he could not. He threw away his sword. Then I returned [sheathed] mine.[25] I said to him, "Are you dead, really?" He answered, "I am in very deed." He opened his [coat or shirt] breast and shewed me the blood. He again desired me to run away, for if I was catch'd, I would be hanged. I desired him to give me what money he had. In a very trembling manner, he put his hand in his pocket and gave me three shillings to carry me off, saying it was all he had. He took me by the hand and said he forgave me, crying, "Make your escape!" When I was about two miles from Perth, in the road that goes to Stirling, I met with my officer, who asked where I was going. I told him my misfortune and that I was afraid of six quarters of St. Johnstoun ribbons,[26] so I resolved to make my escape. He was very sorry for it and gave me half a crown to carry me to Glasgow. He wrote to one Captain Cockburn, who was recruiting for the Royal Regiment of Scots,

---

[22] The Royal Scots in the Netherlands. According to the Regimental history, "The Royal Scots are the oldest Infantry Regiment of the Line in the British Army, formed in 1633 [for service abroad]. In 1661, the Regiment was summoned to Britain to bridge the gap between the disbandment of the New Model Army and the creation of a Regular Army, organised along the same lines as the British units in foreign service. The Regiment was thus the original model for all others. In 1680, the Regiment was sent to Tangier and won its first battle honour, On its return to England in 1684, the title 'The Royal Regiment of Foot' was conferred by Charles II. During Monmouth's rebellion in 1685, five companies formed part of the force concentrated against the rebels who they met at Sedgemoor. The Royal Scots saw service under Marlborough during the war of the Spanish Succession and followed this with garrison duty in Ireland where they it remained until 1742. From this date, the two battalions were usually to be separated and posted far apart. The 1st Battalion moved in 1743 to Germany to take part in the Austrian War of Succession, and was involved in the Battle of Fontenoy. In the following year, the 2nd Battalion became involved in the fight against the Young Pretender (i.e "Bonnie Prince Charlie") which culminated in the Battle of Culloden. In 1751 the army adopted a numerical naming system, and thereafter the Regiment was officially designated the First or Royal Regiment of Foot."

[23] "On September 20, 1697, the Peace of Ryswick (near the Hague) ended the 'War of the Palatinate' with England, Holland, and Spain [against France]." Durant, 699. Louis XIV's decision in 1688 to invade the Rhineland, rather than Holland, gave William III free rein to pursue his conquest of England. Durant, 691-2.

[24] Twenty shillings equal one pound. According to the Durants, a pound in 1779 *might* be worth $50 in 1962. That *might* be equivalent to $500 today. See note 20.

[25] McBane has very strong opinions about how to deal with an injured or disarmed opponent. He discusses them at length in his *General Directions*.

[26] A hangman's noose.

then lying in Ireland. He likeways said he would suffer none to pursue me. I was not much afraid of any man catching me: I was at that time as swift as a Highland horse. I came for Stirling and there met me two soldiers and a Drum.[27] They asked me where I was going and what I was. I answered, it was none of their business. They told me I must give account and better language. One of them drew his shackle and said I was his prisoner. Immediately, I jumped over a ditch and drew my sword. Then they attacked me. I thrust one through the shoulder. The Drum threw his stick at my face and fled. The other one I thrust through the hand. He, fearing further danger, begged pardon. So they made the best of their way to the garrison. I, fearing a party to be sent after me, went to the Tor-wood, where I stayed that night. The next morning I came for Glasgow and found the Captain I was recommended to, who immediately gave me a line to his Sergeant, then lying at Saltcoats with recruits. He shipped me and next morning we set sail for Ireland. Then I was pretty safe.

We arrived at Carrickfergus. We marched to Belfast and from thence to Dublin, where the regiment lay. My pay being small, I went to court a maid in Smoke-Alley, where was one who made me very welcome, carried me into a room, and call'd for wine. She thought I was the man with pockets lined, but found a disappointment in the end. A fellow came in who call'd himself her husband. He drew his sword and in a most furious manner said, "You rogue, what have you to do with my wife?" I begged him pardon, for I knew not she was his wife. He said I must either give him money or satisfaction. Having on coloured cloaths, he knew not I was a soldier. He drew very near, and being afraid he would stick me, I drew my sword and told him what satisfaction he wanted he must take it off the point of my sword. Then we to it. The fellow's heart failed him. Then he took a chair in his left hand to defend, and the pretended wife came behind, and taking me by the hair of the head. I fought and wrought this way for near half an hour. At length a constable is call'd, who took hold of the woman to send her to Brydwell.[28] We gave good words to the constable, desiring him to sit down. I told him I was a re-

cruit. He said I should wear my red cloaths. I promised to do so for the time to come. The fellow that fought with me said, had he known I was a soldier, he would not have troubled me, "For I am wounded both in the arm and thigh." We called for a bottle to make the constable drink. The landlord said, "See you have as much money as pay it, otherways, friend, you must go to the striping room." I pulled out all that I had. It was but two shillings, thinking the price was no more. The landlord said it was three shillings. Likewise, he told me I must pay the other two bottles or leave my coat. I told him that was hard since the gentlewoman had called for them. "That is nothing," said he, "call for them who will, you must pay them. Otherways, go to the striping room." The constable, being a good honest fellow, paid one shilling for me, and made the woman leave her scarf for the other two bottles. The landlady said, "When you come back again, bring more money with you." I told her I would pay her a visit again, which accordingly I did. I asked some of my comrades what kind of a house it was. They said it was a bawdy-house. I put on my livery, and with two of my comrades came to the house. The landlady knew me not, but the young lady knew me. We asked the landlady if she had any young ladies in the house. She answered, "None for soldiers." Meeting with my former antagonist, "Spark," said I, "you and I must have a turn this night." He answered, his arm was so sore he could not fight, but his mistress was at my service any time when I wanted her. Then he called up the landlady and gave us six bottles of wine and told me I was welcome when I pleased, so we parted in peace.

At that time I went to a French [fencing] Master to learn to push. I tarried with him a month. My fellow Scholar and I fell out: he said I was not able to do with the sword what he could do with the foil. We went to Oxmentoun-Green and drew on each other. I wounded him in three places. Then we went and took a pot and was good friends, and I stayed at that school a month longer.

Our turn coming to leave the city, we marched to Limerick, and some was quartered upon the farmers. In the house where I quartered, I fell in love with an Irish girl and would have kissed her, but she would not until she was married. She told me she had twenty shillings, a cow, and a goat. I got three of my comrades and went to the Change-House[29] to send for the priest and be merry. The girl came with her money. The priest was sent for. When he came, he said to me, "This woman is too young for you." (We desired her to say the same words that the priest said.) He said, "Are you willing to take this muckle [great] man? She answered, "Are you willing to take this muckle man?" He says again to her, "What came you here for?" She said, "What came you here for?" The priest answered her, "I came here to marry you." She repeats, "I came here to marry you." The priest said,

---

[27] A drummer. "Though military drumming seems an ancient thing, drums to regulate marching were a late-medieval innovation without precedence. Ancient armies had marched in step, but in time to singing – the Greek paean or war chant is an example – and the music of flutes and trumpets. Before the Swiss, there is only fleeting evidence of medieval soldiers marching in step at all. Significantly the sixteenth-century French military reformer Fourquevaux, who wrote to help refine Francis's [Francis I] legions experiment, specifically identified the Swiss as the inventors of the drum – the cadence of the drumbeat was yet another novel feature of the Swiss way of war, and an integral feature of the new infantry tactics." Arnold, 67-8.

[28] Bridewell. A prison; a reformatory. St Bride's (or Bridget's) Well in London, between Fleet Street and the Thames, where such a building (formerly a royal palace) stood. *The Oxford English Reference Dictionary*, 1996.

[29] An inn that provides shelter and a change of horses for travelers.

"I believe you are a fool." She repeats the same words, "I believe you are a fool." "Get out of the house!" said the priest to her. "Get out of the house!" said the girl to the priest. Out he goes in haste, and was very angry with the landlady for sending for him. We made the girl believe she was married, and got her to pay the wedding dinner out of the twenty shillings. We came home to her mother's house and lived together twenty days. Our men in the country got orders to march into Limerick. I left her with her mother. When I was gone, her mother went and asked the priest if her daughter was married. He told [her], "No." Then she was angry at her daughter, and the daughter was not well pleased with her mother. Then they ended their strife in a battle.[30]

We remained in Limerick about eighteen months. I continued still at the school, and had several turns with my fellow Scholars, and continued still foremost Scholar in my Master's school. There was several other schools in the city with whom my Master's Scholars had several conflicts. At last one of the Masters and I fell out about a sister of his whom I intended to marry. All the Tocher[31] I got was a duel with her brother. After which I set up for a Master myself and kept a school while our regiment lay there.

An order came that we should march to Cork in order to ship for Holland. In our march, a great deal of our men deserted. My Captain feared my deserting, which made him set a Sergeant and four men to look after me. While they pretended to guard me, behold, they deserted themselves. Then my Captain wished he had made me their guard instead of them being mine. Next morning ten regiments went aboard at the Cove of Cork. We were five weeks in our voyage from Cork to Holland.

Now follows an account of my transactions in Holland. During my abode there our regiment went to the Bush [den Bosch] at Brabin [Brabant]. There I met with the Sergeant I had killed at Perth. I asked him if ever he was a Corporal in Perth. He said he was. I said, "Was you not once kill'd at Perth, as you said yourself?" He said, "Almost, but not altogether, by a roguish fellow called Daniel Bane, and I believe you are the man!" I took him by the hand, so we went and took a bottle. He served a Sergeant all the wars of Queen Ann.[32] Now he keeps a public house in Gravesend, about twenty miles from London.

Brabin [Brabant] being very throng, there being eight battalions of English, eight battalions of Dutch and Scots, eight regiments of Horse and Dragoons, which obliged me to hire a quarters. I set up a school for teaching the *Art of the Sword* and had very good business. But there being a great many schools in the town, which caused great envy amongst us, they took all methods and ways to do me a mischief, which obliged me to be constantly on my guard and to fight twenty-four times before they would be perswaded that I was Master of my business. I took one of the Switz soldiers to be my servant (he could speak some broken English). This made me acquaint with a great many of the Dutch and Switz officers, who continued at my school some weeks.[33]

At this time the Switz mocked the English, and called them "beardless boys," and killed several of the English at night when going home. This obliged the English to stand to their defence. A body of them gathered together (being tolerated by their officers) and slew a vast number of the Switzers. This was like to have rais'd a mutiny, and caused a complaint to be made to the States General,[34] who ordered the Switzers to another garrison.

I continued keeping my school. A short time after, I came to know that there was four good swordsmen in the town that kept women and gaming (the Wheel of Fortune and Legerdemain) by which they got vast money. I resolved to have a share of that gain; at least to have a fair trial for it. I fought all the four, one by one. The last of them was left-handed. He and I went to the rampart, where we searched one another for firearms. Finding none, we drew and had two or three clean turns. At last he put up his hand and took a pistol from the cock of his hat. He cocked it against his shoulder and presented it to me, upon which I asked

---

[30] In order for this bit of classic comedy to work, the girl must speak only Gaelic, and not understand what the priest says in English. Which means McBane must have seduced her in Gaelic. The editor thanks Paul Wagner for this interesting insight.

[31] Dowry.

[32] The War of the Spanish Succession (1702-13). The issue was whether a Habsburg or a Bourbon would sit on the throne of Spain, and was

fought between Louis XIV and the Grand Alliance forged by William III, and held together by the Duke of Marlborough. "Practically all of Europe west of Poland and the Ottoman Empire was involved… By 1704 [Louis] had 450,000 men under arms – as many as all his foes combined." Durant, 706. The War would spawn the greatest armies and the bloodiest campaigns seen in Europe since the days of the Roman Empire. The Grand Alliance would ultimately bring France to terms in the Treaty of Utrecht (1713). The peace would settle the wealth, power and frontiers of almost every European state until the advent of World War II. Churchill, v.1, 4-5.

[33] The armies of the Grand Alliance were made up of "English, Scots, Irish, Danes, Prussians, Hanoverians, Hessians, Saxons, Palatines, and Dutch…" Churchill, v. 6, 728. According to McBane, there were also Swiss. The Swiss also fought alongside the French.

[34] The individual assemblies of the seven provinces of the Dutch Republic elected "representatives to a States-General that ruled the interrelations of the provinces, and their foreign affairs." Durant, 165. Their conservative approach to the war would be a bane for Marlborough through all his campaigns.

quarters [mercy]. But he refused, calling me an "English Bouger," and fired at me and run for it. One of the balls went through my cravat. I, thinking I was shot, did not run as I was wont to do, but run as I could after him, crying for the guard. The guard being half a mile distant, I was not heard. At last I overtook him, over against the guard, and gave him a thrust in the buttocks. Then I fled to the flesh market: nobody could take me out there, it being a priviledged place. I tarried there till night, then went home to my quarters and call'd for his comrades that same night, who agreed to give me a brace of whores and two petty-couns [petticoats] a week. With this and my school, I lived very well for that winter.

In 1701 we went to camp at Breda in the Netherlands, where we was received by His Majesty King William. It was a camp of pleasure, so we tarried but fourteen days and was ordered back to our garrisons.

When I came to the garrison I enquired for my mistresses. One of them had taken up with a tinker and said she was married to him. I told her, "Married or unmarried, you must pay me a pistole[35] a week." The tinker gave me my demand for three or four weeks, then he run away with her, which was a great loss to me, having but one. I applied to the Gentlemen who had supplied me before, that they must give me another, who granted my request and gave me two. So then I had three. I kept my school and my wife[36] kept a Change-House and sold wine, so we lived very well. My wife was never jealous of me, for I never was concerned with common women through the whole tract of my marriage life.

In 1702 we marched to camp at Rosondale [Roosendaal], where we heard the sad news of the death of King William. Then France and Spain proclaimed wars against England and their allies. At this same time the Duke of Marlborough[37] was made Captain General of Her Majesty's[38] forces. We had a very plentiful camp.

During this camp there was a great snow in March, and lay until April. The Genever[39] being plenty, we regarded not the cold.

My old trade was still going on: gaming tents, Pass-Banks[40] and whoors, which brought me four pound[41] a week. I was often in danger by protecting them. I risqued my life four or five times in a day on their account.

We marched from this camp to the camp at Cleeve [Kleve], where Lord Cutts[42] commanded us. We had a very plentiful camp. I went on with my old trade. I was still at wars with the Dutch and Switzers. In this camp a great many of our men deserted to the French. But as soon as we catched them they were hanged.

There was a great wood in our front called the Wood of Orleance. It was full of wild creatures. At that time there was a wild man taken by the Brandeburghs.[43] He was drinking at a spring-well about sun setting. He was eight foot high. Before they could take him, they made a net of their forage cords.[44] He received a great many wounds in the taking of him. The nails upon his fingers and toes were a quarter long: if he catch'd hold of any person, he tore cloathes and skin at once. He was brought to the Dutch General who ordered his wounds to be dressed. They called for a Master of Languages, but could not understand him. I can give no further account of him, whether he lived or died.

---

as a statesman conscious of realities and possessed of authority. He was sometimes merciless, and often unscrupulous; he poured out the blood of his soldiers in any quantity needed for success...he was the organizer of victory." Durant, 706. In ten years of hard campaigning, Marlborough never lost a battle.

[38] Queen Anne, daughter of James II and VII, and the last Stuart to rule Great Britain.

[39] The Dutch word for Gin. Franciscus Silvius, a late sixteenth-century Dutch professor of medicine, is generally credited with its invention. With the proscription of French trade, Gin, imported and domestic, gained rapidly in popularity in England, where consumption rose from an estimated half million gallons in 1690 to five million gallons in 1727. Conrad, 123-5.

[40] Gambling operations.

[41] A pound in 1779 *may* have been equivalent $50 in 1962. McBane *may* have been raking in $2,000 a week, in terms of today. See note 20.

[42] John, first Baron Cutts.

[43] Troops of Frederick III, Elector of Brandenburg.

[44] Cords used to bind provender and other supplies gathered by foraging parties.

---

[35] France, Spain, Germany, and the Netherlands all had coins called "pistoles." McBane clearly values it at a pimp's share of a prostitute's wages for a week, in a garrison town. I will let the reader take it from there.

[36] McBane's second "wife." This one appears to be more of a business partner.

[37] John Churchill, Duke of Marlborough. "Perhaps never since Caesar had the genius of war been so combined with the art of diplomacy as in Marlborough: skilled in the strategy of planning operations and moving armies, in the tactics of manipulating infantry, cavalry, and artillery with rapidity of perception and decision, as the needs of battle changed; and yet also patient and tactful in dealing with the governments behind him, the personalities around him, even with the enemies that looked to him

We were attacked by the French. Likewise they endeavoured to get betwixt Namegin [Nijmegen] and our army, which obliged us to march all night until we came in sight of the town. Then we halted a little time upon our arms. Then we espied sixty squadrons of the French Horse and Dragoons, commanded by the Duke of Berwick.[45] Upon this, Lord Cutts drew up his army upon the top of an hill in order to fight them. Buffler,[46] who commanded the French Foot, fell behind, in which time the Dutch General called for my Lord Athlone,[47] where my Lord Cutts was. He asked them what they were minded to do? Cutts answered with courage, brave and bold, he was willing to fight. "My Lord," says he [the Dutch General], "you have too many to lose, and too few to fight, for which reason I desire you to make the best of your way with the army until you get under the walls of the town." He obeyed orders. He left several companies of Grenadeers[48] to guard the rear. My Lord Orkney's Company of Royal Grenadeers was one, in which I was one. The French Horse pursuing so hard, we were obliged to get in to the walls, but the cannon playing upon the French Horse obliged us to lie down until the cannon stopped a little. The French tarried until their Foot and train[49] came up. We retired under the palisades of the town, but this time our baggage and wives were all taken by the French Horse. Then they raised a battery and cannonaded us very hard. One of the balls carried away the half of my cape and the half of my gun, but I received no more damage.

They continued their cannon firing upon us till the next day. Then they striped [beat, or stripped] our wives and sent them to us. Many of us would rather they had kept them. The French, finding themselves at a loss, retired without the reach of our shot. Then were we peaceable in our camp. Having all taken that I had, and my wife strip'd, I went to my Captain and borrowed eight crowns to buy a barrel of beer in order to set up again. In my way to the town to buy my beer, I met with bad company at the Fort. Strangers I knew not were playing at a game called the *Taylor's Invention*, at which I ventured, thinking to gain something. But alas, I lost my eight crowns. I was then worse than ever. I stood amazed, not knowing what to do. At last I fell upon the fellow who got the money and took sixty crowns from him.

Then he called for his companions; they were seven in number. All fell upon me with their swords. I drew my Spadroon in my own defence, with a stick in my left hand. I resolved to die rather than part with the crowns. O, how the bystanders laught to see the battle: swords broken, legs and arms cut, and five of them so wounded that they could do no more. The other two engaged me pretty hard. But I made a retreat until I got to my camp and came to my good wife, who asked me for the barrel of beer, calling me "rogue" and an hundred worse names, saying, "You have drunk the money!" I desired her to call for a surgeon. When he came, he dressed my wounds I got in the skirmish. I took a hearty bottle with the surgeon, and my wife she still scolded me. I went and payed my Captain his eight crowns, and told him what market I had made. I gave my wife thirty crowns. What remained, I went and bought cloaths for myself, and she did the same.

At this time His Grace the Duke of Marlborough came to us with a good number of troops, and the army close besieged Coysaraward [Kaiserwerth], which put us in a case to form a camp against the French.[50] This made them to retire a little further off. Next morning we marched over the Maiz [Maas] by the Grux [Grave]. The French followed us. We not being afraid, we encamped. Next morning we marched for Dunderstake [Dunderslaugh] in the Netherlands. We were not above an hour in camp till the French came in sight. We left our tents standing. When we faced them they begun to cannonade us. We did the same to them. The cannons played from two [in the] afternoon until six a'clock at night. The French had a great water in their front, otherways we had been in the middle of them. In the night time they thought fit to march off, leaving great fires burning and dogs yowling, that we might not hear or see their march. Next morning our Light Horse pursued them and made a great slaughter on their rear.

We camped at the windmill at the side of the Maiz [Maas], where His Grace [Marlborough] made a detachment out of every battalion, with several pieces of cannon and hopits,[51] in order to attack a strong shottoe [chateau], a French garrison. It had a morrash [morass] of water about it. We took it in four hours time with sword in hand. His Grace sent them all prisoners to Holland.

---

[45] James FitzJames, Duke of Berwick, Marshall of France. Natural son of James II and Arabella Churchill, Marlborough's sister.

[46] Louis François, Duc de Boufflers.

[47] Godert de Ginkel, Earl of Athlone.

[48] Grenadier. An elite assault soldier, armed with a slung musket, sword, and grenades. The grenadier was a fearsome component of 17th, 18th, and early 19th century armies.

[49] A train of wagons carrying supplies, artillery, or siege equipment.

[50] Marlborough's goal was always to bring the enemy to battle. This would prove a difficult task, and was at odds with the conventional warfare of the day: an affair of parades, maneuvers, sieges, and the control of foraging areas. The plains of Flanders contained nearly thirty large fortresses of the first class, as many as fifty fortified towns and stongholds, large expanses of water barriers and protective morasses, forming a barrier of immense strength between France and Holland, nearly all of them in the hands of France. Churchill, v. 3, 97-116.

[51] Hobit. A small mortar on a gun carriage, in use before the howitzer. *Webster's Revised Unabridged Dictionary*, 1913.

After this we laid siege to Venlow [Venlo], a French garrison upon the river Maiz [Maas]. The town submitted in a few days. It had a strong fort called Fort France, which we took with sword in hand. The French had a great loss of men. I received some slight wounds, of which I soon recovered.

His Grace caused us to lay siege to another garrison of the French, called Rearmount [Roermond]. It submitted in a few days. The fort held it out until we took all their wood works [palisades], then they yielded themselves prisoners of war. They likewise were sent prisoners to Holland. A few days after, we laid siege to another town on the river Maiz [Maas] call'd Stephensward [Stevensweert]. We took it in a little time with sword in hand, and the fort likeways. Those men were sent prisoners down to Holland. Our army marched to another town (upon the same river) call'd Marcheigh [Maaseik]. Upon our approach the French left the town. We camped there three days. A great many of our men went out a-plundering; I went in company. At last I came to a Bouer's[52] house and got a hog. I tyed a cord to its foot and was driving it home to the camp. There meets me two Hollanders. They would have the half of the hog. I refused. They drew their swords, I drew my Spadroon, and to it we went. I resolved to die ere I would quit my hog. I cut one of them in the face. He could make no more use of his sword, but threw stones at me in the time the other was fighting with me. He gave me many a sad blow with the stones. The other, thinking to kill the hog, cut off its nose. It cryed terribly and alarmed the Grand Guard which was hard by. Two of the Gray Horse[53] came to see what it was, then the Dutch run away. I was conducted safe by the Guard and came to the camp with my booty.

Next morning we marched along the river side until we came to Mastrick [Maastricht]. I being up all night before, in the march I fell drowsy and fell into the river, where I lost my gun and very narrowly escaped myself. The army halted for an hour. As I was coming along the line I took up one of the Hollanders' firelocks [muskets] and came to our company in the front. We encamped hard by Mastrick [Maastricht]. While we lay there I went in to see some of my mistresses that I had there. I asked them if they had got me any money. All I got was three pistoles from six of them. I took a bottle of wine with them and was very hearty until nine at night, at which time I left them and came away for the camp. It was a little dark when I came by the gallows, where a great many were hanging in chains. One of them cryed in French with a loud voice, "Give me a drink of water!" Hearing the voice and thinking they were all dead, it made me run with speed to the camp, where I told the story to my comrades. They could not

believe it. Next morning we went to see the truth of it, and there we found a man hanging in chains alive, with a penny loaf hanging within a little of his mouth. When he would snatch at it, it fled from him and then would hit him on the mouth. He lived this way eleven days. He ate the flesh off both his shoulders. He was a spy from the French, and was design'd to blow up the magazine of the garrison. The Governour ordered this death for him.

Being near the end of the year, our army laid siege to the great city Luke [Luik, or Liége]. They [the city] surrendered to His Grace immediately, but the two citydales [citadels[54]] stood it out. One of them was on the top of a hill. It was the strongest and we attacked it first. In ten days time we were in readiness, then we began to play our cannon and mortar pieces. Before we cut out our trenches, we were within ten yards of their palisades. Our cannons beat down their walls in three days time. Our mortars burnt down their houses. The Governour beat a parley and promised to deliver the citydale to His Grace against ten a'clock next morning. That night the Governour sent to the other fort, desiring assistance from it. The Governour desired him to hold it out another day and he would send to his relief. Next morning, about nine a'clock, the Governour hanged his coffin over the wall and fired upon our trenches. Then we fired all our guns and mortars. We destroyed a great many of them. About three a'clock [in the] afternoon the Duke of Marlborough came to the Grand Battery. He commanded twenty Grenadeers of each company through the whole army, and ten battalions of the first troops to storm the fort, sword in hand. Our orders was to give no quarters[55] to none within the fort. We made all ready for the attack. Every Grenadeer had three grenades.[56] Our word was, "God be foremost." When we came, we came with a loud "Huzza!" and fired our grenades amongst them and small shot without number. We continued thus for an hour and an half, then we jump'd over the palisades. We then made use of our swords and bayonets, and made a sore slaughter upon the French, which obliged them to cry for quarters. Although it was against orders, we had mercy on our fellow creatures and turned them all behind us; then the Dutch used them as they pleased. They hung out their flag in several places, crying for quarters, but none was given. This

---

[52] *Boar, Boer, Boor, Bouer*: A Dutch peasant.

[53] The Royal Regiment of Scots Dragoons, also known as the Grey Dragoons and the Scots Greys (for the grey horses they rode).

[54] "A fort forming part of the works of a town and fortified both towards the town and towards the country. It should always be on the most commanding ground, and should the town be taken it becomes a retreat for the garrison." Hogg, 250.

[55] Quarter: Exemption from being immediately put to death, granted to a vanquished opponent by the victor in a battle or fight; clemency or mercy shown in sparing the life of one who surrenders. *Oxford English Dictionary*.

[56] A pomegranate-sized (hence the name) cast-iron ball filled with gunpowder and metal shrapnel, ignited with a fuse, and thrown at the enemy.

caused them to take courage and beat us two times from the bridge. Then our mortars began to play anew. I was one that made the attack at the sallie-port. An officer at the head of his platoon kneeled down and asked quarters. I gave it him and took his sword, [it] being mounted with silver. After we took the sallie-port, the officer took me to a cellar under the wall where was ten or twelve trunks full of gold and money. He gave me eleven bags of it for saving his life. What I got was all pistole pieces. I made all speed I could to my company, where they were tumbling over the wall all the carcasses that were loaden with hand-grenades. I took up one of them with design to throw it amongst the enemy. But it prevented me, and broke in my hands, and killed several about me, and blew me over the palisades, [and] burnt my cloaths about me so that the skin came off me. I and my gold fell among Murray's company of Grenadeers, flayed like an old dead horse from head to foot. They cast me into water to put out the fire about me. The fort was taken and plundered. Our army got the money that was to pay the French army.

That night our troops took possession of the fort, and looking after the dead and wounded, I was found among them, and carried into a house that the surgeons might dress our wounds. When he saw me he said it was needless to apply any thing to me for before morning I would be dead. My wife came, and when she saw me she clapt her hands and cryed. She ran into the city and got milk and rubbed me with it, putting some of it in my mouth. I continued in this house for some time. When our army laid siege to the other citydale, they immediately surrendered and got honourable terms, marching out with flying colours and drums beating, [and] so went to their own camp. His Grace the Duke of Marlborough ordered his troops to garrisons and ended that glorious campaign, having cleared the Maize [Maas] in Brabant and also Lukeland [the Bishopric of Liége].

All our wounded men were left in Luke [Liége]. The surgeon would not dress my body nor order any thing to be applied to me. I was left to the care of my wife only. She addressed herself to a cloister where were several Englishmen, who came over and saw me. They caused two porters [to] carry me on a barrow to their cloister. They took great care of me. They caused a tub to be made, wherein I lay at my whole length in oil for twenty days. They opened my mouth with a knife and poured in oil or milk. I was all this time blind. They killed two young dogs and plyed their lights [lungs] warm to my eyes, which took the heat out of my eyes in twenty-four hours. Then they put me in a bed and fed me with strong broth and wine. They suffered not my

wife to come near me, but took a room for her near the cloister. In a little time I was in case to travel to the garrison. The English clergymen in the cloister gave me four pistoles, and took a seat for me in the stage-waggon, in which I came where our regiment lay, called the Bush [den Bosch] in Brabant. My Captain made me very welcome, and gave me my pay for the whole time I was away from the company.

When I was perfectly recovered I set up my school. My wife kept an ale-house. I went to look for my bread-winners (the lasses). Finding they were all pickt up by the Hollanders, I was obliged to fight for them and got them and, placing them in good quarters for that winter, they were better to me than six milk cows. I lived after this very peaceably.

In the spring [of] 1703 we took the field and laid siege to Houie [Huy], where there was a very strong castle on the Maiz [Maas]. It lay betwixt Luke [Liége] and Namuire [Namur]. In a few days we took the town. The castle held out about eight days longer. We made ladders to scale the walls and made attempts with them, which obliged them to surrender. Prisoners of war, they were all sent to Holland. The Duke left a good number of men in it to repair the breaches made in it, it being one of the frontiers of the country. Our army laid siege to Sanflight [Sandvliet], not far from Antford [Antwerp]. We took it in fourteen days time, and sent all the men in it to Holland. We had a plentiful camp, and I followed my old trade at the General's quarters, where I had sixteen mistresses that payed me contribution weekly. It was dear bought: I was in danger of my life every day upon their account. One Sunday morning I and my consorts had a man playing at the *Taylor's Invention*. By came the priest to say mass, but seeing the man have a handful of money, and looking on for some time, we made him kneel down and play all the money he had, which was twenty-one pistoles. He went off in a passion, but I know not if he said mass that day.

Next day we marched for Santroy [St. Truiden]. We were two or three nights in camp by the way. We had an alarm that the enemy was near to us, which obliged our army to march to Santroy. The night before our march I was up all night. When I came to my tent I fell asleep. My comrades could not awake me, so they took away the tent and my arms, except my sword. They cast some straw over me and left me, never thinking to see me again. Up comes a French Dragoon seeking plunder and took me prisoner. He took my sword from me sore against my will. He drave me before him until he came to a wood-side where he wanted to ease nature.[57] He alighted and took a pistol with him, commanding me to hold his horse. When his breeches was down I mounted

---

[57] McBane is uncharacteristically dainty about the French dragoon's need to take a piss.

his horse and rode for it. He cryed and fired after me. The bullet came through my hair and cap and grazed on my head. I loosed my sword that was tyed to the saddle, and with it I whipt the horse. He cryed in French, "Stop the English rogue!" A great many wives were before me which cast stones at me, which obliged me to ride the faster until I came to the front where our Royal Regiment was. When my Captain saw me he was amazed, saying he never thought to see me again. I told him the whole story, which pleased him well. We came to Sautrey [St. Truiden] and encamped there and I sold my horse and accoutriments for twelve pistoles. We continued there a good while, and I set up my old trade of gameing. At this time I had twenty-four whores, all of them placed in sutlers' tents. I was still in jeopardy on their account: foreigners still falling out with them obliged me to protect them. Then I got plenty of money, but made a bad use of it.

At this time we had a flying army commanded by Vsadam [Opdam], a Hollander, who beat the French army near Antwerp.[58] At the same time the Duke of Marlborough detach'd an army to besiege Limburgh, which he took in a few days, and sent all the men in it prisoners to Holland, until they were relieved with men or money. In this campaign we made several attempts to get over the Brabant Line,[59] but could not that year. With the taking of Limburgh we finished our campaign and went to our former garrisons where I set up my old trade. My mistresses were reduced at this time to four.

In 1704 we set out for Germany[60] and had seven weeks march, but had plenty of good bread and wine, and the people were very kind to us all along the Rhine. When we came to Cobelands [Coblenz], we found a strong castle[61] on this side of the Rhine, and the town on the other side. The castle saluted our army three times with their great guns round the castle. They fired sharp shot over our heads: they always do so because it was never taken. We came to Myance [Mainz] and camped there by the side of the Rhine. At this place, the German Princes made us very welcome and gave our army a great deal of wine. The Duke of Marlborough marched the whole Cavalry and joined the Emperor's[62] army, least the Duke of Bavaria[63] should engage him with the French army. We marched after His Grace the Duke of Marlborough, and crossed the [river] Main, on the other side of the Rhine. We march'd up great hills and mountains, where we were obliged to draw our train with the strength of men through the Duke of Whitemburgh's [Wittenberg's] land. In few days we joined the Emperor's army, which caused great joy. We rested there four days. The next day we march'd five leagues into the Duke of Bavaria's land, where we saw the French and Bavarian army in camp, close by Denneward [Donauwörth]. The river of Danube was in their rear. They were at work casting up trenches with all expedition. The Duke of Marlborough stopt the army and consulted with Prince Lewis De Bade,[64] in order that the whole army should attack them at once.[65] It seems the Emperor's General refused, by reason his men was fatigate [fatigued] with marching, which obliged the Duke of Marlborough to fight them himself. He commanded ten men of a company to go to the wood and make fascines.[66] Then the French played their cannon upon us from their trenches and likeways from the town. Our gunners soon set the village on fire and dismounted a great deal of the enemy's cannon. Both sides continued thus cannonading one another for an hour and an half until the Foot was in readiness to attack. The ten men of a company who had made the fascines went in the front with the fascines on their breast in order to fill the trenches for the Horse to go over. Brigadier Ferguson commanded the men with the fascines. General Faugle,

[58] General Opdam nearly lost this battle (July 1, 1703), and indeed galloped off to Breda before it was over, thinking all was lost. The Dutch rallied, however, under Jacob Hop, Treasurer of the Republic, and General Slangenberg. They beat back the superior numbers of the enemy, and at dawn of the next day, were marching safely in retreat, leaving the French, under Marshal Boufflers, in possession of the field. Churchill, v. 3, 227-8.

[59] In 1701 Louis XIV had constructed a continuous line of fortifications, sited under the supervision of the military engineering genius Vauban, along a seventy mile crescent from Antwerp to Namur. These impassable forts, entrenchments, palisades, and inundations were known as the "Lines of Brabant." Churchill, v. 3, 105.

[60] "The annals of the British Army contain no more heroic episode than this march from the North Sea to the Danube." In a brilliant feat of surprise and military logistics, Marlborough moved his entire army of nearly 19,000 men, along the Rhine from Flanders to the Danube, and affected a union with the Imperial forces of the Margrave of Baden and Prince Eugene of Savoy. His strategic goal was to strike into the heart of Bavaria to compel the Elector to forsake his alliance with France under threat of the destruction of his country, and to throw the French armies into confusion. Churchill, v. 3, 314-47; v. 4, 42.

[61] "...the majestic rock-fortress of Ehrenbreitstein on the long tongue of land formed by the confluence of the Rhine and the Moselle." Churchill, v. 3, 331.

[62] Joseph I, Holy Roman Emperor.

[63] Max Emmanuel, Electoral Prince of Bavaria. The Elector allied himself with France and traitorously waged war against his neighboring German Princes and the House of Austria. Churchill, v. 3, 191-5.

[64] Prince Louis, Margrave of Baden.

[65] This battle (July 2, 1704) is the "Storm of the Schellenberg," the fortified heights above the city of Donauwörth on the Danube. "The prize had been gained, but the cost of nearly six thousand casualties, fifteen hundred killed outright, was shocking in an age when soldiers were hard to find, and human life narrowly valued." Churchill, v. 4, 39.

[66] Bundles of branches used to fill in ditches, so soldiers may pass over them.

Major General Withers, with ten battalions of Foot and sixteen squadrons of Horse, march'd close after the men with the fascines, under the muzzle of the enemy's guns. The battle was very hot and continued for four hours. We filled up their trenches with dead men and fascines. Then our Horse and Dragoons went over upon the enemy and slaughtered them down to the Danube, wherein a great many of them were drowned. The town continued still flanking us with their cannon. Next morning we satisfied them for their kindness. We took the town and six regiments of Foot that were in it. This pass was several times besieged but never taken before this time. Our company of Grenadeers lost forty-eight men, besides several wounded men. I my self received three stabs of a bayonet and a brace of balls that lyes in my thigh to this day.

After taking the town, we laid our bridges on the water and marched to the Duke of Bavaria's country. Notwithstanding of my wounds, I marched with the army. In our march, we took a town with two regiments in it. They were sent prisoners to Denneward [Donauwörth]. We camped that night in a plentiful country. The people fled and left their houses well furnished. We plundered and lived a jolly life. In a few days march we came into the heart of the country, to a city called Freeburgh [Friedburg]. We camped there a good while. The French camped over against us on the other side of the water at a great city call'd Ousburg [Augsburg]. Being in an enemy's country, we had liberty to do as we pleased in it. Being fully recovered, I resolved to set up my old way of living at the Duke of Marlborough's quarters. I got my comrades, who waited on my command. We set up all sort of gaming tents. We had not above sixty campaign ladies in the quarters. Sixteen professors of the sword resolved to go to the Emperor's quarters, where we got fourteen brave Dutch lasses to reinforce our quarters. Next day came twenty-four swords men and demanded the lasses again, or else give them satisfaction. We made up twenty-four men and drank together; then we fought two and two. There was eleven of the Dutch killed and seven of our men. Our bargain was that if they beat us, we were to give them the lasses and pay them a tribute; and on the contrary, they were to pay us tribute. We fought a second time. I being of the Royal, it fell [upon] me to fight first. The first time, I was soon done, but the second time, before I put up my sword, I fought eight of them. So it ended, and they promised to pay their tribute. We buried our dead and parted. Two or three days after, we sent six pretty men to receive our tribute, but only two came back, and brought no money. The other four, they shot. Our business went on and we prospered. At length I was ordered on a command. I left one to take care of my affairs, for I had always two men's share.

We marched three thousand Grenadeers, with a great many Horse, in order to burn the whole country that belonged to the Duke of Bavaria, which we did. The next day after our return, the whole army march'd, and burn'd their quarters before their march.

We crost the river Danube back again. The French, they crost it likeways, and came to Houston[67] and Blenham [Blenheim], six miles from Denneward [Donauwörth]. Our army march'd within two leagues of them, where Prince Eugene[68] joined us. We marched towards the enemy a little way, and came back to the same ground, and sent all our baggage to Denneward [Donauwörth], and lay on our arms all that night. In the morning, being the 2d of August,[69] by break of day we march'd up within shot of the enemy, and halted there on our arms until Prince Eugene came through the wood upon the right of our army. When we advanced, the French guns played very hard on us. About seven a'clock in the morning we placed our batteries very near their camp. We played very hard on them and burnt a village, wherein we play'd our cannon, which did a deal of damage to them. There was a little water in their front. Our General commanded bridges to be laid over it for Horse to go over. Lord Cutts attacked the right wing with both Horse and Foot. He was beaten several times. He advanced upon them, making a new attack, until the whole army engaged, which obliged the Duke of Bavaria's troops to give way. The French closed to the right, and got into a strong village call'd Blenham [Blenheim]. The Duke of Bavaria, with his forces, fled and crossed the Danube, where a great deal of his Horse were drowned.[70] In the village there was of French thirty-six battalions of Foot and six regiments of Dragoons. We cannonaded on the village until we burnt it about

---

[67] Possilby Lutzingen. The French army was established on the line Lutzingen-Blenheim.

[68] Prince Eugene of Savoy, head of the Imperial War Council. His association with Marlborough was "a glorious brotherhood in arms which neither victory nor misfortune could disturb, before which jealousy and misunderstanding were powerless, and of which the history of war furnishes no equal example." Churchill, v. 3, 352.

[69] The Battle of Blenheim was actually fought on August 13, 1704. It was Marlborough's greatest victory, and would change the balance of power in Europe. Its name was given to the palace at Woodstock built for the Duke by Queen Anne, in token of thanks. The allies brought 56,000 men to the field to attack the French force of 60,000 men, on a four mile front. At the end of the day, the French army was entirely destroyed, suffering more than 38,000 casualties. The allies lost nearly 13,000 men, including 6,000 killed. The Royal Scots were hotly engaged on the extreme left of the allied line, in the village of Blenheim itself. Afterwards, their commander, Lord Orkney, wrote, "I think we did our pairts." Churchill, v. 4, 85-117.

[70] "The bank of the Danube near Sondenheim falls very steeply as much as fifteen or twenty feet. A mob of French horsemen, jammed knee to knee and variously computed at thirty squadrons or two thousand men, were driven headlong over this drop into the marshes and the deep, swift river; of whom the greater part were drowned." Churchill, v. 4, 106.

their ears. We took their head General, Count Tailard.[71] When we attacked them, we were beat several times with great loss. At last, we took them all prisoners. They laid down their arms and marched a mile to the right of our army. We took a great many of their head officers, with the standards, tents, and their whole train and ammunition. In the attacks we made upon the French, I was four times shot with ball in several parts of my body, and five times stabbed with a bayonet, and was left among the dead. About the middle of the night, the Dutch of our army came a-plundering, and stript me of all except my shirt. A little after came another and took the shirt also. I besought him to leave me it, but he gave me a stroak with the butt of his gun because I was not quick enough to pull it off. Thus was I left in a deplorable condition. A little after, the ground took fire. I creept up on a dead man until the fire was past me, then I fell off him and lay among the dead, expecting death every minute, not only by reason of wounds, but by reason of the cold and great thirst that I had. I drank several handfuls of the dead men's blood I lay beside. The more I drank, the worse I was. I continued until day light. Then came a Serjeant and a soldier of our company looking for the wounded men of our company. When the Serjeant saw me, he cast his coat and put it on me, and they carried me on their shoulders to a village where the wounded were and our surgeons. Then they gave me water to drink to cause me vomit the blood I had drunk. I got my wounds dressed, then they gave me a dram, which I received. We continued there a day or two, then our army marched in pursuit of the French, and laid siege to a town call'd Oulham [Ulm]. They left a small army to take the town, but the Grand Army marched hard after the enemy, and laid siege to Lando [Landau], and camped at Crownensburgh [Kronweissenberg].

The wounded men at Hogestead [Höchstädt] lay up and down in the fields with a guard to look over us, until they got waggons to carry us to a town call'd Marelykin [Mahringen] in Swapperland [Swabia], six leagues from the place we fought at. Our Grand Hospital was there, but very scarce of surgeons. There was four thousand wounded men. I had some money wherewith I employed a surgeon for my self, so that in a months time I would have jumpt upon my crutches and walked through the town, where I saw my old trade of gamcing going on very well. I call'd for the Master of the Game and asked him why he gave me not of the profit (he was an Italian in the German service). He told me he had two comrades that were Frenchmen that knew me not; they would give me nothing unless I would fight all the three. I told them I would have a fair trial for it, so sent for a sword. The Italian and I went to it. He was lame of his left arm,

and I of my legs. You may judge how the spectators did laugh to see two lame men fight. I fought him and the other two, and wounded them all three. So I became Master of the Pass-Bank. I gave them what I thought fit. I was kinder to them than they were to me, when they had the power in their hands. We continued very good comrades for fourteen days, then all that were able to go to the camp were obliged to go. I went down the river of Main: the finest country on both sides of the river that ever I saw. At last I came to Lando [Landau], where the siege was very hot. I went to the General's quarters to see how my business went there. I found it went on very well.

We left the Emperor's army at Lando [Landau]. Our army marched down to Holland. I had the good fortune to go to my old quarters, where I set up my old trade. At this time Her Majesty Queen Ann, for our good service in that campaign, ordered every man two guineas, which we called *smart money*.

In 1705 we set out to the Fields. We marched up to Germany upon the river Mussel [Moselle], by a town called Trecar [Trier]. We camped on a hill called Hungry-Hill,[72] where we were not so plenty as formerly. The French Horse lay on our front. Every day our Horse and theirs were charging one another.[73] I set up my old trade and lived very well. But meeting with some new troops that did not know me, I was obliged to fight very often. While we lay here there came an express to the Duke of Marlborough that the French were very strong in the Netherlands, and had beat the Dutch army into Saint Peter's Hall [St. Pietersberg], near Mastrick [Maastricht]. They were obliged to trench themselves. The French at this time took Houie [Huy]. The Duke then ordered all the Grenadeers in the army, and so many men of a company that could march well. We marched night and day until we came to the Dutch. When the French saw us, they retired. In a few days our Grand Army came up, and laid siege to Houie [Huy], and retook it with sword in hand. His Grace sent away the prisoners to Holland, and left a fresh garrison of men there. Then we marched in six lines, making no noise, and attacked the Brabant Line,[74] and took it about break of day, with little or no loss. When we were over on their side, they attacked us with very great loss.

---

[72] The Hunsrück mountains.

[73] The French cavalry placed an emphasis on the long horse-pistol, and were trained to halt and deliver volley fire at the opposing cavalry, using their swords when they came to the melee. Marlborough's squadrons were allowed only three pistol-rounds per man for the whole campaign, and relied more upon their swords. They "were trained to maneuver, to approach the enemy slowly and in close order, and then to ride upon them at a heavy trot in the teeth of their pistol-fire." Churchill, v. 3, 110.

[74] See note 59. After a skillful series of feints, the allied armies crossed the Lines of Brabant below the fortress of Léau, in the early morning hours of July 18, 1705, achieving a complete surprise on the French defenders. The Royal Scots were in the van. Churchill, v. 4, 200-27.

---

[71] Camille d'Hostun, Comte de Tallard, Marshal of France. In addition to the Marshal, eighteen French general officers were captured at Blenheim. Churchill, v. 4, 116.

Then they took retreat to Lovaine [Leuven], to maintain that pass. We took their baggage and several pieces of cannon: some with three bores. We fell upon their rear and took four regiments of them prisoners in Tarlimount [Tirlemont]. They were sent prisoners to Holland. Our army marched near Lovaine [Leuven], where the French frequently cannonaded us. Our picket and theirs did frequently engage over the pass with small shot. We made several attacks on the pass of Lovaine [Leuven], but could not take it. We laid siege to Saintlue [?] and took it. This campaign being ended, His Grace ordered all the troops to their former garrisons. When I came to the Bush [den Bosch], I followed my old trade in all points as I used formerly. I was in great danger from the Italians and French: they put hard on me. It was a very cold winter. Several sentries were frozen to death on their posts.

In 1706, the spring being good, we set out in the end of March with courage, and marched through Brabant until we came near Ramelie[75] [Ramillies], where all the foreign forces joined us. Next morning being Whitsunday, we espied our enemy the French, all in good battle order. We drew up immediately over against them. They cannonaded us very briskly. When our train came up we erected batteries and did great execution among the French Horse. The cannons continued two or three hours, then both Horse and Foot engaged. The Scots Grays behaved well against the enemy's Foot. The Dane's Cavalry fought well against the Household of France.[76] We took many a standard, and all their baggage and bread waggons, with all their ammunition. There was a great many killed, and a great many prisoners taken. We then pursued the chase over the pass of Lovaine [Leuven] into Flanders. That campaign, we took all Flanders. We laid siege to four strong garrisons: Dormount [Dendermond], Minnen [Menin], and Oustain [Houstaing], the city of Ath, which we took with a great deal of difficulty. At the siege of Ath, I was in several storms. I was throwing grenades eight hours together, where I got a ball in my head, which will mind me of it while I live. That city submitted to the Duke, and were sent prisoners to Holland. This campaign ended and we were ordered to our garrisons. It fell the lot of our regiment to go to Bridges [Bruges], where I recovered of the wound in my head. I have a piece of

silver in it. While I was under the cure, my contribution came in to me from my comrades. When I was fully recovered, I set up a school and had very good business. I had several combats in protecting my new ladies I got there.

In 1707 we took the field and camped at Pungdeperie [Pont-Espier]. During this camp I had good business by gameing and with my ladies. There was a wicked fellow who belonged to the Dutch Blue Guards.[77] He was a French Gascoon. He bullied all the swords-men belonging to them. He and I fell out about a mistress. He challenged me immediately to answer him, which I did. So we went out to the back of an old trench where he shewed me five graves which he had filled, and told me I should be the sixth (we had a great many spectators, both Dutch and English) if I would not yield him the lady. For shame, I could not but fight him. He drew his sword and with it drew a line, saying that should be my grave. I told him it was too short for me. Likewise, I did not love to lie wet at night, but said it would fit him better. We fell to it. He advanced upon me so that I was obliged to give way a little. I bound his sword and made a half thrust at his breast. He timed[78] me and wounded me in the mouth. We took another turn. I took a little better care and gave him a thrust in the body, which made him very angry. He came upon me very boldly. Some of the spectators cryed, "Stand your ground!" I wished them in my place. Then I gave him a thrust in the belly. He then darted his sword at me. I parried it. He went and lay down on his coat and spake not. I took up my scabbard and made the best of my way to the regiment, hearing no more about him, but that his comrades were glad he was off the stage, for he was very troublesome.

We removed our camp to a place called Meldor [Meldert], where we continued a long time. There I had thirty-two ladies, and were obliged each of them to pay me a crown a week.[79] My gameing went on apace. There was a Quartermaster of Taps Dragoons came to one of the tents, and took the bobs [earrings] out of the ears of one of the ladies, and ten crowns. He gave her a kick on the back-side and went off. The landlord sent me word. I told him I would see them next morning. I called for the Quartermaster at a sutler's tent. He came to me and told he knew my errand, and that he would give me satisfaction. He and I took a bottle of white wine. So we went out and met a Genever man and carried him with us. We came to a hollow place in a high way

[75] May 23, 1706. In this battle, fought 30 miles south-east of Brussels, the French army was completely destroyed, with 12,000 men killed and wounded, and 6,000 men taken prisoner. It was the scene of the largest cavalry battle ever fought, involving nearly 25,000 horsemen; and opened the way for the allied conquest of Belgium. The Royal Scots, under Lord Orkney, fought at the right of the line, between the villages of Offus and Autréglise. Churchill, v. 5, 102-29.

[76] The Maison du Roi, the household cavalry of the French monarch. "These splendid warriors, the pride of the French nobility…" Churchill, v. 5, 115. They were cut to pieces at Ramillies.

[77] First brought to England as the personal bodyguard of William III, this elite force was exiled to the Continent in 1699, along with the rest of William's Dutch favorites, under pressure from Parliament. Churchill, v. 2, 81, 191.

[78] A time-thrust or arrest, that anticipates and intercepts the opponent's attack. Gaugler, 57.

[79] See note 20.

where he laid out the money and bobs, saying, "Win them and wear them." We took a snuff and a dram. Then we took a turn for the money, but I could make nothing of him. So we took breath a little and fell to it again, and closed one another, and secured one another's swords. But none of us could get advantage of another. We had five such turns, but could make nothing of it. We were four or five times through other's shirts, but could not draw blood. Then I told him I would agree with him. He gave the bobs to the Genever man and desired him to carry them to the young lady. As for the money, we agreed to drink it and let the whore work for more. This Quartermaster was an old Fencing Master in the west of Ireland.

A little after this I got thirty men that was willing to be at my command. So we went to the Duke of Marlborough's Secretary and got a warrant to go a-partisaning. That night we went out very quietly to try what we could make. Before day we came near the French camp and hid our selves in a wood all the next day. At night we went to the rear of the French camp and hid our selves as we could in a little wood by the highway side (about three leagues from Namur). Presently appears a Colonel of French Dragoons with sixteen horsemen and his own baggage. I desired them to surrender, but they were unwilling, which obliged us to fire, wherewith we wounded four and took the other twelve and the Colonel prisoners. We took the sixteen horse and the prisoners and made the best of our way for our own camp. We brought him before the Secretary, and there he [the French Colonel] paid eight pistoles for each horse and servant, and twenty for himself, because he was civilly treated. He and his servants were upon parole, and we were dismissed. So we parted our money. I asked how my affairs went on: my deputy gave me a good account.

After two or three days rest, I and my volunteers resolved to try what we could make of the French. We went to the Secretary for a new warrant. We obtained it, and our orders was to take special care of our selves, and to return in ten days, and make a true report what should happen in the time. We came to the Wood of Orleans and lay close. The day following, I ordered my guide to go to the French camp to see what they were doing or when they were to forage. About twelve at night he returned and told me that the Household of France was to forage near where I and my men lay. They had the best horse in the camp. About five in the morning we removed a little nearer the highway where they were to pass. But when they came we were not able to attack them, but presently they begun to spread themselves and posted their guards about them. My guide and spy was as throng cutting the corn as they were. He had his forage coards about his waist and an old Boor's coat on him. Near night, he came off from them, and told which way they were to return, and in what order. There was a guard of Horse in the front and another in the rear. There was a great distance betwixt the guards. When I viewed them in the hollow of the highway, I thought fit to attack them in the center, which we did, and took sixty of their horse. One of them fired and wounded one of my lads slightly in the face. We went off with all speed, for that shot alarmed the camp. Each of us had two horse. When we came near to Brussels, one of our garrisons, I espyed three squadroons of Horse, so we thought fit to place our selves in a Boor's yard that was well fenced. I creept as far as I could, and found they were French with white paper in their hats.[80] Then I fired among them and ran in to the garden. They all followed me, but could not get at us on horseback, so a squadron of them dismounted and cut down the hedge with their swords. In that time, we kept a constant fire upon them. We fired ten shots apiece and then run for it, losing fourteen of our men in that dispute. When we got over into the wood, they could follow us no further. It was a great rain, and we all resolved to go and shelter ourselves from it under a great tree in the wood. When we came there we spyed a party of the French under it: about sixty men. All the guns were standing about the root of it. We fired and surprised them so that they all run and left their arms. We pursued and took an officer and twelve men. We tyed them two and two and took the flints out of their guns and made them carry them on their backs to a town called Baliedelang [Braine-l'Alleud], where we refreshed ourselves and sold their firelocks for half a crown apiece. Then we marched with all speed to Brussels and presented the prisoners to the Governor, who gave us crowns apiece for the men and four crowns for the officer. He kept them until they were relieved, and we came for our camp and told the Secretary all that befell us. Every one of us went to his own tent, and I went to enquire after my business, and found that two of the men that I trusted with my affairs had carried away two of my ladies to their own quarters, which obliged me to fight them both. So they carried the ladies home again.

At this time, we marched to Newvel [Nivelles], where we pursued the French, and beat up their rear, and took four regiments prisoners. After this we marched to a place called Swinie [Soignies], where we halted for some time. One day as I walked along the lane, I met with a Pass-Bank at the front of the Danes' Horse. I asked a share of the money that was got at the game. The Master answered, he had a point on his sword. I told him mine had another. Then we went to try it in a little wood in the rear of the camp. We no sooner drew but he cryed for help, and cryed, "Follow on, follow on, follow on!" There was a great many of his countrymen grassing their horses who came on me with swords, staves, and clubs and stones, which obliged me to take

---

[80] The cockade. The practice of wearing a device or badge in a soldier's hat, to distinguish him from the enemy. "…in the darkness they wore green boughs in their helmets, as was often done by the allies on battle occasions." Churchill, v. 5, 506.

my heels. I happened with my Spadroon to wound their Quartermaster, which put them in a great rage at me. They followed me hard. In the way as I fled there was a trench by a Boor's house. I thought to jump it, but the ground brake in with me, so I fell in it. Before I got out I got many a stroak. Then they drew me out. The Quartermaster ordered them to beat me, and they did do it to purpose so that I was left for dead. There was a well where they used to water their horses. He ordered me to be cast into it. There was not above a foot and an half of water in it. When I came to my senses, I looked about me but could see nothing but as it were a star above me. Thus I lay in a most wretched condition, being all blood and battery, my cloaths rent off me, my back black with bruised blood. Some time after there came a woman to draw water. I took hold of the chain and came up to the breast of the well. When the woman saw me she supposed I was a devil. She quit her hands of the chain and I went down to my old quarters. The last fall was worse than the first. There I lay, bemoaning my misfortune, and like to perish every moment with cold. I cryed, but no body was to hear me in that pit. The time of watering horse came and I was drawn up. When the men saw me they blessed themselves and asked what I was. I told them I was drunk and fell into it. They asked where my cloaths were. I told them that the Boors took them from me. One of them call'd a Genever man and gave me a dram and shewed me the way to the regiment. I thanked him kindly. When I thought all trouble was over, it but began with me, for as I went along the line all the dogs of the army came out on me. The faster I ran, they followed me the harder. At last I came to my tent. When my wife saw me in such a case, she cryed pitifully. I desired her to get a surgeon. When he came I let blood of both arms and I got a hot drink and went to bed. I did not recover for a month's time. After this I proclaimed open wars with all such base rogues. Then we went to our winter quarters. I set up my school in Ghent.

In 1708 we encamped betwixt Brussels and Lovaine [Leuven]. The French left the ground and marched toward Ghent. We followed them hard and took most of their baggage. A few days after, we fought them at Audinard [Oudinard],[81] where they sustained a great loss. I was wounded in the battle, and was sent to the hospital in Brussels, where I was a month e're I recovered of my wounds. At this time we laid siege to Lyle [Lille], whither I went to camp. At this siege there was great loss on both sides.[82]

In the time of this siege General Web[83] was commanded to go to Ostend with a small flying army to bring provisions to the camp. In our return three thousand, six hundred French, with six piece of cannon, attacked us near Winning [Wynendael][84] in a great plain hard by a wood-side. Our army was but a thousand, three hundred. To their shame, we beat them into the wood and took their cannon. We brought our provisions safe to the camp. I was wounded in this action and sent again to the hospital in Brussels, where I continued above a month. Then I came out on my crutches and set up my old trade of gameing. At this time the Duke of Bavaria laid siege to Brussels, which obliged every man that could go to take arms. We were besieged with fifty thousand men. All that was within the town was thirteen regiments and five hundred men in the hospital. My charge was five piece of cannon. I had sixteen men to assist me. The French broke ground very near our works, which obliged us to stand to it. We continued five days, cannonading one another. They burned several houses with their bombs. The sixth day they stormed us with twelve hundred men. The storm continued from nine at night until seven the next morning. We beat them off and killed an hundred and sixty of the French. We sallied out upon them and leveled a great deal of their works. After this the enemy desired the favour of General Murray, who commanded our forces, to grant a parley until they carried off their dead men, which was granted. No sooner they had carried them off, but we fell a-cannonading one another again. Some of their deserters told us that we were to be stormed next day with sixteen hundred men, and to take the town with sword in hand. About ten a'clock at night the enemy got account that General Cadogan[85] was in his march for our relief. This put them in such confusion that they blew up their magazine and left their train and all their wounded men. About the break of day a great deal of deserters from the French were at our port and gave us an account of their flying. Then our General sent a good party of Dragoons and Huzars to drive up their rear. On their return they brought a great deal of the enemy's baggage. Likewise they brought in all their cannon

[82] Sieges depended largely upon gunpowder: for the artillery battering the fortifications and the batteries attempting to prevent them. In order to succor the beseiged French at Lille, the Chevalier de Luxembourg led 2,000 dragoons, each carrying a sixty-pound bag of powder, in a daring midnight gallop into the town. Nearly half got through before they were discovered. Churchill, v. 5, 506.

[83] General John Richmond Webb.

[84] The relief convoy, carrying much needed powder for the besiegers of Lille, was threatened en route from Ostend by Marshal La Motte, with 40 battalions. Webb, with 24 battalions, caught the French between two woods at Wynendael and repulsed them, although outnumbered two to one. The ammunition convoy passed safely, sealing the fate of Lille.

[85] William, first Earl Cadogan. Marlborough's Quartermaster General, he fulfilled the modern offices of Chief of Staff and Director of Intelligence. Churchill, v. 2, 234.

[81] July 11, 1708. Crossing the river Scheldt on hastily thrown-up pontoon bridges at the fortified town of Oudenarde, the armies of the Grand Alliance caught the French, once again, by surprise, and routed them, inflicting 20,000 casualties. The French commander, Marshal Vendôme, joined in the hand-to-hand fighting on the front line; while the Dukes of Burgundy and Berri, and the English Pretender, James Edward Stuart, watched helplessly from the mill at Royegem as the debacle unfolded. Churchill, v. 5, 404-32.

and an hundred and forty of their wounded men and put them in to the hospital, where they were taken care of. The Governour of the city, Prince Piscal,[86] and the General ordered to every gunner ten pistoles of *smart money* as their reward, and two pistoles to every single man.

After this all of us that were able to travel went to our own regiments. Lyle [Lille] being taken, we laid siege to Ghent. The year being so far spent, we were obliged to take it, that we might winter in it. They seemed not to surrender. Then the Duke of Marlborough ordered a hundred piece of cannon to be mounted opposite to the great-church in order to burn the town with hot balls. Likewise [he] ordered fifty mortars and hobits, and three hundred small mortars, call'd cow-horns,[87] with all the Grenadeers to play at once upon the town in case they would not surrender. When the cityzens saw this, they threatened to fall upon the French if they would not accept of the offer Marlborough made to them. This obliged them to accept. They marched out with flying colours and drums beating. We took Bridges [Bruges] at the same time (in these two garrisons were five thousand French). On Christmas day we marched into Ghent, where I lived very well with my school that winter. Thus ended this glorious campaign.

In 1709 we took the field and laid siege to the city of Turney [Tournai] and the citydale. I was one of the besiegers at the citydale. While we were breaking ground and erecting batteries, they fired very hard upon us with their cannon, but we soon made them keep in their heads. We stormed their out-works in the night-time and took them, and before day we cast a trench to shelter our selves. When they saw what we had done, they planted a gun directly on our flank, through the wall. With one shot they killed forty-eight men. I escaped the shot, but one of the heads of the men that was shot knocked me down and all his brains came round my head. I, being half senseless, put up my hand to my head, and finding the brains, cryed to my neighbor that all my brains were knock'd out. He said, "Were your brains out, you could not speak!" When our gunners spyed where the shot came from, they directed the whole batterie against that place, and beat down the wall, and dismounted the gun before they could fire it again. In a little time after, the city submitted and marched all their men into the citydale. It was very strong, and held out for several weeks, until they sprung all their mines. Then we beat them out of it and took possession of both city and citydale.

The Duke then marched his army towards Mons, in order to besiege it. At this time the French army advanced to the plains and woods of Malplackie [Malplaquet].[88] His Grace the Duke of Marlborough left some troops at Mons and marched the army to give the French battle. When they heard of our march, they intrenched themselves. When we came up they cannonaded us two days. I had two children at this time. Our wives were far in the rear. My wife gave my little boy to a comrade's wife who had a horse. The woman, hearing her husband was dead, she rode until she saw me in the front of the line, then she threw the boy at me. Then I was obliged to put him in my habersack. He was about three years of age. As we were inclining to the right, the boy got a shot in the arm. I then got a surgeon and dressed it. I had neither bread nor drink to give him. I got a dram to him from an officer and a leg of a fowl. Then he held his peace and was very quiet all night. In the morning, his mother took him from me. His Grace the Duke of Marlborough ordered every battalion to go to prayers, but the wicked French with their cannon obliged us to make our prayers short. Then His Grace ordered every man a dram of Genever. Then we marched towards the enemy. The Duke of Argyle,[89] with thirty thousand, made the first attack on the woods and put them out of three trenches with a great loss on both sides. A cannon ball went through my cape and broke my gun. Then I took up another gun and went on. The Earl of Orkney ordered six piece of cannon to be drawn through the wood by strength of men, which was done, and placed in the plain against the enemy. The six piece of cannon did great execution on both men and horse, and obliged them to run, some one way, some another. We returned to the place we fought in and lay on our arms all night among the dead.[90] Next day we

---

[86] During the siege, Colonel Pascal "ordered a pound of flesh, two quarts of beer, and four glasses of brandy to be distributed every day gratis to each soldier. Thus fortified, the garrison resisted with vigour..." Churchill, v. 5, 524. A man after McBane's own heart.

[87] A grenade-mortar named for Baron van Coehorn, the "Dutch Vauban." Chandler, 249.

[88] Battle of Malplaquet (September 10-11, 1709). While covering the siege of Mons, Marlborough attempted to lure Marshal Villars and the French army to battle, but Villars would not take the bait. He entrenched his army and opened an artillery fire upon the allied positions. Early the next morning, Marlborough attacked. His plan of battle was to strike the French wings, anchored on two forests, until Villars was forced to weaken his center. Orkney's troops, with McBane among them, were selected to pierce the French center of earthworks and redans. Mid-way through the battle, Orkney detached a battalion of the Royal Scots to shore up the allied right in the salient of the Wood of Taisnières. "The conditions inside the salient were indescribable. Within a triangle, no side of which exceeded six hundred yards, there were at least seven thousand men lying killed and wounded, more than thirty thousand allied infantry in almost solid masses, and four or five thousand French survivors. The wounded on both sides... were bayoneted and plundered. The screams of the injured, the roar of the mob of combatants, the crash of musketry, resounded form this smoking inferno, in which half the allied foot had become engulfed." The allies prevailed, but at the appalling cost of 24,000 allied and nearly 15,000 French casualties. This day of carnage would not be surpassed until the Battle of Borodino in 1812. Churchill, v. 6, 127-75.

[89] John Campbell, second Duke of Argyll.

marched to the ground we were on before. Then His Grace detatch'd an army to lay close siege to Mons. I bought a fine horse from one of our officers and gave him four pistoles for it. I set a wounded man on him, who kept the horse for me. That night the Duke of Marlborough gave orders to all the Horse and Dragoons that wherever they could get any of the horse they had lost, to pay a pistole and take them again. I mounted my horse with the French furniture on him, in order to sell him. They offered me fourteen pistoles, but I would have sixteen. Then I rode to the rear of the Dutch Horse where the bread waggons were. Two Dragoons, with two Quartermasters, challenged my horse for their own. They ordered me to dismount and they would give me a pistole, according to orders. I told them, "Gentlemen, you see by the French mounting that he is none of yours. I bought him from an officer who shot the French-man off him." I desired them to come along and I would shew them the officer, but they refused. One of them took me by the leg and cast me off the horse. Then I drew my Spadroon and held the bridle in my left hand. They drew upon me. I defended as I could, but some of them was so foolish as to run upon the point of it. Another cut the bridle so the horse got loose, and I ran to the bread-guard, and delivered my sword to the Serjeant, and told him I was his prisoner and the crimes I had committed within the liberty of his sentries. I asked for his officers. He told me they were at dinner. I desired him to save me from the Dutch Guard, and to send me to our own regiment, and to send an account of my crime with me. In the time I was speaking to him the Dutch Guard came, and he delivered me to them without acquainting his officers (for which he was broke). The Dutch used me most barbarously. They beat me with their guns, and cut the head-band of my breeches that I might carry them up with my hands least I should run away. They brought me before their Brigadeer, who would not hear me speak for my self, but swore he would have me hanged as soon as he had dined. He ordered me to be carried to the Standard Guard and to have the Provo[91] in readiness. The Provo came and shewed me his ropes and told me he should soon put an end to the life of an "English Bouger." He went and put a nail in a tree that was hard by and tyed the rope with a loop on it. I saw him doing all this, which bred a dreadfull

fear on me. Kind providence brought the Earl of Orkney's Edecamp [aide de camp] that way. Some of the by-standers told him my case. He rode up to the Guard in haste, but the sentries would not suffer him to speak to me. Then he went to the Brigadeer, who was still in a passion, and fully resolved to put his former orders in execution. Major Whitney desired the Brigadeer to take a bottle of wine, and in the mean time he sent his servant to our own regiment, and brought a party to carry me to our own Quarter-Guard, whither I was immediately carried. Next morning I was try'd and acquit before General Wood. My accusers were found guilty of robbery, and were obliged to pay me fourteen pistoles, as I had been offered, for the horse. This good service laid me under an endless obligation to that Gentleman. We went a little nearer the city of Mons, and it being taken, we ended that campaign, and were sent to our winter quarters. Our lot was to Ghent, where I lived very well that winter. One day as I was walking in the castle, I met a man and his wife who were fighting. I desired the man not to beat down the woman and thrust him away with my hand. The woman got up and call'd me a rogue, saying, what had I to do with her husband? She took me by the hair and he got my finger in his mouth. O! how the spectators did laugh to see her drawing me back and him drawing me foreward by the finger, until the people of the house took them off me. I had no manner of arms about me. That learned me never to meddle my self with the pleas of man and wife since.

In 1710 we set out to camp and laid siege to Dowie [Douai].[92] We made a strong line in the front between us and the French. In this camp I had several skirmishes with foreigners in defence of my mistresses and gameing trade. We took both city and citydale. The French march'd out upon condition.[93] The Duke left a good garrison of men in it, and march'd further into the French country, and laid siege to St. Vinian [St. Venant]. At that same time we laid siege to that great city, Aire. The French was looking on and could make no help. The battalion I belonged to stayed at the siege of St. Vinian [St. Venant]. The other battalion of the Royal went to the siege of Aire. One night I was one of the stormers of the counter-scarf [counterscarp] and half-moon,[94] and took it

---

[90] The Dutch Deputy Goslinga wrote, "There where the Dutch Guard battalions had stood lay about twelve hundred terribly mutilated corpses, most robbed of their clothes, in rows before the French entrenchments. The bodies of those who had been foremost seemed to have been mown down, having toppled forward in their ranks against the enemy breast-works. Behind them the ditch was so thick with corpses that no inch of soil could be seen. Add to such a sight the shrieks and groans and sighs of the badly wounded, and one can get some idea of the horror of the night which followed the battle of Malplaquet." Churchill, v. 6, 173

[91] Provost. An officer of the military police in a garrison, camp, or the field. *Oxford English Dictionary.*

[92] The siege of Douai was to be the first step in the allied invasion of France. "It covered Brabant and the Spanish Netherlands from French counterstrokes, and it threatened simultaneously five or six fortresses essential to the French defense." At the head of one of the French armies opposing the allies in 1710 was the Duc de Montesquiou, who as a young musketeer went by the name of d'Artagnan. Churchill, v. 6, 234-58.

[93] "If, however, the defenders refused to capitulate upon terms they were eventually faced with the alternatives of withstanding a general storm, or surrendering 'at discretion.' In the latter case they stripped themselves of all legal and moral protection, and, in theory, laid themselves open to...cold-blooded execution..."Duffy, 250.

with sword in hand. The shell of a grenade wounded me sore in the side. The next morning they yielded upon conditions. They march'd out with flying colours and drums beating. Aire stood it out some weeks longer, but were obliged to surrender upon terms. This campaign ended, and we were ordered to our old garrisons, where I followed my old trades.

Towards the latter end of winter there was a detachment of every company through all our garrisons to go and cantoon upon the borders of France. When we were all gathered together, Cadogan came to us with a train. Then we march'd to a great city called Orrass [Arras] in Normandy.[95] We placed our guns against their high magazines with hot balls. We set them all on fire, with some houses adjacent to them. This put the city in an uproar. Fearing he should burn the whole city, they sent to see what he was for. He told them to send him twenty years' contribution, and that in the space of two hours. Otherways he would burn it at once. They sent him a waggon loden with gold and silver. So we retired and were sent to our own garrisons.

In 1711 we took the field, and march'd to the plains of Dowie [Douai], and stayed there a few days until our army convened. Then we march'd to leward [leeward], between Dowie [Douai] and Bashaine [Bouchain]. We continued there for several weeks. There I followed my old trade, as well in the Hollands' quarters as in Marlborough's quarters. There was two Hollanders that was angry that I should have a share in their quarters, so they swore I should have it no more. They came to the gameing tent I had there and cut it down and abused my servant. They sent me a challenge to meet them next morning, but being under arms to be reviewed by the General, I could not attend. This offended them because I gave them not a meeting. Both of them came where I was in bed and said if I would not arise and give them satisfaction, they would stab me where I lay. I desired them to go to a tent in the rear and take a glass of wine, and I would be with them in a minute. I sent for a comrade, one Joseph Borrough, an English-man, who came. Then we went to the tent where they were and asked what they designed? They told us they would fight in the front of our army, and that they had provided a waggon to carry us off when killed. The landlord of the tent, as we were going out, searched us for fire arms. He found two pistols upon one of them and one upon the other, but none upon us. So we walked to the place appointed in the front of the army. They stript, and we likeways. Then they took a dram and drunk to

each other. I asked if they would give us a dram, but [they] refused, upon which my comrade drew and engaged his man. I likewise engaged my man. We were not long until we ended the controversie. One lay on the spot. The other was carried in the waggon that was provided for us. We went to our camp and kept quiet a day or two. After this we march'd to a place call'd Shotto [chateau] Broolee [?], where we made several attempts on the French line to draw them from the pass of Orlew [Arleux], but to no purpose. One day we made fascines in order to take their line. This we did by way of feint, but that night we cast them all away and took the pass by day-light. All our army passed over before seven in the morning. We march'd up a hill and camped in sight of the French. About twelve a'clock at night we moved our camp and passed over the river, surrounded Buschean [Bouchain], and laid close siege to it.[96] The French from their camp cannonaded us, but to no purpose, for we secured our selves with good trenches. We took it very soon. Some time after it was taken, I went in to view it. I met with gameing tents in the market-place. I and the Hollanders fell out, then we drew our swords. Some thing extraordinary happened and I was obliged to fly. The Guard followed me and fired several shots at me. I escaped them and came to my Captain and told him what had befallen me. He ordered me into Dowie [Douai] under the protection of Colonel Douglas until he should send for me. In the way to Dowie, it being dark at night, the French took me and stript me and took my money from me. They carried me into a wood where there was a great many more prisoners. By daylight, we were brought to the French camp, where the Partizan knew me and gave me my cloaths and two crowns. We were carried before General Legby, and from him to General Villars,[97] who ordered us all to the Provoes. He caused me to list in his own regiment. The next day I came to the head-quarters, where I pickt up a mistress. I staid with her that night. In the morning she went away with my breeches and my money. When I began to make a noise, the landlady call'd me a rogue. She said, "You brought her in your self, and we thought she had been your wife. You shall pay before you go, otherways we will take your coat." I was obliged to send to my Captain, who sent me a pair of breeches, and money to clear my quarters. Next day I came to the quarters again, where I fell out with some of the swords-men about a share of the gameing money. I got the better of two of them. The guard came and took us prisoners. We were carried before the General, who said I began soon. "If you were not a stranger you should be punished." He pardoned me. Next morn-

[94] The counterscarp is the exterior wall of the ditch below the glacis (the elevated mound of earth that slopes toward the country from the ditch, forcing the enemy to attack uphill). The half-moon, or lunette, is a semicircular fortification facing the counterscarp. Hogg, 250-1.

[95] Arras is in actually in Artois. The important thing to McBane seems to be that it is in the territory of France.

[96] The fortified city of Bouchaine was the eastern anchor of the French "ne plus ultra" lines. Marlborough successfully undertook the siege with an army of 90,000 men, in the face of a French force of 96,000. It was his last conquest and command. A Tory government would dismiss Marlborough and replace him with the Duke of Ormonde. Churchill, v. 6, 440-457.

[97] Marshal Claude-Louis-Hector de Villars.

ing came a Drum Major from our army to relieve those men that were with the Provoes. My name was among them also. The General said, "Take him, for if he stay he will kill all my men."

This was the first time that ever I was taken. I was eleven days with them. I was glad when we went to our own camp. My Captain was very glad to see me alive. In four days after, we were ordered to our garrisons. We lay in Ghent, where I was still busied with my school and old trade.

In 1712 we took the field and encamped at Shotto-geamersie [Cateau-Cambrésis]. While we lay there, the Hollanders laid siege to Landosie [Landrecies]. Then a cessation of arms came.[98] Then we marched to Ghent and left the Dutch troops. The Royal Regiment I belonged to went to Dunkirk. Thus ended our Flanders wars. While I stayed in Dunkirk, I kept a school and had good bread. At length I took the ague and my Colonel sent me to England and recommended me to Chance-Colledge.[99] When I got my foot on British ground, I desired to be thankfull for all the deliverances I met with while abroad. Here ends all my transactions in Holland, Germany, Flanders, and France.

Some time after I recovered, I went and married a wife.[100] I kept an ale-house and a school, and lived very well in London. I fought thirty-seven prizes in Bear-Garden.[101]

At the late rebellion,[102] I left Chance-Colledge and listed in General Honeywood's regiment of Dragoons, where I was made a Serjeant. I had the honour to guard the standard at the battle of Preston.[103] After the battle we were ordered to lye in Balton [Bolton], in the Muire [moor] of Lancaster, where by reason of the long cold winter, my old wounds in my leg broke out, which caused me to draw my discharge, which was granted me, and was recommended to Chance-Colledge as a Serjeant of Dragoons. Yet being willing to serve His Majesty,[104] I went as a gunner to Fort William[105] in the north of Scotland. In 1726 I fought a clean young man at Edinburgh.[106] I gave him seven wounds and broke his arms with the Fauchion [falchion]. This I did at the request of several Noblemen and Gentlemen. But now being sixty-three years of age, resolves never to fight any more, but to repent for my former wickedness.

FINIS

---

[98] The Tory party in England, which had organized the dismissal of Marlborough, further betrayed the Grand Alliance by secretly negotiating a separate peace with France. In July of 1712 the Duke of Ormonde withdrew the British forces from the theatre of battle. "Under an iron discipline the veteran regiments and battalions, whose names had hitherto been held in so much honour in the camps of Europe, marched off with downcast eyes, while their comrades of the long war gazed upon them in mute reproach…when they reached the end of the march and the ranks were broken terrible scenes were witnessed of humble men breaking their muskets, tearing their hair, and pouring out blasphemies and curses against the Queen and the Ministry who could subject them to that ordeal. Others of these rough fellows – the scum, we are assured, of our country – sat on the ground weeping with rage and grief when they thought of all they had dared and suffered, and of "the Old Corporal" [Marlborough] who had led them on." Churchill, v. 6, 554. McBane, who clearly had great admiration for Marlborough, must have shared in these emotions. This may explain why, after so many years of danger and hard campaigning, he has so little to say about the armistice.

[99] This is probably the Royal Hospital, Chelsea. Founded by Charles II in 1692, and designed by Christopher Wren, Chelsea Hospital continues to serve as a retreat for old or disabled soldiers. On parade, the Chelsea Pensioners wear the scarlet coats and tricorn hats of the time of Marlborough and McBane.

[100] Wife number three for McBane.

[101] McBane retired from the wars at the age of 48. In London he became a prize fighter at the Bear Garden, a theatre on the south bank of the Thames, only steps from where Shakespeare's Globe once stood. Prize fighting in those days was done with a variety of real, sharp weapons (including back sword, sword & dagger, sword & buckler, falchion, case of falchions, and quarterstaff), and drew large crowds from all walks of life. That McBane successfully fought thirty-seven of these combats is as remarkable as his surviving the wars. Castle, 265-9; Hutton, 286-309.

[102] The unsuccessful rebellion of 1715 to restore James Edward Stuart to the thrones of Scotland and England.

[103] The Jacobite Anglo-Scottish force marched into England, proclaiming James Edward Stuart as king, and hoping to pick up large numbers of supporters. On November 11, 1715, they reached Preston. Government forces surrounded them, and on the 14th they surrendered unconditionally. Daiches, 65. According to the valedictory verses at the beginning of his book, McBane was serving as a sergeant of dragoons at this battle.

[104] George I

[105] see note 19 above

[106] At the age of 62, McBane fought and vanquished the Irish gladiator O'Bryan at Holyrood House, as described in the poem *To a Scottish Hero* at the beginning of McBane's book.

Martial arts instructor Dale Seago from Bunjin-kan as a Highland swordmaster, appropriately attired in clothing c.1740s.

McBane's Fencing Manual

"General Directions"

Before you take a *Fleuret* from either Master or Scholar, put on both your gloves to save your hands in case you should receive a Batter. And pull off your coat, otherways 'twill incommode you. When the *Fleuret* is presented to you, take off your hat with your left hand and receive the *Fleuret* with your right hand. Then make your salute handsomely by drawing the right foot behind the left, and then the left behind the right to your Guard; then advance again to your adversary by bringing your left foot before the right, and then the right before the left to your Guard. In the salute, as you retire from, and as you advance up to your adversary, turn your hand in *Quart* and in *Tierce*. Stand on your Guard thus: bend your left knee as much as you can to stand firm and easy; keep your right leg right up and down, and bend your right knee a little; keep your right foot pointing directly to the front, to your adversary, and the left foot broadways to the rear, thus:

Ashley demonstrates McBane's footwork position.

Let your feet be two foot distant, one from the other And have them at command ready to advance, retire, traverse, spring to right or left, jump back, or *Avolt* as there is occasion. And not let one foot touch the other in any of these cases, and don't stand wider with your feet than that you can command them, and do as above mention'd. Always keep your body straight up, except when you Push. You must bend it from your adversary's point, or to the contrary side from it, as is hereafter mention'd, when you Push some particular thrusts. For unless you bend your head from his point, you may be hit in the face. And if you bend your body forward to your adversary, besides the danger it

is in by being so much nearer, you can not easily recover your self from a Lunge, nor retire so easy and quick as you ought. Therefore rather bend a little back from him than to him. Let your side be only in his view, for the less mark you give the better. This is call'd *Light*.

Keep your left hand always above your left eye brow, ready to Parie. And when you Push, still keep it there for the same purpose, in case your adversary should *Contre-temps* or Riposte. Keep your right hand breast high, and your point 3 or 4 inches higher, which is the proper *Quart* Guard, and best to play upon. For from this Guard you can instantly go to any other. And Parie with a spring. Or you may easily go to any other and make a thrust. Thus you are in your proper Guard every way.

Let the grip of your Sword or *Fleuret* be no bigger than that you can close your little finger round it and touch the palm of your hand. And let all your fingers be round the grip, and the point of your thumb close to or near the shell; which guards your hand much more than as some people hold it, with the pummel in the hand, and fore finger stretch'd out towards the shell. They then can not command the Sword so well, and all the advantage of holding it so is that they have a greater length from the point to the body than if they held it with the thumb close to the shell. If the grip of their Sword or *Fleuret* be larger than as here mention'd, it will easily be beat out of your hand by a Batter.

When you are to offend, whether at the wall or on the floor, keep your hand breast high, and point rather below your hand. And if you are to defend at the wall, keep your hand as low as your hip, and your point as high as your forehead. But for defence on the floor, keep the proper *Quart* Guard, and by turning your hand you may Parie all high thrusts or thrusts made at the level of your hand and above. For thrusts below the level of your hand, the *Low Quart* and *Seconde* will Parie them.

When you Push at the wall, first take off your hat with your left hand, and make a Lunge at your adversary's breast, to try if you have the proper distance: which is so that at a Lunge you can just touch his breast with the button of your *Fleuret*, but no nearer. Your adversary is to take off his hat at the same time with you, and give you leave to touch him on the breast by dropping his hand and point down a little to his right or out-side. Then recover both to your Guard. Note that when you are going to Push on the floor, before you salute your adversary; and when you are going to Push at the wall, before you take the distance; both

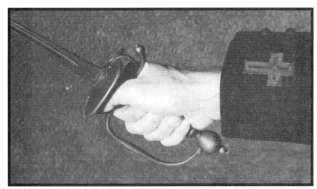

Gripping the Fleuret or Small Sword, per McBane

blade, so that it can not easily be beat out of your hand. Thus the blade will be half-turn'd, or be between being flat-ways and edge-ways. Some people hold the blade flat-ways, or one side directly up level. But then there is nothing to support the pummel, and a Batter will easily beat your Sword out of your hand.

Quart Guard is to guard off or Parie a thrust made on the in-side of the arm, any where between the neck and lower part of the breast.

A *Quart* Thrust is with the hand and blade turn'd as in *Quart* Guard, and made at your adversary any where between the neck and lower part of the breast, or the in-side of his arm.

persons must, if there is any person of rank present, salute the person of rank first, and then the Master. But if there be not any such person present, then salute the Master first, and the Gentle-men present, or Scholars, afterwards. This salute is thus: as you stand on your Guard with your hat on, raise your point and bring your blade almost right up and down. Then (without any stop) drop your point towards the person you'd salute, then bring over and drop it on the other side to the other person or persons who you are to salute, and then recover to your Guard and salute one another, or take the distance.

Quart Guard is with your hand as high as your breast and turn'd inwards, so that the knuckle of your thumb and the upper knuckle of the fore-finger are the uppermost part of your hand; and both level with one another; and the point three or four inches above the height of your hand; the pummel almost under the heel of the palm of your hand, which supports the

Quart thrust and the response; a quarte parry

Ashley demonstrates McBane's Quart Guard.

Ashley demonstrates McBane's Tierce Guard.

*T*ierce Guard is with the hand and point the same height as *Quart*, but the hand so turn'd in that the blade is edge-ways, or the out-side edge up, and the in-side directly underneath it. Don't turn the hand more than to let your blade be exactly thus, for this is sufficient to Parie, and you can command your Sword. But if you turn your hand more, it is awkward, and you can't command your Sword so well as you ought, nor come to another Guard, nor take an advantage so quick and easy as you might, were it only turn'd so much, as here said, which is necessary.

Tierce Guard is to guard off or Parie a thrust made on the out-side of the arm, any where between the neck and the level of the lower part of the breast.

A *Tierce* Thrust is with the hand and blade turn'd as in *Tierce* Guard, and made at the adversary any where between the neck and level of the lower part of the breast, on the out-side of his arm.

A tierce thrust by the right-hand combatant countered by a tierce parie by the gentleman on the left.

Low Quart Guard is to guard off or Parie a thrust made on the in-side of the arm, any where between the level of the lower part of the breast and the level of the lower part of the belly.

A *Low Quart* Thrust is with the hand and blade turn'd as in *Low Quart* Guard, and made at your adversary any where between the level of the lower part of the belly, on the in-side of his arm.

Ashley demonstrates McBane's Low Quart Guard.

Seconde, or Hanging Guard, is with the hand as high as your forehead, and point as low as your waistband, the hand so turn'd in that the thumb is lowermost, and little finger upper-most, and the blade flat-ways. This Guard is dangerous because the Sword hand is exposed, and it is more difficult to come to another Guard from this than from the *Tierce*.

Seconde Guard is to guard off or Parie a thrust made on the out-side of the arm, any where between the level of the lower part of the breast and the level of the lower part of the belly.
A *Seconde* Thrust is with the hand and blade turn'd as in *Seconde* Guard, and made at your adversary any where between the level of the lower part of the breast and the level of the lower part of the belly, on the out-side of his arm.

Ashley demonstrates McBane's Seconde or Hanging Guard.

Ashley demonstrates McBane's Seconde or Hanging Guard.

Seconde Thrust by the fencer on the right; Seconde Parie as a counter

Italian *High Quart* Guard, or Parade, with the hand as high as your face, and with the hand and blade turn'd as in *Tierce*, the point as low as your neck and inclined to the *Quart* or in-side, which is the reason it is call'd a *Quart* Guard, because it guards the *Quart* side.

Ashley demonstrates McBane's Italian High Quart Guard

In your Guard, you should keep continually traversing round your adversary in the Round Parade. And don't let him feel your blade if you can possibly avoid it. And make offers as if you were going to Push, sometimes at his face and sometimes at his breast. And shew as if you were going to dart your Sword at him if he goes down to the *Portugueze Guard*, or gives an opening with design. And sometimes spring up as if you were going to Push or hit him in the face, or somewhere above his Sword. And sometimes drop your self low on a sudden, as if you wou'd come under his Sword. This dodging and continual motion will, 'tis likely, make him give an opening. And when he thrusts at your breast or belly, if you have a mind to Batter him, your hand and Sword, being so much raised above his, will come down with such force as will probably beat his out of his hand, or be very near doing it, and put him so much off his Guard that you may have time to hit him before he can recover that firm hold of his Sword, which your Batter deprived him of.

Portugueze Guard is with the hand and blade turn'd as in *Quart* Guard, but the hand down near and clear of the outside of your thigh, and the point within three or four inches of the ground, on the out-side of your foot. You now must Parie all thrusts with your left hand. If you are tired and your adversary will not give you time to rest or draw breath, you may in this Guard rest and recover your self; and there are few that will venture to attack you in it, unless they have an extraordinary dependence on the left hand. But take care, least your adversary dart his Sword at you, to be ready to Parie it. It is good to take your scabbard or cane by the middle, or something short like a dagger, and hold it in your left hand and parrie with it, all by Batter.

Mark & Ashley in Italian High Quart Guard

Mark & Ashley in Portugueze Guard

Ashley demonstrates McBane's Portugueze Guard.

The *French Guard*, which they commonly use, and call *Quart* Guard, is our defencive Guard at the wall, so that they are obliged to cut, Disengage, or Change over the point; which I think is neither so quick nor so safe as Disengaging under the blade with our Guard. Besides, it takes more time to bring your Sword on the level on the line when they are going to thrust; and when feeble, may easily be forced; and their Sword hand is more exposed to be pricked.

Ashley demonstrates McBane's French Guard.

Besides the aforemention'd Guards, there are three others, call'd *High Quart*, *High Tierce*, and *Low Tierce*. But as they are all very open, dangerous, and unnecessary, therefore I take no further notice of them than just to mention them.

There is no particular thrust more than an other to be made from the *Italian High Quart Guard*. You may thrust any thrust as you have an opportunity.

From the *Portugueze Guard*, *Quart* and *Low Quart* are the easiest thrusts to be made. And you may prick your adversary's hand, wrist, or arm from this Guard under his shell easier than from any other Guard.

Mark & Ashley in the French Guard

Quart Over is a thrust with the hand and blade turn'd as in *Quart* Guard, and the same height, and made at your adversary any where between the neck and level of the breast, on the *out-side* of his arm. It is to be Parie'd as *Tierce*.

Re-Quart is a thrust with the hand and blade turn'd as in *Tierce*, and the same height, and made at your adversary any where between the neck and level of the lower part of the breast, on the *in-side* of his arm. It is to be Parie'd as *Quart*, but requires a wide Parie. This thrust is more likely to take upon a skillfull person than an unskillfull one, because the former al-

ways takes care to Parie close and not go far off the line with his point, and the close Parie is not sufficient for this thrust.

Boar's[1] Thrust is thus: as you are in either *Quart* or *Tierce* Guard, draw your arm and Sword down as quick as possible, the hand as low as in the *Portugueze Guard*, and the point

---

[1] Boar, Boer, Boor, Bouer: a Dutch peasant.

Quart Over Thrust

Re-Quart Thrust

you. Then is your time to Push above his blade, either in *Quart* or *Quart Over*, according as he gives the open. This is a deceitful thrust, but must be done with all the quickness imaginable. And if he does answer the call or drop his point, you may Push home below.

Flanconade is a Riposte to be made on your adversarie. As he recovers from Pushing *Quart*, you having Parie'd it, bear his blade down as you thrust with your hand and blade turn'd as in *Quart* Guard, but both lower, and with your blade across his. And direct your point to his flank, belly, or any where else where you can hit. You may make a Riposte in the same manner, as he recovers from Pushing *Tierce*, with your hand and blade turn'd as in *Tierce* Guard, but both lower.

A Flanconade

level with your hand, towards your adversary; then make your thrust either in *Quart*, *Tierce*, or *Low Quart*, by bringing your hand and point up to your adversary, and Lunge at the same time. Do both as quick as possible, without regarding where the point hits on one side or the other, or whether it hits his hand, wrist, arm, face, or body. This going down and returning with such quickness, and in a contrary manner from the usual school play, is apt to put your adversary in confusion, not knowing where the thrust will come, or how to guard against it. And unless he retires as soon as you go down, 'tis very probable that he will be hit. For besides the uncertainty where it comes and the quickness, it goes with great force when return'd against him. This is what is call'd a *Poke*, which many find fault with. I would never make use of this thrust but when engaged with a Ruffin [ruffian], or some person that I had a mind to kill, or was indifferent about the consequence of it.

To thrust with an *Appeller*, do thus: make a small advance, and at the same time make an offer as if you were going to thrust at his face, then instantly drop your point as low as his breast, or upon part of his belly. This dropping is the *Appeller*, or call for your adversarie to drop his point to Parie you below. But you must be so quick as not to let him feel your blade below to Parie

Always keep a spring in your arm and wrist, to make your thrust go the quicker, and your Parie the more sure. And as soon as you have done either, recover them again. [2]

Always observe your adversary's wrist and point, which you may do both at the same time. And sometimes observe his eyes to see how he is in temper. This last you need do very seldom. If you do it often, or think by his eyes to discover where his intentions are, you very possibly may be deceived, for he may look at one part when his design is at another.

Never look another way from your adversary when within reach, or when engaged, for he may take that opportunity to hit you. Nor do you believe him if he should say any thing to you to perswade you to look another way, for many do it on purpose to take that opportunity to hit you, when perhaps they can't effect their design otherways. If you have occasion to look about, be sure first to retire, or get some ways or other out of his reach.

Never over Lunge your self, because one or other of your feet may slip, and you can't recover your self to a Guard so soon as

---

[2] Return to your guard.

Mark begins a Boar's Thrust against Ashley's Quart position

Mark finishes the Boar's Thrust against Ashley's Quart guard

you should, and may be hit in that time. Therefore make but short Lunges, that if you have a Sword in your hand, only three or four inches at most may enter, and that will be sufficient.

If at any time you happen to totter or are likely to fall, jump up from the ground, and you will readily come down to your Guard, firm on your legs as you ought to be.

Always keep the distance of a good Lunge from your adversary that he may not surprize you any way.

On wet or loose ground, raise or turn up the out-side of your left foot when you Lunge, and bear on, or support your self on the in-side edge of the said foot. For then your foot will not readily slip back, as it would were it flat. But on a board floor keep it flat always.

When you have made a Lunge, which must be as quick as possible, make not the least halt or stop, but recover to your Guard as soon as you can, or spring off to right or left, or jump back out of the reach of your adversary's Lunge, least he should Riposte you. For should you make the least halt, if it be with Swords, unless he be kill'd dead by your thrust, he will either seize your Sword, or else stab you for revenge.

Parie all thrusts with the same edge, *viz.* the *Quart* or in-side edge.

Particular Directions for Pushing at the Wall.

If you are to Push at the wall, you must keep an offencive, and your adversary must keep a defencive Guard, as directed before. And to Push *Quart* from the *Tierce* side, do thus: incline your hand to his *Quart* side, it being turn'd in *Quart*, and take your aim at the place you would hit, over the upper joynt of your fore-finger; then draw in your arm to clear your point from his blade, or Disengage, close and quick, and Push *Quart*. To Push *Tierce* from the *Quart* side, do thus: incline your hand to his *Tierce* side, it being turn'd in *Tierce*, and take your aim along the ball of your thumb, &c. You may make a single Feint after every single thrust, so Push *Seconde* at the same place.

At the wall, or Pushing on the floor, if after any thrust your adversary quits your blade from the Parie, Push home on the same side again. Or if he does not keep a good Guard, Push home on the same side.

At the wall, the defender may Riposte with his arm only, and not Lunge, for this will make the other take care to Push true, quick, and recover the moment after he has made his thrust, else he may be hit. The defender may Parie by Batter at the wall, or by single Round Parie.

You may force a thrust at the wall. Or Push in the Round Parade, single or double.

General Directions.

The moment after you have received or given a *Fleueret* and have saluted; or with Swords, as soon as you have advanced near enough and come within reach of one another; either give your adversary's *Fleueret* or Sword a single or double Batter, or make a single or double Feint and Push. And be carefull at coming near that he does not Batter yours out of your hand, or thrust at you before you are aware of it. Endeavour to catch him thus first if you can, some way or other. For after points are presented, you must take care of your self, and may take all advantages of surprize, for there's no time given. When you Push any *Quart* on the *Quart* side, you must bear off, or clear your adversary's point from the line towards you with your Sword in your thrust. And keep your hand high to guard your face; and look over your arm, bending your head to the contrary side from his point. For unless you clear his point off the line, you will pin your self upon it. When you Push any *Tierce* on the *Tierce* side, you must do the same as before *Seconde*, and look under your arm, bending your head to the contrary side from his point. In short, you must at all times when you Push, if your adversary does not of himself have an open, clear his point off from the line, or else you'll be in great danger.

Endeavour at all times when you Parie any thrust, to keep your point towards your adversary, and Parie with the fort of your blade: that part from the middle to the shell is call'd the fort or strength of the blade. If you do this rightly, and he makes a home Lunge, or Lunges so far that if he were not Parie'd he would reach you, he will run himself upon your point. When you Parie a thrust, be cautious of quitting his blade least he Push as soon as you quit. For your quitting him makes his blade come to the line with a great spring. And it will follow yours so close, that if you are making a thrust, that spring will Parie you off the line and carry his direct. Or else it may be a *Contre-temps*. So to prevent the worst for your own safety, if you do thrust, do it only at his arm or hand, by which you will be in little or no danger.

Never Parie wide if possible you can avoid it, for you then are open and may be deceived by a Feint. Therefore endeavour to Parie close, for the other is too apt to become a custom.

Be cautious of Parieing with a greater spring and force than ordinary. For if you miss the Parie, and your adversarie did not carry his point as he should do, or did not Push home, before you can recover to your Guard he will have time to give a second thrust. And if you perceive a strong thrust coming, rather than stand to Parie it with that force that is requisite, *Avolt* contrary, or from it, by which you will not only avoid the thrust, but may hit him before he recovers to his Guard.

Avolting is very proper to avoid a thrust, and at the same time you may give one safely. It is thus: as he Pushes a home thrust on the *Quart* side, step back off the line with your left foot, or contrary from his thrust. As he Pushes a home thrust on the *Tierce* side, bring up your left foot as far as the fore-part of your right foot, or step with your left foot foreward on your own *Quart* side. This secures your body by carrying it off the line he Push'd on, and his Lunge brings his body on the line you then are on, which you may safely do before he can recover.

Avoid *Contre-temps*, for they are often mortal to both parties. This is when both Push together on the same line. As your adversary turns his wrist, or Disengages (which is Changing his point from one side of your blade to the other, and under your blade), if he does it wide; or as he cuts over the point (this is Changing his point from one side of your blade to the other, by raising his point till it is clear of yours, then dropping it on the other side); or if he Feints wide; you may Push home at his arm as he does any of these. This Pushing is call'd Timeing, because you do it as he does any of the above-mentioned.

Wide Feints are dangerous, except it be sometimes with an unskillfull person. For it is very likely he will answer your wide Feint and follow your Sword, which gives you an opportunity to

hit him. A skillfull person will not answer a wide Feint, but will Time you. Therefore Feint close from one side of his blade to the other, and endeavour always to keep your point within three or four inches of his blade, and as much from his shell. But not within his shell, least he seize your blade and break it. This you must observe at all times on your Guard.

Never let your adversarie bear upon you. And if he offers it, Slip him. And if you can do it quick, you may have a thrust to him on the contrary side, or part where he beares. If he bears you down, Slip and Push above. If he bears you up, Slip and Push below. If he bears on you in *Quart*, Slip and Push in *Tierce*. And if he bears on you in *Tierce*, Slip and Push in *Quart*. And if you don't Push, Slip and present your point to him against his breast, to prevent him from offering to advance or close. If you can't Slip him, retire back, or spring off to right or left, else he will command your Sword.

If he offers to Batter your Sword, Slip, and you may have a thrust at him before he can recover to his Guard again.

After you have made a thrust and are recovering, or as soon as you have Parie'd a thrust, if you are nimble to spring on one side or other of your adversarie, you may have a thrust at him, be it in his back or any where else. For all is fair play whil'st Swords are presented and you're disputing the victory.

As you recover from a Lunge, be sure to Batter your adversarie's blade, or go off in the Round Parade, or bearing on his Sword.

When you advance upon your adversarie, step forward with your right foot a little, and immediately draw your left foot after you to your Guard. When you retire, step back with your left foot a little, and immediately draw your right foot after you to your Guard. You may repeat either, as you have occasion to advance or retire. And when you traverse, step with your left foot first, foreward or backward, as you do when you *Avolt*, just as you have occasion, to right or left.

When you advance upon your adversarie, make only half-thrusts at him, to prick him in the Sword hand, wrist, or arm. But don't Push beyond the length of his elbow, unless you have a very fair open at his body. This is very safe, and a few wounds in the hand, wrist, or arm may effect what you desire, to get the better of him, with little hazard to your self. You may prick him in the afore-named places in *Quart*, *Tierce*, or *Low Quart*, by dropping your hand and point a little, so prick him under the shell. This you may also do as you retire or traverse. And at any time when you have Parie'd *Quart* or *Tierce*, you may Riposte at his hand or arm. Pricking him in any of those places will make him go off the line with his blade to Parie you when too late. He then gives an open to his body. After any thrust, you may Riposte a thrust at his arm or body, just as he is recovering.

If your adversarie advances upon you, step back with your left foot so far as to be in the posture of a Lunge, and at the same time Push with your arm only at his arm. And if he still advances, draw back your right foot and arm to the posture of a Guard, then step back with your left again, and Push as before said. This you may repeat as you have occasion or think proper. This will stop him from advancing so furiously as he would, and perhaps he will be hit or disabled. The stepping back carries your body out of the reach of his Lunge and is very safe.

If your adversary will not stand you when you have Lunged, bring up your left foot, and recover your arm to the posture of a Guard. Then thrust again, and repeat this as you have occasion or think proper. But take care least he close you or command your Sword. When you thrust and are on your Lunge, perhaps he will retire on purpose with design to take such opportunity.

'Tis less dangerous to retire than to advance upon your adversary, and not at all scandalous. For you may Time him every time he advances, and so get the better by disabling his Sword arm, hand, or wrist.

When you attack, never make more than one thrust at the same place in the same manner, but change your method, *viz.* from a plain thrust to a single or double Feint; or to a single or double Batter; or first make a half-thrust to hit the arm *&c.*, then thrust home, or at the former place; or force or make an *Appeller*; or if you want to hit in *Quart, Tierce,* or *Low Quart*, try the *Boor's Thrust*, and Change the thrust, and Push at some other part, then return to the former. These are to deceive him, that he may not guard your part so well as he might, which you have the design at. And if he does perceive your design to be at any particular part, and guards accordingly, you may then surprize him in another part. Try all thrusts, for some may answer your intent. If they don't answer standing, try advancing or traversing. Or retire a little, and endeavour to catch him as he advances.

If at any time you observe your adversary to be in confusion, be sure not to let him recover it, but take the advantage of it, and keep him so by a brisk attack: by *Avolting*, Slipping and retireing, and giving the point. In these cases, a weak man is a match for a much stronger. And it is certainly best to do these if your adversary be *Fool Hardy* and press foreward, whether he understand the Sword or not, for he may run himself upon your point. Or when he has tired himself you may then play with him and do what you please. Commonly, those people who are unskill'd do thus. They think (and indeed with reason) that they must not let you attack, because they do not know how to defend as they

ought, for the defencive part is the most difficult. Therefore they drive on with great fury (whil'st they have strength) to put you out of your play. But when once that is over they are at your mercy.

Some men care not (at least don't think of it, being only intent upon hitting their adversary) if they receive a thrust, if it be not immediately mortal, so that they can but give one. But this may properly be called rashness or *Fool Hardiness*.

At any time, if your adversary keeps an High Guard, make an offer to thrust at his face, then Feint below, and Push above his Sword. If he keeps a Low Guard, make an offer to Push low, then Feint above, and Push below his Sword. Be cautious of making a home thrust above or below, for you then give a great open. And don't do it unless your adversary's Sword is far off the line. And in that case 'tis better to Push upon the level at the breast or arm, for that is nearest and you readier to Parie should he Riposte.

Command your temper and you will do much better than if you give way to your passion. And if you do command it and are engaged with a person that can not, you will have very much the advantage of him. For his passion will make him play wild and wide, and consequently exposes himself to be hit very often. Whereas your thoughts not being in hurry and confusion, you may defend your self with ease and judgment, and take an advantage readily when ever you have a mind. You are the more capable of doing this because your strength, mind, and spirits are not spent or exhausted.

When you have a *Quarrel* with any man, and have not opportunity to decide it immediately, don't trust him within reach unless others be present or near. And when you are going to fight, or returning from it, having got the better, don't trust your adversary behind you nor any way within reach, least he give you foul play and stab you for revenge, or takes a villainous way of getting the better of you when you are not provided or ready to defend your self. And during your dispute, if it happen that you both consent to rest to take breath, don't quit your Sword out of your hand, nor look from him, nor stand within his reach. And if he submits and offers to deliver his Sword, don't let him come near but with the point of his Sword in his hand and [the] mounting presented to you. And should he desire to be reconciled, and the Swords are drawn, whether you have exchanged any thrusts or not, don't suffer him to come near, tho' in a friendly manner, unless he throw his Sword down on the ground. And if after you have disarmed your adversary, or he submitted and delivered his Sword, you return him his Sword again, be sure [to] give it with the point towards him. And be ready in all the aforemention'd cases with your own Sword. And take care least he spring in upon you, and trip you up; or by being stronger, he may disarm you of your own Sword, or break one or other and stab you with the piece. That is when you have disarm'd him, or he has delivered his Sword. I mention these to caution you on all occasions to be on your Guard, and not to trust any man whatever who is your adversary. For many have been deceived by not taking care of themselves in these cases, tho' their adversaries have been men of strict honour, as they thought, and that they would not be so base and villainous as to be guilty of any thing below the character of Brave Men and Gentlemen. *Experientiæ Docet.*

Disarm against a Quarte Thrust described above

Accepting an opponent's surrender: "...and not to trust any man whatever who is your adversary. For many have been deceived by not taking care of themselves in these cases." Although opponents may be gentlemen--many a good man has lost his life from a foul blow--another of McBane's 'real-world' bits of advice.

Another disarm against a Tierce Thrust. Note--McBane says to step in with the left foot behind the opponent's right.

When your adversarie Pushes a home *Quart* and does not recover immediately, or slips with either of his feet, or is tottering, or you can be quick enough to close him upon his thrust, you may disarm him thus: *Avolt* a little in *Quart*, or step with your left foot to the contrary side from his point, and Parie him low, and seize his blade close to the shell, with your thumb on the upper edge of it. Then give a Batter with the in-side or *Quart* edge of your own blade on the foible of his blade (note, from the middle of it to the point is call'd the foible), which will force the Sword out of his hand, be he ever so strong. And then present the point of it towards him, that he may not offer to close you. And as soon as possible present your point to him also. Take care he does not seize your Sword, either whil'st you are disarming him, or as you recover from so doing. And that he does not close you and trip you up. If he Push an home *Tierce*, you may bring him round by the Round Parie to the *Quart* side, and disarm as already mention'd.

Note that when joyn'd disarm in *Tierce*, you must bring up your left foot and place it behind his right foot, to be ready to trip him up if you have a mind, or there is occasion. And at all times when you seize your adversarie's Sword, it is to be done with the left hand, not the Sword hand. But to disarm in *Tierce*, at the same time that you step up with your left foot, seize his Sword hand and mounting together, and bring it down close to the lower part of your belly, and present your point to his breast. This is to be understood that your adversarie has Pushed *Tierce*, and you Parie and close him before he can Slip or recover to his Guard.

Another way to disarm in *Tierce*: thus you may seize his wrist underneath by turning your left hand down and outwards, so that the palm is up. Then bring his Sword and hand over your head, and hold the blade under your left arm, close to your left side. And still keep your hold of his wrist, and point your point. Another way to disarm in *Tierce*, thus: seize his blade fast, a little from the shell. You may then easily force it back over his own head, and perhaps out of his hand. And stick the point of it into his back if he offers to close you upon it, or if he does seize your Sword so that you have not the command of it. If he Push an home *Quart*, you may bring him round by the Round Parie to the *Tierce* side, and disarm as already mentioned in the first way of disarming in *Tierce*, which is the easiest. There are several other ways of disarming, but more difficult and dangerous. You may close when he Pushes *Seconde* by Parieing in *Seconde*, then

Ashley (right) begins a Tierce thrust. Mark begins the disarming counter described above.

Mark steps forward and grabs the sword-hand, lifting it while keeping his point on line.

The disarm is completed as Mark....

seize his hand and mounting together. You must not step foreward with your left foot in this case, but only step foreward with your right foot as on a Lunge. And take care he does not stun you by a knock with his head in your face. [3] Note, at all times when you

---

[3] McBane's Swordplay is not the polite, gentlemanly fencing of the salle; but the practical, rough and tumble, head-butting, heel-tripping combat of the real world.

disarm, you must Parie first, and when you have hold, take care to secure his Sword fast. And keep your own out of his reach, with the point ready to hit if he struggles or offers to close. And when both are closed and command one another's Sword, you should part upon Honour, but take care how ye go off. And that he does not forfeit his honour, beware of being trip'd up. And endeavour to serve him so if you can. Take care you are not deceived by a Feint or false thrust, and so be hit instead of disarming him. For in disarming you give a great open. You may disarm advanceing, retireing, or traversing.

If your adversarie have a much longer Sword than your self, and you are nimble and Parie well, 'tis not amiss to endeavour to gather him up and take the advantage when you are within the length of his Sword, by disarming or otherwise as there is occasion. For whil'st you are at full length of his Sword, you have no chance to hit him and can only act on the defencive, whil'st he acts entirely offencive. A good way to get in is thus: from the *Tierce* side Disengage to the *Quart*, and continue the motion, if he does not Slip, and bearing on him with a spring, force his Sword aside to his *Quart* or your *Tierce* side. As you do this, turn your hand and blade to the *Seconde*. You may Push *Seconde* if you throw his blade aside, or you advance and close him. But take care to seize his hand and mounting together fast that he may not seize it with the other hand, or else seize the blade close to the shell.

When you would make a thrust in the Round Parade, be sure not to go above twice round at most, for if you go more you may be Tim'd. And if your adversarie attack you in the Round Parade, and you don't Time him at the first charge of his point, then follow his blade once round. And if he goes more than once, after following him once round, Parie single or plain Parie. Never let him stand idle any time, but keep him in motion. For when he is standing still, he waits to Time or surprize you, or perhaps is tired or out of breath, which time you should make the best use of. And don't be fond of disarming.

If you are engaged with a *Ruffin* [ruffian], or a stranger, be watchfull that he does not throw his hat, dust, or something else at your face which may blind you, upon which he will take the opportunity to make a home thrust; or perhaps if he sees an open, he will dart his Sword at you; and if he misses, trust to his heels.

I would not advise you at any time to do the last mention'd. But with a *Bravo* or *Ruffin* [ruffian], I would throw any thing in his face to blind him, and then take the advantage of it. Such fellows as those often carry dust in their pockets, or something on purpose for that end. But no Gentleman ought to use such methods unless with such people who often carry pocket Pistols about 'em. So to prevent the worst to one's self, I think 'tis not amiss to get the better of them as soon as possible by blinding them, or by any other means whatever, before they shew a Pistol. For fair play is what they ought not to have.

If you fight in the dark, make continual use of the Round Parade, and as soon as ever you feel your adversary's blade, Push along the same, and recover again in the *Contre-Parie* or *Round Parie*. And avoid having any light in your face, and traverse round from it if there be. And in the day time avoid having the Sun or a great wind in your face.

These *Directions* are for right handed men, and the same will serve for left handed men, only where the right side, arm, foot, &c. is mention'd, they must understand it as for the left side, arm, foot, &c. And so where the left is mention'd, they must understand it as for the right. And if a right handed man and a left handed man engage, they should endeavour to keep the outside and Push *Quart* over the arm, or *Quart* under the arm, all on the out-side, which are the safest thrusts for each at that time, and the Round Parade on the out-side. To do which they may take all the different ways of Feint, Batter &c., to Push their thrusts at one another, as when engaged with persons that use the same hand as themselves. They may also use the *Boor's Thrust*, and the *Appeller*, and the *Portugueze Guard*.

After this, you may give Directions how a man with a Small Sword must act with a man that has a Broad Sword.

Keep a low Guard with your Small Sword out of his reach, and always Slip as he strikes, still Pushing at his arm, letting his blow [go] to the ground, keeping always above him. And if he attacks you very rash, raise your hand to a Cross Guard before your face, and receive his blow upon the strength of your Sword. And before he can recover, you can hit him in the *Seconde* as often as you please. Take good care of your Sword hand, and you have ten to one odds. For I compare a thrust of a Small Sword to a Pistol ball, for it kills. And suppose you receive by chance a cut, it's soon cured. But a thrust of a Small Sword is very dangerous, especially in the body.

If you meet a man with Sword and Target, and you with your Small Sword, take off your coat and roll it about your left hand, and take a wet napkin and put it under your hat, and that will prevent his cuts, in case he hits you either on the arm or head. Save the blade of your Sword as much as possible by Slipping from his blows. And your Sword hand making always high Feints to his face, then he will raise his Targe and blind his sight, that you may have an easy opportunity to take him in the belly. I reckon a man that does not understand a Target, better to want it than to have it. It would have been better for him to have a cane or scabbard in his left hand to Parie a Small Sword, than a

Target to blind him. And when a man with a Broad Sword draws against a man with a Small Sword, let him stand upon a high Hanging Guard at great length, and then he can Parie by the way of *Quart* or *Tierce* by moving his hand. And as he Paries, let him make a small stroke constantly to his Sword hand, or making a back stroak or under stroak to keep him off, and in constant motion, for he will be soon tired because his Sword is heavier. And have the left hand always before his breast to defend. And if he understands to Parie, he may Change to a *Medium*, and Slip and throw. But still the Small Sword hath great odds of the Broad, for the Small Sword kills, and you may receive forty cuts and not be disabled.[4]

Hanging Guard

[4] This is a controversy already ancient in McBane's time. Here are two opposing views from past fencing Masters.

"Without all doubt, the thrust is to be preferred before the edge-blowe, as well because it striketh in lesse time, as also for that in the saide time, it doth more hurt…blowes of the edge, though they were great, yet they are veric fewe that are deadly, and that thrustes, though litle & weake, when the enter but iii fingers into the bodie, are wont to kill." Giacomo di Grassi, *His True Art of Defence*, 1594, p. 21 verso.

"And for plainer deciding this controversie betweene the blow and the thrust, consider this short note. The blow commeth manie wayes, the thrust doth not so…The blow requireth the strength of a man to be warded; but the thrust may be put by, by the force of a child. A blow upon the hand, arme, or legge is a maime incurable; but a thrust in the hand, arme, or legge is to be recovered. The blow hath manie parts to wound, and in everie of them commaundeth the life; but the thrust hath but a few, as the bodie or face, and not in everie part of them neither.." George Silver, *Paradoxes of Defence*, 1599, p. 22.

Lessons with the Small Sword

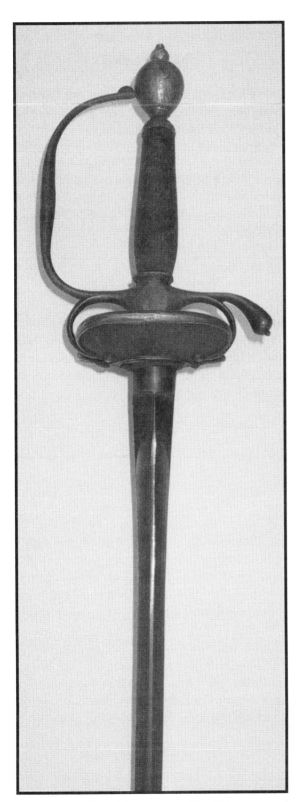

Smallsword characteristic of the 1700s
Photo courtesy W. Kevin Dougherty

The First Lesson of the Small Sword begins as thus.

Take your hat off with your left hand, and deliver the *Fleuret* to your *Scholar* with your right hand, and the pummel foremost, putting him firm on his Guard. Advance in *Quart*; advance in *Tierce*; *Quart* to his right and *Tierce* to his left, either coming on or going off. Retire and Parie *Quart*. Retire and Parie *Tierce*. Salute with your hat in your left hand, drawing the right foot behind the left and coming to the same posture again.

Batter upon the *Tierce* side if possible, and go off. And stand firm upon your Guard, bending well upon your left thigh; and when you Push, upon the right thigh, with your nails up in *Quart*, and down in *Tierce*. In case it were a Sword, draw your Sword with your right hand and cock your hat with your left hand, keeping your hair from your eyes, and your left hand over your eyes in order to Parie, your Sword at quarter-Sword[5] and a straight arm. There is no occasion to move [remove] hats at sharp weapons. When your adversary advances with the right, retire you with the left, still keeping at quarter Sword, either coming on or going off. For half-Sword is dangerous, for fear of a *Contretemps*.

The Second Lesson.

A standing lesson begins as thus: Push *Quart*. Push *Tierce*. Push *Seconde*. Recover in *Quart* and Push *Quart*. Push *Flanconade* and then *Quart*. Push *Low Quart*, which the French call *Quart Cuppy*. Recover well in *Tierce* to the Sword, and Push *Tierce*, still Parieing and Pushing, keeping close to his shell. Break Measure well when he advances with a straight arm, in going off and a Batter.

The End of the Second Lesson.

[5] "Quarter Sword" is the position in which one's Sword crosses the opposing Sword at the first quarter of one's blade, measured from the point. Likewise, "half-Sword" is the position in which one's Sword crosses the opposing Sword at the mid-point of one's blade.

The Third Lesson.

Advance in *Quart* and Push *Quart* along the blade. Advance in *Tierce* and Push *Tierce*. Advance in *Quart* and Push *Low Quart*. Advance in *Tierce* and Push *Seconde*.

Retire in *Quart*, Parie and Push *Quart*. Retire in *Tierce*, Parie and Push *Tierce*. Retire in *Quart*, Parie and Push *Low Quart*. Retire in *Tierce*, Parie and Push *Seconde*. And go off with a Batter on the Round Parade upon all occasions.

The End of the 3d Lesson.

The Fourth Lesson.

Advance in *Tierce* close to the shell and Push *Quart*, Batter and go off. Advance in *Quart* and Push *Tierce*, Battering in going off. Advance in *Quart*, Push *Low Quart* under the arm, Battering in going off. Advance in *Tierce* to his right eye and Push *Seconde*, likewise Batter in going off.

The End of the Fourth Lesson.

The Fifth Lesson.

Feint *Tierce*, Push *Quart* close to the Sword, going off with the Round Parade. Feint *Quart*, Push *Tierce* close to the Sword. Feint *Low Quart*, Push *Quart* over the arm. Feint *Seconde* and Push *Quart* over the arm, always going off with the Round Parade or a Batter.

The End of the Fifth Lesson.

The Sixth Lesson.

Double Feint in *Quart*. Double Feint in *Tierce*. Feint *Quart* and *Tierce*, and Push *Seconde*. Feint *Seconde*, Feint to his eye, and Push *Seconde*. Go off with a Batter or the Round Parade upon all occasions.

The End of the Sixth Lesson.

The Seventh Lesson.

Attack the Round Parade in *Quart*. At the Round Parade in *Tierce*, go to the Round Parade. Attack the Round Parade in *Seconde* and go off with a Batter in *Tierce*. Attack the Round Parade in *Quart* over the arm, still going off with the Round Parade or a Batter.

The End of the Seventh Lesson.

The Eighth Lesson.

Four *Quarts* from the *Tierce* side. *First*, attack a single *Quart* and go off with a Batter. *2d*, Attack a *Low Quart* and go off with a Batter. *3d*, *Quart*, bind in *Quart*, and Disengage *Quart* over the arm. *4th*, *Quart*, a half-thrust to his face, stamp the ground with an *Appeal* [*Appel*], and Push *Quart* over the arm.

Four *Tierces* from the *Quart* side. First a single *Tierce*. Then *Tierce* and *Seconde*. Then a *Low Tierce*, which the *French* calls *Tierce Cuppy*. *4th*, a half-thrust in *Tierce*, and a full thrust in *Quart*, without turning hand for losing Time. And then going off with the Round Parade or Batter upon all occasions.

The End of the Eighth Lesson.

The Ninth Lesson.
Of Revolting and Binding, likewise of Slipping

When your adversary Pushes *Quart*, Time him and Slip back your left foot, your left hand before your face in order to *Parie*. When he Pushes *Tierce*, come up with your left foot to the front and Time him with your hand in Tierce. And when you are going off, Push *Quart* when he feels your Sword. And when he offers to feel you, Slip him in *Tierce*. And when he feels you in *Tierce*, Slip him in *Quart*. When he feels you in *Low Quart*, or mounts your Sword at any rate, Slip him in *Seconde*. When he bears down upon your Sword, Slip him in *Low Quart* along the blade, going off in *Tierce* upon all occasions.

The End of the Ninth Lesson.

The Tenth Lesson.

Advance along the *Tierce* and Push *Quart*. Advance along the *Quart* and Push *Low Quart*. Recover to his Sword in *Tierce* and Push *Tierce*, then go off. Advance in *Tierce* and Push *Seconde*. Advance in *Seconde* Parade and Push *Seconde* over his arm. Advance in *Quart* close and Disengage *Quart* over his arm, along the blade, without turning hand. And when you lie in *Quart*, beat up his Sword, and sink your body with an *Appeal* [*Appel*]; and Push *Quart* over his arm, with your hand high-mounted; beat and go off.

The End of the Tenth Lesson.

The 11th Lesson.

Advance in *Quart* with a half-thrust. And when he Paries, turn your hand *Tierce*-way upon the same side, your hand well mounted. Advance along the *Tierce*. And when he Paries, keep close to his Sword, and turn your hand *Quart* over the arm, upon the *Tierce* side. The *French* calls the above thrusts *Recart* and *Retierce*. Turn your hand in *Tierce* to the *Quart* side, with a Round Parade, inclining off the line with your right foot as much as possible to his left side, your left hand before your face in order to Parie.

The End of the 11th Lesson.

The 12th Lesson.

Make a half-thrust in *Tierce* and Push *Quart*, and incline off the line to your right side as much as you can to keep out of his point's way. Make a half-thrust in *Quart* and move to your left, and Push *Low Quart* with your right foot off the line to your left and his right. Make a half-thrust to his face in *Tierce* and drop the same *Tierce* upon him under his arm. Make a half-thrust in *Quart* to his left eye, and when he draws back his head, drop your point upon his breast at the same time, Batter and go off.

The End of the 12th Lesson.

The 13th Lesson.
Either Pick [pike] *or Halbart* [halberd], *against Sword, Target, or any other Weapon.*[6]

When a man Feints upon a line, there is Time to be taken; or when he Feints wide. When he shires[7] his Hand in *Tierce*, Push *Quart* at him. If he shires his hand in *Quart*, Push *Tierce* at him. If he offers to Push *Low Quart*, Push *Flankeneath* [*Flanconade*] at him; for *Flankeneath* is no thrust, but a good Riposte. If he Pushes *Tierce* at you, down with your head and take him in *Seconde*. If he Feints wide, Push him in the mean time.

The End of the 13th Lesson.

The 14th Lesson.

Four attacks off the line. A small Feint in *Tierce* and Push *Quart* under his arm, inclining off the line for fear of Time or a *Countertang* [*Contre-temps*]. A double Feint going off the line, or a double Batter going off, then Push *Quart*. A double Batter upon his blade in *Quart* and Push in *Quart*, going off the line as much as possible. A double Batter in *Tierce* and Push in *Seconde* towards his back, and inclining still off the line very much from his point. If he is a left-handed man, keep to his out-side as much as possible: either single thrust or Round Parade. Make a half-thrust to his left eye if he keeps a high Guard, and Push *Quart* under his arm. If he keeps a low Guard, make a small Feint and come over his arm, for there is no other thrust safe upon a left-handed man. Neither has he any more upon you but two. There is three ways to bring him in: a plain thrust, and a Feint, and the Round Parade. For his *Quart* is your *Tierce*, and your *Tierce* his *Quart*; keeping always the out-side of him.

The End of the 14th Lesson.

The 15th Lesson.

Keep a strong Guard and a straight point, and your left hand above your face in readiness to disarm. And when a man Pushes *Quart*, Parie *Quart* and take away his Sword with your left hand, laying your thumb upon his shell. And give a small Batter with your Sword to his blade, and shew both points to his breast. If you return his Sword, give it by the point. But I do not approve of returning it at all. When a man Pushes *Tierce* at you full home, close him with your left hand and left foot, and secure his Sword by the hilt with your left hand, and put the point to his breast, having your left heel in readiness behind his right to trip up his heels. Likewise if he Pushes *Tierce* at you, run your hand as if you would catch him by the nose, and seize his Sword hand with the left, and bring it under your arm, with your heel to his right foot and your point to his breast. Likewise when he Pushes *Tierce*, Parie and turn his point over his right shoulder with your left hand, and shew your point to his breast. And when he Pushes a *Seconde*, Parie it to the ground, and secure his Sword hand with your left, taking care of your head from his. Likewise when he Pushes *Tierce*, if he closes you, secure his Sword hand with your left hand, and take care that he does not trip you down. And when you get at liberty, attack him as soon as possible with a small Feint. And when you are tired, sink your right hand and Parie with your left, and Push as he advances towards you, keeping always good distance.

The End of the 15th Lesson.

Footnotes from previous page:

[6] This caption is obviously misplaced, as the following text is a continuation of the Small Sword instruction. However, McBane does not include directions for the use of the pike or halberd in his book.

[7] With main force, mightily; sheer or straight down. *Oxford English Dictionary.* McBane may be using "shires" in the sense of making a down-right blow. Or it could possibly be a misprint for "shews."

Lessons on the
Spanish Rapier and Poinard

The 1st Lesson.
Of Rapier and Poinard, after the Spanish and Portugueze fashion. [8]

Take care to hold your Rapier very low, the point within three inches of the ground on the out-side of your right foot. And keep your Poinard in your left hand as high as your left eyebrow, defending still with the Poinard in your left hand, and offending with his Rapier in his right hand. You must Parie by the descent of your Poinard, and thrust your Rapier with an ascent, and return very quickly to your former Guard. While engaged, hold constantly in quick motion with your adversary and give him no delay.

The 2d Lesson.
The Small Sword, Contra Rapier and Poinard.

To play this, you'll take (if your scabbard be not sufficiently strong) your hat by the lineing and Parie therein pretty quick until you find his Rapier, binding him still because of the length of his Rapier beyond your Small Sword, until you gain ground of him and come within his reach, holding the same Guard against him that he holds against you (your Sword still being a hollow blade, and consequently lighter than his, which is long and heavy). Then feeling his blade and seeing an open in his body, you'll thrust along his blade, *Quart* or *Tierce* as you see the open, and return nimbly to your Guard without ever quitting his blade in the motion. And when you are recovered, spring off to the right or left as you please, out of his reach.

The *Portugueze* guard with their *Spadoes* [swords], with their points within an inch to the ground, and their Poinards in their left hand above their left eyebrow, one still going up and the other down, offending and defending at the same time.

---

[8] The rapier is a sword with a complex hilt and a long, narrow, two-edged blade, used primarily for thrusting. Spanish rapiers typically had very long blades and cup hilts. The poniard is a long dagger used defensively to parry and offensively to stab. Rapier and dagger were used by the Spaniards long after these weapons had fallen out of fashion with the rest of Europe.

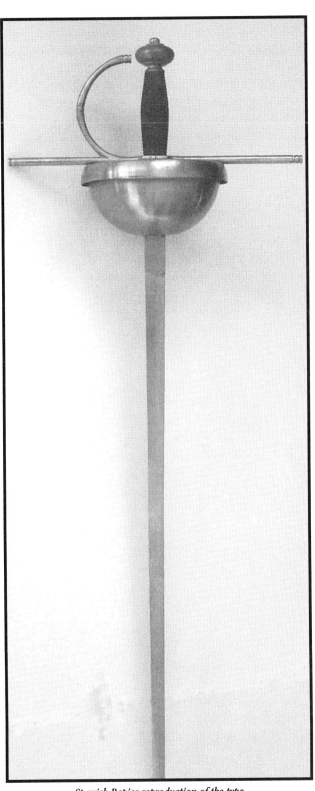

Spanish Rapier reproduction of the type Dennis L. Graves of Boulder, Colorado. Brian R. Price Collection.

General Directions of the Guards of the Spadroon or Shearing Sword.

There are Four Guards belonging to it. The *First* Guard is a *Low Quart* Guard to cut upwards towards your adversary's belly, with your wrist a little turn'd and your nails up. That will cut or thrust. The *Second* Guard, to the out-side of his Sword with a low point, with a *Seconde* Parade with your nails down, in order to cut upwards or thrust. The *Third* Guard, you'll hold your Sword towards your adversarie's face to the in-side, and there you may cut to his face or thrust a *Quart* to his breast. The *Fourth* Guard, Change to the out-side of your adversarie's Sword, and keep the point to his right eye in order to cut him in the face. And if he draws back his face, thrust at his breast or any other part of his body that is nearest you. Especially drive to cut at his Sword hand if he has a Small Sword. For if your Spadroon or Shearing-Sword be light, you are upon a level with the man that has the Small Sword. And you can traverse either back or foreward with your Spadroon after the form of a Broad Sword, and may thrust or cut (your Spadroon being sharp on both edges). And if your adversarie advance on you with what Sword he has in his hand, whether Broad or Small, keep a straight point, looking under your Sword with your nails downward. And from that you may come to any Guard you please of the Four.

McBane's first guard of the Spadroon

McBane's second Spadroon guard

McBane's third Spadroon guard

McBane's fourth guard of the Spadroon

The 2d Lesson.

Lie upon a Hanging Guard, well straitched [stretched] out with your point, if he has a Back Sword. Make a cut to his right eye with your Spadroon. Guard your self immediately with a *St. George's Guard*.[9] And instead of a cut, which he will expect from your Guard, being a *St. George Guard*, return a quick thrust under his Sword arm by way of *Seconde*, and then come to a *St. George Guard* immediately again. Then make a cut to his face, jumping backwards, inclining to his left and your right. And then guard your head from his cut with a Cross Guard, most commonly called *St. George*, and Push a *Low Quart* to the undermost part of his belly. And then guard your head immediately again, for every second Parade must be a thrust. And after you make your thrust, come quick to your Guard, which must be a Hanging Guard, with your left hand betwixt your legs.

The 3d Lesson.

Lie upon your *St. George Guard*. With your Spadroon make a thrust to his right eye. And if he makes a defense for his eye, cut at the out-side of his leg, and come off with a straight point. Make the same Push at his right eye, and cut him on the left side of the face, then come to the *St. George Guard* immediately. And if he returns a blow to your head, which he will certainly do if he have any life in him, then return to him again. And guard your face with an in-side Guard. And instead of a cut, return a quick thrust to his breast or any part of his body, and then go off with a straight point, for fear he should advance. And if he do advance, retire with your left foot and Push at him.

The 4th Lesson.

If you meet a man with a Small Sword, play at him under hand till you get a blow on his Sword or Sword arm, which will disable either Sword or Sword arm. And if he advances, keep a straight point, that you may be capable to Parie him either *Quart* or *Tierce*, and to Parie and Riposte either *Quart* or *Tierce*, your Spadroon being as light as his hollow blade.[10] And if he makes a *Seconde* at you, Parie it by way of a Hanging Guard, which is easy done. And as soon as you have Paried him, make a cut at the right side of his face or Sword arm. And if he Paries that, make a thrust at him under his Sword arm to his ribs, by way of *Seconde*, and give a slap on his Sword or Sword arm on the outside, and come off with a straight point.

---

[9] The name for this guard is taken from depictions of the patron saint of England slaying the dragon.

[10] The hollow-ground, triangular blade of the Small Sword. This profile allows the blade to be light, but extremely stiff and strong for making thrusts.

The 5th Lesson.

Begins this, by way of *Fence* or *Falsifie*. The Fence comes under the Sword arm and the Falsifie goes over the point. When you have a mind to spare a man and not kill him, make a half-thrust to his belly and cut him over the head. And then make a Feint to the out-side of his Sword to his ribs, by way of *Seconde*, which he will be apt to Parie. Then give him a cut over his head, which seldom or never misses. Then return to a Hanging Guard, or *St. George*. Then make a Falsifie to the left side of his face and cut him on the right ear if you can, or any way downward to his heel, for you have a very good opportunity. And be very sure to keep a straight point on all occasions, with your thumb downwards, with a long streach [stretch], by way of a Hanging Guard. And when you have a mind to give him a thrust by way of Falsifie, make a cut at his nose and he will draw back his face, then give him a thrust under his Sword arm. And if he Paries that thrust, give him a cut over his head or face, which [ever] you can, let him have what Sword he will. Then going off with a straight point, giving him a slap on the Sword arm, face, or body, which [ever] you can most conveniently hit. And you may double those Fence or Falsifies either right or left, by way of traversing either right or left with a quick motion, or springing up to his head. And when you are hard put to it, make a thrust to his mouth, which he will strive to defend. Then turn your hand, give a back cut to his throat. When you meet with an enemy this never fails. The Italians makes very much use of this thrust and cut, and likeways the Piemontiers, Valloons, Switz, and Gaskoon French.[11] Which I know very well by experience, by being often engaged with them. And I never found any nation make use of this weapon but the above-named.

The 6th Lesson.

When you meet with a man with a Broad Sword and Targe, take off the right slive [sleeve] of your coat and roll it about your arm, and that will defend his cut. Put a wet napkin under your hat and another about your neck. Then you may attack with your Spadroon either Highland-Man and his Targe, or a horseman and his Broad Sword. A man with his Targe will certainly attack you. Keep your left side foremost, and receive his cut on your left arm, your arm being well guarded with your coat. Raise your arm as high as your head, for he cannot cut neither arm nor head. Then make a very quick thrust to his left eye above his Targe. He will recover his Targe to save his left eye, which will blind his sight. Then you have a great opportunity to run him through the body or cut his legs. A man that does not understand the Targe is better without it than with it, for it blinds his own eyes. So that he that has the Spadroon or Shearing Sword has the better, and very capable to attack the horseman, keeping away fire arms, and he is able to cut his bridle reins, and dismount the horseman. And if he have a Pistol, do you take another, and then you will be on a level with him. For this is an extraordinary weapon that none can compare with it. Neither has there ever been any such [treatise for the use of this] weapon printed in Great Britain or Ireland before, for the benefit of all readers.

---

[11] Piedmontese are people of the mountainous region of northwestern Italy bordered by France, Switzerland, and Lombardy. Walloons, or Flemish, are from southern Belgium. Switz are obviously Swiss. Gascons are from the province of Gascony in the southwest of France.

Back Sword.

After you take up your Sword, you are to lodge it on your left arm, then retire to an Out-side Guard with a gracefull air. Then Changing to an Out-side Guard with a quick motion, both foot and your hand, with your left hand down on the knee, shewing your point in a direct line to your adversarie's right eye, covering well your out-side, the point of your Sword over your right knee to save your leg.

The next Guard is a Medium.

Shewing your Sword in a line with the center of your body, an eye in each side of your blade, and point to your adversarie's right eye (but if a left handed man, to his left eye), your foot and hand in a direct line in order to cover your leg. If he offers to Change, Slip foot and hand, and through [throw] to his head. Be very quick and guard your own head with *St. George's Guard*, which is a Cross Guard to cover your face, taking care to keep in your wrist for fear of a cut there, and return him the same cut.

McBane's original illustration for the Medium Gard position.

Dale in McBane's ready position: "...After you take up your Sword, you are to lodge it on your left arm, then retire to an Outside Guard."

...And from that position transitioning smoothly to the Outside Guard he later describes.

4thly, turn to a Hanging Guard, the pummel of your Sword upward, the point down, covering your left knee for fear of the *Pope's Eye*.[12] And keep your head close to your Sword arm. If he strikes at your head, raise your hand; if at your ribs, turn your point from you (this is a Guard of Defence). Take care to save your self as directed, and return him the same cut, covering your head as above.

5thly, raise your Hanging to *St. George's Guard*, crossing your face, looking under your hilt, which is to cover your head; your point, your left shoulder; your head close to your Sword arm to defend it. If your adversarie strikes at you, return him the same stroak, and come quick to the same Guard, and strike to his face. Come quick to your Guard and keep to your Guard. Follow those three stroaks and come quick to your Guard. Note, the first cut at his head, the *2d* at his face, and *3d* at his ribs. Apply much to this Guard, it being the most securest. For though you miss his face, you have a hazard to reach his belly or thigh. If he stops you there, Change quick to his out-side, and you have a chance to reach him from his ear to his heel. But still apply to the same Guard when he opposes you, it in my opinion being the securest Guard of the Back Sword. For you do not only defend your face and head, but lie in a readiness to secure all other parts of your body. Whosoever follows this Guard as directed may assure himself he is half learn'd, though he were never come to school. Experience hath taught me the knowledge of it. And if occasion offers, it is the Guard that I shall depend on.

Photos Page Previous:

p. 74: McBane's Hanging Guard: *"...the pummel of your Sword upward, the point down, covering your left knee...and keep your head close to your Sword arm."*

p. 75: McBane's St. George's Guard: *"...crossing your face, looking under your hilt, which is to cover your head; your point, your left shoulder; your head close to your Sword arm to defend it."*

Photo Opposite:

McBane's Medium Guard: *"...Shewing your Sword in a line with the center of your body, an eye in each side of your blade, and point to your adversarie's right eye (but if a left handed man, to his left eye), your foot and hand in a direct line in order to cover your leg."*

The Lessons, or Traversing of these Guards.

When you rise to your In-side Guard, bring up your right foot, with your left hand close to your left ear, taking care to keep your Guard low, for fear your adversary cuts you under your hilt or catches you at Changing. Care must be taken that the Back Sword is reverse to the Small, for all Changes at it are over the point, and at the Small all are under it.

Traversing to your out-side must be done thus: *viz.* you must take great care that your enemy does not cut you on your Change,

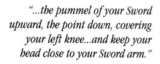

"...the pummel of your Sword upward, the point down, covering your left knee...and keep your head close to your Sword arm."

---

[12] Dr. Johnson wrote, "Popeseye, the gland surrounded with fat in the middle of the thigh: why so called I know not."

falling briskly back with your left foot behind your right, your hilt to cover your right knee in order to save your leg, your point directed to his right eye upon all those Changes. All traversing are by the In-side and Out-side Guard, still beginning with the In-side.

The Advanceing upon a Line is by throwing quick at the in-side and out-side of the face, taking great care to cover your self at all those occasions, having the same reason to defend your self coming off as you had of offending going on.

When standing on an Out-side Guard, make a quick motion at his face with an in-side cut. And if he moves, Change as quick as possible and cut him on his out-side.

If at an In-side Guard, make a quick motion at his out-side and thrust home to his in-side.

The Falsifies in this case are to be doubled over the point, as the Feints of the Small Sword are under the shell.

When you Fight Sword and Dagger.

You are to keep your Sword as directed, at a good Out-side Guard, your Dagger above your brow in order to defend your head, often having them a cross. But take great care to have your Sword out-side. For should your Dagger be out, you may be cut in the face or head in Changing. At Sword and Buckler, keep your left hand extended with your Buckler, at such a rate as not to hinder your fight, taking care to cover your Buckler with your Sword, and as much on your Out-side Guard. And if you cut at his leg, take care to cover your head with your Buckler.

The Difference between Buckler and Target are as follows.

The Buckler extended as above. The Target, being much broader, is fixed from the wrist to the elbow in order to cover the left side, and was much used formerly as a defence against Cut, Thrust, Shoat,[13] Halbert [halberd] and Pike, Lochaber Ax, or Horseman.

This Target is of great use to those who rightly understand it. But to unexperienced people is often very fatal, by blinding themselves with it, for want of rightly understanding it. Therefore who has mind to use it must take care to have it upon an edge so as to cover his left side, from which is a defence against ball or any weapon.

Fauchions[14] are weapons that no person can get any credit by. For whoever understands the Back Sword, must be Master of them. And whoever are spectators where those weapons are made use of have no pleasure in seeing it, tho' single or double, by reason there is but one Guard belonging to them. And he who makes use of them, and can save his knuckles without his head is broke, may without control say he was not hit at all.

The Quarter Staff is a weapon that has been made much use of and is now much in request. For whoever is Master of the Staff may defend himself against any one man with Back or Small Sword, as has been often experienced. It is generally seven foot long and of Ash, if it can be had.

The raising the Staff is thus: taking it in your right hand about a foot from the end, bring the other end over your left ear, and secure it with your left hand. Then change foot and hand, to his left ear that opposes you, throughing [throwing] quick at this head, either advancing or retiering. If he offers to close you, or come any ways to half-staff, slip your hands about a yard asunder, always observing to have one hand under and the other over, still guarding your head. If you strike at his head, slip your right hand down. And when he returns, slip it to former distance. Bring your left hand to your right, and return him a quick blow either on his ribs, arm, or leg, coming quick to your former posture, raising your right hand a little above your left. If he presses hard upon you, cover your self by changing your hands up and down to cover your head and body, returning blows at half-staff from right to left. If you meet with any game-keeper or rustical fellow, when you engage him close, dart your Staff at his face with your left hand. Which he endeavouring to stop, slide your right hand to your left, and at full length hit him on the left side of his head, which is scarce to be defended.

The Hollanders who fight with their knives have no legal Guard. For they, by Slipping when their adversaries strikes at them, saves themselves. And the supplest man often carries the victory in their scandalous way of butchering one the other.

---

[13] Shot; i.e., pistol or musket shot.

[14]The falchion is a short, curved, single-edged sword, with a clipped point and a simple cross guard. "The word comes from the Latin Falx, through the Italian *Falcione,* meaning a scymitar, or the French Fauchon, diminutive of Faux, a scythe." Castle, 321, n. 1.

"This Target is of great use to those who rightly understand it. But to unexperienced people is often very fatal, by blinding themselves with it, for want of rightly understanding it."

Richard Brown & Diarmid Campbell of the *Highland Mercenaries*, showing one instance of how an opponent can be killed by blinding them with their own target.

"And if you cut at his leg, take care to cover your head with your Buckler."

Richard & Diarmid begin the play described on the page opposite.

Richard Brown & Diarmid Campbell of the Highland Mercenaries in another play of the sword based on McBane's commentaries on the Buckler. Here, Diarmid strikes Richard's head to draw the shield upwards--but he does not commit to the attack, instead withdrawing the sword. When Richard lowers the target once more to see where the sword is...

Patrick McKee & Roman Guelfi-Gibbs of Bunjinkan San Francisco interpret McBane's advice for using the target against the Lachaber axe. The original illustration appears below.

Sword and Pistol is what is too often practised on Desperate Occasions on Foot.

When Gentlemen are so desperate as to engage in this manner, they in honour ought to have regard to do one another justice, and each to take a fast hold of a cloak or plaid, holding it so high in the left hand that they cannot see their adversary, and cock on the other if he be ready. So by cocking their Pistols they may be so advertised, as by Slipping to the right or left they may very probably avoid each other's shot. Then may they apply to their Swords for the decision of their quarrel.

If you fight with Sword and Pistol on Horseback, take care your Pistol or Pistols be in good order, your Sword slung on your right arm, Pistols cocked in your holsters, that you may be in readiness. Shorten your bridle reins, mount your horse-head to cover yours, face your horse-head directly to your enemy, bowing your head in a line between his ears that your head may not be seen. You may discharge one Pistol at your first rancounter to start his horse, which will put him out of the posture he was in. If you miss him and horse, take care to have your horse-head in a direct line with him so as to be on your guard that way. Pistols discharged, take care to have your Sword ready. And above all things, guard your bridle reins. And if possible, to have the right hand so that when your enemy makes a cut at your head you may defend it with an out-side or *St. George's Guard*, at the same time giving him a back stroak, which often proves fatal.

To avoid those desperate combats, my advice is for all Gentlemen to take a hearty cup and to drink friends to avoid trouble.

FINIS

Mark and Ashley recreate McBane's plate on pistol duels using the cloak, "each to take a fast hold of a cloak or plaid, holding it so high in the left hand that they cannot see their adversary, and cock on the other if he be ready. So by cocking their Pistols they may be so advertised, as by Slipping to the right or left they may very probably avoid each other's shot."

Of
ORDINANCE
For
Land Service.

*O*dinance for *Land Service* are of different kinds; such as are for Garrisons, are, or ought to be of *iron*, and made of good Lengths and well Fortified, that so your Enemy may be Annoyed at a Considerable Distance, to prevent their near Approaches.

Ordinance for Service of the *Field* and Battering must be of *Brass*, being less subject to Casualties, and are more proper for Marching and General Uses; besides if a *Gun* happen to split, the same Mettle is ready to be converted into a *Gun*, so for the same Service.

Ordinance for *Field Service*, are used according to the Opinion of the General, having Regard to the Ways and Passages in the Countries, through which they are to March. However Ordinances from 12 Pound Ball to *Saker*, which is 5 ¼ Pound, are the most Proper Artillery for open Countries; if your Country be Hilly or deep Ways, and your Expedition requires a quick March, you must use *Guns* of small dimensions, as *Mynion* of 4 Pound Ball, and 3 Pounders.

Ordinance for *Batteries* must be of larger Dimensions, such as *Demy Cannon* of 24 Pound Ball, 18 and 16 Pound Ball, the last are very much used in Forraign Service; the Lengths of these Guns never exceed Ten Foot, and are often not above Nine Foot, but well Fortified; having spoken of what *Guns* are proper for *Garrison* and *Field Services*, you are now to observe the following *Directions*.

First, You are to take Notice, that there is much more Trouble in your Duty on *Field Service*, in Regard every Days March Imploys your Care in keeping your *guns* in good Order, and that all Things belonging to them be at Hand, and that your *Gunner* and Assistances be Sober, and Diligent in their Attendance and re-spective Duties. It is true your Superiour Officers have the same Care over you, but this must not Excuse your Watchfullness; for Diligence will save you a great deal of Trouble, obliging all Men that know their Business to be Active and ready for Service.

Your Carriages being different from *Sea Service*, and daily Marching, must be well observed whether the *Iron-work* continue firm, as well on the Bodies as Wheels, and whether your Axeltrees be sound, that they be well Greased before you March from any Garrison or Incampment.

That such Waggons, Tumbrels of Ammunition, or Shot-Carts under your Charge be Sound in all Degrees, as spoken of before, especially such as have Powder, these must never want good Greasing, to prevent Fireing the Axeltree and Nave; which Accident may blow up your Powder, and do further Dammage to your Train.

That your Ladles, and Spunges, and Worms, may be Lasht and plac'd on the side of the Carriage of the *gun*, and the Lockers that are made in the Train of your Carriages, have more or less Powder and Ball with other Necessaries, as may Defend you upon any Surprize of Ambushment, till you can more Conveniently have the rest of the Ammunition which must March near your Ordinance.

As for Cartridges, with all other Matters incident to the use of Ordinance, are made as on Board for *Sea Service*, and your care in searching your *Guns*, and to fit the Formers for making them; but this Trouble is general made Easy, Cartridges being made ready in the Magazines for the Service of your Campaign.

You must be Carefull in supplying your self with good large *Powder Horns*, with good *Priming-Irons*, and *Drifts* to Clear the

Vents of your *Guns*; you must likewise have *Budg-Barrles, Cases of Wood* and *Tinfunnels*, all these are necessary to secure *Powder* from Accidents of Fire, in time of Service.

Handspikes and *Crows* must be at hand, for quick Traversing your *Guns*; all these Utensels are the most Material about your *Guns*, either in the *Field* or on *batteries*, all other Emptions are used as in the *Sea Service*, and therefore need not mention the applying them, having given a full Direction of their Use.

As for all other Habiliments of War, which you find in the Inventory given you for a Train of Ten *Guns*, will be employed as the General Officers of the Train or Engineers shall Direct, either for making of Bridges, or repairing of Passes for Marching the *Cannon*.

Such Stores as *Horse-harness*, and what are incident to the use of Waggons, *Tumbrels* or the like, are applied according to the Directions of the Officers, that have that Charge Committed to them.

To proportion your Horses, either for *Guns* or *Waggons*, it is generally allowed according to Weight, as Two Hundred Weight to each Horse, allowing the Carriage, this Weight is certainly enough considering daily Marching, with other Hardships Horses must endure; if your Ways be Hilly or extraordinary Deep, you must add to the number.

You are often obliged to make use of Men, and then there is allowed Six Men for each Horse, as an Equivalent to their Service, but this is very rarely Acted unless in narrow Passages, where Carriages are taken in Pieces and the *Cannon* and Carriages drawn upon Sledges; many other Contrivances are made use of, to get *Guns* over narrow Mountanious Passes. Upon such Occasions as this, a *Gunner* is obliged to be very Active, that he may Deserve his General Officer's Favour.

You are obliged every Night in all Encampments to receive Orders from your Principal Officer, or Adjutant as shall be appointed to give out Orders; strictly observing the Sobriety of all *Gunners* and *Matrosses*[1], whither on or from Duty, that you have your *Matches Lighted*, and secure from Weather; that your *Guns* be decently plac'd, with all Necessaries fitting for immediate Service, or for quick Decamping.

Having Briefly spoken of a *Gunner's* Duty, with Directions in Managing himself in a Marching Train; I shall now acquaint him how to Erect his *Batteries,*

Advancing and Directing of *Batteries* in former Wars, were very far different to our present Times; Old Authors Direct you to

Place your *Batteries,* Two or Three Hundred Paces Distant from the Town Besieged, and Erected their *Batteries* extream Lofty. This Method was to Batter Houses; but that Service was Expensive and Tedious: *Morters* are more Expeditious, and far more Terrible to the Besieged. All *Engineers* Covet to Advance their *Batteries* as near as possible, before they proceed to a General *battery*, which is about an Hundred Paces, if farther you spend your Shot in Vain; at this Distance you will be sure to Place every Shot to do Service required, and your Enemies Cannon will be soon Dismounted, which gives you Liberty of being Masters of all Out-works.

Your *Batteries* must be made on Rising Ground to carry off Water; and you must Intrench them to prevent Water lying within your Works, which will spoil your Ammunition; you must Cover your *Guns* from the Enemy, with good Fences of Earth Eight or Ten Foot thick, faceing your *Parrapets* in the inside, with Three Inch Plank Nail'd to good Posts set into the Ground, so you will always have your Earth stand firm, without which it will slip down by your *Guns* Fireing; if you cannot be supplied with Plank, you must make a Fence of Rattling, by Bowes or such like; your *Parrapet* must be Nine Foot high, your *Ambrazure* or Port hole need not be above Two Foot wide in the inside, and slopt to Four Foot on the outside which is enough, your *Guns* having no Occasoin of being Traversed upon the Place you design to Batter, the rest of your *Guns* assisting the said Service: Your *Ambrazures* need not stand above Ten Foot wide from each other; let your *Platforms* be well laid and Plank'd, that your *Guns* may be used with greater Expedition.

Whil'st your Battering *Cannon* are at Work, you have some other *Batteries* Commodiously Plac'd to Divert the Enemy; these *Guns* are used by Skilfull *Gunners* that they may Annoy the enemy the better; *Morters* are also used to Incommode the Besieged, all which gives Life to the *Grand Batteries*, and saves Men.

Necessary Rules to be Observed, when your Guns *are Mounted on your* Batteries.

First, That your *Powder* and *Match* be securely kept in different Places, to prevent such Accidents as may Deprive you of all your Ammunition at once, and not only that, but Disorder your Batteries, and give your Enemy Reason to make a Salley, and secure your *Cannon*, or at least Spoil them by Spiking or such like Methods.

2dly, That your *Round-Shot, Crows*, and all other Material Stores, ly so in time of Service, that no Shot from the enemy can Prejudge them, or cause them to be Hurtfull to your selves; you must therefore Place them below that Danger.

3dly, You must have *Tan'd-Hides*, and *Tarr'd-Paulins*, to Cover your *Powder* from Weather, and also small *Tarr'd-Paulins* to lay over the Breech of your *Guns* in Extream Rains.

4thly, That you always be provided with good *Match*, and preserve it well from being Wet; and likewise prevent its doing any Dammage, by laying it any where negligently.

5thly, That your *Powder-Horns* be always fill'd, and good *Priming-Irons, Drifts*, and *Bits*, be Annexed to the Horn, that if the Vent of your *Guns* want Clearing, it may be readily performed.

6thly, After you have with all the Care imaginable put all Things in Order, and you have Orders to Play your *Cannon* against your Enemies Walls; you must then observe, whether your *Guns* will do the Execution intended, by Shooting by the Dispart Line, (if not) then find out how much you fall short, and so cut your *Dispart* for your use; this Way is a good Direction; but if you observe how your Bed and Coins ly in the Carriage and Mark them, and so run out the *gun* to the Port to the usual Distance, this will give you less Trouble, then placing your *Dispart*, and you may Fire with greater Expedition, observing sometimes with your Eye, some Object on the Place you Batter, that your Shot may not be Shot to Loss; this is the way which must Direct you if you Batter in the Night.

7thly, That every *Gunner* and others Imployed on the Batteries, behave themselves quietly without Hurry, laying all Things they make use of in their proper Places, so will your *Guns* perform the Service intended: Lest the *Ordinance* in *Land Service* may prove something Difficult, I therefore have given you an *Exercise* hereafter, which words of Command will make the Use more easy to you, and yet little different from that of *Sea Service*.

An
EXERCISE
For
Guns on *Batteries*,
Supposing them Unloaded.

Silence.
Handle your *Crows* and *Hand spikes.*
Run back your *gun* from the *Ambrazure.*
Draw forth the *Tampeon.*
Unside your *Vent.*
Handle your *Ladle.*
Put it into the *Gun.*
        observing to keep the open part upright.
Examine Home to the *Breech.*
Draw forth your *Ladle.*
        and discharge it from Filth *&c.*
Lay down your *Ladle.*
Handle your *Spunge.*
Put it into the *Gun.*
Stop the *Vent*, with your Thumb.
Put Home the *Spunge* to the *Breech.*
Turn it about Thrice.
Draw forth your *Spunge.*
        keeping it turning.
Strike it on the Muzzle.
Exchange your *Spunge* for the *Rammer.*
Handle your *Cartridge.*
Put it into the *Gun.*
Handle your *Wadd.*
Put it into the *Gun.*
Handle your *Rammer.*
Put it into the *Gun.*
Ram Home *Wadd* and *Cartridge.*
Give Three Strokes.
Examine with the *Priming-Iron.*

Withdraw your *Rammer.*
Handle your *Shot.*
Strike it on the *Muzzle.*
Put the *Shot* into the *Gun.*
Handle your *Wadd.*
Put it into the *Gun.*
Ram Home *Wadd* and *Shot.*
Give Two Strokes.
Draw forth your *Rammer.*
Lay down your *Rammer.*
Handle your *Priming-Iron.*
Handle your *Powder-Horn.*
Unstop your *Powder-Horn.*
Hold up your *Horn.*
Prime your *Gun.*
        carrying the Powder foreward.
Stop your *Powder-Horn.*
Join you Left-hand to the small end of the Horn.
Bruise your *Powder.*
Return your *Horn.*
Cover your *Priming* with the *Apron.*
Handle your *Spikes.*
Run Home the *Gun* to the *Ambrazure.*
Lay your *Gun* right in her *Carriage.*
Point your *Gun* to the *Object.*
Handle your *Linstock.*
Take off your *Apron.*
Blow your *Match.*
Fire.

The *Gunners*, and *Matrosses* attending the *Gunner* of each *Gun*, must have their *Hand spikes* ready to Heave the *Train* off the *Carriage* when Ordered, that so the *Gunner* may make quicker Dispatch in laying the *Gun* to Pass.

FINIS.

A LIST,
of the several Regiments of *Horse*, *Dragoons*, and *Foot*, in his *Majesty's*[1] Service.

Horse Guards

1st Troop	Lord Herbert
2d Troop	Earl of Hertford
3d Troop	Earl of Cholmondeloy
4th Troop	Lord Shanon

Horse Grenadier Guards

1st Troop	Collonel Fane
2d Troop	Collonel Berkly

Foot Guards

1st Regiment	Lieut. Gen. Wills, 3 Battal.
2d Regiment	Earl of Scarsborough, 1 Bat.
3d Regiment	Earl of Dunmore, 2 Bat.

Regiments of Horse

1st Royal Regiment	Duke of Bolton
2d Royal Regiment	Lord Cobham
3d Regiment	Duke of Argyle
4th Regiment	Lieut. General Wade
5th Regiment	Lieut. General Wywn
6th Regiment	Major General Napier
7th Regiment	Lieut. General M'cartney
8th Regiment	Lord Liganier

Dragoons

1st Royal English	Major General Gore
2d Royal Scots	Collonel Campbel
3d King's Regiment	Lieut. General Carpenter
4th Regiment	Lieut. General Evans
5th Regiment	Collonel Sydney
6th Regiment	Earl of Stairs
7th Regiment	Brigadier Ker
8th Regiment	Brigadier Sir Robert Rich
9th Regiment	Major General Crofts
10th Regiment	Brigad. Charles Churchill
11th Regiment	Major General Honeywood
12th Regiment	Collonel Bowls
13th Regiment	Collonel William Stanhope
14th Regiment	Collonel Nevill

Regiments of Foot

1st Royal Regiment	Earl of Orkney, 2 Battalions
2d Regiment	Brigadier Kirk
3d Regiment	Lord London-Derry
4th Regiment	Lord Cadogan
5th Regiment	Collonel Kane
6th Regiment	Major General Dormer
7th Regiment	Ld. Killmain, Earl Tirawley
8th Regiment	Brigadier Pocock
9th Regiment	Liut. General Windram
10th Regiment	Major General Groves
11th Regiment	Collonel Montague
12th Regiment	Lieut. General Wetham
13th Regiment	Major Gen. Lord Mark Ker
14th Regiment	Brigadier Clayton
15th Regiment	Collonel Harrison
16th Regiment	Earl Delorain
17th Regiment	Brigadier Tyrrel
18th Regiment	Collonel Crosbie
19th Regiment	Collonel Graves
20th Regiment	Collonel Edgerton
21st Regiment	Sir James Wood
22d Regiment	Collonel Handisyde
23d Regiment	Lieut. General Sabine
24th Regiment	Collonel Howard
25th Regiment	Collonel John Middleton
26th Regiment	Collonel Anstruther
27th Regiment	Collonel Molesworth
28th Regiment	Collonel Barrel
29th Regiment	Collonel Disney
30th Regiment	Lieut. General Bisset
31st Regiment	Major General John Ker
32d Regiment	Brigadier Dubourgay
33d Regiment	Collonel Hawley
34th Regiment	Collonel Hayes
35th Regiment	Collonel Charles Otway
36th Regiment	Collonel Lanoe
37th Regiment	Collonel Murray
38th Regiment	Collonel Lucas
39th Regiment	Brigadier Newton
40th Regiment	Collonel Richard Philips

The Independent Company in Scotland.

Collonel Grant. The Right Honourable Lord Lovat. Sir Duncan Campbel of Lochnell.
Captain Monroe. Captain Campbel of Skipnige. Captain Campbel of Carrick.

---

[1] King George I.

Hope's New Method of Fencing

Milo Thurston

In his last work on the Art of Defence, Hope wrote: "I am perswaded, [that my writings] will be much more valued when I am gone, and mouldering in the grave, than they are now; however acceptable they may have been hitherto to the more curious."[1] With the first re-printing of his *New, Short and Easy Method of Fencing* for nearly three centuries, there is a distinct possibility of his words coming true. It seems likely that he made this comment in relation to his attempts to reduce the prevalence of duelling and control the teaching of the art by introducing a society of sword-men to act as court of honour and judge of the competence of instructors.[2] Though there is at present much discussion on the certification of instructors, Hope's methods of controlling charlatans (fines and imprisonment) are unlikely to be used. It is his method of fencing that is of interest, and will hopefully become more widely studied.

What aspects of Hope's work would appeal to the 21st century reader? There are perhaps several points of interest to his work, but the one that seems foremost in my mind is his emphasis on the true purpose of learning the art of the sword - to defend one's life when fighting with sharps. Hope is quite open about this, and this interest is more pronounced in his later books. The only book not to mention this topic (if one excludes *Observations upon the Gladiators' Stage Fighting*, which has yet to be found) is *The Fencing Master's Advice to His Scholar* (1692). *Advice* is purposefully set out to describe recreational fencing, presumably because there were many gentlemen who would enjoy salle fencing for its own sake, and to ignore their interests, even when pursuing such a worthy end as self-defence, would not make sound business sense.

Hope had his first book, the *Scots Fencing Master* (1687), published at the age of 27 and it appears to be little different from other works published in the late 17th and early 18th centuries. Though the terminology is somewhat quaint and less precise than is seen in more fashionable works on the small-sword (for this is the only weapon covered in this first book), it contains the germ of what would become his New Method. Amongst the rules for fighting with sharps are the beginnings of the "Abstract" that featured in all later books where sharps were discussed. One may also see the hanging guard in seconde appearing in the *Scots Fencing Master*, although described as the "guard of tierce with a sloping point" or the "second parade in tierce." In fact, much of the New Method can be traced back to this first book. *A Vindication of the True Art of Self Defence* (1724), written shortly before his death, presents the same system as the New Method with a few trifling changes and an involved discussion of matters of honour. As Hope's ideas developed, he did not completely discount what he had done before. Usually, he would point out that it was quite an acceptable solution given his knowledge at the time, and still workable even though he would recommend his later system instead.

What seems to have happened during Hope's long career as author and fencing master is a change, or more accurately a development, of focus and philosophy. It is clear that in the *Scots Fencing Master* he has gathered together all that he knows, and there is little order underlying it. By the end of his career, his writings are tightly focused upon the subject of using any form of single hand sword then available to defend one's life from ruffians or others attacking with sharps. I would expect this to appeal to the modern practitioner, given the interest in the practical aspects of swordplay that is often expressed in discussions of today.

---

[1] *A Vindication of the True Art of Self Defence*, p. 99.

[2] Hope's *New Method of Fencing*, present edition, pp. 180-1.

The first indications of this trend came in a work by the name of *The Sword-Man's Vade-Mecum* (1691), published about four years after the *Scots Fencing Master*. The sole purpose of this book is a discussion of self defence, though it is not yet using the hanging guard described in the New Method. This is the first book to feature the "Abstract;" general rules to be followed with "Calmness, Vigour and Judgement," at sharps.[3] An interesting and revealing point about this book is that Hope confesses to having been ignorant of the back-sword when he wrote his previous book, and to have begun studying it since that time. He goes on to recommend that all gentlemen also study this weapon, as it will enable them to employ techniques learned from it to defend themselves against a back-sword if they are attacked whilst armed with a small. This is a great change from the slipping and time-thrusting method of defence he previously described. During the next decade, it is certain that a gradual realisation that the two weapons (now the rapier, or small-sword, was a handy length) were similar, and that the appropriate system to use with them was that of the back-sword.[4] This back-sword system would appear to be something common to the British Isles, and it is true that many things described by Hope would fit nicely with the principles of the "true fight" described by George Silver. Combining the teaching of the two weapons, the main thesis of the New Method, also has the benefit of simplicity. A simple system would be quicker to learn and more efficient to use, as a great many superfluous and overly fancy techniques would not be of assistance to a man defending his life when assaulted with sharps on the field of honour or elsewhere. Hope's opinion of the unnecessary complexity of some other systems can be seen in his reference to the "specious, hard-seeming names" that masters may use to impress their scholars.[5]

A considerable portion of the New Method discusses not only the art, but the attributes of those who are to practice and teach it. What constitutes a good master has been a topic of interest of late, and readers will be pleased to see that Hope appreciates what is necessary to fit one for this qualification. The main qualification he admires is an ability to understand and communicate theory behind the art, and would rather have a master who is a less skilled fencer, but who can impart all that he knows with good reasoning behind it, than one who is an expert sword-man but lacking in knowledge of the theoretical grounds.[6] This is quite in keeping for a master whose works (with the notable exception of the *Scots Fencing Master*) were mainly books of theory and principle rather than technique - quite a contrast to his contemporary, McBane.

I have one other point to make on the topic of why Hope is an interesting author to read; his style is often entertaining and written in a witty manner. His books are frequently enlivened with bad poetry, although not only does he admit that it is perhaps not the best written verse he also states that he will "sleep not a whit the worse" should the reader dislike it. His verbosity does sometimes obfuscate the principles he is trying to describe, and some sections may need explanation by an instructor for students less interested in slogging through several repetitive paragraphs; a good example is the discussion in Chapter VII on "Distance." Essentially, these are the "true times" described by Silver, though not put so succinctly. It is interesting that Hope claims that this information was "never made known by any author." I have found both the study and practice of Hope's system to be time well spent. I trust that readers of this book who are willing to spend their time in the pursuit of the art described within will find it similarly rewarding.

Milo Thurston
Oxford, 2001

---

[3] *The Sword Man's Vade-Mecum*, p.11.

[4] *New Method of Fencing*, present edition, pp. 176-8.

[5] *New Method of Fencing*, present edition, p. 162.

[6] *New Method of Fencing*, present edition, pp. 176-8.

A
NEW, Short, and Easy
METHOD
OF
FENCING:
Or, the ART of the
Broad and Small Sword
Rectified and Compendiz'd.

WHEREIN,

The Practice of these Two Weapons, is reduced to so Few and General Rules, that any Person of an indifferent Capacity, and ordinary Agility of Body, may in a very short time attain to, not only a sufficient *Knowledge* of the *Theory* of this Art, but also to a considerable *Adroitness* in *Practice*; either for the Defence of his Life, upon a Just *Occasion*, or Preservation of his Reputation and Honour, in any Accidental Scuffle, or Trifling Quarrel.

By Sir WILLIAM HOPE[1] *of* Balcomie, *Baronet,*
Late Deputy-Governour of the Castle of Edinburgh.

Gladiatura, non solum ad Honoris, Vitaque Conservationem; sed etiam ad Corporis, atque Animæ Relaxationem, perquam necessaria.

EDINBURGH:
Printed by *James Watson,* in *Craig's*-Closs, on the North-side of the *Cross.*
M. DCC. VII.

---

[1] "The most important treatises extant in the English language on the swordsmanship of that period are the various works of Sir William Hope. This celebrated swordsman was a son of Sir John Hope of Hopetoun by his second marriage with Lady Mary Keith, eldest daughter of William, seventh Earl Marischal [see Hope's dedication to Lord Keith below]; his eldest brother was the father of the first Earl of Hopetoun. Born in 1660, he was knighted between 1687 and 1692, and created a baronet in 1698. He was first designed of Grantoun, afterwards of Kirkliston, and in 1705 he purchased the land of Balcomie, in Fifeshire. He served some time in the army, and was for many years (previous to 1706) Deputy Governor of the Castle of Edinburgh. He died in Edinburgh, 1724, in his sixty-fourth year, of a fever caused by having overheated himself in dancing at an assembly. Dancing, fencing, and horsemanship were his most ardent pursuits." Castle, 268-9.

To the AUTHOR,

*Upon his Publishing this New and Easy,
as well as Most Useful Method of Fencing.*

Nature and Art with all their Pow'rs combine,
To make thy Name for Skill in *Fencing* shine.
O'er all the *Nation*, the shrill trump of *Fame*,
Shall sound the growing Glories of thy Name.
O'er all the Nation, nay, o'er all the World,
In Renown's Chariot, shall thy name be whirl'd.
No Pestilential Blasts, from putrid Lungs,
Tho' dissipated by more pois'nous Tongues;
Shall Blast thy Name, No! thy renown by Fame,
Shall soar on High, and Eternize *HOPE's Name*,
For this *Essay*; by which thou do'st impart
Secrets, till now unknown, of thy Great *Art*.
Whereby *Our Youth* are Taught, with *Ease* and *Skill*,
To *Defend Life and Honour* more, as *Kill*.
This! many times, is an *Unlucky PART*.
But to *Defend*; not *Kill*; *That! That* is *ART*.
May then the *Reader*, wholly Trust *Thy WORD*;
And by this *Method, Boldly wield his SWORD*.

J.B.

To the Right Honourable,

WILLIAM
Earl Marischal,

Lord *Keith* and *Altire*, Great Marischal of the Kingdom of *Scotland*, and Heretable Keeper of the *Regalia* of That Kingdom, *&c.*[1]

MY LORD,

Having of late discovered the *Short and Easy Method of Fencing*, contained in the following sheets, and which I am persuaded, will be found by practice, to be as useful as it is New; I was not long a making choice of your Lordship, as the person to whom I ought in Justice to offer it.

For not to mention, at present, your Lordship's many Personal Endowments, which I the more willingly forbear, lest I should be thought too much interested therein, not only upon account of that Great but just Esteem, which I have always had for your Lordship, but also (and which is indeed my greatest Honour) with respect to my near Concern in, and Relation to, your Lordship's most Ancient and Noble Family.

Therefore, not to insist upon These, which are already so well known; there are Two Motives, which chiefly induced me to present to your Lordship this Small Essay; which I dare Boldly affirm, contains the Greatest and most Useful Improvement, that ever was made in the Art of the Sword.

The *First* is, A Generous and Publick Spirit, whereby your Lordship always endeavours to Assert the Rights and Priviledges of the Subject, as well as to promote the Publick Good and Wellfare of your Country; For Which, your Lordship has the Approbation, and general Applause, of all truely good Country-men; Which when your Lordship is gone, will add an Everlasting Lustre to the already most Noble and Illustrious Family of the KEITHS.

The *Second* is, The most Honourable Office of Great Marischal of Scotland, of which your Lordship's worthy Ancestors, were thought so Deserving in former Ages, that it has now been Hereditary to your Lordship's Family for above these Seven Hundred Years.

And what Family could so well Deserve it, as That, which has upon all Occasions, not only Asserted and Defended the Rights and Liberties of the People, but even in the last Great Rebellion, did after a wonderful manner Preserve the Honours and Regalia of the Sovereign? For which the Convention of Estates in the Year 1661, ordered their Thanks to be given to your Lordship's Uncle, Earl William[2] of worthy Memory, declaring, That the Preservation of the Crown and Scepter were owing to Him; and gave Orders that it should be insert in the Records of Parliament, as an Everlasting Evidence of your Family's Loyalty.

For whatever some Nice and Narrow Spirited Politicians may pretend, certainly the Power and Prerogative of the Prince, and Right and Priviledge of the People, are Reciprocal; so that the One cannot possibly subsist long, and in safety, without a reasonable Condescendence to, and Allowance, of the Other.

And, My Lord, allow me to say it, without the least Flattery, your Lordship's Family hath signalized it self as to Both: For by Preserving the Regalia, it declared it self sufficiently Loyal, and beyond all exception Monarchical; and by Asserting the Rights and Priviledges of the Subject, of which your Lordship gives daily singular Instances, it proves it self to be abundantly for the Good and Prosperity of its Country, and the Liberty and Prosperity of the People: So that the Subject-matter in this Essay corresponding so naturally with these Two Extraordinary Characters, the one of your Lordship's Person, and the other of your Eminent Office, you are certainly, My Lord, (all other Considerations laid aside), the most proper Patron I could possibly make choice of. For,

---

[1] This is William, Lord Keith, the 9th Earl Marischal (d. 1712), and a cousin to Hope's mother. "The important hereditary office of Great Marischal of Scotland was held by the family of Keith, from the 12th century." *Burke's Peerage*, 1897. "The Marischal of Scotland was an hereditary office entrusted with the military affairs of the sovereign." *Oxford English Dictionary*.

[2] Hope may be referring to William, Lord Keith, the 7th Earl Marischal (d. 1661), Lord Privy Seal to Charles II, and Hope's maternal grandfather. However, it was the Marischal's younger brother, the Hon. Sir John Keith, Earl of Kintore (d. 1714), who is credited with safely conveying the Royal Scottish Regalia from Dunottar Castle and burying them in the Church of Kinnef, to keep them out of the hands of Cromwell. After the Restoration, he was appointed hereditary Knight-Marischal of Scotland in consideration for his loyalty. Both his son, William, 2nd Earl of Kintore, and his nephew George, 10th Earl Marischal, would be stripped of their lands and titles for their participation in the Jacobite uprising of 1715. *Debrett's Illustrated Peerage*, 1966.

First, the Art it self being a material Branch of Honour and Chivalry, falls most naturally under your Lordship's Jurisdiction and Protection; because as Lord High Marischal, all Debates about, and Decisions of Points of Honour, come under your Lordship's Cognizance, and are Determined by your Lordship's Sentence when in Judgment. And,

Secondly, the chief Design of this *New Method of Fencing*, being for the Safety and Preservation of Men's Honour and Lives, tends certainly so far to the advancement of the Publick Good, as it lays down a Rational and Easy *Method* for that End: And This alone I know is sufficient to Recommend it, and make it Acceptable to your Lordship, who I know have always taken such a great deal of Pleasure and Satisfaction, in such Gentlemanny and Useful Exercises. So that, both a Man's Honour and Reputation, which are indeed all his Regalia, and in place of a Crown to him, being hereby Preserved; and his Life, which is his Right and Property as a Subject, being Protected and Defended: It could not, My Lord, have possibly thrown it self under the Protection of a more Proper, as well as Generous, Patron.

Having thus given your Lordship a short Account of the Reasons, which prevail'd with me to give you this Trouble; I humbly lay it before your Lordship. And as according to your Lordship's Just and Virtuous Devise, *VERITAS VINCIT*, Truth and Sincerity does always hold Foot, and at last Vanquish and Triumph: So I am persuaded, that the Extraordinary Improvements contain'd in this Piece, will sufficiently Convince your Lordship of my Sincerity in Writing it, and the good Effects it will have hereafter upon the Gentry of This Nation for their more certain Defence, give your Lordship an evident Demonstration of the Truth of all I have advanced in It.

And I do further ingenuously declare, That I had no other Aim in Publishing of it, next to the Safety and Preservation of my Country-men's Honour and Lives, by Rectifying in it many Imperfections, which have creept into the Art as commonly Taught, than to give my self an Opportunity, wherein I might discover to your Lordship and the World, the great Respect and Esteem I have for your Lordship's Person and Family.

That therefore the most Noble and Ancient Family of the KEITHS may be Preserved and Flourish, not only for Seven Hundred, but Seventy times Seven Hundred Years; nay even to the CONSUMMATION of all Things, is the most sincere Wish, and hearty and most fervent Desire of,

     My Lord,

        Your Lordship's,
            Obedient and most
              Humble Servant,

            Will. Hope.

ADVERTISEMENT

Especially to Fencing-Masters,

*A*nd such who being very Curious, are resolved by their own Industry, and the Assistance of a Comrade, to improve themselves in the most Useful Art of Defence; by this *New Method of Fencing*.

It is not to be doubted, by the great Alteration that is designed to be made by me, in the *Art of the Sword*, by this *New Method of Fencing*, will startle a great many People, as well Masters and Professors of the Art, as others; the Attempt being no less Great and Bold, than New. For to endeavour at one dash, wholly to alter and reverse an Old, though bad and pernicious Practice, is no easy Matter.

I very well know, that it is one of the easiest things in the World to pretend Faults, where there are but few or none, and a very common thing, to cry down, or discommend Books, without ever going further than the Title Page, or but taking at most, a Cursory View of some of the Titles of the Chapters. A most discommendable and unreasonable, as well as Ungentlemany Custom; (though daily practis'd by many, who pretend to be no mean Judges in matter of Books,) Because, before a Man either approve of a Book as good, or condemn and reject it as bad and useless, he ought in Reason before he pass his Verdict upon it, not only to read it [thoroughly and] attentively, and without Prejudice; but if he intend to play the Critick, reflect seriously upon the Design of the Author, and Arguments he brings for what he would advance; and all this without the least *Pique* or Prejudice against him.

Therefore I expect this Justice from All, especially from Fencing-Masters, that before they disapprove and reject this *New Method*, they will take the trouble to thorowly peruse it; not only with regard to the Advantages which a Man may have by it, against any of the Ordinary Guards belonging to the Small Sword, and which will still more and more appear, and be better discovered, the more frequently this *New Method* is made use of, and put in practice against them; but chiefly with respect to all the other great Benefits which a Man will reap by the constant Practice of it. Such as, that it will not only prove a sufficient Guard and Defence, against all the Thrusts of the Small Sword, and Blows of the Sheering, or Back Sword in a single Combat; but also against the Thrusts and Blows of all other *Pointed* or *Edged Weapons* whatsoever, and that not only a-Foot, but on Horseback, as well as in a Battel as in a Single Combat.

I say, if my Readers, especially those who make profession of Communicating their Art to others, consider it seriously under this general View; and not out of a Cavilling Temper, pick out, and insist upon some particular and trifling Imperfections in it, from which no Guard whatsoever is free; because it is impossible for any one particular Guard or Parade, to answer exactly and equally all Circumstances. I make no doubt, but it will answer sufficiently for it self, and give them such an intire Conviction of the Unsufficiency of their former *Common Method*, for a sure and general Defence against all Weapons, that they will hereafter wholly reject That, and take themselves to this *New One*, which I am persuaded, will be attended with such good Consequences, as will make it hereafter prevail, not only in the Fencing Schools of these Islands, but over all, where it shall have the good Fortune to be made known.

A dexterous Small Sword Man, how adroit soever he may be at the handling of his Rapier in a Duel after the *Common School Method*, will, when he comes to Engage at Close Fight in a Field-Battel, either with Foot or Horse, find himself extremely put to it, and almost as much to seek, as if he had no Art at all, if he be Master of no better Defence, whereby to secure himself, than the *Ordinary School Parades* of *Quarte* and *Tierce*, which belong only to the Small Sword or Rapier; & whereof the unsuccessful Practice, (even in Duels, laying aside their Insufficiency in a Crowd, or Field Battel) hath no doubt made many People value less the *Art of the Sword*, than otherwise they would have done; judging thereby, that there could be no better nor securer Defence drawn from it: For in such a Juncture, I mean in a Crowd or Battel, a Man hath neither Time nor Bounds, nicely to Ward off his Adversary's Blows or Thrusts, nor to Break his Measure, as he would have, were he engaged only in a Duel. Here he is a little more at Large and Freedom; but there, perhaps surrounded by two or three Stout and Vigorous Single Soldiers, or Troopers, who are with all Fury Sabring, and Discharging Blows upon him.

I say in such a Case, this *Hanging Guard* with the Cross-Parade from it, is the only One in the World he can rely upon; and if he be Agile and Vigorous, and can perform it Nimbly and Dexterously, (especially that Parade upwards and across his Face as in Fig. 16. returning alwise Smart Plain Strokes or Thrusts from it, so long as he has the Strength to renew them) it will certainly, if any Art can, and as much as Human Nature is capable of, (for no Man is infallible) save him from many a Wound, although not from all, for that, without being Armed *Cap a pe*, [armoured "head to toe"] is in a manner impossible, where there are perhaps, Two or Three against One; but certainly, the dexterous Use of this *Guard* and Cross Parade from it, will save him from a great many, he would have otherwise received, had he been ignorant of it, and necessitate to make use of his Imperfect, or rather School-Play Parades (for in such a Juncture they deserve no better Name) of *Quarte* and *Tierce*.

So that all this being duly considered, I am fully persuaded, (if there be any such thing in Nature, as that a True, Sure, and General Defence may be drawn from any Single Weapon) that I have hit right on it; and that this Cross Parade I so much recommend is it; at least, the very best that Art can furnish a Man with, against all kind of Edged or Pointed weapons whatsoever; a thing so very Useful, yet so much wanting amongst our British Youth: And therefore, if there be any Failure hereafter in their Defence, it will be found to lie, not in the Unsufficiency of this *New Method*, but either in the want of a sufficient Strength or Vigour, or in the bad Execution of its Rules; which last, I beg such Masters will take special Care to prevent, who shall be so just to me, and kind to their Scholars, as henceforth to communicate it to them; for the Security and Preservation of whose Honour and Lives, it was chiefly made publick.

To which End they are entreated, not to mix and jumble the *Two Methods* together; particularly the Parades or Defensive Part; that is, Teach their Scholars sometimes the One Manner of Parieing, and sometimes the Other; for that is the ready way to render them dexterous at neither. But if they will obstinately keep to their *Old Method*, let them wholly reject *This*; And if they are pleased to make Trial of *This*, then let them make a True and Thorow Proof of it, especially with respect to the Defensive Part or Parade, (wherein the great Advantage of this *New Method* consists) without so much as letting their Scholars practise any part of the Parades, nay, nor even the Pursuits belonging to the other, except in so far, as *Both Methods* shall jump together in the Offensive Part; because in it, that Nicety needs not to be so much regarded, as in the Defensive, which from this *Hanging Guard* is indeed most admirable, by reason of the great Cross it Forms upon the Adversary's Sword in Opposing and Defending it.

If Masters punctually observe this, I dare promise to their Scholars, not only a Great and Sudden, but even Surprising Success in the *True Art of Defence*, of which it may be most justly asserted, that hitherto we have only possessed the Name, not its good and salutary Effects, towards the redressing of which, 'tis hoped that the Publication of this *New* but *Secure Method of Fencing*, will not a little contribute, especially if duly Encouraged and put in Practice by such, as have the Instruction of our Youth in this most Gentlemany and useful Art entrusted to them, I mean the

Adroit and Judicious Fencing Masters, as well Back Sword as Small Sword-Men of these Islands.

For here both their Arts, which have been of a long time most unreasonably, as well as unluckily separate, and in a manner Rent asunder, are by the improvement of the following *Guard*, and Parade naturally flowing from it, join'd and reunited; So that hereafter Gentlemen shall no more need to enquire after *This* Master to instruct them in the *Art of the Back Sword*, and such another to render them Dexterous at the Small, but only see for one who is really Master of this *New Method*, that is, who is thorowly Master of the *True Art of Defence*; And this Master, nay, when such an one cannot be had, this very Piece alone, if duly considered, and its Rules exactly put in Practice with an Assiduous Application, assisted by the help of a judicious Comrade, will in a very short time make them such Masters of it, as is for the most part needful for the Defence of any who intend not to make the Art their Profession, by gaining wholly their Livelyhood by it.

And that they may attain to this with more Ease, I advise all Masters, who shall undertake the Teaching of this *New Method*, with Success, that they order their Scholars, to provide themselves with *Fleurets* having Hilts, with several neat Bars, both lengthways and a Cross upon them, resembling somewhat the Close-Hilts of Back Swords, for the better Preservation and Defence of their Sword-hand and Fingers, when they shall be obliged to ward the Blows made against them; because to Teach this *New Method* Methodically, and with all its Advantages, the Blow must be taught at the same time with the Thrust, that the Scholar may be rendered alike dexterous at both; so that although a Scholar, after some Practice, may come to defend his Adversary's Blows very safely, and with a kind of Assurance and Certainly, upon the Blade of his *Fleuret*; yet at first Teaching, and also in Common Assaults for Diversion, such Barr'd Hilts as I am Recommending, will be found most Convenient and Useful, as well for the Preservation of the Sword-hand from irregular Blows, as to render the Scholar so much more Lively and Brisk in his Assaults, as he knows that his Sword-hand is pretty well secured, against his Adversary's irregular Blows, should he himself at first Assaulting, fail to receive them upon the Blade of his *Fleuret*, which with a little Practice, he will not fail for the most part to do. Neither will such Hilts, after he is once used with them, at all hinder or retard the swiftness of his Thrusts; because he is to hold his *Fleuret* in his Hand after the same manner with them, as he does the Small Sword; and consequently will by Practice, Thrust as swiftly with a Sheering Sword, kept in his Hand after this manner, as he could do with a Small Sword or Rapier.

Now after all, it will perhaps be objected by some, that this Essay does not exactly Answer, nor Correspond with its Title, because in the Title, the *Art of the Sword* is said to be therein not only rectified, but also compendized, and yet this Exact Compend [i.e synopsis] consists of near 36 Sheets of Print: A very brief and short Compend indeed!

To which, for the Objector's greater satisfaction, who, I must say, is a little more nice upon this Head than is needful; I will easily Answer, and make it appear, that I have made good the Title to a Nicety: Because, although this Essay swells to near 36 Sheets of Print, to which I was obliged by reason of the exact Explications I resolved to give to most of the *Terms of Art* belonging to Fencing; besides the Addition of a whole Chapter of Principles, whereupon I found the *True Art of Defence* with both Back Sword and Small, which hath never been done heretofore by any: As also, of the nice Theory I all along intersperse, with the Excellent Rules and Explications, which likewise is not to be found in any other Book of this kind: Yet the whole of the Art, as well Back Sword as Small, is really contained in about seven Sheets, that is, in the First, Fifth, and Sixth Chapters: So that notwithstanding of my prolixness upon other Heads, especially with respect to the explication of the *Terms of Art*, and consequently the Rectifying of a great many Material Escapes, in the *Common Method* of Teaching and Practice, for which this Essay will be also very useful, though not so particularly compil'd for it, as for the Illustration of this *New Method*: The Title Page is therein made good, because of the Substance of the *Whole Art of Fencing*, as well from the Common Guards as this *New One*, being in effect contained within the three above-mentioned Chapters.

As to that other Objection, of *This New Method's* not being my own invention, because Founded upon a very Common and Old Guard; I think I have sufficiently removed it in my Answer to the sixth Objection against this *New Method*, page 113. and shall therefore only add here, that how easy soever the Discovery, or rather Improvement of this *Hanging Guard in Seconde*, may appear to some, who are perhaps no Well-wishers either to me, or the Art I improve by it; yet it is somewhat like the Famous *COLUMBUS*, his desiring of some of his conceited Company, (who slighted his discovery of America, as a thing of small moment, and what another might have done as well as he) to make an Egg stand alone upon its little End; which when they had tried, and were not able to perform, he took the Egg, and gently bruising the little End of it, made it presently to stand upon it, saying to the Company, *There, now I suppose you can do this too, now that you have seen it done*. The Application I leave to the Reader; but with this Difference, That Columbus's Discovery was indeed of a *New World*, whereas mine is only of *A New Method of Fencing*.

This much I judg'd fit to premise by way of Advertisement, as well to Masters, as others, who have an Itch to Object and Criticise; as also for other Ingenious Persons, who would gladly improve themselves in the *True Art of Defence*, but cannot conveniently have the Benefit of such Masters; for the supplying of which Inconveniency and Want, let them have Recourse to the *Directions* set down to them for that purpose in Chap. 5. where I have been as plain as possible.

I have likewise for the Reader's greater Ease, caused engraved in a Print, (which is placed at the end of the Book) the most necessary Postures of Defence and Pursuit, flowing from this *New Guard*, which will make my Directions be understood a great deal better, and with more Ease, than if the Book had been altogether without them; For let a Direction in Writing, especially for any Practical Art, such as Fencing, be never so plain, yet a well drawn Figure adds Life to it, and makes it not only more intelligible, but also more readily retain'd by the Reader, for whose Ease as well as Benefit, and Security in an Occasion with Sharps this Piece is chiefly designed; neither do I doubt, but (as Horace *De Arte Poet*.) *Quo propius stet, eum capiet magis.*

THE SCHEME

By this Scheme is demonstrated, the great advantage a Man hath in making a great cross upon his Adversarys Sword, whereby the swiftness of his Thrust is considerably retarded, and which alone is sufficient to vindicate the reasonableness of This

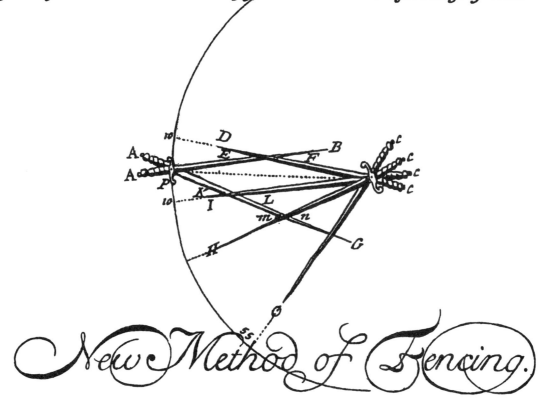

New Method of Fencing.

FIG. 1.

One standing to the hanging Guard.

FIG. 2.

One opposing the hanging Guard with the same posture.

HOPE's
New METHOD,
OF
FENCING &c.

Introduction.

'The Art *of Fencing*, being not only a very gentle and diverting exercise, but also most necessary and useful upon an Occasion, which few Gentlemen but once in their Life find it their fate to meet with; and many worthy and deserving persons, not only in this Kingdom, but elsewhere, having done me the Honour to pass an obliging character upon me with respect to my dexterity and knowledge in this Art; which preceeded chiefly, I presume, from the great esteem and liking I have alwise had for it from my youth; I judged myself in some measure obliged, as well for their vindication, that they might not be said to bestow altogether undeservedly such a character upon me, as out of gratitude to them for it, to make good that character by giving to the publick three small Essays[1] upon this subject, all which had the good success to meet with a general approbation.

And as it was my opinion at the writing of these, so it is still: that as to the Common Method of Fencing, both abroad and in this Kingdom, nothing can be rendered more plain and easie, by rules and directions in print, than the whole Guards, Parades, Lessons, and Contraries to them, are in these three small Pieces.

For does a man desire to be informed of all the different Guards belonging to the Small Sword, with the Method of defending and pursuing each; or of the Parades and various Lessons, with their Contraries? He hath them all, most distinctly described, in the *Scots Fencing Master*. Or does he incline to behave himself dexterously, and with a graceful address in the Fencing Schools? *The Fencing Master's Advice to His Schollar* will bring him to it, as well as inform him of many other useful things belonging to the Art. Or, in fine, is his chief design to (and indeed a very commendable one it is) only make himself Master of a true and sure defence at Sharps? He needs then only consult and diligently put in practice the excellent directions set down to him, with all possible exactness and brevity, in the *Sword-Man's Vade-Mecum*; and then he shall not fail to acquire it. For there, in a very few singular rules, is contained the very marrow and useful part of Fencing: I still mean, with respect to the Ordinary Method of teaching and play.

But the longer a man lives, the more experience he acquires, Which duly reflected upon, makes way not only for the finding out of several imperfections which may have hitherto lain undiscovered in any Art or Science, but also to fall upon such Methods as may raise them to the highest pitch of perfection. And as this generally holds in meditating upon other subjects, so does it no less upon the *Art of Fencing*, which hath given rise to the following sheets.

I intend not here to make an encomium upon this Art by discovering its usefulness, and how much it concerns every Gentleman to understand it, at least so much of it as may be of use to him on an Occasion, either for the defence of his Person, or only for the preservation of his Reputation and Honour, having done that sufficiently already in those above-mentioned pieces, to which I refer the reader. Altho' perhaps I may give a little further anent it in a few paragraphs towards the close of this. And to tell the truth in one word, Fencing never was nor will be undervalued and rejected by any, but by such as, either for lack of inclination or capacity, cannot come at the True Practice of it, and who, because of their own want of Art, would therefore gladly wish all other people to be as ignorant and unskilful as themselves. For I really never knew a good Sword Man who ever repented him of his Art.

Therefore, not to dip any further at present in this matter, I shall in this introduction confine myself to these two heads: *First*, discover the motive that induced me to enquire after and publish this *New Method of Fencing*; and *Secondly*, show the useful advantage of it to all who intend to be Masters of the useful part of Fencing: that is, either the defence of their Persons and Lives, or the preservation of their Reputation and Honour.

As to the *first*, when I seriously reflected upon the Common and Ordinary Method of communicating this Art, I found it so defective, especially in the defensive part, that I concluded one of two: either what the Masters taught for the *Art of Defence* had in it really no true defence, or if there was a true *Art of Defence*, it was to be sought in some other Method of practice than what was commonly seen in the Schools.

---

[1] See the Bibliography for a list of Hope's works.

For, *First*, to find that Art which they called the *Art of Defence* to consist chiefly in thrusting and offending, was what I did not approve of, being perfectly opposite and contradictory to the very meaning and import of the term *Fencing*.

Secondly, to find the generality of people who pretended to be Fencers, not capable by their Art reasonably to defend themselves against the vigorous and irregular thrusts and blows of Ignorants, and yet to maintain that they understood and were Masters of the *Art of Defence*, was what I did as little understand. For although, as I have elsewhere acknowledged, the very best of Sword Men cannot pretend to an infallibility in their defence, yet it is a reflection upon them, and argues a great weakness and imperfection in the Art, to be altogether uncertain; of which I have seen but too many instances while I frequented the Schools, and which I have known some, no well wishers to the Art, to take advantage of, and make an argument against it.

Therefore I concluded that the generality of Fencing Masters had hitherto either designedly kept up and reserved, as a secret to themselves, the true and easie *Method of Defence* on purpose to detain Gentlemen a longer time at their Schools, which is a piece of disingenuity I could never suspect them guilty of, especially their very best and oldest Schollars' defence proving for the most part imperfect and uncertain. For to be sure, if they had a more secure Method, I concluded they would communicate it to these. Or otherwise, that in place of Fencing or defending (the true meaning of the word and design of the Art), they had, through an unvoluntary mistake, been hitherto alwise teaching the Art of thrusting and offending. Whereby they did not only ignorantly rob their Schollars of their money, but, in a manner, their Lives, seeing they taught them chiefly, tho' at the second instance, and I am persuaded without any bad design, to take their adversaries' Lives, not to defend their own.

However, after all, I was fully convinced that it was indeed only their not knowing a better Method that made the Fencing Masters practice the Common One. And that altho' the most part of them did know somewhat of this Guard I am to discourse of, yet they had not thoroughly examin'd it, nor considered the great benefit of it. Otherwise they had never so long neglected its improvement. And that which confirmed me the more in this opinion was my sometimes hearing the most judicious amongst them, as well abroad as in this Kingdom, regret that the Art did not furnish them with a more sure and general defence than what they commonly taught. But notwithstanding of all this, I was fully persuaded that the imperfection did not at all lie in the Art it self, but in the bad application of its rules. For that there was a true and real *Art of Defence*, I made not the least doubt of it. But where to find it, lay the difficulty.

This made me run through all the Postures people commonly make use of, both for Guards and Parades, as well natural as artificial. And I found the generality of them very defective as to what I was chiefly enquiring after, which was *a sure and true defense against the blows and thrusts of all weapons*. At last considering that the most part of Arts serve only to assist and perfect Nature, I turned my thoughts to that Posture which I found Nature prompted most people without Art to take themselves to, upon a sudden and vigorous attack. And I found it was the *Hanging Guard*, with the point sloping generally towards a man's adversary's advanced thigh, altho' sometimes higher or lower, or without or within it, as occasions require. I considered it again and again; compared the defences and pursuits flowing from it with those made use of from the other Guards; and after all the difficulties and objections I could start against it, I found it had by far the advantage of them all, especially for a general defence.

These were the motives that first put me in a quest of a good and sufficient Guard. And being very hopeful that I have fallen upon it, I fancy few people will be surpris'd at my offering it to the publick. For man being a sociable creature, designed not only for himself but for the benefit and advantage of the community wherein he lives, it would have been, in my opinion, a strange piece of reservedness in me, whatever some morose criticks may fancy to themselves, if I should have kept such an extraordinary and useful improvement as this is, and which may tend so very much to the benefit of the Lieges, as a Secret, and altogether undiscovered.

I confess I have alwise had something more of a publick spirit than that comes to. And although I am none of those who have the greatest opinion of their own performances, yet rather than that the young Gentry of this Kingdom should lose the benefit of so great and useful a discovery in an Art I may say peculiarly belonging to them, I am ever resolved, and chiefly upon their account, to venture a kind of publick censure by appearing again in print upon this Gentlemany subject.

It may likewise be thought by many people somewhat strange that after all I have formerly writ upon this subject, and the great value and esteem I put upon those former treatises, I should after all this take now quite another Method, and in a manner renverse and condemn what I before approved of and so much recommended. But such persons may be pleased to know that as it was alwise my opinion that a man should never so fix his judgement, but that upon stronger and more convincing reasons he might alter it. So experience discovering to me the great advantage this Guard and play from it, if rightly prosecuted, may have over all other Guards whatsoever, for the security of a man's

Life and Honour; I am not at all out of countenance to own that I am proselyted to it, and for a sure and general defence against the blows and thrusts of all weapons, do prefer it very much to them all. Besides, that which I writ then still holds good, with respect to the Common Method of Fencing. Whereas now I am designing a new and considerable improvement of the whole Art, and therefore am obliged to alter a great deal of my former Method, which otherwise I do declare I still approve of as much as ever.

What I have been saying, does, I think, sufficiently answer the *first* branch of my division, which was the motive that induced me to enquire after and publish this *New Method of Fencing*. And as to the *second*, which is the advantage those persons may have by it, who chiefly intend to be Masters of the useful part of Fencing, that is, the true defence of their Lives, I shall only say that by exactly practising this *New Method*, they have in general these following advantages.

First, They thereby acquire a universal defence, both a-foot and on horseback, against the blows and thrusts of all weapons whatsoever. Which cannot, in my opinion, be obtained by the Common Method, but by a very great application and long practice in both weapons: I mean the Back Sword and Small.

Secondly, It is an excellent Posture against the irregular pursuits of Ignorants, as well half-skilled as others. For a very forward half-skilled person is worse to deal with than one altogether ignorant of the common principles of Fencing.

Thirdly, They thereby save a great deal of time, seeing by following this Method they may acquire as much, nay more, knowledge and practice in the Art in three months as they possibly can in the Common Method in twelve. As for any other advantages, I willingly omit them in this place, seeing they come all in more properly in the Second Chapter, to which I refer you.

Having thus given a brief account, of my design in writing and publishing this new, and in my opinion, great improvement in the *Art of Defence*, I shall endeavour to prosecute it in the following method, which shall serve as titles to so many chapters.

First, I shall show you as plainly as I can in writing how the *Hanging Guard* is to be kept.

Secondly, Discover some considerable advantages it hath over the other Guards.

Thirdly, Propose some of the chief objections that may be made against it, and endeavour to answer them.

Fourthly, Explain, and give a few short, tho' not ordinary, remarks upon the most difficult *Terms of Art* made use of in Fencing. And that the rather because I intend this piece shall be useful to young beginners by itself, and without the assistance of any of my former.

Fifthly, Show how a man ought to defend himself upon this Guard.

Sixthly, How he ought to pursue his adversary from it, by describing some of the principle Lessons, as well for blow as thrust, that most naturally flow from this Guard, and which are abundantly sufficient for any man to practice upon an Occasion.

Seventhly, Lay down some few principles upon which, in my opinion, this most useful *Art of Defence* ought to be indispensably founded. Otherwise the superstructure must of necessity prove altogether weak and false. For a man who is not Master of a true and sure defence, founded upon reasonable and solid principles, had much better totally abandon such a false Art, and take himself wholly to the plain and simple dictates of pure Nature. Which, upon a pinching necessity, he will find of far greater advantage, and more serviceable to him, than an uncertain and precarious Art founded upon false and erroneous principles.

And how close I have kept to those principles in this following Method (so far as the nature of my improvement will allow of), I leave to the determination of my judicious reader. But however I may have failed in my performance, yet I am hopeful that my sincere endeavours will be sincerely accepted of, and that this Essay will at least excite some more skilful pen to prosecute the improvement of it. This much I thought fit to promise, by way of introduction or preface.

FIG. 3.

How the ordinary Quart Guard is to be oppos'd by the Hanging Guard.

FIG. 4.

One standing to the ordinary Quart Guard

FIG. 5.

One standing to the Quart Guard with a sloping point.

FIG. 6.

How the Quart Guard with a sloping point, is to be oppos'd by the hanging Guard.

CHAPTER I
Of the Hanging Guard,
and how it is to be kept with
the Back Sword, Sheering Sword, or Small Sword,
either a-Foot or upon Horseback.[1]

THE SCHEME

Being to establish the *Art of Defence*, in a manner, upon quite another foot and Method than what it hath been formerly; security and safety being my only aim. The reader must not be surprised if in place of a neat and graceful posture (such as that in the 4th Figure on the Plate 2 [p.100]), and genteel method of play, so much admired by some people, he meet only with a good, secure, and homely posture, and a firm and solid defence and pursuit flowing from it. For provided a man defend himself well by making a good cross upon his adversary's sword (which is the only true source from whence all certain defence flows), it is in my opinion no great matter whether it be in *Quarte* or *Tierce*, or with a genteel and graceful deportment of the body or not.

And altho' I do acknowledge that a comely and graceful address be very agreeable and taking with by-standers, especially in a School-Assault, yet I have alwise observed that when a man is really concerned to make a true defence for his Life, he appears in such an earnest posture, his limbs and other members so much concerning themselves in the celerity of the motion designed for their defence, that it clearly appears that what goes under the name of graceful Fencing is for no other use but only for such as, for divertisement, counterfeit a fight with blunts: that is, who only Assault in the Schools with foils. For in a real Occasion, all that variety and quaintness of play is so much neglected, that it is easily perceived by the eagerness of the motions, and concern of the look and gesture, that it is only safety and self-preservation, not a good grace, which a man in such a case chiefly aims at, and is concerned about.

Therefore leaving that genteel and graceful kind of play for the diversion of Schools, I shall endeavour to recommend in its place one of quite another nature; and whose gracefulness consists chiefly in its security for a man's defence. There, and there only, in my opinion, lyes the gracefulness of Fencing. And if it do, I hope to make it appear that the Method I am about to discover is as genteel and graceful a method as any hath ever hither to been made use of.

Short and easie then shall be the rules upon which I shall establish it. And as I intend to lay down directions for the blow as well as for the thrust, I shall so order it that the rules for thrusting shall alwise go before and preceed the directions for the blow. But seeing that before a man can either thrust or strike, he must of necessity bring his blow or his thrust from some one posture or other, I shall therefore begin this *New Method* by showing how a man ought to stand to his Guard. For it is chiefly from hence that all the benefit of a sure defence does proceed, as you will easily discover by the sequel.

In standing to this Guard, which in effect is but an improving of the ordinary *Hanging Guard*, a man is to keep his feet at a pretty good distance from one another, for his more firm standing; his right knee a little more bent than the left; is to show as little of his left side to his adversary as possible, without constraining and weakening too much his posture; is to present his sword, with his hand as high as his head and in *Seconde*, which is with the nails of it almost quite down; his sword's point must slope towards the middle part of his adversary's advanced thigh, but sometimes higher or lower, as occasion requires; and either without or within it, according as his adversary presents his sword. And this for the better securing of himself upon one side. For 'tis a general rule in Fencing, and punctually to be observed, never to present one's sword without perfectly covering or securing, as we call it, one side of the body.

The sword being in this posture, he is to keep his head a little beneath his sword-arm with his breast inclining forewards, which is as well for the securing of his head as the keeping of the lower parts of the body at a little distance from his adversary. And the more earnest he is upon his pursuit or defence, the more he must stoop and incline forewards with his head and shoulders. His left hand is alwise to be kept in readiness for the opposing or putting by of an irregular or straggling thrust; and for its position, ought to be kept advanced within the hollow of the sword-arm, the points of the fingers pointing slopewise upward, and its

---

[1] In addition to being a master of swordsmanship, Hope was an expert on the equestrian arts. In 1696 he published *Le Parfait Marechal, or the Compleat Farrier,* a translation of Sieur de Solleysell's book on horsemanship. This places Hope firmly in the tradition of horsemen/swordsmen that reaches from the fifteenth century, with Dom Duarte, King of Portugal (*Livro da ensinanca de bem cavalgar*), to the late eighteenth century, with the elder Angelo. Castle, 269; Sydney Anglo, *The Martial Arts of Renaissance Europe*, 2000; J.D. Aylward, *The House of Angelo*, 1953.

palm declining a little from him, toward the right side, but with as little exposing of the left side, as I said, as possible. And all this as much as he can without constraint, for never was there any posture of defence yet good that was too constraining. See the Figures 1, 2, & 14 [p.96 & 171].

Thus have I shown you exactly how this excellent *Hanging Guard* is to be kept, with any kind of weapon, either a-foot or horseback. From which I intend to draw such a secure and general defence against the thrusts and blows of all weapons, that, without contradicting reason and evident demonstration, it shall not be in the power of any, even the greatest criticks, to deny the advantages it has over most of the other Guards, which shall be the subject of the next Chapter. But for such as have neither the patience nor curiosity to read those advantages, and who, relying upon my judgement, take them upon trust, and are only anxious to be informed of the true defence and pursuit naturally flowing from this Guard, they may skip the three following Chapters and go to the Fifth, where they will certainly find what they desire. Altho' if they take my advice and intend to understand the theory as well as practice of this excellent Guard, I do indeed recommend to them the regular reading of this piece from beginning to end, whereby they will understand my design, and the arguments I found it upon, to the full. And also be the more capable to reason upon it when any person, who perhaps is no well-wisher to either the author or it, shall offer to impugn the great use and benefit of it.

Fig. 7.
One parieing without and below his Sword, upon the hanging Guard.

Fig. 8.
One thrusting without and below his Adverfary's Sword from the hanging Guard.

CHAPTER II
Of the Advantages that the Hanging Guard
hath over all or most of the other Guards.

Advantage I

By reason of its sloping position, which takes in almost the whole length of the body, the lower parts thereof, particularly the belly and thighs, are better defended. And consequently, a man is not obliged to sink so low upon this Guard for the defence of those parts as he is necessitate to do upon most other Guards in which the position of the sword is quite contrary: to wit, either streight and in a level, or pointing a little upward.

I have alwise found upon the ordinary Guards, the lower parts of the body most difficult to defend, and that for two reasons. *First*, because upon these Guards a man stands for the most part pretty straight; and when thrusts are given in upon those lower parts, as very commonly they are, then he must either keep his sword-hand very low to make the Parade or cross, which exposes him much to thrusts above the sword, if his adversary should make a Feint beneath it; or he must, as the thrust is coming home, slope his point to make a cross; which taking up a considerable time, renders his Parade slow, and thereby makes him more liable to receive the thrust. *Secondly*, the upper parts of the body are in some measure naturally defended with cartilages, gristles, and bones, so that a weak or spent thrust will not easily pierce them, even altho' a man should not defend at all; whereas the lower parts of the body have no such natural bulwark, but, consisting chiefly of soft membranes and entrails, are easily pierced by reason of the small resistance they make. As also the thrusts of most people, when at a stretch, fall low, so that where one man is wounded in the trunk of the body, many are wounded in the belly or thighs.

These very reasons were the cause of my so much recommending, in the *Scots Fencing Master*, etc., the sinking low upon the ordinary *Quarte* Guard. For upon that Guard, I found the lower parts of the body to be so much exposed and so difficult to defend, most people in Assault receiving thrusts in them, that to make a good cross for their defence, there was a necessity either to sink low and to keep the sword-hand but a little above the right knee, which is but an uneasie, altho' most secure, posture upon that Guard; or otherwise to alter the Guard. But to what posture I did not at that time know, not having fallen upon the usefulness of this Guard I now recommend. So that the sinking low, supplying that defect of the ordinary *Quarte* Guard, I did alwise practise it my self and recommend it to others. And I still do so, when a man resolves to play from the ordinary *Quarte* Guard, but willingly passes from, and dispenses with, the not making use of it, when he shall take himself to this excellent

Hanging Guard. Which, because of its sloping position, is most safe, defending thereby easily all the lower parts without constraining the body to a low and sinking posture, which upon the ordinary *Quarte* Guard was in a manner absolutely necessary, and at that time a very considerable improvement.

Advantage II

The defensive part of the Art of the Sword, or Parade, being most difficult, and the pursuit or offensive part most easie; the keeping this Guard quite renverses that by rendering the defensive part more easie, and the offensive more difficult. Which new and extraordinary alteration is no small advantage to the Art.

The defense of all weapons consists in the cross they make with the adversary's weapon when he is giving a thrust or blow. So that the greater the cross is, the more sure is not only the Parade, but the slower the thrust or blow, either made against a Guard, or after a Parade which makes such a great cross. For that which, upon ordinary Guards, makes the offensive part easie and the defensive difficult is the great uncertainty of Parieing variety of most quick and subtile Feints; which a man is encouraged to make by reason of the extraordinary conveniency and ease he finds in Disengaging upon the pursuit; and which is occasioned by the small cross that is made by the two weapons upon the Parade. To obviate which is the general direction of all good Masters (especially the French, who neither make much use of Binding, nor of the *Contre-caveating* Parade) when they would have their Scholars to prevent and put a stop to their adversary's Feints; to order them, upon their adversary's making of such Feints, immediately to *baisser la pointe*, as they term it, or to slope their sword's point: the only sure defence and preservative upon the ordinary *Quarte* and *Tierce* Guards, in place of the *Contre-caveating* Parade, against multiplicity of Feints, and which is a kind of imitating unawares this excellent and useful posture. For as I said, the more streight and level the sword is kept, with more ease are the Feints made, because of the great readiness a man finds to Disengage, by reason of the small cross that is made betwixt the two weapons.

For upon those Guards, the two angles made by the weapons, and which respect the adversaries, are very acute or sharp, as you may see in the Plate at the Scheme, in the middle thereof where the two lines A-B and C-D represent two swords crossing one another, as upon an ordinary *Quarte* or *Tierce* Guard, and by their cross make Angles E and F, respecting the adversaries, acute or sharp. And consequently the two lines or swords make but a small cross.

And it is a mathematical demonstration that the nearer an angle made by two streight lines, or which is equivalent, by two swords, approaches to a right angle, the greater is the cross made by those two lines or swords, because the arch [arc of a circle] included betwixt them is so much the larger. And the further it is from making a right angle, keeping still within the quarter of a circle, the more acute or sharp it is; and so likewise makes the smaller cross, because the arch included is so much the less. And consequently the Disengaging is thereby made the more quick, as the arch is in smallness; which is the cause of the pursuit, either from or against such Guards, being a great deal more easie than if the cross approached nearer to a right angle, and the arch consequently larger.

But to make this a little more plain and intelligible, observe narrowly the above-mentioned Scheme, which represents six lines or swords crossing one another, two whereof, A G and C H, represent the posture of this Guard I am discoursing of. Now it is evident that the two angles M and N, made by the crossing of these two swords, and which respect the adversary's sword-hands A and C, approach nearer to right angles than the angles K and L, made by the swords A G and C I. Because the arch betwixt 30 and P, which is 30 degrees, contains more degrees than the arch betwixt 10 and P, which is only 10 degrees. And consequently, if the sword C I were to thrust at the point or hand P, it would have a shorter way to make to hit it. Or could more easily Disengage to thrust at the number 10 above P because of the smallness of the arch betwixt 10 and 10, whereby its thrust is made more short, and consequently more quick, and so would come sooner home than that made by the sword C H. Because the arch betwixt 30 and P, containing more degrees, *viz.* 30, is larger than the arch betwixt 10 and 10, which is only 20, and therefore comes nearer to a right angle, whereby the thrust of C H will be longer, and consequently slower in performing, than that made by C I. But if the sword C O were to thrust at the Number 10 above P, it would still be longer a-coming home, and consequently the thrust slower, and so more easily Paried. Because the cross it makes upon the sword A G forms a greater angle, being 65 degrees. Which is 25 degrees more, the other angle being only 40.

I know that most thrusts form a part of a parabolic curve, not an exact arch of a circle. Therefore it is only for the more ready understanding of my demonstration that I call the line which a sword makes in thrusting, a part of the arch of a circle, and that I might thereby more easily form my Scheme.

Having thus demonstrated that the greater the cross made by the two swords is, so much the longer, and consequently so much the slower, is the thrust given against such a Guard, because of the largeness of the arch included betwixt them, or the great way the sword offending hath to make before it can make its designed mark, which is what I chiefly intended; I shall now give one reason more why all thrusts made against this Sloping Guard must be more slow than thrusts made against Guards with a level or high point: and that is the natural tendency all peoples' sword-hands have to fall low in Disengaging or thrusting, and the great difficulty they have after Disengaging to thrust high. All who have the least knowledge in Fencing know the truth of this assertion. Which being granted, it will then follow that upon all the ordinary Guards with a level or high point, the Disengaging beneath the hilt of the adversary's sword being more easie, it will consequently be more quick, by reason of the sword's point being obliged, in Disengaging, to fall or sink. Whereas upon this Guard, the hand being necessitate to raise the point in Disengaging, in place of letting it fall, it makes it more difficult, and consequently the thrust more slow, as may be proven by the preceeding Scheme.

For suppose the sword C D, which is in the posture of an ordinary *Tierce* or *Quarte* Guard, were to thrust at the point P, and were but ten degrees from it; and likewise that the sword C I upon this *Hanging Guard*, were but as many degrees from that same point. I say that by the natural tendency and inclination of the hand, the sword C D would hit the point P sooner than the sword C I which keeps this Sloping Guard, even altho' the thrusts were to be performed by the same person. And there can be no other reason given for it, but that in Fencing, the thrust that is performed by raising the hand or point is alwise found to be slower than that wherein the hand or point must a little fall or sink.

And this is also the reason why the common thrust in *Quarte*, or within the sword, is more quick and difficult to Parie than that given in *Tierce*, or without and above the sword. This is known to be true by all who frequent the Fencing-Schools. And I never heard any other reason pretended to be given for it, but this natural tendency and disposition of the sword-hand rather to fall as to rise, either in Disengaging or thrusting. By all which I think I have made good the Second and very considerable advantage this *Hanging Guard* hath of most of the other Guards, which is the renversing, in a manner, the whole Art by rendering the offensive part or pursuit more slow, and consequently more difficult, and by that very reason of its slowness, the Parade or defence more easie.

I am very sensible that the slowness of the pursuit against this Guard, occasioned by the greatness of its cross, and for which I so much recommend it, will be by some persons made a great objection against it. Because, say they, a man cannot attack his adversary with so much certainty of execution as he can do upon other Guards. But as this can very easily be answered, so resolving to set down all the objections together that can be made against it, I shall defer the answering of this until I come to discourse the rest. For it being a common thing to start objections against anything that is new, I am resolved to answer the best I can what may be said against this Guard, being fully persuaded that the advantages redounding from it will very far counter-balance any objections can be made against it, even by the most prejudged, and critical Masters, whom I intend, if possible, to convince and satisfie that so great and general an improvement, and of such advantage to persons of all ranks, may not, for lack of being supported both by Art and reason, be neglected by those who profess to instruct our youth in the defence of their Honour and Lives.

Advantage III
Parades against all the Lessons of the Sword, both Back Sword and Small Sword, are easily deduced from this Guard, they being reducible to Two.

The posture of other Guards, by reason, as I have said, of the small cross they make with the adversary's sword, renders the Parade not only uncertain upon them, but also the positions of the sword, in performing it, more numerous. So that for different Lessons, a man is necessitate to use different postures in his defence. For upon those Guards, the sword being presented almost level and streight towards the adversary, there are generally Four Opens for a man to thrust at: to wit, without and above the sword, and without and below the sword, towards the right-side; and within and above the sword, and within and below the sword, towards the left-side. So that to defend the various Lessons that may be play'd upon all those Opens, a man is necessitate to use different positions of his sword, sometimes with the point high, and sometimes low. As also the great opportunity his adversary hath to make Feints upon those Opens, makes his Parade still the more uncertain, and that because of the conveniency his adversary hath of easily and quickly Disengaging, by reason, as I have already proven in Advantage II, of the small arch his adversary hath to make in performing his thrust.

Whereas in using this sloping posture with the sword, there being a great cross made with it, almost from head to foot, there are only two sides exposed to thrust at, *viz.* without and below the sword towards the right-side, and without and above the sword towards the left. Which renders his Parade a great deal more certain than upon the other Guards, the whole motions he

is to make for his defence against all kinds of thrusts being reduced to two. That is, moving his sword-hand a little (without altering its position) either towards his right-side or his left: to his right, when the thrust is given without and below the sword, and to his left, when it is given without and above the sword. So that all the Lessons that can be play'd against this Guard terminating in those two thrusts, it follows of consequence that there needs no more different positions nor motions for the Parade than these two, which are but half the number, and a great deal more certain, than those used upon the ordinary *Demy-Quarte* and *Tierce* Guards.

Again, for Parieing the blows of the Back Sword, nay of any other edged weapon whatsoever, such as the Pole-Ax, Lochaber-Ax, Halbard, or Quarter-Staff, the position of the sword and motions of the hand are the very same. And altho' it is not possible for any man to ward off with one hand a full discharged blow of any of these two-handed weapons I have named, because of the great force they carry along with them in delivering it, yet it still shows the excellency of this posture for a general defence, that altho' a man hath not the strength to Parie and put by those violent stroaks with one hand, yet he shall alwise meet with the adversary's weapon when he is delivering a blow. Which makes it clear that it is only for lack of strength that he cannot ward it, but is necessitate to receive it, because of his being overpowered with its force; and which signifies nothing at all against the usefulness of this posture, because if his one hand had strength equivalent to his adversary's two, it would certainly ward and defend him.

Advantage IV
Because of the great Cross this Guard makes upon the Adversary's Sword, it is a most safe Guard against all Ignorants and Ramblers, who Thrust alwise irregularly, and for the most part at a distance from the Sword.

Nothing hath been a greater reproach to the *Art of Fencing* than the unexpected success many Ignorants have had over such as pretended to a considerable share of skill in this Art. And altho' it is evident that a compleat Sword-Man, especially such an one as is exactly Master of the defensive part, will be very rarely, if at all, baffled by any (even the most foreward and irregular) Ignorant; yet it cannot be denied but many who have got the character of Sword-Men (how deservedly I shall not say; many indeed passing for such who do not in the least deserve that character), I say it cannot be denied but many such persons have had the misfortune to be worsted when they have engaged with Ignorants of a forward and resolute temper.

And the only reason that can be given for it is the deficiency and imperfection of their Parade. For it hath been hitherto the great misfortune of this Art to be chiefly designed for offending, altho' the very word *Fencing*, as I have shown in the Introduction, does in my opinion chiefly imply warding or defending. And there are at present few Fencing Schools wherein this does not visibly appear to be their chief design, there being scarcely a Lesson given wherein the Scholar shall not be ordered to push or discharge, perhaps, half a dozen or half a score of thrusts before he is desired to Parie one.

Now when it is the Fate of such a person to appear in the field, his dexterity in the pursuit prevails with him to take himself to the offensive part, as upon the other hand the insufficiency of the Ignorant's defence obliges him likewise to take himself to the pursuit. So what can in reason be expected from the engagement of such two persons, but continual *Contre-temps* and Exchanged Thrusts. Both which would have been certainly prevented, to the great reputation of both the Art and Artist, had he been obliged, when at the Fencing School, to apply himself more to the Parade.

And even in that case, as the Art is now commonly taught, there is a great defect in the method of Parade, as I have demonstrate, by reason of the small cross it makes upon the adversary's weapon. Whereas this Guard, making not only a greater cross upon the adversary's sword, but also in a manner securing, upon one side, the whole length of the body, it follows of consequence that upon that very account it must be a more secure Parade and better defence against the thrusts of all Ignorants than any other ordinary Guard or Parade whatsoever.

For as I said, the thrusts of Ignorants are not only irregular, but generally given at a distance from the sword, and upon the lower parts of the body. Now the ordinary Parades in *Demy-Quarte* and *Tierce*, making but small crosses, it is not possible for them to meet so easily with the adversary's sword, and to ward his thrust or blow, as it is for this Guard, which not only easily rencounters the adversary's sword, and so opposes it, but also makes a considerable cross, almost from head to foot. Whereby not only the Ignorant's thrusts above the sword, but also his straggling and irregular thrusts or blows at the lower parts of the body or thighs, and which are the most dangerous, are more certainly warded and defended.

It is also a most convenient posture when a man comes to be attacked in the dark. Because without altering the position of the sword-hand from *Seconde*, he may perform the *Contre-caveating* Parade. By which circular motion he will seldom fail to meet with and cross his adversary's sword, a conveniency much to be valued in a dark or mid-night rencounter. By all which it is evident that this Guard is one of the safest and most secure Guards that can possibly be made use of against Ignorants of all constitutions, even from the most cold and slothful to the most forward and resolute pursuer.

Advantage V
The Art of the Sword is by this Guard rendered a great deal more easie to be acquired, by reason of the pursuit being reduced to very few Lessons.

Certainly the fewer directions are required for the perfecting a man in any Art, and the fewer rules it can be reduced to, by so much the sooner, and with greater ease, will a man be made Master of it. Which advantage is likewise to be found by the constant practising of this Guard. For there being but little variety of play, either from or against it, it follows that there can be but few Lessons; and the fewer Lessons there are, the sooner will a man be made Master of them, and so consequently of the offensive part. So that I dare venture to say that any man of an ordinary disposition, agility, and vigour, shall in six months time acquire a sufficient dexterity for the defence of his person. Whereas by the Ordinary Method of teaching, a man cannot be perfected under at least two or three years assiduous application and constant practice. A very long time indeed for Gentlemen to attend! who are not to make it their profession and employment, but only to acquire a competent skill and address for the defence of their Honour and persons. And no doubt this tediousness of the Common Method hath rebutted a great many Gentlemen who would have been otherwise very great Sword-Men.

For upon the Guards commonly taught in the Schools there is a great variety of Lessons that can be played either from them or against them. So that for a man to be dexterous in performing them, it requires a long and constant practice. Otherwise he shall never execute them with that life and vigour that he ought. And altho' I cannot deny but that most of the Lessons may possibly be play'd both from and against this *Hanging Guard*, yet they do not so naturally agree to it, as a very few, which I shall hereafter recommend. Upon which account it is that a man can be made a great deal sooner perfect in the Art upon this Guard than upon any other. And that not only in the pursuit or offensive part, as I have been saying (and which, as I formerly said, I do not, strictly speaking, allow to be the true *Art of the Sword*, that indeed chiefly consisting in the Parade), but also in the defensive part. Which is indeed the true Art, by reason of the great cross it makes with the adversary's sword, and simple and easie motions that in Parieing are to be performed by the hand. So that if certainty in the Parade, and being exposed to few and slow Lessons, can in any measure recommend a Guard or Parade, then they needs must this Guard, which is indeed also a Parade, and that one of the very best and most secure that I know of.

Advantage VI
Any Man who uses this Guard Dexterously, may with a great deal of more ease and certainty, save both his Honour and Life, than he can possibly do, using any other ordinary Guard;

upon which Account alone, it is highly to be valued and preferred.

It were certainly a very great piece of kindness done to the young Gentlemen, in an age wherein rencounters and drunken scuffles are so frequent, if some method could be fallen upon whereby they might, in a manner, certainly both defend their Lives, and save their Reputation and Honour, when in an Occasion. For such a notion have people got now a-days of this word Honour, that a man dares scarcely suffer a wry look or anything like a frown, let alone threatening words, but he must immediately either resent it, by demanding Satisfaction in the Field, or suffer the reproach of passing for a coward. And yet in both those cases how unlucky, at best, is a man circumstantiate.

For if he sit with the affront without duly resenting it, he infallibly loses his Reputation and Honour by being repute a Cully.[2] And if he go to the Field to take reparation for the injury and affront done to him, then in saving his Honour, he not only hazards his Life against his adversary, which no good man will decline, but which is indeed hardest of all, in saving of his Life by mastering his adversary, he runs a great risque (without a pardon) to lose it by contravening the laws. So that what way soever his Fortune turns, he is at a great disadvantage and loss, because in being overcome by his enemy, he runs the hazard of being killed; and mastering him, of being hang'd.

What shall a man of Honour do then in such a juncture? For fight he must to save his Honour. And whether he vanquish or be vanquished, without a pardon, as I said, it comes much about one. For let him behave himself never so well or ill, he still runs the hazard of dying. And that either by the weapon of his adversary or by the sentence of the Judge. A hard and cruel necessity indeed upon any man of Resolution and Honour!

> *Hard Fate of Man! who either, if he flyes,*
> *Hopeless of e're retrieving Honour lyes;*
> *Or if he Vanquish, still expects to find*
> *The Stroak of Justice, or Remorse of Mind.*

Now altho' there be no great difficulty in such a case to determine which side a man of Honour ought to embrace, there being few Gentlemen of any spirit and mettal who (notwithstanding of the many severe laws against Duelling) will not rather venture the gaining of the gallows by appearing with sword in hand in the Field than the losing of their Reputation and Honour by declining the Appeal. Yet were it not much better for them that they could, with some measure of assurance, affirm that by their skill they are so much Masters of the *Art of Defence* that without some very extraordinary accident they are in a manner

certain either to overcome their enemy, or at least to save both their own and their adversary's Life.

I shall not positively assert that any Guard or Parade made use of, even by the most dexterous Sword-Man, can infallibly promise this. But this I will affirm, that if there be any Guard of the sword that is capable of yielding this benefit to a man, I am fully persuaded 'tis this in *Seconde* I am discoursing of, and recommending. For by reason of the great cross it makes with the adversary's sword, it renders not only all pursuit more slow, and consequently the Parade against it more sure and certain. Also, by that great cross which is made, there is a fair opportunity frequently offered to either side to inclose or grapple when ever they shall please, and that with very little or no hazard of receiving either a *Contre-temps* or an Exchanged Thrust.

Must it not then be acknowledged by all that here is a very great improvement of the Art, and that this *Guard in Seconde*, above all others, is highly to be valued and preferred? Sure it cannot possibly be denied by any thinking & considering person, especially by such as have the least knowledge of the looseness and openness of most of the other Guards, and the great difficulty and hazard that a man is exposed to in attempting to close and Command upon them.

May this singular advantage then of this *Hanging Guard* so recommend it, as that all who have their Honour and Life at stake may make boldly use of it. If not as a certain, yet at least as a most probable Method to save both. Which in all engagements ought to be their chief aim and design, not only as good Christians, but as Men of true Generosity and Honour.

Advantage VII
It is a Natural Guard, all Ignorants or Naturalists generally taking themselves to it, so soon as they offer to present their Swords; but particularly when they offer to defend themselves.

It is a received maxim that Art ought never to thwart or cross Nature, but rather to encourage and assist her, if possible, in her own natural road and means. And I may say it were a very happy thing if, in all Arts and Sciences, we could as easily trace her, and concur in our assistance with her designs to preserve us, as we can do in the *Art of Fencing*. But to observe the Common Method of teaching the *Art of Defence* hitherto made use of in Schools, one will be apt to think that either Nature points not out to us any such rational way for our defence, or otherwise, that the generality of Fencing-Masters are deaf to her admonitions, and so prepossessed with their old rote. And that rather than let her have the Honour of it, they will prefer and make use of other unnatural postures, and awkward and constrained motions, the product and effect of their own fancies and invention. Whereby the persons and Lives of many young

---

[2] A dupe, silly fellow, simpleton. *Oxford English Dictionary.*

Gentlemen are, as I have said, upon an Occasion mightily exposed and endangered. I say a man is ready to conclude from their practice that they rather intend to do this, as to give ear to her, in the natural method she discovers to us for our defence. And which when known, ought certainly to be encouraged and improven.

Now, that Nature makes an offer of this *Hanging Guard* to all persons who never had any other posture, I may say, obtruded or forced upon them by Art, I appeal to all, as well Artists as others. For I would gladly know of any man, what other posture he has ever observed any person, who was never at the Schools, to take himself to, when he hath been to engage. And if he has not alwise observed such persons, especially upon their defence, to make use of this posture, with the hand in *Seconde*, and the point sloping towards the adversary's thigh. If this be so, as to my certain knowledge it is, why ought we not to follow and improve Nature, when she offers so easie and so secure a posture for our defence?

Let Artists then for the future take this one Lesson, at least, from naturalists. And let them practice and improve this natural posture, altho' used by Ignorants. So shall they have the benefit, not only of a better defence for the security of their persons, but also have the Honour to defeat such Ignorants at their own weapons and with their own homely and natural posture. Which so far from diminishing, will, as I said, for the future, as well mightily secure the person of the Artist, as improve and increase the Reputation of the Art and this *New Method* of teaching.

Advantage VIII
As it is a Natural Guard, so it is a General Guard, both a-Foot and upon Horseback, against either Rapier, Shearing Sword or Back Sword.

Altho' all the preceeding advantages I have been discoursing of are very great and considerable, yet if I can make it appear that this last advantage is peculiar to this Guard, this alone is sufficient to recommend the practice of it. Even altho' all the other were false, or totally struck out and rejected.

And indeed when I consider how frequently I have seen such as pretended to be Sword-Men baffled and confounded for lack of a general defence against either a thrust or blow, it puzzles me to determine whether or not it were not better for a man not to fence at all, as to be ignorant of and not know how to use a general defence against all weapons, as well edged as pointed. For how strangely out of countenance does a man look when in the place of a thrust that he expected and prepared to Parie, after the common form, he is saluted with a sound and firm blow over the head? Or instead of a stroak, which he fancies was designed against him, he is suddenly and unexpectedly whip't

through the lungs? And this for not understanding to Parie both blow and thrust.

I know it will be urged that without making use of this Guard, a man may prevent that inconveniency of being surprised by either a thrust or blow by making himself Master of both Parades, as well that against the Back Sword as that against the Small.

This I grant. But then it cannot be denied but that it will cost him a considerable time and practice to become Master of both Arts, which very few Gentlemen have the patience to acquire. Whereas in the using of this Guard, the defence of both weapons are joined in one. For both thrusts and blows are, upon this Guard, Paried after one and the same manner, and with the same very position of the hand, as you may see in Advantage 3d. So that whether a man's adversary give in a thrust, or discharge a blow, it comes much about one, for he defends both with the same ease and dexterity. Which except upon this Guard, cannot (without being taught both the Arts) be dexterously and exactly be performed by any man.

Again, when a man comes to engage with his sword upon horseback, how strangely is he put to it if he has not been acquainted with the particular postures and defences most useful and proper in such a juncture? Which, to my certain knowledge, few people are at the trouble and charges to be instructed in. Altho', I must say, as necessary a part of defence as any a man can possibly be taught.

Now the making use of this posture removes all that difficulty. For without the least trouble, it naturally leads a man to a defence upon horseback, as well as a-foot, either against a Rapier, Shearing Sword, or Back Sword. So that I may venture to alter the proverb a little and say that here, without any difficulty, *fit per pauciora quod frustra fieri potest per plura*.

Seeing then this posture is not only a natural Guard, but a general one too, how willingly should we all embrace the advantages it offers to us, and endeavour by any means to bring so good and safe a Guard in request as may not only be a means to save our Reputation and Honour, without much exposing of our persons. But if they are briskly and vigourously attacked, can even very easily defend them, and that not only a-foot, but also upon horseback, against all single weapons whatsoever.

I could have insisted, not only much longer upon each of these advantages I have named, but could also mention several others that really belong to no other Guard save this alone. But as I design to be as brief upon each head as possible, so those few advantages I have slightly discoursed of will be to any judicious and considering person a sufficient proof of the great benefit all persons may reap, by an assiduous and frequent practice of it.

Without which, tho' a man should write like an angel, it would signify nothing, but be so much labour to no purpose, and as the beating of the air.

For it is in writing of Fencing, as it is with all other practical Arts which have been already both fully and learnedly treated of in print. There are many books of the Art of War, Evolutions or Drilling of men, Riding, Fencing, and even of Dancing, of late. All which are excellent in their kind. But then it is not only the reading of them will make them useful. For I never heard of either a good general, engineer, or horseman, made so only by book. It is then the reducing of the good directions of such curious books to practice that render them useful, as well as diverting. And that also, after a man hath been well grounded by a Master, and not the simple perusing, nay, nor even getting by heart the substance and marrow of such books, altho' most useful, as I said, in their kinds, that will make a man Master of any of those practical Arts.

All then I can promise is to lay down easie and good rules for a safe and true *Method of Fencing*, which we in this age stand so much in need of, and to recommend to you the putting them in practice. For when a man comes to the Field, he is not to make use of his book, but of his sword. And it is his hands which must then put in execution what both his judgement hath before-hand digested after reading, and practice accustomed his body and nerves to. So that altho' I had said a great deal more of the advantages flowing from this Guard, yet it would have been but to little purpose, seeing it is only practice, not discourse, that can make a man perfectly sensible of, and Master of them. I shall therefore proceed to the chief objections that can be made against it.

Fig. 9.
One thrusting without and above his Adversarys Sword, from the hanging Guard.

Fig. 10.
One paricing without and above his Sword upon the hanging Guard.

CHAPTER III
Where some Objections are Answered,
that may be Stated against the Usefulness of this Hanging Guard.

Man is naturally so selfish and invidious a temper, that except what flows from himself, he can suffer almost nothing to pass without either playing the critick upon it, or starting objections, altho' never so frivolous, against it. And this certainly hath its rise from a selfish pride. Because upon no other ground, for the most part, do people criticise and censure, but only out of, I may say, an ungenerous concern that another person should receive the commendation and applause which they would unjustly claim a right to themselves. So that it galls them to the very soul to think that others are taken notice of, while they are overlookt and neglected.

For did not this un-Gentlemanly, as well as un-Christian, temper flow from such an impure and diabolical fountain as this of self-interest and pride, we should, in place of condemning and criticising other people's works, which perhaps we can scarcely ourselves parallel, far less out-strip, be rather daily encouraging and exciting each other to discover and improve the talent Nature hath bestowed upon us. So that in place of the clamorous noise of critical and anti-Christian censuring which resounds over all, we should hear nothing but the still and gentle voice of Unity and Concord, and be so far from ridiculing and exposing the failings of others, that we would use our outmost endeavours to conceal, or at least, to alleviate them. Especially when it is to be supposed that their design is really good, whatever may be their performance.

For besides that it is one of the easiest things in the world, to censure and criticise, many people's talent lying this way, who are otherwise but of a very ordinary reach and capacity, so I still find, for the most part, that it is a token of some smartness and mettal in the person's work, who is thus taken to task and canvassed. For as mean and contemptible things are commonly overlookt while those of more value are taken notice of, so men generally censuring, more out of a private and selfish envy and pique, than out of any good design for the publick interest, it is a shrewd token that pride and passion prevail more with such persons, and have a greater ascendant over them than the most convincing rhetorick and solid reason. And seeing most part of persons and books are liable to this misfortune, and that we never want a sett of such froathy and cavilling sparks among us,

I cannot let myself escape. Therefore concluding that objections will be made against it, I have thought fit to draw together such as I judge to be most material. And which, if sufficiently solved, will render all others ineffectual and of no force.

Now the objections of any weight that can be started against it (particularly with respect to this *New Guard*) may be reduced to these six following.

Objection I

First, say they, the Posture of this Guard is constrained and weak, and so a Man can neither continue so long upon it, nor pursue so vigorously from it, as he can do from the Ordinary Guards, with the Point either level or a little elevate.

To which I answer that no posture can be constrain'd and weak to which most people naturally take themselves for their defence. But most men who have never been instructed in the *Art of the Sword* do naturally (as it hath been already proved in Advantage 7th) take themselves to this posture for their defence. Therefore it can be no such weak and uneasie posture as some would pretend. Besides, people in a rencounter stand not so long dallying to advise what they are to do, but on a sudden engage briskly. So that, for the most part, before half a score or dozen of thrusts or blows are vigorously discharged, the business is in a manner decided, and in so very short a time, a man scarcely loses his wind, far less the strength of his arm or sword-hand.

But grant that this Guard were indeed somewhat constrained and weak, as it is not, it being, as hath already been told in Advantage 7th, the natural Guard and defence of all unskillful persons when necessitate to fight. And sure Nature would never prompt them to that which is unnatural and constrained. But, I say, grant it were a little so. Can that be of such force and weight to any considering man as to prevail with him to undervalue and neglect a posture which may be of such use and benefit to him for the defence of his Life and Honour, as this Guard is, which is made most evident by the preceeding advantages? No, certainly. For let it be never so uneasie and weak, yet a little custom and practice will render it, as it does most things else, natural and easie to him. And he will Parie as firmly, and pursue or thrust from the Riposte as smartly or swiftly from this posture or Guard as from the most easie Guard in the Common Method.

If any person who had never lifted a bowl nor handled a racket should attempt to play either a sett at tennis or a match at bowls, he would certainly, at first, acquit himself but very weakly at either. And yet with what a genteel ease and dexterity do persons who are accustomed to those divertisements perform them? With such a surprising address, I may say, that it would seem they had been brought into the world with a bowl in one had and a racket in the other.

Nay, this irresistible power of practice does not only master and overcome the unflexibleness of our bodily members, but also affects and prevails very much, even over our more dull and ignorant judgements. For so great and universal an influence hath custom and habit upon the faculties of mankind, that I scarce know any thing, whether Art or Science, that he is Master of, but what, in a great measure, he owes to it. For I may say that without it he could neither walk, speak, read, nor write distinctly. Nay, I may further venture to affirm that he is beholden to it for much of his understanding and judgement. For whatever some people may talk of innate ideas, and whether we have any such or not (that I leave to be determined by the wise), yet we certainly know by experience that our understandings are improved by reflecting and meditating. And by the use of these, are as much practised as either our tongues or hands are by speaking and writing, or our limbs by crawling about and walking. And did not people daily see the surprising tricks of legerdemain, and feats of activity, performed by jugglers, rope-dancers, and tumblers, they could never believe that it were possible in nature for men to perform with any assurance such astonishing tricks and postures as they do. And which it is very well known, they only attain to by an assiduous and daily practice. I shall give a few very singular instances, some of which I was an eyewitness to myself.

I remember Montaigne, in his *Essays*, I believe towards the end of his first volume, where he is discoursing of manag'd horses, and the firmness and dexterity of some horsemen, hath the following passages, which I shall give in his own words:

I have seen, says he, *a man ride with both feet upon the saddle, take off his saddle, and at his return take it up again, refit, and remount it, riding all the while full speed; having gallop't over a bonnet, make at it very good shots, backwards with his bow; take up any thing from the ground, setting one foot down, and the other in the stirrup.*

There has been seen in my time, at Constantinople, two men

upon one horse, who in the heighth of his speed, would throw themselves off, and into the saddle again by turns. And one who bridled and saddled his horse, with nothing but his teeth.

Another, who, betwixt two horses, one foot upon one saddle, and another upon the other, carrying another upon his shoulders; would ride full career, the other standing bolt upright above him, making very good shots with his bow. Thus far Montaigne.

The fourth is of a rope dancer, whom I did see myself in a tennis-court in Paris, first walk up a stretch't sloping-rope to the top of a pole 5 or 6 yards high, upon the top of which was fixed a level circular board, betwixt two and three foot diameter. When he came near to the board, quitting his pole, he pitch'd himself a-top on't, upon his head, by the help of his two hands. Then with a spring he recovered himself to his feet, and standing bolt upright, with a sudden jerk threw his heels over his head, and stood upright again upon his feet, to the surprize and amazement of most who were present.

But why need I go abroad for singular instances of ease and agility acquired by mere custom and practice, when we have had lately in this kingdom the famous posture performer Higens, by far the most adroit and dexterous that ever my eyes beheld: being, I do verily believe, the most expert, and agile in that manner of way, of any man now alive. For not only I, but most persons of quality in this nation, have been witnesses to his performing such postures as were not only surprising and astonishing, but in a manner miraculous, to be performed by any who had either a bone or an articulate joint in their whole body. For he said (taking hold of a piece of his shirt, and plying it backwards and forwards with his two hands) that he had as much command of his joints as he had of that piece of cloth, and that it was as easie for him to perform most of his postures as it was for any present to walk about the room.

Many such incidences may be given of the prevalency of custom and practice. But these few being very odd and surprising, I made choice of them as examples, to show what degree of ease and dexterity an assiduous and daily practice will bring men. *Nil tam difficile* is an old but true saying. And indeed what will not a constant habit bring a man to?

Great care then ought all young people to take, what first ply or bent they give to their more tender or yielding inclinations. And good is it, and thrice happy for them, when they make choice of, or accidentally fall into, any of the paths of virtue. Whereas upon the contrary, most misfortunate they are, and very much to be regretted, who either themselves make choice of, or by the bad examples of others are led aside, or decoy'd, into the crooked and by-lanes of immorality and vice. For in this case, *Quo semel est imbuta*, very rarely fails.

But to return to our subject, and to give one single instance wherein Fencing is only concerned. I affirm that to the knowledge of many young Gentlemen in this kingdom, and particularly my own experience, I have known the sinking very low upon the ordinary *Quarte* Guard, which, at best, is but a constrained and uneasie posture, to become as familiar and easie to many, by a little practice, as any the most unconstrained and natural Guard they could have stood to. Let never then the pretended constrainedness and weakness of this most useful Guard be longer urged against it as any imperfection when, *first*, it is much to be doubted if it be so to most part of men, particularly to such as wanting Art make commonly use of it for a natural defence. *Secondly*, when, tho' really it were so, yet it is evident by the above-mentioned instances that a man by a little practice may very quickly strengthen and confirm himself in it, and that as well for the pursuit against his adversary as for his own defence against any single handed weapon whatsoever.

I have not only begun with this objection, but have also insisted the longer upon the answer to it, because I find it is that which occurs to, and startles many persons, which may perhaps retard their more frank acquiescing to, and approving of, the great benefit and advantage arising to people from this Guard. Therefore if, notwithstanding of the foregoing most pregnant instances of the prevalency of custom to render not only the posture of this Guard (if it were really very constrained) easie, but also any other a man shall resolve to ply and take himself to, some persons will still insist, upon the strength of this objection, and maintain that it is not sufficiently removed. I must be so free and plain to tell them that it argues one of two: either an extraordinary obstinate and opinionative temper, or a very weak and shallow judgement. So in God's name e'en let them enjoy their opinion. For to endeavour to convince such unreasonable persons by the strength of reasoning, is but just so much time spent, but to no purpose under the scope of heaven. But for such as will give ear, and yield to reason and experience, I am persuaded my arguments will prevail with them. As for others, they are not to be valued nor regarded, so not worth any man's while to trouble himself or be concerned about them.

Objection II
Secondly, the pursuit from this Guard is very slow, which altho' an Advantage to the Defender, is a very great disadvantage to the pursuer.

It is indeed somewhat strange that the advantages which naturally flow from a Guard should be made some of the chief

objections against it, as appears by this and the two following objections. For one of the greatest advantages I pretend this *Hanging Guard* hath over most others is the rendering of the pursuit slow, and consequently the defence more easie and certain. And as it cannot be denied but this is one of the most considerable advantages this Guard yields, as I think I have most sufficiently proved in the Second Advantage. So altho' the assertion as to the first and second part of this objection holds good, and be acknowledged, yet it is denied as to the last. For it is certainly a great deal more advantage to a man, when engaged for his Life, that his Parade or defence be rendered the more certain by the slowness of his adversary's pursuit, than it can be a disadvantage to him that his own pursuit is a little slow against his adversary. For by the first he hath a very fair opportunity given him to defend both his Honour and Life, and by the second he only runs the hazard, by his adversary's saving of himself, of being free from manslaughter. A very great blessing in my opinion, as well as an advantage. For assure yourself, no man in a Duel or rencounter ever killed another, but after a little serious reflection would, with all his heart, have given a good deal of what he was worth to have had him alive again. So pitiful and false a foundation are the common points of Honour whereupon to build a just resentment. and from which a man shall not afterwards have a check in his mind. Therefore a man ought to consider well, and have very just grounds and provocation to it, before he draw his sword in good earnest.

So that I still affirm that instead of any disadvantage a man can have by his pursuit being rendered slow, he reaps ten to one a greater benefit by it, in having a fair opportunity, both as a man of Honour, of defending himself, and as a good Christian, of saving his adversary (Honour, as well as Religion, obliging him to both). And by means of a not too subtile and quick pursuit against his adversary, which would in all probability tend to the inevitable ruin and destruction of both, but which is easily prevented by the use of this most excellent Guard. And therefore the slowness of the pursuit from it is so far from being an objection against it, that it is one of the greatest and truest advantages that naturally flows from it; and for which it ought to be, by all truely Good and Honourable persons, most esteemed.

Objection III
Thirdly, there is but little variety of Play, either from or against this Guard, which takes quite away, or at least lessens a great deal the pleasure of Assaulting in Schools.

There is a vast difference betwixt Assaulting in a School with blunts for a man's diversion, and engaging in the Fields with Sharps for a man's Life. And whatever latitude a man may take in the one, to show his address and dexterity, yet he ought to go a little more warily and securely to work when he is concerned in the other. For in Assaulting with *Fleurets*, a man may venture upon many difficult and nice Lessons, wherein if he fail, he runs no great risque. And if they take not at one time, they may succeed at another. But with Sharps, the more plain and simple his Lessons of pursuit are, the more secure is his person. Whereas by venturing upon a variety of difficult Lessons he very much exposes himself, even to the hazarding of his Life, by his adversary's taking of time, and endeavouring to *Contre-temps*, which are not so easily effectuate against a plain and secure pursuit.

For it is at Sharps, as in the Art of War: *Non licet in Bello bis delinquere*. A man may indeed, in School-play, recover a mistimed thrust. But here, a great escape being once made, is irrecoverable. There is no retrieving of it. And therefore a man had need to be very cautious, as in his Parade or defence, so particularly in his attacking and method of pursuit. So let us Guard never so much against precipitancy and too much forwardness (yet when once engaged), we are so much mastered by our passions, notwithstanding our strongest resolutions to the contrary, that our blood will boil up and force us to extravagancies. For which we cannot, in cold blood, but mightily condemn ourselves.

Therefore, altho', as I have elsewhere said, the most part of Lessons may be play'd both from and against this Guard, yet the small number of Lessons which naturally flow from it is rather to be lookt upon as an advantage peculiar to this Guard, than any objection against it. And that because altho' variety and diversion be our great aim in School-play, yet plainness and security ought to be our chief design when in an Occasion with Sharps.

Objection IV
Fourthly, this Guard gives frequent Opportunities of either Commanding or Enclosing, which also abates a great deal of the Satisfaction which People have when they Play from the Ordinary Tierce or Quarte Guards.

This objection being much of the nature of the former, the preceding answer takes away, I think, sufficiently the later part of it. But as to the first part, I am so far from looking upon the opportunity this Guard gives of Enclosing to be a disadvantage, that, upon the contrary, I take it to be one of the chief advantages for which it is to be recommended and made use of. For can there be a greater satisfaction to a good man (who, to save his Honour, is necessitate, perhaps contrary to his inclination, to go to the Field), I say can there be anything more acceptable to such a person than a fair opportunity not only to save his Reputation and Honour, but also to defend his Life with that of his adversary's? When, it may be, nothing brought them to the place appointed but a trifle or some pitiful drunken scuffle. Which 'tis like both of them are ashamed of, and yet neither of them dares pass it over without showing a kind of resentment lest it should reflect upon their Honours.

Now by making use of this Guard, and the great conveniency from it of Enclosing, a man is rendered secure not only as to his Honour, which is saved by his keeping the appointment and appearing with sword in hand, but also, in a manner, as to both his own and his adversary's Life, by the fair and frequent opportunities offered to both for Enclosing, and which is occasioned by the great crosses made by their weapons upon this Guard. So that if by using this Guard they lose a little pleasure of variety in School-play, they reap it by the advantage of having a fair opportunity, when in an Occasion, to save both their Honours and Lives. A very extraordinary benefit in my opinion, and an advantage only peculiar to this Guard. For which it ought to be so much more esteemed, as Enclosing and Saving is to be preferred to Estocading [thrusting] and Killing.

Objection V
Fifthly, whatever Disadvantage a Man may put his Adversary to, by keeping of this Guard, he is liable to the same Disadvantage himself; and consequently, he can reap no benefit by his taking himself to it.

This objection is so much the more easily answered as it is of less weight than any of the preceding, seeing as it may be leveled against all the other Guards, as well as against this. For I would gladly know what Guard or posture it is possible for any man to make use of, but his adversary, if he be equal in skill, may take himself to the same. And there being an equality supposed in the persons, both as to courage and dexterity, it is impossible for any of them to have the least advantage by any Guard over the other, but what that other person may have over his adversary. So that this objection reaching all kind of Guards or postures whatsoever, ought not in the least to be regarded.

I shall only add that according to this supposition of a perfect equality as to the Art betwixt two persons engaging, none of them can ever have the least advantage over other. But as this exact equality in Art is a chimerical supposition, so one man's judgement or agility, exceeding or overpowering another's, gives alwise a fair opportunity to such a person, upon any Guard, to catch, or force an advantage over his adversary, altho' upon the same Guard. And yet that the one shall not reap the same advantage by it that the other shall do. Which I think is a very full and sufficient answer to this objection.

Objection VI
Sixthly, and Lastly, this, say they, can never be called a New Method of Fencing, because it is founded upon a very Common and Old Guard, to wit, the Common Hanging Guard of the Back Sword.

Altho' I am far from pretending to attribute to my own invention the posture of this Guard, yet I will be so vain as to assert that I am the first person who has ever found out and improved the many great and singular advantages which naturally flow from it, for a sure and general defence against all single weapons. So that albeit it may not perhaps be allowed that I am the first inventor of this Guard, yet it must be at least granted that I am the first improver of it. And altho' *facile est inventis addere* be a true proverb, yet I have not so very small an opinion of my addition and improvement, but that I think that Art is considerably beholding to me for it.

For altho', strictly speaking, improving cannot be called inventing, yet where, for lack of canvassing and improving a Guard, the benefits which might arise from it are buried in oblivion, and in a manner quite lost, he who endeavours to bring such advantages to light may be said, I think, in some measure to discover such a Guard. Then I being so fortunate as to find out and bring to light again the many and singular advantages which a man may reap by rightly using of this Guard, and which might have continued for ever undiscovered if the great liking I have for the Art had not prompted me to turn my thoughts that way, I think in this case that I may very justly lay claim to the invention of this *New Method of Fencing* in general. Tho' not to the particular posture of the Guard from whence it is derived. For altho' many Masters mention this Guard, particularly Monsieur de Liancour,[3] who calls it a German Guard, yet they all say so very

little of it, particularly himself (who in his time was one of the most celebrated Masters in France), that it is a clear demonstration they did not know the singular advantages of it. Upon which account it is that some have but just in a manner named it, and the rest quite pass it over. Therefore I think I may very justly, as I said, pretend, if not to the invention of the posture or Guard, yet at least to the improvement of the benefits or advantages flowing from the right use of it, and so consequently to the discovery of this *New Method of Fencing*, which is founded upon it.

And altho' some people may look upon all I have said upon this head as not deserving the pretensions I would justly claim, yet I must let such persons know that whatever may be in the invention, yet the improvement is of such consequence that I will be bold to say it is the most useful, and consequently the greatest and most considerable, that ever happened to the *Art of Defence*. Nay, if I should go a greater length and positively affirm that no greater improvement ever will, or can possibly be made in the Art, especially as to the defensive part, than what may be drawn from this *New Method*; yet however confident and paradoxical this assertion may appear, I am fully persuaded. And it is also a demonstration that it is true, because the defence I draw from it runs all upon the forming of a good cross, and no cross can be better nor greater than that which forms a right angle. But the defence from this Guard goes that length (for which, observe the crosses made by the Figures 7, 10, & [p. 102, 109, 172). Therefore it is impossible for any other defence whatsoever to exceed it in security and safety.

FIG.11.
One comanding his Adversarys Sword, from the hanging Guard without and below his sword.

FIG.12.
One upon the hanging Guard haaving his sword commaded.

[3] André Wernesson de Liancour, *Le Maistre d'armes, ou l'exercice de l'espée seulle dans sa perfection.* Paris, 1686.

But however, this may not prove at first view so obvious to many persons who are already prepossessed of the benefit arising from the Ordinary Method of defence. Yet I am perfectly persuaded that in a little time they shall not only approve of this new one, but discover daily more and more of its security and use, especially for a true and general defence, for which I chiefly admire and recommend it. So for a full and satisfactory answer to this objection, provided this improvement answer my expectation as to the security and preservation of people's persons when in an Occasion, I shall upon the matter be very little concerned whether I be allowed the Honour of being called the inventor, or only the improver of this Guard and the defence flowing from it; my country-men's safety, and not my own applause, being what I chiefly aimed at, in my search and enquiry after this *New Method*. This is the last objection wherewithal I shall trouble my reader, any other being so weak and frivolous that they are not worth mentioning, far less the trouble of refuting.

CHAPTER IV
An Explication of most of the
Terms of Art made use of in Fencing.

If this piece were only to fall amongst the hands of knowing Sword-Men and true Artists, I should not trouble my self with the explication of the following *Terms of Art*, seeing it is to be supposed such persons do already understand the true meaning and import of them, having also done it already, but after a much shorter method, in the *Scots Fencing Master*. But seeing it is not only designed for such, by reason that, no doubt, many novices will be curious to know what new discoveries it contains, and it were hard wholly to disappoint them.

Therefore, not only for their greater ease and satisfaction, but also that this small treatise may be of use alone and by it self (even in the Ordinary Method, for such as will still adhere to it), without the assistance of any of those I formerly published upon this Gentlemanly subject, I have thought fit to explain in this Chapter most of those *Terms of Art* which are of greatest import to be known. And without the understanding whereof, the following rules and directions, would not be perhaps altogether so intelligible. I shall also take care to explain them after such an unusual, tho' plain, manner as, to my knowledge, hath never been done hitherto by any writer upon this subject. And I doubt not but the perusal of them will be not only diverting and useful to Scholars, but even grateful and acceptable to Masters themselves.

But before I proceed, I think fit to acquaint the reader that the most part of the modern *Terms of Art* made use of in Fencing are derived from the French language, altho' the French themselves were at first beholding to the Italians and Spaniards for them, who were certainly the first great improvers (the invention, whatever some nations may pretend to, being certainly owing to the old and warlike Romans) of this most useful *Art of Defense*, as well as of that other heroick and Gentlemanly exercise of Horsemanship, or *Riding the Great Horse*. So that for the better understanding the true derivation of some of the terms of both those Arts, a man ought to understand a little these two languages. Which knowledge not only upon this, but several other accounts, is lookt upon now a-days as a very Gentlemanly improvement and qualification.

It may be also thought by some, and not without appearance of reason, that the explication of these *Terms of Art*, many of which are also Lessons in the Art, and frequently practised in the Common Method, would have come in more properly at the beginning of this Essay, and immediately after the First Chapter, wherein the keeping of this *Hanging Guard* is explained, than here, where I have placed them. Because it is generally usual in explaining of any Art to begin with the terms belonging to it.

This I readily acknowledge, and would also have done it if my great design in this piece had not been to recommend this *Hanging Guard* by discovering its advantages and the objections that might be made against it. But that being my chief intention, I judged it more proper to begin with these, that so the reader's curiosity might be the more quickly satisfied with respect to the usefulness of this *New Method*, and not kept in suspense as to his information of the great benefit and advantage redounding to him from this Guard, for a general defence.

So this being the reason of my delaying the observations I had to make upon the *Terms of Art*, I hope it will sufficiently remove this objection. Especially seeing I bring them in, in this Chapter, which is immediately before those wherein I give any directions, either for the defence or pursuit from this *New Guard*. Which being the chief heads in this book, and to which the *Terms of Art* have the greatest and more immediate relation, I cannot see but I have brought them in as seasonably as I could possibly have done any where else, notwithstanding of the common practice of writers upon other Arts, who for the most part begin with the explication of theirs.

Now amongst the *Terms of Art* belonging to Fencing, some respect the weapon, which altho' of several kinds, yet I shall here confine to the sword in particular. Others again respect the person who is to make use of that sword, and which are to flow from the several members of the body. For some are general, in which the whole body, or several of its members are concerned in executing them; and others more particular, wherein only the sword-hand or the leggs are chiefly concerned in the time of performing them. I say chiefly, because if taken in a stricter sense, it is scarcely possible for a man to move either hand or foot without making the rest of his body in some degree concerned in their motion, such a mutual dependence have all our members upon each other.

I shall therefore first name such as I intend to discourse upon, as near as I can in the order I have mentioned, that the reader may have them all at once under his view. And then shall proceed to the explication of each, altho' not in the same order as they are set down in the following list, but as they do more naturally flow from, and depend upon these which immediately preceed them.

For altho' they are pretty exactly classed in the list, according as the particular members of the body are concerned in them, yet it sometimes falls out that the explication of a term belonging to a particular member will fall in a great deal more naturally to be discoursed of immediately after a term which is more general, than it would do after a particular *Term of Art*, even belonging to the same member. And therefore in my explication I judged it a great deal more proper and methodical to follow the very same method that I would take were I to teach and communicate them to a Scholar, than confine my self to the order of the following list. Which, however, has its own use, because of the easie and regular method I have taken to class the *Terms of Art* for their more ready retention in the reader's memory, and which is altogether new. I shall also, in setting down the list, mark such as are Lessons, that the reader may the more readily distinguish betwixt such as are only *Terms of Art*, and such as are both Lessons and *Terms of Art*.

A List of the most material
Terms of Art made use of in Fencing.

First. *Terms of Art* relating to the Weapon.
1. Fort
2. Foible   Of the Sword.

5. *Quinte*.
6. Within
7. Without   The Sword.
8. Parieing.
9. Parade.
10. *Contre-caveating* Parade.
11. *Caveating*, ……... Lesson.
12. Feint, …………... Lesson.
13. Time, …………... Lesson.
14. *Contre-temps*.
15. Exchanged Thrust.
16. Beating, ………... Lesson.
17. Binding, ………... Lesson.
18. Riposte, ………... Lesson.

Secondly. Relating chiefly to the Body in general.
1. A Guard.
2. Measure or Distance.
3. Judging of Measure.
4. Thrusting, ……... Lesson.
5. *Ecarting*.
6. *Elongeing*, ……... Lesson.
7. Pass, …………… Lesson.
8. Half-Pass, ……... Lesson.
9. *Volting*, ………... Lesson.
10. Enclosing, ……...Lesson.

Thirdly. Relating chiefly to the Sword-Hand.
1. *Prime*.
2. *Seconde*.
3. *Tierce*.
4. *Quarte*.

Fourthly. Relating chiefly to the Leggs.
1. Approaching.
2. Retireing.
3. Breaking of Measure.
4. Redoubling, …… Lesson.

Here are no less than thirty-four *Terms of Art*, thirteen whereof are Lessons. For altho' strictly speaking, all the *Terms of Art* may be so far called Lessons, as they must be descrived and communicate by a Master to his Scholar when he is a-teaching him, yet in this list I only name such for Lessons as either directly belong to the offensive part, or at least being a means whereby a man may prevail over his adversary, have a tendency to it.

Having thus reduced the *Terms of Art* into four Classes, according as they chiefly relate to either Weapon, Body, Sword-Hand, or Leggs, I shall now go through them in a more gradual method, as if I were to descrive them to a young Scholar. And in descriving them, shall make such true remarks as I have gathered from near thirty years experience and observation.

I
Of a Guard in general.

The word *Guard* has succeeded in the *Art of Fencing* to the old term *Ward*, which signifies a place of security. For long ago, to say that a person was *under ward*, was as much as to say he was *under custody*; from whence also *Warden*: a *Guardian* or *Keeper*. And so, when a man is said to be *in Guard*, or *upon his Guard*, is as much to say that he has put himself into the most secure posture he can for the defence and preservation of his person. Also, when a man is *taken up* and *secured*, we say his is *under Guard*. For a man may be secured or under custody upon two very different accounts, either when he hath committed some crime, and then he is secured that he may undergo the just and legal punishment he deserves; or a man may be secured and put under custody or Guard for his preservation, when engaged in any quarrel, or when there is any bad design against his Life. And it is in this last acceptation that I here understand and explain the word *Guard*. The old term *Ward* is no more in use amongst Sword-Men, and therefore I shall say no more of it; it is enough that I have shown the importance of the word.

As for this modern term *Guard*, it is in Fencing alwise taken for *that posture of the body, wherein a man puts himself for his greater security, when he has occasion to make use of his weapons.* Now altho' a man's Guard may be justly reputed a posture of security, yet it is not his Defense, albeit it may contribute much to it. It is only the Parade flowing from it which can justly be called his true Defense. For one man may keep a very good and close Guard, and have an exceeding loose and uncertain Parade or defence; whereas another may have, and sometimes also of design may stand, to a very open Guard, and yet have a most firm and secure defence.

So that I may properly enough compare a good *Guard* to the place wherein a man is to be kept safe from any bad attempt against him, the *Sword-Hand* to the keeper or sentinel, & the *Sword* from whence the *Defence* or *Parade* flows to the key that locks in and secures all. For as a person may be put into a very close room for custody or security, and yet if the door be neither lockt, nor a sentinel put upon him, he is almost as loose and unsecure from the malicious attempts of his enemies, as if he were at large and no safeguard about him. So may a man keep a good and close Guard, and yet be very unsecure from the vigorous Assaults and attacks of his malicious and ill designing adversary, if he be not Master of a firm and sure defence whereby he may exclude his adversary from having access (notwithstanding of his most cunning and subtile addresses) upon him, to the hazard and prejudice of his person.

And therefore, as the only way to keep any person safe and secure from the bad and malicious designs which may be intended against him, is not only to put him into a good close room with sentinels upon him, but also to secure him absolutely by turning of the key, and so locking him in, that there may be no access to him but by those to whom the sentinels or turn-key shall grant liberty; so the only way to preserve a man's person at Sharps from the quick and subtile attacks of his adversary is, besides his putting himself into a good Guard, to be Master of such a firm and sure Parade, as that his sword-hand, which is the sentinel or keeper, may at pleasure turn the key or sword, and so lock him up safe from his adversary's having any access to him, for the prejudice and hurt of his person. Except when he shall himself comply with it, and voluntarily grant an Open, which he judges may tend to his own advantage.

This is a homely but natural allegory, whereby it will clearly appear that altho' the keeping of a neat and close Guard be good, yet if it be not accompanied with a firm and sure defence, a man's person can never be secure. The keeping then of a close Guard is good, but it is the Parade flowing from it which is a man's defence and security. Therefore never have so much regard to the posture of defence to which a man at first pitches himself, as to the Parade you find him draw from it. Neither is it the posture of the body and position of the sword, in this *Hanging Guard* which I so much admire and recommend, as the secure and safe Parade, or general defence which most naturally flows from it, and which the more a man reflects upon, the more he will still value and approve of.

There is not that posture which any man can put himself into, but may properly enough be called a Guard, if he draw a defence from it. And the reason is because, as I said, the posture of a man's Guard is not at all his defence, but the Parade he draws from it. Altho' the more close the posture be, the more readily will he draw a good and secure Parade from it.

It is upon this account that there may be as many Guards as there are postures of the body, or positions of the sword-hand. But because such a prodigious number would but amuse and confound people, therefore Sword-Men have reduced them to five, *viz. Prime, Seconde, Tierce, Quarte*, and *Quinte*, which is more than the ordinary positions of the sword-hand, as you will immediately understand.

I here only name them, that you may know there are so many. And of the five, you see I have pickt out, rejecting all the rest, the *Seconde* as the only true Guard, and pure source from whence all true defence must proceed, as I think I have made sufficiently appear by the preceeding advantages. I shall likewise, in a few words, give my opinion of the other four by only naming them, as I judge they ought to be preferred, conform to the security of the defences that may be drawn from them.

Next then to this excellent Guard in *Seconde*, I prefer the *Quarte*, with the point level or a little elevate, the body sinking very low; then the *Tierce*; then the *Quinte*, which is nothing but the *Quarte* with a sloping point; and last of all the *Prime*, of which I may say we have nothing but its name, for this *Seconde* is alwise made use of in place of it, because of the most constrained position of the sword-hand when a man attempts to pitch himself to it.

So that if the reader intend to reject the Guard in *Seconde*, which I with so much earnestness recommend to him because of the general and excellent defence may be drawn from it, I cannot but, out of the great regard I have for his safety, recommend to him in its place (if he will still jogg on in the common road of Fencing) the Guard in *Quarte*, with the body sinking very low, equally posed upon his two leggs, and with his sword-hand in *Quarte*, and kept but just above his right knee, which perfectly secures all the lower parts of the body, a direction much to be observed at Sharps. This, next to the *Hanging Guard in Seconde*, whose great advantage is the chief subject of this *New Method*, is what I do earnestly recommend to him. But then it is only in case of his totally undervaluing and rejecting this *New Method*, for which I should be heartily sorry after all the perswasions and convincing arguments I have used for it.

II

Of the different Positions of the Sword-Hand, viz. Prime, Seconde, Tierce, and Quarte.[4]

When a man presents his sword perfectly streight or, in a manner, upon a level, he may, by keeping of his arm stretched & turning it, as it were, upon a center from its articulation in the scapula or shoulder-blade (for in this case the whole arm must turn, as well as the wrist, tho' not quite so much), form a perfect circle. So that with respect to this circle, the sword-hand may have as many different positions as there are degrees in a circle, which are 360. But such a number of different positions being of no great use in Fencing, the Masters of old were satisfied to reduce them to four, that so they might answer, tho' not altogether exactly, to the four quarters of a circle. And this division has been kept by most Masters even to this day, and are called *Prime, Seconde, Tierce*, and *Quarte*. Which is as much as to say the First, Second, Third, and Fourth position of the sword-hand, altho' some of late have added a Fifth, which they call *Quinte*.

The *Prime*, or first position, is reputed that position of the hand with which a man draws his sword at first out of its scabbard, but indeed falsely. Because if it be strictly considered, people do really alwise draw their swords with their hand in *Seconde*, and not in that which is truely the *Prime*. For in the true *Prime*, the nails of the sword-hand are turned up as much as possible, toward the right side outwards, and is a most constrained posture, no man being able to keep it any considerable time, therefore is scarcely ever made use of. So that we have, in a manner, only its name in Fencing.

Seconde, or the second position, is that position of the sword-hand which is performed by holding the sword with the thumb quite downward; the nails of the hand quite outwards, towards the right side; and the back of the hand towards the left or inside. This position is a great deal more easie than the *Prime*, and is exactly the position of the sword-hand wherewith people commonly draw their swords, and wherewith this *Hanging Guard* I have been so much commending is also to be kept. And truely I may say it serves for both *Prime* and *Seconde*. For when ever *Prime* is ordered, the position is so constrained that the hand falls naturally from it into the *Seconde*. See the positions of the sword-hands, of Figures 1 & 2 [p.96].

The *Tierce* is the third position, and the sword-hand in forming it makes a full quarter of a circle from the *Seconde*, whereas from the *Prime* to the *Seconde* it alters but a very few degrees. This position is yet more easie than the *Seconde*, and is kept with the back of the hand and Knuckles quite upwards, and the nails down; and is that position of the hand wherewith the thrusts without and above the sword, in the Common Method, are generally performed, altho' they are also many times given in with the hand in *Quarte*.

The *Quarte* or fourth position of the hand is still more easily kept than the *Tierce*. It is kept with the thumb quite upwards,

---

[4] It is interesting to note that Hope's hand positions differ from those in traditional rapier and small sword theory, in which *Prime* has the thumb at 6 o'clock, *Seconde* has the thumb at 9 o'clock, *Tierce* has the thumb at 12 o'clock, and *Quarte* has the thumb at 3 o'clock.

the back of the hand outwards, towards the right-side, and the nails of the fingers towards the left, but inclining a very thought upwards. See Figure 4 [p.100]. The sword-hand in forming the *Quarte* altereth also from the *Tierce* a full quarter of a circle, as the *Tierce* did from the *Seconde*; and is the strongest position of any, seeing a man can keep his sword longest firm upon it without wearying of his arm. It is also that position wherein, in the Ordinary Method of Fencing, most of the thrusts within the sword are performed, as likewise that very position of the hand wherein a man keeps the *Quarte* Guard with a sloping point. See Figure 5 [p.100].

Now it is to be observed that the position of the sword-hand in its circular passing forwards from one of those four quarters of a circle to that next it, retains still the same denomination it had when it was in the immediately preceeding quarter. As for example, when the hand is in *Prime*, it is said, notwithstanding of its being a little altered towards the *Seconde*, to be still in *Prime* until it fall in to the exact *Seconde*; and when it is in *Seconde*, it continues in *Seconde*, notwithstanding of its varying from it, in its turning towards the *Tierce*, and never alters its denomination until it be fully upon that quarter which forms the *Tierce*; and so of the rest.

It is therefore a mistake, which some Masters fall into, when they call the true *Quarte* the *Demy-Quarte*, and that only *Quarte* which is nothing but a variation of the sword-hand from the true *Quarte* point, towards a greater degree of *Quarte*, or towards the *Prime* quarter, wherein the nails of the hand are kept quite upwards. And which is so very constrained a posture, that a man can scarcely turn his hand to it, let alone keep it for any considerable time.

I confess indeed that this position is still a *Quarte*, until, as I said, the position of the nails of the hand arrive at, or at least near to, the other quarter of the circle wherewith the *Prime* begins, altho' the hand be in a quite opposite position than when it formed the *Prime*, being now almost quite turned about. But still this is no more a *Quarte* than what they call a *Demy-Quarte*, and is so very difficult that we have really no more of it in Fencing, but its name, altho' many Masters order their Scholars to deliver their thrusts within and above the sword in this constrained position. Which is not only a considerable error, but almost impracticable, the position being so constrained, as I shall make it appear when I come to discourse of thrusting. Therefore what those Masters call the *Demy-Quarte* ought to be called the true *Quarte*, as well as that variation of the hand towards the *Tierce* quarter which they call only the *Quarte*. This is an observation wholly new, and very well worth noticing for the better and more ready distinguishing of the four different positions of the sword-hand.

There is also a *Quinte*, or fifth position, as they pretend, of the sword-hand mentioned by some Masters, particularly Monsieur de Liancour. But seeing it is not so properly a different position of the sword-hand, as a different situation of the sword, whereby it is kept with the point sloping towards the ground, the hand being in the same position with *Quarte*. And is also, as I said, the very same posture with what we call the *Quarte* Guard with a sloping point. I shall say no more of it, seeing it is enough that I have, by naming it, discovered that another distinct position of the sword-hand is not in the least meant by it, but only a different situation of the sword. For which see Figure 5 [p.100].

Having explained the four different positions of the sword-hand, *viz. Prime*, *Seconde*, *Tierce*, and *Quarte*, I must tell you that, for the most part, two of them are rejected in this *New Method* I am about to establish. So that in place of the four, I only make use of two: to wit, the *Seconde*, in which this *Hanging Guard* is kept; and the *Quarte*, which is sometimes for the thrusts given without and above the sword. So that I wholly reject the *Prime* and *Tierce*, and make only use of the *Seconde* and *Quarte*: the *Seconde*, both for the posture of the Guard, and the thrusts as well within and beneath the sword upon the right-side, as without and above the sword upon the left; and the *Quarte*, now and then for thrusts without and above the sword towards the left-side, as the practitioner shall judge it most convenient.

Altho' to give my own opinion frankly in this matter, I have very little regard to the particular positions of the sword-hand. Because, provided a man make a good cross with his weapon upon his adversary's for his defence when upon the defensive part, or wound his adversary with his thrust when upon the offensive part, and recover himself quickly again to his cross or opposing posture, I think upon the main it is no great matter whether it be with his hand in *Seconde*, *Tierce*, or *Quarte*, seeing with safety he performs what he designed. For it is the cross upon his adversary's sword, not the position of the sword-hand, that procures safety to a man in either defending or thrusting.

III
Of the Fort and Foible of a Sword.

There are few people but know the parts which compose a sword, therefore I shall but just name them, for the information of the younger sort of Scholars. A Rapier[5] hath its hilt and its blade. The hilt hath its pommel, handle, shell, and cross-bars. And if it be a Shearing Sword, hath commonly also a back-ward as a kind of preservation or defence for the hand. Every man pleases his own fancy, both with regard to a round or square,

---

[5] Hope is using "Rapier" to mean a Small Sword.

full or small handle, as well as the other furniture of the hilt. But as for the blade, whatever kind it be, whether Rapier or Shearing Sword, certainly the lighter it be, provided it be stiff enough, and of good tough mettal, so much the better. For any blade had much better continue in the bend (which is what we call a *poor man's blade*), than be so brittle as to be apt to break and fly in pieces upon every little stroak or stress it may meet with.

But whatever kind of sword a man make choice of for the pleasing of his fancy, yet there are two things which it is absolutely requisite that he take notice to. The *First* is that his sword be well mounted, which is known by laying it cross his fore-finger, within two or three inches of its hilt. And if the hilt, with the assistance of these two or three inches, counter-balance the rest of the blade, then it is well mounted. Otherwise not, seeing it will be too weighty before the hand.

The *Second* is that whenever he has an occasion to draw it for service, he alwise keep it fixt and firm in his hand so that it be not beat out of it by every sudden jerk or stroak that his adversary makes upon it. Nothing is more unseemly, nor makes a Sword-Man look more out of countenance, than when his sword either drops accidentally, or is really of design, by his adversary, beat out of his hand. Therefore every good Sword-Man ought to prevent it, not only for his own greater safety, but even for decency, that he may not be smiled at.

Having thus briefly given an account of the parts of a sword in general, I shall now show how a sword-blade is divided by Sword-Men when they come to discourse, or make use of their Art and Skill.

The Fencing Masters of old divided the blades of their swords, from the hilt to the point, sometimes into twelve parts or divisions, and sometimes into four. Which served for no other use that I know, but to perplex and embarrass their Scholars. Upon which account, I wholly disapprove and reject it, and shall with the *Moderns*, who have a great deal of more reason for it, divide the blade into two equal parts. So that I generally call the *Fort* or strong part of the blade that division or half which is betwixt the hilt and the middle of the blade, and the *Foible* or weak part that which is betwixt the middle of it and the point.

The Fort is so called because it is of greatest strength, as being nearer to the hand or center, and is therefore most proper for the Parieing, or putting off, thrusts or blows.

The Foible is so called because it is of least strength, by which, as it is less capable to defend or Parie a thrust or blow, so it is most proper, because of its quick and surprising motion to offend, either by thrusting or striking.

But the division of the sword in the middle into the Fort and Foible must not be understood so strictly, but that with respect to either the strong or weak operation of the adversary's sword against it, or of it against the adversary's, that which was at one time the Fort may not be at another time the Foible, and that which is now the Foible may not become at another time the Fort. This being occasioned really, not only by the impression and power which one sword hath over another, according to the degrees of weight, whereby it over-powers and masters its adversary's when it hath crossed or over-lapped it, but even according to the strength and impulse it receives from the hand and wrist of the person who is making use of it. As, for instance, if with eight inches from the point of my sword, I overlap only five or six of my adversary's, which it overlaps, it may very well be called the strong, because it hath the same effect upon my adversary's sword as if it were really that part which is properly called the Fort.

Again if my Fort, for instance, a foot from the hilt, should be overlapped with only eight or ten of my adversary's from its hilt. In that case, I say my Fort, with respect to the impression and command of my adversary's sword hath over it, may very properly be called the Foible.

And which is yet more surprising, this ordinary division of Fort and Foible is not only altered, as I said, by the impression and power of one sword over another, according to the degrees of weight, whereby it masters and over-powers its adversary's after it hath overlapped it, but even by the different degrees of strength and impulse made use of by the adversary's sword-hand, either in Parieing or Binding. So that, in such a case, my foot or 12 inches of Fort from the hilt shall even master my adversary's eight or six from his. Or my five or six of Foible from my point shall, by the strength and impulse I add to it from my wrist, master eight or ten of my adversary's from its point, he noways assisting to resist me by the strength of his sword-hand or wrist. So that after all, strictly speaking, the Fort and Foible of a sword, notwithstanding of the former division, can only really be called such according as either my sword operates upon my adversary's, or my adversary's operates upon mine. So that the most part of the blade of a man's sword, even almost from the hilt to within five or six inches of the point, may become either all Fort if it overpowers its adversary's, or all Foible if it be mastered and overpowered by his, either by its own weight and pressure, or by the strength and impulse of his sword-hand. And this is the only true explication I can give of the Fort and Foible of a sword; the former, altho' generally true, being yet at bottom so variable as not to be wholly rely'd upon. However for the more ordinary sort of players I shall keep to my former division. But for those who are more expert, and consequently greater criticks and more nice as to this point, I earnestly recommend this extraordinary and useful observation I have made, which is not to be found in any author.

IV
Of Within and Without the Sword.

Within and *Without* the sword may be considered with two respects: either with respect to the division of a man's body by his sword-arm, or with respect to the particular position of his sword-hand, when he either presents his sword without and above, or when he forms the cross of his Parade. If with respect to the division of the body by the sword-arm, then that part betwixt his sword-arm and left-side (if a right handed man) is alwise called *within the sword*, as the opposite side is called *without the sword*. And they never alter, let the position of the sword-hand be what it will. But if they are considered with respect to the particular positions of the sword-hand, or cross made in Parieing, then they are not so fixed. Because what was *within the sword*, with respect to the division of the body by the sword-arm, or that distance betwixt the sword-arm and left-side, by the alteration of the position of the sword-hand into Seconde, will become *without and above the sword*; and that which was *without the sword*, will be either *without and above*, or *without and below the sword*, just as a man's adversary Paries him. And this is the reason that there is no *within the sword* to thrust at upon a person who takes himself to this *Hanging Guard*.

But it being chiefly with respect to the division of the body by the sword-arm, and not with respect to the positions of the sword-hand, or cross made by the Parade, that Masters commonly denominate the within and without of the sword. Therefore I shall generally give them their denomination from the same ground, except where I particularly otherwise mention it. Atlho' I do really think it were more agreeable to reason to have only regard to the positions of the sword-hand in these two terms (as I have classed them in the list), and cross formed in Parieing. But seeing so great an alteration of these two terms would be fair to startle a great many Masters who cannot willingly quit with any old rote, tho' never so much contrary to reason, I shall therefore comply with them so far as generally to keep to the old denomination.

And yet strictly speaking, even with respect to the ordinary division of the body by the sword-arm, and if we decide according to the nicest rules, which is by considering both how people generally present their swords, and how every thrust terminates with respect to the cross made upon the weapon Paried, there is hardly any such thing to be found in Fencing as a true within or without the sword, either to thrust at, or terminated in by a thrust, which I make evident thus:

To make an exact within or without the sword, a man must (whatever Guard he pitch himself to) keep his sword exactly level. And his adversary must also oppose it with his sword perfectly parallel to it, as to its heighth, upon what side soever he present it. For if the adversary's sword make the least cross upon his sword, then there is no more an exact within or without the sword. But immediately what might have been properly enough called *within* the sword, while the two swords were parallel, must now, if the cross be made with the point a little elevate, be called *within and above* the sword, if the adversary's sword was presented towards the left-side of your sword. Or *without and above* the sword, if it was presented towards the right. And if the cross be made with the point sloping, then it will be either within and above or beneath the sword, or without and above or beneath the sword, according to the cross which the Parade makes. So great an alteration does either the different positions of the sword-hand, or the cross made by the Parade, make upon the termination of a thrust, that it may have its true denomination. But this position of parallel swords so rarely happening, even when person's swords are at first presented to one another; and I may say almost never in the performing or finishing of any thrust, because of the adverse party alwise endeavouring to defend himself, and whose Parade framing still a cross, either towards the left or right-side, makes it so fall out that all thrusts terminate either within and below, or within and above, or without and below, or without and above; and never almost in an exact within or without the sword. Whereby it may be clearly perceived by what has been said that an exact within or without the sword is but, in a manner, a supposition, and what *possibly* may happen; but I may positively affirm does not once, in the performing of several thousands of thrusts; and has really a false denomination from the division that is made of the body with respect to the sword-arm in general; but which would be perfectly rectified were the particular positions of the adversary's sword-hand and cross formed by the Parades more regarded, and the within and without regulate only according to these. But this being a little nice, I despair to get it wholly rectified. Although what I have said is most agreeable to reason, and may perhaps convince the more judicious.

V
Of Measure, or Distance.

When two persons are to engage, either for their diversion or in earnest, there is alwise a certain space or distance betwixt them. Which distance is termed by Sword-Men, *Measure*. And although, generally speaking, this Measure or distance may be only distinguished into that which is greater, and that which is less; yet seeing this division agrees equally to all the kinds of distances I am to explain, I shall therefore here take

Measure in a stricter sense, in which I reckon three kinds wherein Sword-Men are chiefly concerned; and in one of which the adversaries will alwise of necessity find themselves, which ever of them either offends or defends. Which is the reason that I have brought in this *Term of Art*, as well as the next following, before these of Parieing or thrusting. Because before a man can either defend or offend, there is a necessity that he and his adversary be not only separate from other by one of the three following Measure*s* or distances, but also (by one of them, at least, approaching or advancing; which is the next *Term of Art*) bring themselves into it, if they chance to be altogether without Measure or reach.

The first whereof is when a man is so near to his adversary that he can reach him without *Elonging* or stepping out, by only stretching out of his sword-arm and inclining forwards with his body, without moving in the least his advanced foot.

No good Sword-Man who regards his own safety will make use of this kind of Measure, because it obliges him to be so very near to his adversary that he may readily be surprised by him, either by a quick plain Thrust, a subtile *Feint*, or a sudden Commanding.

Therefore, in place of it, Sword-Men make more frequently use of the second kind of Measure or distance, which is as it were a *Medium* betwixt the first, which needs no stepping out, and the third distance, which is alwise performed by approaching or advancing, although not constantly by stepping out or *Elonging*. Because the approaching may bring a man so near to his adversary, that there is no necessity for him to step out, but only to make a stretch with his body and sword-arm, that so he may reach his adversary.

This second kind of Measure is that which is most commonly made use of by good Sword-Men, especially those who regard their own security, when they have an Occasion with Sharps. For this obliges their adversary to come to half-sword,[6] as we say, whereby a man's true skill and dexterity is a great deal better discovered, especially in the defensive part, than it is possible for it to be when playing at the third kind of distance, or *without distance*, as it is commonly termed in the Schools.

The third kind of Measure is that wherein a man is necessitate to advance a step or two, yea sometimes more, before he can reach his adversary. And although it be less dangerous for the person who makes use of it than the first kind of distance, being not so subject to surprise, yet it is not near so secure and safe as the second kind of distance: because a man is very much disordered

by approaching, let him perform it never so warily. Whereas when he plays at half-sword, or *within distance*, as we call it, he neither disorders himself so much before he discharge his thrust, nor is so liable to be surprised by the advancing motions of his adversary, which are much prevented by his keeping him alwise engaged at half-sword. So that in such a cause, the victory depends chiefly upon the surest and firmest Parade, and the quickest Riposte: the only true and secure method of fighting upon an Occasion, not only from the Ordinary, but even in this *New Method of Fencing* from the *Hanging Guard in Seconde*.

So that of the three above-mentioned distances, the *First* is the most dangerous; the *Third* the next best; and the *Second* the most secure of all the three: being that which is generally made use of by the greatest Sword-Men, by reason of its great benefit and use in an Occasion with Sharps, where all nice breast-plate Lessons,[7] and other such like School-Tricks, (for they deserve no better name, being only proper for a diverting Assault with blunts) are to be avoided, as a man tenders his own preservation and safety.

VI
Of Approaching, or Advancing.

As there is alwise a certain distance betwixt two persons before they engage, so they must of necessity be placed at that distance or Measure by either the one or both of them *Approaching* or *Advancing* upon each other. So that, as unless two antagonists be in the first or second kind of Measure, it is impossible for either of them to Parie or thrust, because of their adversarie's not being within reach of them. Even so it is impossible for them, without one or both of them first Approaching or Advancing, to place themselves in any of the three above-mentioned Measure*s*. And consequently it is no less proper to discourse of this Approaching before Parieing or thrusting, than it was to explain before them the different kinds of distances immediately preceeding.

When a man is within reach of his adversary, or in the first or second Measure above described, there is no need of his Approaching. It is then only when a man's adversary is out of his reach that he must come within distance of him before he offer to launch out a thrust. Because if he should offer to discharge his thrusts before he be within Measure or reach of his adversary, they would be all lost in the air, and consequently his mettal and vigour would be spent to no purpose. To prevent which, when a man finds himself without distance, he is indispensably obliged, if he intend to be the pursuer, to Approach or Advance

---

[6] The position in which the opposing blades are engaged at the midpoint, bringing the adversaries into close distance.

[7] Lessons with a Fencing Master or other Scholar, wearing a breastplate or plastron. In other words, academic fencing.

so much, until he judge himself sufficiently within Measure to reach his adversary with an *Elonge*.

Indeed, if he design that his adversary shall be the pursuer, then the Advancing of his adversary will bring him likewise within Measure, without his moving of himself in the least until he deliver his thrust. Which I must confess is an excellent method of play, because it is a great token of a man's being absolutely Master of the Parade, whereby he not only keeps himself in a firm posture of defence, and puts upon his adversary the disadvantage of Approaching, whereby, at best, he is somewhat disordered; but also procures to himself the advantage of playing from the Riposte, which of all methods of Fencing is the most commendable and safest. But then, as I have said, it is only to such as are Masters of the Parade. Which is a quality rare enough to be found, even amongst the greatest Sword-Men.

Now there are two ways of Approaching or Advancing towards a man's adversary. The *First*, and indeed most natural, is that by which all persons who have never been instructed in the *Art* advance towards their adversary when they are out of Measure from him: which is by an ordinary walk, such as people commonly make use of in going from one place to another. But Masters, finding that a man, in making use of this ordinary step, was subject to advance too much his left side and shoulder, whereby his body became the more open, and consequently in greater danger by being thereby exposed to his adversary's thrusts, I say being sensible of this disadvantage, they not only ordered a man, when making use of this ordinary step, to keep back well his left shoulder or side, that he might thereby make his body a narrower mark for his adversary to thrust at, but also fell upon...

The artificial, or *Second* and most safe way of Approaching, called the *Single Step*. Which is by keeping the legs still in the same position wherein a man stands to his Guard (that is, the one alwise behind the other), and only making the hind foot advance as much, by slipping as it were along the ground, as the right or foremost foot advanced, or stept, forewards. And by this method they found that not only a man did not so much expose his body by the advancing of his left shoulder, which is alwise forced in a manner forewards upon the ordinary *Double Step*, but also that it was kept a great deal more firm, while performing this *Single Step*, than when he made use of the former. So that ever since, this method of Approaching hath been look't upon as not only the most becoming and graceful, but also the most secure and safe for a man's person, that so he may not receive a wound, as it were, by surprise in Approaching.

I cannot indeed deny but Masters are in the right on't as to this determination, when a man is almost within Measure of his adversary; or even being within Measure, would yet come nearer

to him. So that in these two cases, this last method of Advancing with the *Single Step* is much preferable to, and hath the advantage of the former, because the left side of the body is not so much exposed by it in Approaching as it is by the *Double Step*.

But if the matter be considered a little more narrowly, it will be found that there is no more disadvantage in advancing with the *Double Step*, when a man is a great way out of his adversary's Measure, than there is in advancing with the *Single*. For seeing a man is only to Advance with the *Double Step* until he be almost within his adversary's Measure, and not until he be quite within it (the *Single Step* being indeed only proper for that), he is certainly all that time a good deal without his adversary's reach. And if he be so much without his reach, it is no great matter if he approach not only with his left shoulder and side exposed, but even with a full body upon his adversary, seeing at that distance he is in no hazard of being hit by him. But it is alwise with this provision, that so soon as ever he judges himself within five or six yards of his adversary's Measure, he immediately *Thin* his body as much as possible, by throwing back of his left Shoulder, and taking in the remainder of the Measure, for his greater security, with the *Single Step*, and all this without the least constraint. A rule to be strictly observed in all the directions of Fencing.

From whence I conclude that a man may very safely make use of either of the preceeding steps without the least hazard, so long as he is at a great distance. But if he be pretty near to, or even within his adversary's Measure, and yet would approach nearer to him to make his thrust the more effectual, in this case he is indispensably obliged for his greater security not only to prefer and make alwise use of the *Single Step* (unless he have some little furrow or strand to step over, for which the *Double Step* is most proper), but also, in performing it, to endeavour as much as possible to prevent his adversary's surprising of him by Thrusting in Time.

And this brings me to a very useful direction to be punctually observed upon all occasions when a man shall draw his sword in good earnest. Which is that instantly upon drawing it, he jump or go back five or six yards, if he have so much free space, that so he may not be surprised by his adversary's sudden attack. And then immediately Advance towards him upon a good Guard, and with the *Single Step*, either to attack or receive him. The exact observation of this direction will many times prevent more than can be expressed: a man's being surprised by his adversary's sudden and vigorous attack, before he hath well put himself in Guard.

But if a man, when he quarrels, shall be so near to his adversary, and so straitned with room, that he cannot possibly observe the above direction without perhaps running himself into a greater inconveniency, of either going close to a wall, or falling into a more disadvantageous ground, or part of the street, if it be a rencounter in a town; then he is, upon drawing of his sword, immediately to pitch himself to his Guard, and engaging firmly his adversary's sword, make a vigorous half or whole pursuit upon him from the Binding or crossing of the sword, having alwise his left hand in readiness to prevent a *Contre-temps*. And thus he will not only keep his ground, which, when a man is thus straitned, is very precious, but also force upon his adversary the disadvantage, unless he be a very great Sword-Man, of becoming the defender. And if his adversary should prevent him by becoming the pursuer, then if he have space enough, he is either to break his Measure a little, until the violence of his Attack be over, and then to become the pursuer. Or if he be confined in a narrow bounds so that he cannot conveniently break his Measure, then he is to defend himself the best way he can by a firm and dry beating Parade, attacking him from it by the Riposte, and assisting his Parade by the dexterous use of his left hand. Which in such a juncture he will find very serviceable to him, it being one of the most difficult circumstances wherewith a Sword-Man can be tristed [involved]. That is, a rude, irregular, and passionate antagonist, having a most violent pursuit, joined with a very narrow and small limited bounds.

These two or three last directions are of such singular use to Sword-Men in an Occasion with Sharps, that I cannot but earnestly recommend them to the reader.

VII
Of Parieing and Parade.

Whatever Guard a man designs to ply and take himself to, after he once understands the preceeding *Terms of Art* it is full time for him to be taught, first to Defend himself, and then to Offend his adversary. Which are the significations of the two following *Terms of Art*: *Parieing* and *Thrusting*. For to Parie is to turn or keep off a blow or thrust, so that a man is nowise prejudiced or wounded by it. And from hence is the word *Parade* derived, which signifies not only the defence of any particular blow or thrust, but even the whole defensive part belonging to the Art. Thus we say such a Parade is good against such an Attack or such a Lesson, when the person makes use of a peculiar and proper defence against the thrust that was discharged against him. Again, when it is made use of in a general acceptation, we say that such a person hath a good, sure, and firm Parade. That is, he is much Master of the defensive part of the Art.

There are two considerable Errors that have by degrees creept into the Common Method of communicating the *Art of the Sword* with relation to the Parade or defence which I would gladly convince the Fencing Masters of, that they may be hereafter rectified. Because it is not to be imagin'd what great prejudice the arguing for them, as well as the putting them too frequently in practice, have done to the true *Art of Defence*.

The *First* relates to the Parade or defensive part of the whole Art in general. The *Second*, to the manner of performing every particular Parade against any blow or thrust that a man shall be obliged to Parie for his better preservation and defence.

As to the *First*, I cannot but affirm that the great neglect of the Parade, or defensive part, that is generally observed in the Schools, hath been one great reason of the uncertainty which most people have had hitherto in the defence of their persons in an Occasion. And consequently the chief ground of that unreasonable neglect and contempt which many persons have of late had for the Art.

If a man will but a little frequent the Schools, he cannot fail to observe that in most of them the offensive part, or pursuit, is much more recommended and put in practice than the Parade, or defensive. And yet it is from the great usefulness of this Art in defending that it is justly termed the *Art of Defence*.

The offensive part is no doubt very useful, but its chief design ought not to be to destroy our adversaries. But rather a kind of means whereby a man may the more certainly effectuate the compleating of his defence, according to the maxim *that the best way to defend a Man's own Property is to incroach upon and invade his Neighbour's*. So that I don't at all condemn or diswade Masters from teaching the pursuit. But only advise them to regulate, or rather renverse, their method, and allot that long time (which formerly they allowed to their Scholars, for rendering them dexterous in the pursuit) for making them adroit and firm in their defence. And the very inconsiderable moment that they used commonly to give to the practicing of the Parade, that they would bestow only that, to teach them how they may handsomely destroy and kill according to the rules as they pretend. For which I am persuaded there were never any designed by either GOD or Nature. But such is the pravity of Mankind, that we cannot so much as think of doing our selves the least good, if at the same time we do not endeavour to plague and do our adversaries all the evil and mischief we can possibly contrive and invent.

And this pernicious custom of making the usefulness of the Art to consist chiefly in the pursuit hath had no doubt its rise from those who were the first Improvers of the *Art of the Sword*. That is, who from making only use of the edge or blow for a pursuit, added to it the great benefit of the point, as a surprising and most destructive offense.

For without all doubt, the *Art of the Back Sword* is the Fountain and Source of all true defence, and that of the Small [Small Sword] only a branch proceeding and separate from it. And had the improvement of the Small been kept within its just bounds, it would certainly have been a very great addition to the Art. But so bent are most people, after the prosecution of any thing that is New, and so fond of pushing their own inventions to the greatest heighth, that by their daily refining upon it that which was at first designed as an aid to, and improvement of, the true *Art of Defence*, hath had this quite other effect: that it has tended much to its disadvantage by lessening (by reason of its fickle and uncertain defence) a great deal of its reputation. So that it may be but too justly asserted that the greatest benefit the *Art of Defence* reaps now a-days in most Schools is that by having the Parade or defensive part too much neglected, and the benefit of the point or thrusting too far pusht, the generality of Masters are like to push and thrust all *True Defence* out of their Schools.

However if, notwithstanding of what is past, Masters would be for the future but so kind to themselves and just to their Scholars as to follow the candid advice I just now gave them: of making their Scholars ply more the defensive and less the offensive part in their School Lessons (for believe it, all of us naturally incline but too much to offend; and the pursuit, so much at least of it as is needful for the making good of our defence, will, without giving our selves much trouble about it, force it self upon us, whether almost we will or not), we should in a very short time find the *Art of Defence* recover its ancient reputation, the Masters and Professors of it had more in esteem, and their Fencing Schools so crowded with Scholars of all degrees and ranks, that no Gentleman would be thought really to deserve that epithet who were not desirous to be an advantageous sharer in the possession of the most heroick and useful *Art of Defence*.

The *Second* Error respects the manner of performing every particular Parade, and which the Masters of the Back Sword are more guilty of than the Professors of the Small. And that is the making the hilts or shells of their swords for the most part defend the blow or thrust that is discharged against them, in place of making that true cross with their sword-blade, which is absolutely necessary for the performing of a true and secure defence.

Whatever Guard the Back Sword Masters take themselves to, whether this *Hanging Guard in Seconde*, or the Medium Guard, this error in Parieing or defending alwise upon the hilt is most visible. For they never almost make a true cross, but receive all upon the hilt of their sword. So that they are beholding more for any defence they draw (according to the Common Practice) from those Guards, to the strength and thickness of their sword-hilts, than to any true cross or Parade they draw from them.

To make this the more evident, I will only ask them this question: How they would defend themselves, either with a Rapier, Shearing Sword, or Sabre (none of which have close-hilts, and yet are the swords now a-days most commonly made use of, not only for walking about the streets, but the two last also, in time of War) in a Battle? They certainly could not answer me that they would defend themselves with the common Parades, which they usually draw from the Hanging and Medium Guards. Because if they did attempt to do it once, they would perhaps scarcely have a finger wherewith to hold their sword, against the second or third blow their adversary would discharge against them, if smartly delivered and planted with a true edge: so much is their sword-hand, in making use of such a false Parade, exposed to the adversary's weapon.

And this hazard to which the sword-hand is exposed, is much more so upon the Medium Guard than upon the *Hanging Guard*. Because in the Parade, which they commonly make from the *Hanging Guard*, they sometimes form a little cross, and so receive the blow now and then upon the sword's blade, altho' not once in many stroaks. But in the common Parade they draw from the Medium Guard, they almost never form a cross, but receive all the blows upon the in or out-side of the sword-hilt. So that had they not a good and close-hilt[8] upon their sword, their fingers would be immediately shaved away, seeing the adversary's sword would, in striking, slide alwise along their sword-blade, and fall upon their sword-hand and wound it. By all which it follows of consequence that there can be no certain defence from any of these Guards, but what is made by forming a *true cross* upon the adversary's sword in Parieing. And that those Parades commonly drawn from the Hanging or Medium Guard are most imperfect and false, by reason of their being for the most part performed by the sword-hilt, and very rarely by the forming of a good cross.

For so very little is true Art concerned in this kind of defence, that any man who is furnished with back, breast, and head-piece[9] may as well be said to defend himself by Art from the thrusts and blows that are made against him, as such persons who make their defence with their close-hilts and without forming a good cross may be said truely to defend themselves by Art, and according to the just rules of defence. Because the latter owes no less his defence to the trueness of the mettal whereof his hilt is made, than the other does his, to his proved armour. And therefore all such false defences ought to be rejected by true Artists. And that only approved and made use of which forms a true and safe cross, such as I all along draw from the *Hanging Guard* in this *New Method*.

---

[8] A basket or cage hilt.

[9] A cuirass (body armour) and a helmet.

The very same may be said of the common Parades within and without the sword, drawn from the *Quarte* Guard, when they are only performed by the angle the adversary's sword makes upon the shell of the hilt, or by the breadth of certain kind of German blades, called *Koningsbergs*.[10] And which breadth is no advantage under heaven in Parieing, as some people fancy, because if I make a true cross in Parieing, I will defend my self as well with a blade no bigger than a *Lark-Spit*, provided it be stiff enough, as I can possibly do with a *Koningsberg* blade. Yea, or with one of three inches broad in the blade, which is double the breadth of any *Koningsberg* I did ever see. For as none of these Parades make a true cross, so none of them are safe and secure, even when a man's adversary thrusts close by his sword. But far less so when he thrusts at a distance from it, and very irregularly. Which is an error in the Parade that most Fencing Masters are guilty of, particularly the French.

For they scarcely know, in Parieing a plain Thrust within or without the sword, what it is to form a good cross, but only to turn their sword-hand a little, either to a *Quarte* when they Parie within the sword, or to a *Tierce* when they Parie without. So that if their adversary thrust any way out of the straight line and at a distance from their sword, or fall low without, and observe not alwise a regular method in thrusting close by their weapon, they are in a perfect confusion, and know not where to meet with his sword. Which is the reason of so many *Contre-temps* and Exchanged Thrusts passing betwixt persons in an Occasion, who altho' very dexterous at the pursuit, know no other method of defence. But which would certainly be prevented, did they apply themselves more to the forming of a good cross upon their adversary's sword, by which they could not fail of a true and sure defence.

For to my certain knowledge I can affirm that no people in the world have a swifter hand in thrusting, nor any a more loose or uncertain Parade, than the French. But now that the error is discovered, and may, perhaps by this piece or some other means, come to their ears, I doubt not but they will quickly rectify it. No people on Earth being more capable to do it than they, when they once earnestly set about it, and especially when I hope they shall have the good example of some of our most candid and judicious British Masters to show and lead them the way.

For to have a firm and sure Parade from the ordinary *Quarte* Guard, a man ought not only to form a good cross, with a firm and dry Beat or jerk. But to render it, especially upon the inside of the sword, the more certain, is many times obliged even to make that cross upon his adversary's sword with his sword-hand close almost to his own body, that so he may gain the more readily the weak or Foible of his adversary's sword. Which, should he only turn his wrist with his arm almost streight, which is the common French Parade from the *Quarte* Guard, he would certainly miss, and so receive the thrust. Because his cross, in place of meeting with his adversary's Foible, would fall upon his adversary's Fort, which would render his Parade or defence altogether imperfect. This is a Nicety in Parieing, not only from the ordinary *Quarte* Guard, but even from this *Hanging Guard in Seconde*, which not one Scholar in a hundred knows. Nay, not even many Masters who think themselves most topping and skillful in their profession. And therefore I earnestly recommend the practice of it to all such as are desirous to become Masters of a good and sure Parade. Which can only be such when a good cross is performed by it. And that not upon the Fort, but upon the Foible of the adversary's sword. And many times also almost close to a man's own body (especially, as I said, when the thrust is given within the sword), to render it the more certain.

Altho' I have been pretty long already upon this *Term of Art*, yet seeing it relates to the chiefest part of the Art, to wit, the Defensive, I cannot quit with it until I have spoke a little to that Parade in the Ordinary Method which I have alwise so much admired, and to which, in my former pieces upon this subject, I have given the name of *Contre-caveating* Parade.

VIII
Of the Contre-caveating Parade.

This Parade was called long ago by many Masters *Contre-Gavache*, which is as much as to say *A Parade against all Clownish, Pitiful, or Ignorant Fellows*, it being supposed that none but such kind of people would neglect to improve themselves in the true and useful *Art of Defence*. For *Gavache* in French signifies a *Scoundrel* or *Pitiful Fellow*. And such persons being commonly very forward and irregular in their pursuit and thrusts, because of their ignorance and want of Art, and this Cross Parade being the only best defence against them, therefore it seems the ancient Fencing-Masters did chiefly appropriate and recommend it as a sure defence against them.

Now altho' I am abundantly well satisfied as well of the usefulness as justice of this appropriation, yet I cannot but declare, because of the excellency of this Parade, that I think the derivation of its name is taken from too mean and despicable a source.

---

[10] This is the Colichemarche small sword blade, named after the Swedish Count Königsmark, who is credited with its invention. "The characteristic of the Colichemarde blade is the very great breadth of the forte, as compared with the that of the foible. The change is very abrupt; the blade which is stiff and broad in the portion near the hilt, suddenly becoming excessively slender about the region of the half weak." This type of blade was popular between 1685 and 1720, and then disappeared. Castle, 336-7.

And therefore in my former pieces upon this subject, I endeavoured to derive its denomination from a more rational, as well as generous, spring. So that in place of *Contre-Gavache*, I called it the *Contre-caveating* Parade. And my reason for it was that its former name in a manner supposed that it was only necessary and useful against such as were wholly rustick and ignorant of the Art. Whereas by experience we find the quite contrary. And that it is as much, if not more useful against such as have the most subtile Disengagement, as well as the greatest dexterity in making of Feints. And therefore Disengaging and variety of Feints, which depend much upon quick and subtile Disengaging, being that kind of play which is most difficult to oppose in the most expert Artists who take themselves to that method of point-play. And this Cross Parade being the only sure one against it, I was fully convinced that I had a sufficient reason to alter its mean and rustick name of *Conter-Gavache* to the more refined and genteel one of *Contre-caveating* Parade. For indeed it is the only true crosser and opposer of all Disengagings or Feints flowing from them. And therefore being a certain Contrary and Parade for them, it has very justly, I think, acquired from me the name of *Contre-caveating* Parade.

This *Contre-caveating* or crossing Parade is a *Circular* Parade. That is, a man in performing it forms with his sword not only one, but sometimes (according as his adversary shall *Caveat* or shun it) two or three circles, without in the least altering the position of his sword-hand, until he meet with and cross or oppose his adversary's sword. Which is the reason that it is so very excellent a Parade in the Ordinary Method, both against multiplicity of Feints, and also against the wide, irregular, and straggling thrusts of forward and rambling pursuers, as well Ignorants as others. And consequently excellent in an evening or night rencounter, when a man has not much the benefit of his sight, and therefore is necessitate to supply it with that of feeling. Which is done by making dexterously use of this Circular Parade. Whereas the other Parades in *Quarte*, *Tierce*, and *Seconde*, forming but a very small part of the arch of a circle, a man's adversary may the more easily *Caveat* and shun his sword, especially in the dark, and so give home the thrust upon that open. Which, had this *Contre-caveating* Parade been made use of, would have been quite closed and secure.

So that, as I have said in discoursing of a Guard, if any Parade whatsoever may be properly enof compared to a Key which locks up and secures a man from the pursuit or offending designs of his adversary, then this *Contre-caveating* Parade may most justly be compared to a strong Key with a *double cast*, as we say, or which hath *two turns*: so very secure and safe are all such persons who have the practice and address to perform it dexterously. For against all the pursuits from the ordinary Guards, it is a most certain and general defence, and no particular Parade can be compared to it.

Nay, even upon this *Hanging Guard in Seconde* it may very well be made use of, tho' not altogether with so firm and strong a jerk or spring as when the sword-hand is kept in that position which is called the *Quarte*. And the reason of its being not so strong from this Guard does not proceed so much from the position of the sword-hand in *Seconde*, as that in forming the *Contre-caveating* Parade from this *Hanging Guard*, the adversary's sword is only carried aside and upwards. Whereas against the pursuit from the ordinary Guards, the adversary's sword is by this *Contre-caveating* Parade beat violently, not only aside, but downwards.

Now all motions of the sword-hand which tend downwards being both more quick and strong than those which are carried upwards (as I have made evident in the reasons for Advantage Second, to which I remit the reader), it follows that it is chiefly the tendency of the motion of the sword-hand to raise the adversary's sword a little, in carrying of it off, and not the position of the sword-hand in *Seconde* that is the cause of this *Contre-caveating* Parade being somewhat more weakly performed from this *Hanging Guard* than when it is performed with the sword-hand in *Quarte*. Therefore it may be very well made use of in this new *Method of Defence*, as well as in the ordinary one. Altho' not with such a firm and masterly spring. And that for the above-mentioned reason of the oblique elevating motion which the sword-hand makes in performing it.

And indeed it is too good and excellent a Parade to be wholly shuffled out of any *Method of Defence* whatsoever, when a man can possibly make use of it. Which has made me frequently admire why the French Masters, who know very well the great use and benefit of this excellent defence, yet never almost make use of it. But I judge the reason of it to be this: that they are generally much taken (altho' very often to their cost, because of its looseness and uncertainty when they have any Occasion with Sharps) with that method of play which is not only most genteel, but also yields greatest variety of pursuit to themselves, and diversion to the spectators. And this the constant use of the common Parades in *Quarte*, *Tierce*, and *Seconde* sufficiently allows to them, because they can play readily enough all the Lessons against a person who frequently makes use of these Parades. Whereas the truth is this *Contre-caveating*, circular, or Cross Parade confounds all. And if rightly made use of so crosses and opposes all the common Lessons designed against it that a very good Swordman is many times put to his shifts to contrive and find out means, not only to pursue it, but even to Disengage and rid himself from it.

Therefore I earnestly recommend it in all engagements with Sharps, especially against foreward ramblers, or when a man shall be engaged either in the twee-light or dark, when being most uncertain of finding out and opposing his adversary's sword by any of the other Parades, he must despair of certainly meeting with it unless he take himself to, and wholly rely upon this, which is a most secure and general Parade, and such a one as I can never enof recommend to all truely lovers of a good, firm, and certain defence. For in such a juncture a man ought only to regard his own safety and preservation, not the satisfaction and diversion of the spectators by making use of a more genteel, tho' not near so secure and general a Parade as this most certainly is. And which, when judiciously and dexterously made use of, will rarely fail any man upon a pinch, let his adversary's skill or temper be what it will.

IX
Of the Riposte.

This *Term of Art* comes most properly in after the Parade, and depends so very much upon it that without it there would be no such thing as a *Riposte* in Fencing. For a man may have many opportunities of attempting and performing other Lessons and thrusts. But for the Riposte, it is impossible for a man to give it until his adversary either voluntarily, or by compulsion, offers to launch in a thrust; seeing it is consequential to, and must of necessity be performed immediately upon the back of a man's own Parade, and after the adversary's thrusting. Otherwise it absolutely loses its denomination and becomes quite another kind of thrust.

Riposte is an old French word, and signifies *a sudden returning of an answer*, or rather, *a quick and smart Repartee*. It is now a-days rarely made use of except in the *Art of Fencing*, where its signification is much of the nature with the former. For amongst Sword-Men, Riposte (which in the Schools is commonly called *Parieing and thrusting*) is a quick and smart returning of a thrust after a man hath Paried his adversary's. For if a man do not first Parie his adversary's thrust, then it will be either an Exchanged Thrust, or a returned thrust in the time of the adversary's recovering of himself or going off, and not a true Riposte. Which excellent method of play shows a man to be a great Master of the Parade. And together with Binding, as shall be more fully shown hereafter, is the only true battle (especially upon the Ordinary Method) with Sharps.

For in performing any of the other Lessons, a man cannot promise to himself but that he may receive a *Contre-temps* or an Exchanged Thrust upon his pursuit, unless he oppose very dexterously his adversary's sword with his left hand. Which is indeed very useful at all times, but requires a great deal of practice and long habit to become dexterous with it. Whereas if he play from the Riposte, he in a manner incapacitates his adversary from exchanging a thrust. And that by reason that his adversary's

thrust is spent, and his body thereby somewhat disordered before he offer to attack him from the Riposte. So that his adversary being upon his Stretch, and consequently disordered, his body being off its true posture of defence, it is almost impossible for him to prevent a wound from the Riposte, especially if rightly timed, unless he be more than ordinary dexterous at opposing and Parieing with his left hand. The which, together with a most quick recovery of the body, are the only best, altho' I cannot say certain, Contrarys that I know of against a thrust truely and smartly given in from the Riposte. Which is the only Lesson I may say in the *Art of the Sword* which, when right timed, swiftly delivered, and exactly planted, cannot be with certainty prevented. Altho' as I said, it may be now and then by chance, by the most dexterous use of the left hand.

I cannot therefore enof recommend this excellent and secure method of play from the Riposte, in using this *New Guard*, and more especially when playing from the Ordinary Method. But then it is only to such as are Masters of a quick, firm, and sure Parade, which may be very soon acquired by this *New Method of Fencing*, by reason of the great cross performed in Parieing. So that by a little practice, the Riposte will come as quickly from it as from the ordinary Parades in *Quarte* and *Tierce* above the adversary's sword, altho' I must confess not altogether with such a firm and strong spring. Whereas if novices or half-skilled persons should attempt it, it would but lead them to their more quick and certain destruction, seeing they endeavour a pursuit from the Parade which they are not as yet absolutely Masters of. However the sooner any man accustoms himself in School-Play to this excellent and safe pursuit from the Riposte, the sooner will he become Master of it, to adventure upon it in an Occasion with Sharps, especially when he truely designs prejudice to his adversary.

Because if he have not a real design upon his adversary's Life, but only to master him by a more gentle method, he ought to take himself to some less bloody pursuit and offense, such as Commanding, or making thrusts at the wrists, thighs, or leggs (any of which will disable), and wholly forbear this, which, flowing from the Riposte, is a most strong, sure, and destructive kind of pursuit, seeing the thrusts from it come alwise very full and smartly home, and are therefore with great difficulty defended.

X
Of Thrusting and Ecarting the Head.

A man is said to *Thrust* when he makes an attempt to hit his adversary with the point of his weapon. It differs from the following term, *Elongeing*, in this: that a man may Thrust without offering to *Elonge*, because he may be so near to his adversary that the very spring of his sword-arm (especially when accompany'd with the inclining of the trunk of his body forewards) may carry the point home to his adversary's body. Whereas *Elongeing* is very seldom performed without attempting to Thrust. But this nearness to a man's adversary falls out so rarely that when people generally talk of Thrusting, *Elongeing* is almost alwise understood to accompany it.

There are several Errors committed in the Schools with relation to Thrusting, which I shall name that Masters may consider upon them and advise whether they are so material as that it will be worth their while to rectify them. For my own part, I think they ought to be rectified, seeing they are no less contrary to reason than to the rules of Art.

The *First* is their ordering all plain Thrusts to be given in alwise close by the Foible of the adversary's sword: a thing that can only be performed upon a Master's breast-plate because it is scarcely possible almost to get an opportunity to do it in Assault, or at Sharps, unless a man resolve never almost to hit or wound his adversary at all. For it is most certain that the Thrusting or Disengaging close by the Foible of the adversary's sword retards the swiftness of the Thrust extremely. Whereas if a man design to make a swift Thrust, he should be so far from attempting to Thrust close by the Foible of his adversary's sword, that he ought indispensably to cut beneath the hilt. And never offer to Disengage to Thrust until his sword point be advanced upon the same side it is presented, even beyond the adversary's hilt. And thus he cannot fail to make a swift and subtile Thrust, either within and above or below, or without and above the sword, but especially within and below, if he also observe to make the trunk of his body and hand move together, and both of them alwise before his advanced leg, if he is to *Elonge*.

Yea, to make a Thrust the more effectual, a good Artist will not only cut or carry his Thrust home swiftly beneath his adversary's hilt, but to make it resist the better his Parade, and take more upon his body, will also many times Thrust with a *Quarte* position of the sword-hand, without and above the sword, carrying his hilt high and point low towards his adversary's left side; and with a *Tierce* position of the sword-hand, within and beneath it, carrying his hilt low and, as it were, from his adversary's sword, towards his adversary's left side, and the point high towards his right; which will take so very much upon the adversary's body, within and beneath the sword, that unless he have an exceeding quick and firm Parade, especially in the Common Method of Parieing from the other Guards (for upon the *Hanging Guard*, this manner of Thrusting cannot possibly be performed), he will be fair to receive the Thrust. Whereas the ready way to render a Thrust slow and of little effect is, according to the imperfect direction of most Masters, to attempt alwise to Thrust or Disengage close by the Foible of the adversary's sword. A direction most ridiculous, and which I admire they have not of themselves rectified long e're now.

What I have said against Thrusting close by the Foible of the adversary's sword in performing any plain Thrust, holds much more when a man shall either play from Binding or from the Riposte. For in these cases he ought to be so far from keeping by the adversary's sword in Thrusting, that he should immediately, after Binding or securing his adversary's sword, quit with it, and launch home the Thrust as strong and swiftly to the body as possible, and then immediately recover again to his defensive posture. The same is also to do when he plays from the Riposte.

The *Second* is the ordering them alwise to plant or Thrust high, and with the sword-hand also too much in *Quarte*, which is just of a piece with the former. For by Thrusting with the hand so much in *Quarte*, and carrying the sword so high, a man creates to himself three Disadvantages. The *First* is that he directs his Thrust to that part of the body, I mean the breast and ribs, which are strongest, and consequently most difficult to penetrate or wound, being defended with strong cartilages and bones. The *Second* and *Third* are that his Thrust is rendered thereby the shorter and weaker, the further his sword-hand is turned to *Quarte*, and the more high the thrust is planted.

For it is a nice but true rule in planting a Thrust, to endeavour, as much as the nature of the Thrust will allow, to keep the sword and arm constantly upon a level with the shoulder. Which makes not only alwise the longest line, that being likewise the shortest distance betwixt that part of your adversary's body and you, when upon your stretch, but it also falls to be directed and planted against those parts of the body which are not only most difficult to defend, but also a great deal more easily pierced: I mean the lower part of the stomach and belly. Also, when the hand is kept in the true *Quarte*, and the fingers not too much turned up, the Thrust is the stronger, the sword kept the firmer in a man's hand, and consequently not so easily beat out of it. Which is a fault no less undecent in an Assault, than dangerous in an Occasion. Therefore it is good thus to prevent it.

The *Third* is the ordering their Scholars alwise to *Ecart* their head and shoulders at the performing of every Thrust they design within and above or below, or without and above their adversary's sword. Giving for a reason that this *Ecarting* of the head (which they also wrongfully term *Decarting*), together with the thrusting close to the Foible of the adversary's sword, saves them from a *Contre-temps*, or a Thrust at the same time. Whereas there is nothing more false.

For this *Ecarting* of the head, which in French signifies to keep it from the straight line, or out of the way of the enemie's sword, is of little or no use at all for the preventing of an Exchanged Thrust if a man's adversary design it. No more than the attempting to Thrust close by the Foible of the sword, or with the sword-hand in such and such a position of *Tierce*, *Quarte*, or *Seconde* do. Because *First*, however a man may be humor'd to Thrust by the Foible of the sword upon a Master's breast-plate, yet he shall not perhaps in several Assaults get one opportunity to do it, especially if his adversary understand to cross and Bind his sword. *Secondly*, suppose he should Thrust by the Foible of the sword and *Ecart* his head. Yet that can only save him upon one line. And his adversary has no more to do but to shift and alter his sword, and catch him upon its point in another line. For a man's sword cannot be in, nor, when he is Thrusting, Guard or defend two different places at one and the same time.

Therefore the only true and swift way of Thrusting a plain Thrust, either within and above or beneath the sword, or without and above, is, as I before said, by alwise Disengaging or cutting, as we say, beneath the hilt, let the position of your sword-hand be what it will, and carrying the sword as level home as possible, with the head directly above your sword arm. Unless you intend to Thrust in *Quarte* without the sword. In which case you are, as I said, to carry your hilt high and point low towards your adversary's left side. Or in *Tierce* within the sword, and then you are to carry your sword arm and hand low towards your adversary's left side, and point High towards his right. Now in these cases your head cannot be directly above your sword arm, because of your putting your sword-hand voluntarily out of the straight line in Thrusting, that it may take the more upon your adversary's body. And for preventing of an Exchanged Thrust, if your adversary design one, there is no other more certain method under Heaven than to oppose and carry off his sword with your left hand, in the time you are delivering your Thrust.

These directions are good and safe, as they are great rectifications in the Common Method of teaching. And are also kind of Secrets, if there be any such in Fencing, whereby to Thrust swift and subtily most kind of Thrusts, especially upon the inside.

And this brings me to the *Fourth* Error, which is the ordering their Scholars to throw the left hand either behind them, or to stretch it out along their left-side at the delivery of every Thrust. And the reason they give for it is because, say they, it balances a man's body, and so makes him the more firm when he is upon his *Elonge*.

I shall not deny but this keeping back of the left hand may balance the body a little. But I am very certain a man sustains a far greater prejudice by his losing in a manner the benefit of his left hand for the opposing of his adversary's sword, and thereby preventing a *Contre-temps* or Exchanged Thrust, when in an Occasion, than he can possibly reap advantage by the assistance it gives him for the more easie balancing of his body. Because when a man's left hand is thus thrown out of the way upon the delivery of every Thrust, he loses almost a whole Time before he can bring it forward again, either to oppose his adversary's sword for the better defending himself from a *Contre-temps*, Exchanged Thrust, or Thrust from the Riposte, if his adversary should design any of these against him; or, before he can be ready with it, to catch hold of his adversary's sword when himself intends either to Enclose and Grapple or Command.

So that the only true way for a man in an Occasion is not only to make use of a good and firm Parade when he is upon the defence, but also to assist it with the left hand, when needful. And which he ought therefore to have alwise in readiness upon the delivery of all his Thrusts, and not to bring from behind his back when he does perhaps need it, either to oppose his adversary's thrust, secure himself upon his own, in case of a designed *Contre-temps* and Exchanged Thrust (against which it is absolutely one of the best remedies Sword-Men have), or to catch hold of his adversary's sword if he should resolve to Enclose upon and Command him.

These are the benefits which a good Sword-Man reaps by a seasonable assisting himself with his left hand, all which he is frustrate of when it is, contrary to all reason, thrown behind him. Therefore I wish this abuse, or rather neglect, of the assistance of the left hand, may be rectified with the above-mentioned Errors in Thrusting. For the right placing of which hand, either when a man pitches himself first to his Guard, or when Thrusting, see the positions of the left hands of Figures 1, 4, 5, & 9 [p. 96, 100, 109].

The exact method of Parieing dexterously, and Thrusting swiftly and subtily a plain Thrust being the foundation of all true Fencing, has been the occasion of my being more particular upon these two *Terms of Art* than upon several of the rest. And indeed they are of such consequence to all who really intend to become good Sword-Men that it were in some measure better for them to be almost altogether ignorant of many of the other branches of Fencing than of these two. Because altho' a man be pretty expert in the performing most of the other Lessons commonly taught in the Ordinary Method, yet if he be imperfect in the practice of these two *Terms of Art*, the understanding of the rest will avail him but very little, especially in an Occasion with Sharps. Whereas if he be absolutely Master of a firm and sure Parade, and of a quick and subtile method of delivering a smart plain Thrust, he may very well dispense with a great many of the other Lessons which are taught in the Schools more out of form, and for the rendering a man more adroit and dexterous at the delivering of a true plain Thrust, than for any other great benefit can redound to him from them in an Encounter with Sharps.

Therefore I entreat my reader that for his greater & more certain improvement in this most useful Art, he would chiefly apply himself to the practice of them; either while he is at School, under the conduct and instruction of a Fencing Master; or in his own chamber, where he is only assisted by the natural address, and assiduous application, of a smart and judicious comrade. And let him rely upon my word for it that he shall not be long without reaping the benefit I propose to him by it. For not to be Master of a good and sure Parade, and of a quick and subtile method of delivering a plain Thrust, and to be a good and dexterous Sword-Man, are, in my opinion, very incompatible.

XI
Of Elongeing, or Making an Elonge.

When a man is not so near to his adversary as that he can reach him by only stretching out of his sword-arm and inclining forewards with his body, without moving of his advanced foot, then there is a necessity for him to step out with his right foot, that so his thrust may take effect. And this is what we call an *Elonge*.

Elongeing then, is a vigorous, sudden, and quick moving foreward of the right foot, keeping at the same time the left immoveable, and is performed with a pretty violent kind of stretch, occasioned by the eager desire of the pursuer to hit or wound his adversary, and without which he could not many times reach him. It is derived from the French word *Alonger*, which signifies to lengthen, or to stretch out. And indeed in this action, a man both lengthens his thrust and stretches his Limbs many times to the full. Otherwise he would often come short of his adversary, and so thrust in vain.

Some Masters advise their Scholars that they may the better keep their left foot fixed (which is a very material circumstance in *Elongeing*), to couch the inside of it towards the ground, pretending that they are kept thereby more fixt, and not so apt to stumble or fall forewards towards their adversary. Others again disapprove of this method, and direct the keeping only of the left heel close to the ground, and affirm that this keeps a man altogether as firm upon his limbs in an *Elonge* as the former doth.

And in my opinion, of these two methods, this last is the best and most sure. Because it is by fixing of the left heel, and not the toe, or couching the foot, that all the body is kept firm upon an *Elonge*. For if the heel be loose, a man can never have any assurance of a quick recovery from a stretch, which is the only end for which it is directed.

Again, there are other Masters, and those of the greatest esteem, particularly M. de Liancour, who condemn both the former methods of either couching the left foot, or keeping its heel fixed in an *Elonge*. And in place of both, order a man to keep his left foot flat and firm upon its sole, without altering of it, and maintain that a man is not only as firm upon an *Elonge* this way, but also that he will *Elonge* or stretch as far this way as when his foot is couched to one side.

As to this last assertion, of a man's stretch being fully as long this way as when his foot is couched, I confess I cannot agree to it. Because certainly, when a man's foot is upon its sole as he is stretching, there is a kind of angle formed at the ankle, betwixt the inside of the foot and leg, when he makes his stretch, which certainly shortens his *Elonge*. Whereas the couching of the foot advances a little the left leg in stretching, and so takes away the above-mentioned angle. Which if it do, must certainly so much lengthen the *Elonge*, as itself was advanced. But as for the other, which is a man's being as firm and fixed upon it as when the heel only is kept fast, I altogether approve of it, especially in an Occasion with Sharps. Because whatever large stretches a man may venture upon in a School-Assault by couching of his foot, yet it is dangerous, either in the Fields or upon a street, to make such overreaches from whence a man can scarcely recover himself without the assistance, sometimes, of his left hand upon the ground, to keep him from falling forwards.

For altho' in the Schools, great and long stretches make a good appearance and are mightily cryed up, yet in an Engagement nothing can be more dangerous, because of the opportunity it gives a man's adversary to Riposte him before he can recover to his defence. And therefore one of the chief directions at Sharps is never to couch the left foot, nor to *Elonge* too unreasonably. The first keeping a man firm and fixed, and the other assisting him to a quick recovery of his body after his *Elonge*, that thereby he may prevent his adversary's thrusts from the Riposte.

All *Elongeing* ought to be performed vigorously and with life; at which the French are most dexterous; which gives them generally so swift a hand in performing a plain Thrust, that it comes home upon a man with such swiftness as if it were darted from a cross-bow. For nothing is more unbecoming, and appears more dull, than to see a man *Elongeing* as if he were half asleep, and had neither strength nor spirits. And as the stretching is to be performed with mettle and earnestness, so with no less vigour and quickness ought the recovery to be finished. Without which a man can never pretend to come off safe from an Exchanged and Riposted Thrust.

XII
Of Caveating, or Disengaging.

Whether it was the observing the natural but cunning motions which cocks make with their heads in fighting, to shun and evite the strokes of their adversary's beaks, or some other such like observation that gave the first rise to this *Term of Art* in Fencing, is neither certain, nor very material to be known. But to give a short and true definition of it, is, I think, altogether proper and necessary. And the rather, that it was this very *Caveating* or *Disengaging* which gave the chief rise to this *New Method of Fencing*, or *New Guard*, I have all along been so much recommending.

Caveating or Disengaging is a motion whereby a man brings in an instant his sword, which was presented upon any side of his adversary's, generally beneath its hilt, to the opposite side. And this he can do so often as he pleases, from within to without, and from without to within; from having its point high to be low, and from having it low to be high; either upon the same side it is presented, or upon the opposite side.

It is so very necessary a motion in Fencing, that without it there could be scarcely any offensive part or pursuit at all; at least it would be but very slow. And it is also so easily and quickly performed against the ordinary *Tierce* and *Quarte* Guards, that it gives a constant opportunity to make variety of most quick and subtile Feints against them. Which, by reason of the small cross made by the weapons upon these Guards, makes the pursuit very easie, and the defence or Parade extremely difficult. As I have clearly demonstrate in the Second Advantage, to which I remit the Reader.

It was indeed the great opportunity those Guards alwise give for a sudden Disengaging (which is the source of all quick and subtile Feints, and consequently of a great uncertainty in the defence) that first put me upon the search of this *New Method*. Which by reason of its great cross upon the adversary's sword, renders the Disengaging or making of Feints more slow, and consequently the pursuit or offensive part, and for the very same reason, the Parade, more certain. So that hereby the Ordinary Method is quite renversed, and in place of the pursuit being quick and the Parade uncertain, whereby a man's Life was in continual hazard, the pursuit is now rendered slow and the Parade a great deal more certain. And thereby a man's Life not in near so great danger, which was my whole and only aim, and which I hope will

meet with an approbation as general as the Parade or defence flowing from it is secure and universal. I shall therefore say no more in commendation of it here, having done it sufficiently by a mathematical demonstration in the Scheme, in the middle of the Plate, to which I refer the reader. And which I take to be a sufficient warrant for all I can possibly offer or say in its behalf.

XIII
Of Feints.

A *Feint* is much of the same nature with Caveating or Disengaging, and is a motion whereby a man's adversary, with any kind of weapon, endeavours either only to make an Open upon him whereby he may have an opportunity to thrust, or to make him believe that he designs to give home his thrust at one part of the body, when he really intends to give it in upon another. It is but an uncertain kind of play, and not much to be ventur'd upon in an Occasion, except when it is preceeded by Binding.

As there are two methods of making of Feints, so there are several kinds of Feints. Which I shall but just name, that this may serve as a common place where they may be all found at one view, having descrived them exactly in the *Scots Fencing Master*. It is certain that a man may make a Feint towards any part of the body. And in this respect, there may be as many Feints as there are different parts of a man's body to aim them at. But as this would but lead men into confusion, therefore it hath been thought fit to restrict them chiefly to these seven following.

1*mo*. There are the *Single and Double Feints Within and Without the Sword*. For a Triple Feint is not to be made use of, by reason of the great opportunity it gives to a man's adversary to take Time upon him. Which is alwise most conveniently done, either upon a man's advancing, as he is a raising of his advanced foot to approach; or as he is making of any Feint which is not preceeded by a securing of the sword, or Binding.

2*do*. The *Single and Double Feints Above and Without the Sword*, commonly called the Single and Double Feints at the Head or Eyes.

3*tio*. The *Low Feints at the Belly Without the Sword, Single and Double*. And

4*to*. the *Single Feint Within and Above the Sword*, called in the Schools *Volte Coupé*; but improperly, for the true name in French is *Botte Coupé*, which is as much as to say a thrust cut short of its expected reach. For *botte* in French signifies a thrust. So that this Feint, being made within and above the sword, with the hand turned a little more in *Quarte* than ordinary, and then instantly falling low with the thrust towards the belly, the sword-hand but altered a little more to the *Tierce* than when the Feint was made, it is very properly denominate a cut, or foreshortn'd thrust because the Feint, which was expected to be the motion of the thrust, is stopt and converted into a thrust at the belly, within and below the sword.

These are the most frequently practiced Feints in the Common Method of Fencing. And although a man may invent many more Feints to other parts of the body, yet the most of them will alwise terminate in one of these seven I have named. But indeed this *New Method* I am now upon will not well admit of so many, for I restrict it chiefly to the Single and Double Feints Without and Above, and Without and Beneath the sword; seeing many would but embarrass a man, and not answer so well my design, which is to set down no directions or Lessons but what are in a manner absolutely necessary.

Now as there are several kinds of Feints, so there are, as I before hinted, two methods of making Feints. The *First* and least secure are these I have named, by reason that they are only simple motions made with the sword (without being preceeded with any spring or securing cross upon the adversary's sword) to deceive and cheat a man's adversary out of the security he puts himself into by keeping a good posture of defence, from whence he may bring a firm and sure Parade. And therefore, as I said, a man may be readily surprised, and catch'd upon the performing of them, by a right tristed [engaged] Time. Whereas the *Second* and most secure method of making Feints is by first engaging, as it were, the adversary's sword, either by Binding or a springing cross, which are much about one, before a man attempt to make either his Single or Double Feint. For by thus securing of his adversary's sword before he make his Feint, whether Single or Double, but also very much incapacitates his adversary from catching him upon Time. Therefore if a man will make use of Feints, let him make chiefly use of these last mentioned, which are alwise preceeded by a Beat, Binding, or a springing cross. And then he may venture upon them, not only with the more confidence & assurance, but also rely upon them for a greater success than if he should wholly attempt them without any such pre-engagement of his adversary's sword.

There is also another point in relation to Feints which deserves to be decided. And that is whether a man, in making of his Feints, should accompany each motion of his sword with an *Appel*, as the French call it, or with a beat upon the ground with his advanced foot, or not?

Those who are for it, assert that the *Appel*, or challenge of the advanced foot, surprises a man oft times more than the motion of the sword, and so obliges him more certainly to give an Open than if the *Feint* were only performed with the sword alone. Because that motion may be sometimes so very quick and subtile,

as scarcely to be discerned. Whereas the noise of the adversary's foot upon the ground, when the challenge or *Appel* is given to answer it, is a kind of advertisement and alarm, which a man can scarcely resist or refrain from answering.

To give my opinion in this matter, I think both methods are good, according to the adversary that a man hath to deal with. For if it be with an unskillful person, then certainly an *Appel* or challenge, sometimes with the foot, accompanying the motion of the sword, can never do prejudice, but rather make the alarm the stronger, whereby the Open will be the more readily given.

But if the adversary be an Artist, and especially if the Engagement be upon the street or in the Fields, then in both these cases I am altogether against the *Appel*, or motion of the advanced foot, accompanying the motion of the Feint, and that for two reasons.

First, the *Appel*, or motion with the foot, certainly retards the swiftness of the Feint. Which being thus rendered slow, makes the thrust long a coming home, and so will but very rarely take against a good Artist. And that it does retard the motion of the *Feint*, is what cannot be denied by any having the least knowledge in Fencing. For it is most evident that a quick and swift handed Artist is capable from the *Quarte* Guard, without the *Appel*, or motion of his advanced foot, to make so subtile a Feint that it shall appear but as the twinkle of an eye, and not take half the time that a man must of necessity take to raise his foot and set it down again, which he must do in an *Appel*.

Secondly, If the Engagement be upon the street, or in the Fields, then the *Appel*, or alarm of the advanced foot, is still of less use; because in this case it cannot be heard, as upon a Fencing-School floor, and therefore all it would signify would be to render slow the Feint, and thereby give a man's adversary the better opportunity to Parie it.

From whence I conclude that when a man designs only to make a slow Feint, as if it were to sift and try his adversary, to know how they will take with him; in that case, he may accompany the motion of his sword-hand with that *Appel*, or alarm of his advanced foot. But if he intend to make a Feint, that execution may really follow upon it, then he is not only not to give any *Appel*, or challenge with his advance foot, but also to make the motion with his sword as quick and subtil as it is possible for him to perform it. That so he may the more certainly delude his adversary.

This is my opinion as to Feints made from the ordinary *Quarte* and *Tierce* Guards. But such quick and subtile Feints cannot be performed against this *Hanging Guard in Seconde* I so much commend, by reason of the great angle it makes with the adversary's sword, which certainly retards them. And therefore the constant use of it is an excellent Contrary to Feints, by reason of its sloping point. For which it ought to be mightily valued and esteemed before any other Guard whatsoever; especially seeing this sloping position of it answers exactly the greatest Contrary which the French Masters have against the common Feints within and without the sword, when they order alwise their Scholars, upon variety of their adversary's Feints, either to take Time and thrust out upon him, or otherwise to *baisser la pointe*, or stop their sword's point: in my opinion, the much more rational, as well as secure, direction and Contrary of the two.

XIV
Of Time.

In the language of Sword-Men, by *Time* is not meant that continual flux of moments whereof our short duration in this world is composed. For certainly in this acceptation there can be neither motion, nor thrust, but what is truely performed in Time. That is, there are alwise some moments of Time required wherein to execute them. But by Time, in the *Art of Fencing*, is understood a certain opportunity which a man takes the benefit of, either to perform some kind of Lesson or thrust while his adversary is not as yet thrusting, or even the preventing of his adversary, by wounding him and saving of himself in the very same instant of Time that his adversary is advancing upon, or thrusting at him. And this without so much as offering first to cross or secure his adversary's sword, before he attempt it. And it is alwise, as I said, performed upon the first moving of the adversary's advanced foot.

Now as there is nothing more commendable in an expert Sword-Man than his never losing, but, upon the contrary, his performing alwise his designs upon the first kind of artificial Time. So, in my opinion, there is nothing more uncertain and dangerous than for a man frequently to make use of this last for prevention. Yea, I am so much against it, that whatever may be allowed to a man for his divertisement in School-Play, yet in an Occasion the taking the opportunity of it ought to be so much condemned, that in such a juncture it should not be so much as thought of, let alone put in practice.

For even in taking the first kind of Time, no man can be sure, except it be from the Riposte, or that he oppose his left hand, but he may receive an Exchanged Thrust before he recover to a posture of defence from his discharged thrust. How much uncertainty then must there be, and to how much evident and unnecessary danger does a man expose himself in an Occasion with Sharps, by making use of the last and most uncertain kind of Time, which is performed without the least securing of the adversary's sword?

I know that the taking this kind of Time, tho' most dangerous, is much approved of and admired by many, even great Masters in this Art. For my own part, I wish them good success in it, but shall never advise my friends to make use of it out of an Assaulting School, unless they intend that their Life shall be of as short continuance as the uncertain Time wherein they designed to bereave their adversaries of theirs.

Therefore, wholly disapproving of such an uncertain, deceitful, and dangerous kind of play, especially with Sharps, which does many times occasion the loss of men's Lives, many people, by reason of the wrong notion they have of it, being frequently induced to make use of it, even with sword in hand, I earnestly recommend to all skillful persons who have any regard for their Lives, that in an Occasion with Sharps, they never so much as think (except upon the greatest pinch imaginable) of thrusting upon Time. That is, without first Engaging, crossing, or securing their adversary's sword, or forcing it out of the way by a springing beat, before they thrust themselves. It being impossible for any man to venture upon it without at the same time hazarding his Life, and in a manner, by a seen disadvantage, exposing himself to his enemy.

Let then this ventorious, uncertain, and dangerous play upon Time, never take place (except, as I said, upon a great necessity), but only for a man's divertisement when he is Assaulting in the Schools. And even then let it be accompanyed with the assistance of the left hand, for the better preventing of a *Contre-temps*, or Exchanged Thrust. This advice is of very great importance to such as intend to become truely great Sword-Men, by being Masters of a firm and sure Defence, and consequently of a secure *Method of Play*, against all kind of humors whatsoever, for the better Preservation of their Honour and Lives.

XV
Of a Contre-temps, and an Exchanged Thrust; and How They Differ.

In Fencing Schools, by a *Contre-temps* is commonly understood a thrust given in at the same time that a man's adversary thrusts. Which I think but a very imperfect definition of it. Because certainly for any man to thrust without having an Open, as we commonly term it, or some part of his adversary's body so discovered as that he has reason to make a thrust upon it, or without having, by the neglect of his adversary, or by his own forcing it upon him, a reasonable opportunity to give in a thrust, is as much to thrust in *Contre-temps*, as to thrust at the very same time a man's adversary is discharging of his thrust against him. And therefore by a *Contre-temps* is to be understood every attempt to thrust without having a convenient opportunity offered, either voluntarily by ones adversary, or thro' his ignorance and neglect. Or without having at least forced an Open upon him, which is certainly the safest of any; because a man's adversary may discover the first out of a design. But this last kind of Open, or opportunity, is what he cannot prevent, it being in a manner altogether forced upon him, and he compelled to it, quite contrary to his inclination. So that by this explication you see the signification of the word *Contre-temps* is of greater extent than what hath been allowed to it formerly by most Masters. And indeed nothing discovers more a man's ignorance in Fencing than to be frequently guilty of offering thrusts in *Contre-temps*, when himself hath neither forced, nor his adversary given, any opportunity or Open, or by alwise thrusting upon his adversary's thrust without offering first to Parie. Whereby *Contre-temps* and *Exchanged Thrusts* do most frequently follow.

Many people confound a *Contre-temps* with an Exchanged Thrust, fancying that whatever is an Exchanged Thrust must also be a *Contre-temps*. In which they are mightily mistaken. For tho' it cannot be denied but where there is a *Contre-temps* made, there may also proceed an Exchanged Thrust from it, and *vice versa*, a *Contre-temps* may be very rightly denominate such upon the giving of some certain Exchanged Thrusts. Yet, strictly speaking, there may be a *Contre-temps* where there is no Exchanged Thrust, and an Exchanged Thrust given which was not at all in *Contre-temps*.

For instance when a man, as I said, thrusts upon his adversary without any design, or having the least opportunity for it, then he certainly thrusts in *Contre-temps*, altho' no Exchanged Thrust follow upon it. Again, when a man's adversary thrusts upon him and wounds him, yet he, before his adversary recovers his body or goes out of his Measure, gives home a thrust upon him whereby he wounds his adversary. In this case it cannot be denied but that here is a fair Exchanged Thrust. But I am sure, without the least appearance of a *Contre-temps*. For there could not be a more proper opportunity for him to return the equivalent of the wound he received, than in the time his adversary's body was recovering from his thrust with which he had wounded him, and with which his adversary's body was certainly disordered, not only as he gave it in, but also in the recovering of the body to a posture of defence after it.

But to make this yet more clear, you are to know that there are three very different kinds of thrusts which any man may receive upon his pursuit, besides that upon Time, and which few Masters know how to (at least do not) distinguish as they ought. Which neglect or inadvertancy hath been certainly the rise of the foregoing mistake, and of the false definition of a true *Contre-temps*. And these three are: *First*, a thrust from the true Riposte, or back of a man's own Parade; *Secondly*, a thrust upon the adversary's recovering of his body, or going off, when he hath not given the wound; and the *Third* is an Exchanged Thrust upon the adversary's recovery, or going off, after he hath fairly given a thrust or wound. Now you see all these three thrusts differ. And yet they are taken by many for one and the same kind of thrust, and, except that from the true Riposte, go for the most part under the name of a *Contre-temps*. Whereas there is nothing more false, because the other two Time*s* for returning a thrust have not only nothing of a *Contre-temps* in them, but are also very true and good Time*s* to return and repay the equivalent of what a man may have received from his adversary. So that it is hereby very evident that a true *Contre-temps* and an Exchanged Thrust are not alwise one and the same thing, altho' sometimes they indeed are. And therefore I judged it not amiss to discover this distinction, which many have hitherto disputed.

I remember also that I have often heard it debate whether or not an Ignorant could possibly take Time, and consequently give an Artist a *Contre-temps*. It was my opinion, and still is, that no man altogether ignorant of the Art of the Sword can either certainly take a true Time upon an Artist, or *Contre-temps* him. And my reason for it was that being ignorant of, and not sensible when his adversary gave Opens to him, he could not reap the advantage of these opportunities.

But to be ingenuous, this is but Fencing-School quibble. For altho' an Ignorant cannot, as an Artist doth, either certainly take a true offered Time, or *Contre-temps*, upon his adversary's taking of one against him, yet he can do that which is equivalent. Which is, he may either by chance thrust at the same time his adversary is thrusting, by which means both may come to receive a wound. Or he may thrust by chance so seasonable, after his adversary has spent his thrust upon him, that before his adversary recovers to his defence, he may receive a thrust from him. And I hope a thrust is a thrust, whether it be given by way of *Contre-temps*, or Exchanged Thrust.

So that if an Ignorant can wound an Artist any way, tho' but by mere chance, then it is as ridiculous to say that he hath not thereby gained an advantage over the Artist, altho' the thrust can neither be said to be given in a true Time, nor upon a designed *Contre-temps*; as it was folly in a certain person, as the story goes, to be extremely dissatisfied at himself because of his wounding his adversary with the sword-hand in *Quarte*, whereas, in his opinion, the thrust ought to have been given according to the rules, with his sword-hand either in *Tierce* or *Seconde*.

And this also discovers another mistake many Masters are in, who maintain that a true taken Time hath no Contrary. 'Tis true, strictly speaking, and according to the nicest rule, a true taken Time has no Contrary. But then it may meet with that which is equivalent: that is, with an Exchanged Thrust. For as I have said, after a man hath taken most exactly and nicely a true Time upon his adversary, yet if he do not recover quickly enof after his thrust to a true defence, or more properly defend himself by opposing his left hand in his going off from his thrust, he may come to receive a wound. By which it appears that upon a true taken Time, a man can receive an Exchanged Thrust. Which, altho' strictly speaking, it be no Contrary to it, nor is indeed occasioned by his taking of the Time, but by his slow recovering of himself. Yet seeing he received it upon that occasion, it is of the same nature with a true Contrary to Time, and brings the same prejudice to his person as it were one, or as if the taking this dangerous and uncertain Time had been the cause of it. For wounds are still wounds, let a man receive them as he will. And altho' they may differ with respect to the artificial distinction given to them by some too nice and critical Artists, which at best is but a jangle of words, yet upon the matter, by their effects, and with respect to the person who has the misfortune to receive them, they are the very same as if they were true Contrarys to the taking of Time, and do alike bring many times certain and inevitable Death along with them.

Therefore, wholly disapproving of such quibbling and fallacious distinctions, which are of no other use but to deceive people many times out of their Lives, I wish sword-men would rather endeavour to support and defend their Art by solid reasoning and a firm and secure method of play than by such weak sophisms. Which, in place of encouraging and advantaging, do rather a great deal of prejudice both to the Art and those who profess it.

can never be approved of at Sharps by any, but such whose judgements are as little to be relyed upon as the fickle, dangerous, and uncertain play which they so fervently, but indeed most unreasonably, patronize. So I leave them to enjoy their beloved opinion, in which, altho' I may wish them, yet I am certain they can never have very great success. Especially in an Occasion, wherein it is not possible for any man to be too wary and secure in the method of his pursuit, because of the bad consequences which may attend it, were it otherwise. That is, being dangerous as well as uncertain, by running all upon taking of Time, or *Dequarteing* alone, or *Dequarteing* and *Volting* after other. All very diverting Lesson*s* indeed with Foils in a School, but most uncertain and dangerous pursuits at Sharps in the Field. Besides, that the thrusts commonly delivered from them are so feeble and weak that they are may times scarcely capable of piercing to the ribs, far less through them, or the cartilage of the breast, the ordinary parts people plant at (altho' very disadvantageously), according to the common directions for planting. Whereas I never value a thrust but what, by the smartness and strength of it, is capable to enter the body at least five or six inches, and even pierce the edge of a rib or cartilage, should it meet with them in its passage.

For this strong and manly method of thrusting not only penetrates to the quick, but even to the noble and inward parts. Whereas the other, upon Time, is in a manner only superficial and scurfing: that is, more proper for diversion in an Assault, than for obtaining a just Satisfaction in the Field.

XVI
Of Dequarting and Volting.

Dequarteing and *Volting*, being both of them performed upon Time, and also off the straight line. The *First*, by *Volting*, or turning the body backwards upon the foot next one's adversary, as the center, giving him at the same time the thrust (and opposing the left hand to prevent a *Contre-temps*) in the time the adversary is either passing, or giving in a plain Thrust within or without the sword: which are the most proper times for this Lesson. And the *Second*, by making a kind of circular leap toward the adversary's left-side in giving in the thrust, as he is also either a-passing, or thrusting upon you. I place them in the same categorie with Time, and advise no man to make use of either of them upon an Occasion, unless, that by his thus ventorious and dangerous turning from the straight line (the only true line at Sharps, when a man is not to break Measure), he resolve to have his soul very quickly and suddenly turned out of its fickle and circulating habitation.

For certainly such an uncertain, dangerous, and pyroiting [pirouetting] kind of play is only proper for a School Assault, and

XVII
Of Binding, or Securing the Sword; and Beating.

Having discovered the uncertainty and danger, as well of playing frequently off the streight line by *Dequarteing* or *Volting*, and of much using what Artists call *Taking of Time*; and disswaded people from the frequent practice of either, especially at Sharps; I shall now proceed to a *Term of Art* from whence a much more secure and safe method of pursuit does flow than from that of either Taking of Time, *Dequarteing*, or *Volting*. And it is *Binding*, *Securing*, or *Crossing* the sword with a pressure, accompanied with a spring from the wrist as it is a-performing.

You are to know that by these three different words, I mean one and the same thing. And as the play flowing from this is diametrically opposite to that of Taking Time, so as that from Time is (as I have frequently said, and cannot repeat it too often) a most uncertain and dangerous method of pursuit; this is a most masterful and secure one. For unless a man by some kind of cross secure, as it were, or render his adversary's sword incapable to offend him during the time of his performing a Lesson upon him, it is impossible for him to be certain but that he may receive from his adversary either a fortuitous *Contre-temps*, or an Exchanged Thrust before the recovery of his body, or going off, after a thrust. But if he disorder his adversary's sword by Beating it, with a crossing kind of spring, out of the streight line before he deliver his own thrust, then he may look upon himself in such a condition, as that he may safely perform his designed Lesson. And that still with the more certainty if it be judiciously accompanied at the time of its delivery with the opposing of the left hand.

In this excellent method of crossing with a spring the adversary's sword before the performing most Lesson*s*, does wholly consist the true and safe *Method of Fencing*, especially in an Occasion. And whatever Lesson*s* are not preceeded by this, are not to be reputed of any security. So that a man can never attempt the performing of them, particularly those upon Time, but at the same time he mightily exposes himself. Whereas by his first Binding or crossing his adversary's sword with a kind of spring, he is much more secure, and in a manner defended, in the very time that he is offending, by rendering his adversary in some measure incapable, not only to offend him in the time of his pursuit, but also himself better prepared for his own defence. Which he is not at all, when he plays upon Time.

Besides, it is worth observation that when a sword-man who understands it, quits this secure method of play from Binding or securing his adversary's sword, and offers frequently at the catching him upon Time, especially at Sharps, it is, I say, a very shroud [shrewd] token that he is brought to a great pinch. And being sensible that he is not capable to make good either his pursuit or defence, according to true Art, because of his own imperfection therein, is therefore resolved, by thus abandoning it, to rely more upon Chance than Skill, either for his own preservation, or for the overcoming his adversary. A method so very uncertain and desperate that it ought not to be so much as thought of, far less put in practice by a good sword-man, until he be reduced to the greatest extremity, and as it were, beyond the very utmost limits of all true Art and Skill, so that it can be of no use to him. Which is a circumstance not to be supposed. Because when a man fails in the certainty of his defence, it proceeds alwise from his own frail weakness and maladroitness, and never from any imperfection or unsufficiency in the Art. Which if judiciously put in practice, is undoubtedly capable to furnish a true and most certain defence. Besides that, it is always more sure, as well as more reasonable, for a man, so far as he can, to keep still by the principles and true rules of Art, than wholly to abandon them, and by frequent catching at Time, inconsiderately submit himself, for his preservation or victory, to the uncertain determination of a blind and fortuitous Chance.

I know that the great objection made by some people, particularly those Time-Catchers, against the frequent use of Binding, is that when a man, in performing it, cleaves too much to his adversary's sword, he is liable to his adversary's Slipping of him, and consequently of receiving either a plain Thrust, or one from a *Feint*. But this objection is easily answered. For *First*, it ought to be a man's chiefest care, who makes much use of Binding, to prevent as much as possible his adversary's Slipping of his sword, while he is in that action. Which he may easily do, if he perform it with judgement, and with a springing motion, as I said, of the wrist, so that he suffer not his sword to go too far from the straight line of his adversary's body. *Secondly*, if thro' eagerness he do cleave a little more to his adversary's sword than is needful, yet he ought always to be so ready with the cross, or circulating *Contre-caveating* Parade, as still to be in readiness to meet with, and cross his adversary's sword, should he offer to Slip him when he is going to Bind. And whoever neglects these two most useful precautions in Binding or securing his adversary's sword, is guilty of a gross escape in Fencing, according to its strictest rules.

But why should we by surprised at peoples making many Times great escapes in Fencing, contrary to all its safe injunctions and excellent rules? Especially when what they are to execute, either by way of prevention or otherwise, is for the most part so quick and sudden that they have scarcely time allowed them for a thought, far less to consider and reflect upon what ought to be done, according to its nicest rules; when even the best of men make frequently gross and most unaccountable escapes in point of morals, notwithstanding of their having the opportunity and time for a sedate and serious reflection, whereby they might with the more ease prevent them. The proverb then is but too generally true, and holds no less in Fencing than in other subjects: *that it is far more easie to give, than to take or follow, a good advice and counsel.*

Seeing then the frequent taking of Time is not only uncertain, but most dangerous in an Occasion where a man's Life is at stake. And that a man, by so doing, bids, in a manner, a voluntary *Adieu* to all true and sure Art by Fencing, as we say, at random or hap-hazard, and without the least certainty. I say, seeing this hazardous, or rather Lottery method of play (for it deserves no better name) is so very little to be relyed upon, especially at Sharps, because of its fickleness and uncertainty, may the security proceeding from a springing cross upon your adversary's sword, commonly called Binding, highly recommend to you, notwithstanding of the former weak objection, the frequent practice of it. Whereby you will not only prevent many a *Contre-temps* and even Exchanged Thrust, before recovery or going off, after your thrust, but also acquire that which is the chief scope and design, not only of this essay, but truely also of the whole Art itself. That is, *A Judicious, Safe, and Regular Method of Of-fence*, and *A Firm, Vigorous, and Secure Defence*. Which are all necessarily requisite before a man can justly pretend to that very desireable and much wished for, but indeed rarely deserved character, of being really a great Master of the most *Noble, Heroick, and Truely Useful Art of Defence*. An Art possessed by very few, tho' coveted by many. An Art that will never deceive or fail any who practice it truely and judiciously. And which is con-temned by none, but such as are wholly ignorant and destitute, not only of its worth and use, but also of that couragious bold-ness and assurance it gratefully bestows upon all who admire and with judgement practise it.

For what I have said more relative to Binding, and which is very material to be known, I remit the reader to the *Terms of Art*: *Fort* and *Foible*, explained in the 3d. Article of this Chapter. As for Beating, the difference betwixt Binding and it consists chiefly in this: that Binding is performed not only with a kind of spring, but also a man in performing it keeps by and engages (by a kind of pressure) more his adversary's sword than when he Beats. For which reason Binding is mostly proper when a man intends to become the pursuer. Whereas Beating, being performed by a kind of jerk or dry stroak, it is chiefly designed for the defensive part or Parade. That so a man may return the quicker Riposte from it, seeing his sword, if the Beat be rightly performed, will in some measure rebound, as it were, from his adversary's sword, and so assist him to make the quicker Riposte. Besides, that this jerk or dry Beat upon the Parade forces the adversary's sword considerably out of the streight line, which makes the Riposte still the more certain, and which cannot be done with near that certainty nor strength with the Ordinary French Parades within and without the sword from the *Quarte* Guard. Which is the reason I so much condemn them in an Occasion.

There are two kind of Beats. The *First* is performed with the Foible of a man's sword upon the Foible of his adversary's. Which in the Schools is commonly called *Baterie*, from the French word *Batre*, and is proper enof to be made use of upon a man's pur-suit, to make an Open upon his adversary. But this is not compa-rable to Binding for this purpose, because this Baterie is not only performed at a pretty distance, only a little out of the streight line of the body, so that he quickly brings it in again. Whereas Binding, being performed not only with a spring, but a kind of cleaving to, or pressure upon, the adversary's sword, it is there-fore the only true and certain method upon a man's pursuit to force an Open upon his adversary. And therefore I much prefer it to this first kind of Beating, which goes under the name of Baterie.

The *Second* and best kind of Beat is performed with the Fort of a man's sword upon the Foible of his adversary's. Not with a spring, as Binding is, but with a jerk or dry Beat. And is there-fore most proper for the Parades without or within the sword, as I said, because of the rebound a man's sword has thereby from his adversary's, whereby he procures to himself the better and surer opportunity of Riposting. Altho' it may be also made use of in the pursuit to force an Open, as well as Baterie. But neither of them being so strong, or rather forcing, as Binding, I therefore prefer it far to either of them for the procuring an Open from the adversary upon a pursuit. And this second kind of Beat (that is with the Fort upon the adversary's Foible, or with a dry Beat or jerk) before the other, for a good, sure, and firm Parade upon the ordinary *Quarte* Guard; the ordinary, or French Parade, in *Quarte* and *Tierce*, by only turning of the wrist of the sword-hand, without forming this dry Beat, being most false and uncer-tain, especially in an Occasion when a man's Life is at Stake, and where his Safety and Preservation depends in a great measure upon his good, firm, and certain Parade. Which can only be such when it is performed by forming a good cross, with a strong, firm, and dry Beat upon the adversary's sword.

XVIII
Of Judging of Measure, or Distance.

Having in the Fifth Article discoursed of *Measure* simply, I shall now consider and lay down the most exact rules whereby a man is to judge of it. For the truely judging of Meas-ure, which is the *Distance betwixt a Man and his Adversary*, is perhaps one of the nicest, as well as most useful things in the whole *Art of the Sword*. Because, as the understanding of it per-fectly may save a man many times from being wounded by his adversary, so the slighting or not duly observing it with that just-ness that it really requires, may cost a man his Life.

It should be therefore the business of every adroit Sword-Man to be able to judge of it to a nicety. Because, let him be never so adroit and nimble, and also Master of a very firm and sure Pa-rade, yet if he fail much in the just computation of Distance, especially at Sharps, he may come to lose any benefit he might really have by his Art. And that by his being unexpectedly sur-prised with his adversary's thrust reaching him, which he cer-tainly lookt upon to be out of Distance, or without reach of him. To prevent which inconveniency, it will not be amiss to lay down a few plain and easie directions for a man's more exactly judg-ing of it.

'Tis true that when persons, either in a School-Assault or at Sharps, play at half-sword, then there is no need of their having so great regard to the Distance betwixt them and their adversary.

Because in such a case, they are always within Measure of other. But in all other methods of play, except when engaged at half-sword, a man is indispensably obliged to have regard to it, and endeavour to judge it as exactly as possible.

Therefore, the *First* thing that a man is to consider in judging of Distance, is whether he be to judge of it with respect to his own thrusting upon his adversary, or of his adversary's thrusting upon him. For altho' it be most certain that a man may so order it that (upon his adversary's standing fixed to his Guard, and only discharging a thrust at him without the least Approaching) his adversary cannot reach him, and that nevertheless he himself shall be within reach of his adversary, yet the directions for both these circumstances are very little different. But seeing I know this will seem a paradox to many: how a man may so order his position to his adversary that he may reach his adversary, and yet at the same time his adversary not be in a condition, without approaching, to reach him; I shall first explain how that may come to pass, before I proceed to the directions for each circumstance.

The Secret then consists in this: when a man designs to set himself so as that he may reach his adversary, and that at the same time his adversary shall not, without Approaching, reach him, after he is on Guard, and that he has judged how far he thinks his adversary, by *Elongeing*, may reach him (to do which shall be immediately taught), he must instantly, either by Approaching or Retireing, place his advanced leg about a foot without that Distance from his adversary (for I would not have any man to allow himself less, neither is this trick to be ventured upon at Sharps), bringing at the same time his hind-leg, or that farthest from his adversary, within half a foot or thereby of the other. By which means you may easily perceive, that having a fuller *Elonge* to make them ordinary, which is occasioned by the nearness of his two feet, he will certainly reach his adversary, seeing he judged his adversary's *Elonge* upon him within a foot, and that his own *Elonge* not only takes in that foot, but a full foot more: an ordinary person's full *Elonge* from most Guards being about two foot. Whereas if his adversary should have thrusted, he would, after his *Elonge*, been about a foot short of him, according to the judged distance. And the very same may a man's adversary practise against himself, if he take not care to prevent it. Now this being so pretty and nice a circumstance in Fencing, and known to so very few, nay, not to many who profess the teaching of it, I judged the discovery of it would not be ungrateful, especially to such as are curious and desire to improve themselves in all the niceties of the Art. I shall now proceed to the directions for judging of Distance.

In the *First* circumstance, when a man is to judge of it with respect to his own thrusting upon his adversary, he is chiefly to consider two things. The *First* is that if he and his adversary be standing to their ordinary Guards, without any extraordinary position of their legs or sword-hands, and that he can over-lap a foot and a half or so of his adversary's sword, then he may conclude that he can reach his adversary with a full *Elonge*. The *Second* is that even altho' he can scarcely with the point of his sword reach that of his adversary's, yet if his own feet be very near to one an other, he will still reach his adversary's body with a full *Elonge*, his adversary being still upon an ordinary Guard, which is occasioned by the position of his hind foot being so close to that of his advanced. Whereby, altho' strictly speaking, his *Elonge* can be no longer than when he is upon the ordinary posture of a Guard, for no man can *Elonge* further than the distance betwixt his two feet, when at his full stretch, yet his hind foot being thus advanced so much further than it would do upon an ordinary posture, that he thereby reaches his adversary, which otherwise he could not possibly do without advancing. Which is all that is meant by his *Elonge* being longer than upon an ordinary Guard.

Again in the *Second* circumstance, where a man has respect to his adversary's reaching of him, then he is to consider *First*, that whatever position his adversary's legs are in, yet if his own be at a pretty Distance from each other, he can easilyer shun his adversary's thrust by the bending back or declining of his body from his adversary (which is indeed a kind of breaking of Measure, as shall be immediately explained), than if his own feet were placed very near to other. For being so very near, it is impossible for any man to decline his body considerably from his adversary without being in hazard of falling. Because his body, being much off the equilibre upon his left haunch, he would have nothing whereby to support it, which his hind leg does abundantly well when it is kept at a pretty Distance from the other. *Secondly*, as to his adversary's position, he is chiefly to consider what Distance his adversary's hind foot is from him.

For to be short, and to make the judging of Distance most easie to you without multiplying of directions which, altho' true and useful, would yet but perplex: the whole Mystery of it consists in the exact observing how far your adversary's hind foot is distant from you. And then you are to compute if his *Elonge*, which, as I said, in men of ordinary stature is about two foot, and the length of his arm and sword, will all of them together make up the Distance betwixt his hind foot and your advanced thigh. If you think it will, then is your adversary within reach of you. And consequently it will be fit for you to retire a little with the Single Step, to set your self without his Measure. But if you are persuaded that his *Elonge*, arm, and length of his sword will not all of them together make up that Distance, then you may conclude that he is without Measure of you, cannot reach you, and that consequently you are safe from any thrust he can make upon you, unless he first approach. This is a short, sure, and infallible rule for the judging, not only if your adversary can reach you, but if you can reach your adversary. And therefore I beg it may be thoroughly understood and practiced by all who intend to be Masters of this so very nice and useful a point in Fencing.

XIX
Of Breaking of Measure.

Breaking of Measure is but a genteel term Sword-Men have given to a moderate retiring, or giving of ground. And is no less needful to be understood by a compleat Sword-Man, that thereby, in a strait, he may evite and shun his adversary's thrust, than it is absolutely fit for him to understand exactly the judging of Distance. Both to prevent his spending his own thrusts in vain, and that he may be without the reach of his adversary's, when they are directed against him. So that in a manner, they mutually depend upon each other. But because many people have a wrong notion of Breaking of Measure, and look upon it as the same with still going back and losing of ground, I shall, before I proceed to the directions relating to it, endeavour a little to undeceive them.

As there is nothing more unbecoming a man of Honour, and who is dexterous at his weapons, than an unreasonable, untimely, and preposterously confused retreat, or yielding of ground, so in the whole *Art of Fencing* there is not any one thing sometimes of more use, and which discovers more of a man's Art and adroitness, than a moderate and judicious Breaking of Measure.

I know some people have such an aversion to it, and look upon it as so cowardly a practice, that they think it reflects upon a man's courage if he give the least ground. And they fancy a man is obliged to forbear it if his adversary only call to him to stand. But such persons would be pleased to know that the Breaking of Measure, neatly and judiciously, being as useful a branch as is in the whole Art. So they may as well call to a man not to defend by Parade the thrust they design against him, as oblige him, by forbearing to Break Measure, to continue immoveable in one place and become a fixt butt for their irregular and violent pursuit. Because both of them being defences allowed by Art, I know no reason why the one should be more condemned as the other. For valour has no doubt its bounds, as well as other virtues, which once transgressed, the next step is into the territories of vice. So that by having too large a proportion of this heroick virtue, unless a man be very perfect in its limits, which upon the confines are very hard to discern, he may very easily unawares run into temerity, obstinacy, and folly.

Montaigne in his first volume of *Essays*, discoursing of constancy, hath a very apposite passage to this purpose, which I shall set down in his own words, that other people's judgements, and those none of the meanest, may be known in this matter, as well as my own.

There is, says he, *no motion of the body, nor any Guard in the handling of arms, how irregular or ungraceful soever, that we dislike or condemn, if they serve to deceive or defend the blow that is made against us; in so much, that several Warlike Nations have made use of a retiring and Flying way of Fight, as a thing of singular Advantage; and by so doing, have made their Backs more dangerous than their Faces to their Enemies.*

And Socrates, in *Plato*, laughs at Laches, who had defined fortitude to be a standing firm in their ranks against the enemy. *What*, says he, *would it then be reputed cowardice, to overcome them by giving Ground?* Urging at the same time the authority of Homer, who commends Æneas for his skill in running away, that thereby he might catch advantage of his enemy.

And even with respect to firearms. Altho' as to what concerns cannon shot, when a body of men are drawn up in the face of a train of artillery, or to maintain an advantageous post against another battalion, as the occasion of war does often require, 'tis unhandsome for any man to quite his post to avoid the danger. And a foolish thing to boot. For as much as, by reason of the violence and swiftness of the bullets, we account it in a manner inevitable; and many a one by shifting his post, ducking, or stepping aside, and such other motions of irresolution and fear, has been sufficiently laugh'd at by his companions, yet we have examples where they have succeeded. For instance, Lorenzo de Medici, Duke of Urbin, laying siege to Mondolpho, a place in the territories of the Vicariat in Italy, seeing the cannoneer give fire to a piece that he judged pointed directly against him, it was well for him that he ducked. For otherwise the shot, that only raz'd the top of his head, had doubtless hit him full in the breast. Thus far my author. I shall only add that Colonel Bringfield was not so sharp sighted last campaign, else he had preserved his head, which was struck off at the Battle of Ramellies by a cannon bullet, as he was a-remounting His Grace the Duke of Marlborough.[11] But it seems he was then more intent upon the preservation of his General's Life than upon the saving of his own. Wherein he

---

[11] At the Battle of Ramillies (May 23, 1706, a year prior to the publication of Hope's *New Method*) the Duke of Marlborough personally led two cavalry charges against the Household of France. The second charge was routed, Marlborough was dismounted, and he was compelled to run a considerable distance to gain the safety of Major-General Murray's battalions. Some time later Colonel Bringfield arrived with the Duke's second charger. As he was holding the stirrup for the Duke to mount, Bringfield was decapitated by a cannon ball. This scene was depicted on the ten of diamonds of a contemporary deck of playing cards. Churchill, v. 5, 118-120. Donald McBane was present at this battle.

discovered himself to be no less a faithful soldier than a man of true generosity and Honour, for which his name will stand recorded to posterity; as well as His Grace's, for the glory of that great victory obtained over the French wherein he showed himself to be no less brave and foreward than fortunate.

But to return. However such inconstancy and irresolute-like motions may be condemned in persons who are obliged to engage in a body with others, particularly in officers who have the conduct and charge of leading on their soldiers committed to them, or of commanding in a detachment, by reason that it would not only give bad example to their fellow soldiers, but also be a means, by reason of such continual irregular motions and inconstancy, to bring them into confusion. And also that the same kind of motion, by which Fortune favoured their apprehension, to make them evite the shot at one time, may be a means at another time, as well to make them step into the danger, as to avoid it. Yet in a Single Combat with firearms, either a-foot or horseback, that fixedness and constancy of body is, in my opinion, no more to be required than it is in a Duel or rencounter with swords. And there are, in that case, such measures to be taken, as if execute with judgement and that presence of mind, as in such a juncture is necessary, may be very useful (I will not say certain) to make any man a great deal more difficult aim to shoot at, than otherwise he would, did he altogether neglect them.

And now seeing I am upon firearms, I think it will be neither improper nor unacceptable to the reader to make a short digression wherein I shall give three or four of the very best rules that I know for his more dexterous behaviour when he shall be obliged either to make use of his pistol, in place of his sword, or of both immediately after other. I have, it's true, been pretty particular as to this point in the *Scots Fencing Master*, to which I also refer him. But, however, that shall not make me omit at present any thing that is absolutely necessary in such an Occasion. Besides, that my directions now differ considerably from what I gave then.

I do it also the more willingly, because good Sword-Men are frequently threatened with it. As if a man's being a good Sword-Man did undoubtedly incapacitate him from being likewise a good marksman. Altho', according to the nice rules of giving Satisfaction, I see no tye, nor Point of Honour obliging any man more to answer his adversary with firearms, if his adversary pretend to any advantage by them, than his adversary was obliged to answer him with the weapon he is most dexterous at. But the person who receives the Appeal [challenge] being alwise Master of making choice of his weapon, which wholly removes that debate. Therefore I would have every Sword-Man so adroit, not only at his weapons, but also with firearms, that he may never be taken at a disadvantage, let the arms pitch't upon be what they

will. The directions I am to give will be also very useful in Pickeering[12] (which altho' now a-days much out of fashion, yet a man may come to be engaged in it), and therefore upon that account, they are not to be contemned nor neglected, especially by those who serve in the Army, whether Horse or Dragoons, as well officers as others.

In the *First* place then (after you have drawn your sword and hung it by a riband upon the wrist of your sword-hand; cock'd both your pistols, which I alwise suppose are in good trim; and put one of them into your bridle-hand, betwixt the fore-finger and thumb, for your greater readiness, to make use of it when the first pistol shall be discharged; which, before fireing, you are to keep with its muzzle up; and put your horse to a gentle hand-gallop for engaging), never advance upon your adversary with a full body, but alwise with your side towards him, which will make your body but half the aim it would be, did you come up full breast upon him. For which end it will be fit to keep your horse's side, not his head, as much towards your adversary as possible. And so make your horse advance side-ways upon him. Therefore, in this case, a ready and well mouth'd horse is most necessary and useful. And when a man cannot have the conveniency of such a horse, my advice to him is not to let him go off the trot. Because in such a juncture it is much safer that a man be Master of his horse, than his horse Master of him. Which if he should be put to a gallop, he might (not being well mouth'd) very probably be.

Secondly, you are not only to advance sideways upon your adversary, but you are also to do it in a serpentine line, and not in a streight one. That is, you are to make your horse gallop gently, first to one hand and then to the other, about two or three of his lengths each time, according to your distance. But still with his and your side respecting your adversary, and not with a full and open body.

Thirdly, you are to endeavour as much as possible to attack your adversary alwise upon that side opposite to the hand wherewith he holds his pistol. Which will likewise much surprize him, and make his aim the more uncertain, not being accustomed to shoot over his left arm. And therefore to be dexterous your self in that way of shooting, accustom your self much to the shooting at a mark, both a-foot and horseback, with your opposite side towards the mark, and not that side with the hand whereof you hold your pistol. By practice, a man will find this direction a great use to him.

---

[12] Making a raid for booty; marauding; skirmishing in advance of an army. *Webster's Revised Unabridged Dictionary*, 1913.

Fourthly, never offer to fire your self until you be within two or three yards at most of your adversary. Nay, even nearer if you have resolution enof to wait it. This the French call *tirer a brule pourpoint*, or to *singe the doublet*. And perform it alwise with a brush, and with your arm stretched and at full length, whereby you will seldom fail to make a good aim, and consequently a sure and bloody shot. Firing at a greater distance is but spending, in a manner, your shot in vain. Therefore observe not only this of firing near, but also as much as your courage will permit, keep up your shot. But do it with so much judgement and presence of mind as not to give your adversary the least advantage by it. Therefore when you come to your true and desired Distance, which the nearer the surer, discharge upon him. And when you do intend to keep up your fire a little, make your horse perform his serpentine motion as quick and lively as possible, that you may thereby render your adversary's aim still the more uncertain, until you gain the advantage of him which you intended. Remembering alwise as you pass your adversary, whatever side it be upon (altho' I indeed prefer the left), to cause your horse, after his brush or career, turn suddenly again upon him by a kind of half-pyroit [half-pirouette], both to prevent his gaining of your rear, and for your more ready gaining of his. Which is termed by the French, *gainer la croupe* [gaining the crupper], and is, when obtain'd, a singular advantage, if the person who has got it knows how to prosecute it.

Fifthly, if it shall happen that both of you have discharged both your pistols without doing execution, which will rarely fall out if you fire so near as I order, then you are immediately to take hold of your sword (which is already drawn and hanging by a riband upon your wrist) and pitch your self with it to the *Hanging Guard in Seconde*, recommended in this *New Method* (for which see the Plate at Figure 14 [p.171]). And make use of your Art from it, both for defence and offence, according to the directions given in the two following Chapters; and as your judgement shall direct you, it being the only true and safest Guard that any man can possibly take himself to, who is engaged with his sword; either singly, or in a tumultuary confusion and crowd; either a-foot or horseback, where they commonly come to close sabreing; no other Guard in the sword for a general defence being in the least to be compared to it. And therefore I cannot but again recommend it to all serving in the Army, who are many times concerned in such engagements. There is only one thing to be chiefly observed, that when both your pistols are discharged, and your adversary has one of his yet to fire, that you are not then in the least to hesitate, but with a sudden brush run full tilt at him with your sword. Nay, many are of opinion that at first engaging it is no great disadvantage to a man thus to make use of his sword and forbear making use of his pistols at all. But this I look upon to be too ventorious, and therefore would alwise first make use of my fire.

The very same directions which I have desired to be observed upon horseback will serve a-foot, either with pistol or carbine. Only, the better to imitate the swift motion which a horse makes, you are to quicken and accelerate your own motion a-foot, that thereby your adversary may be the more uncertain of his aim, by both advancing upon him, as I said, in a serpentine line, and with your side, not your full body, alwise opposite to him. I had almost forget to tell you that whenever your first pistol is discharged, you are (that you may lose no time) to drop it, and immediately to take the other pistol from your bridle-hand, and continue your fight according to the former directions.

By the exact observation of these few directions, if a man be a compleat Sword-Man, and has also accustomed himself to shoot dexterously at a mark, and frequently over his left arm, he may appear in the Field with either sword or pistol against any man. And seeing Art can never take away or abate true courage, his being likewise a good marksman will make his Art in the sword to be the more beneficial and useful to him, and prevent people's so readily undervaluing of his skill as a Sword-Man by alwise threatening him with a pistol or other firearms. And thus much for the making use of firearms either a-foot or horseback, which was the occasion of my digression. Let us now return to the Breaking of Measure when we are to make use of our sword only. Of which I shall also very freely give my own sentiment, and then proceed to the directions for it.

I confess there is nothing more unbecoming, and which discovers more the want of resolution and courage, than a continual giving back. And no man can condemn it more than I do. But then that feint-heartedness is down right a timorous retreat, not an artificial Breaking of Measure. And as this is to be practiced and valued by all knowing Sword-Men, so is that as much to be contemned and derided by all men of courage and true Honour. They differ also in this, that a constant giving of ground produces a retreat. Whereas a judicious Breaking of Measure is so far from deserving that name, that it not only procures a sure defence, but frequently also produces an occasion for a true and vigorous pursuit. Losing of ground then, or retiring, is only so far to be allowed and approved of as it resembles the truely useful, and artificial breaking of Measure. And only so far to be disapproved of and condemned as it resembles the dishonourable and cowardly practice of constantly giving ground, or retiring.

As for the directions for Breaking Measure according to the nicest rules of Art, they are as follows. *First*, when you judge that your adversary's thrust, without his approaching (for indeed when a man's adversary approaches before he makes his thrust, it is most difficult to determine how far his *Elonge* will reach; and therefore in that case, this first method of Breaking of Measure is not to be ventured upon), I say, when you judge that your adversary's thrust, without his approaching, will over-reach the nearest parts of your body only the matter of six or seven inches, then you may easily Break that Measure and evite his thrust by only declining or bending back your whole body, supporting it by your left leg and thigh. And this is to be done without the least retracting of your right leg, because the keeping the right foot firm is a kind of stay or counter-support to your body. The which, should you make it follow the motion of the rest of your body, would inevitably procure an advantage to your adversary by your falling backwards. Which by such a sudden motion of the body can scarcely be prevented, but by keeping the right foot firm and steady. Which must be alwise observed in this first method of Breaking Measure.

Secondly, if your adversary approach upon you before he thrust, then there are two methods of Breaking Measure which you may make use of as you think fit. The *First* whereof is upon a Streight Line, and the *Second* upon a Circular.

If you design to Break his Measure upon the Streight Line, then as he approaches or gains ground upon you, which is commonly performed with the Single Step, you are at the same very time to recover as much Distance again from him by Breaking his Measure with the Single Step backwards. But if he reiterate often his approaching and press you hard, then you are not to humour him so much as still to Break his Measure. For that were indeed to convert your Breaking of Measure into a perfect cowardly retreat: a practice alwise to be condemned and avoided by a man of Honour. But are instantly to put a stop to his violent pursuit by encouraging him to thrust, if you are much Master of the Parade, and then take him upon the Riposte. Or otherwise, making use of your left hand for a defence, immediately become the pursuer by thrusting upon him at the same time you are Parieing with your hand. There is no better method than this for either Breaking your adversary's Measure upon the Streight Line, when he approaches upon you, or for putting a stop to a violent and furious pursuit by whom ever it may be attempted against you, whether Artist or ignorant rambler. And therefore I earnestly recommend the practice of it: a great deal of a man's safety, in an Occasion with Sharps, depending upon it.

The *Second*, and indeed best method of Breaking your adversary's Measure when he approaches upon you before he thrust, is upon a Circular Line. And the reason of it is because when a man Breaks Measure much upon a Streight Line, he not only loses much ground, which, as I said (in the opinion of the vulgar), is a kind of reflection upon his courage, but he must also have a considerable bounds to perform it in. Otherwise he is immediately driven to his utmost limits, and perhaps fixed against some wall, fore-stair, or in some corner of a room, if the quarrel

be within doors, where he can go no further, altho' he would. Whereas, when he makes use of a circular motion with his feet, or Breaks Measure Circularly, he not only requires less space or bounds for it, but also prevents the appearance of an unmanly retreat, and comes as well to his purpose in eviting his adversary's thrust by that method of Breaking his Measure, as if he had broke it upon the Streight Line. Neither is there any difference in performing the one and the other. But only that in the one, the hinde foot moves backwards in a Streight Line, and is so followed by the advanced foot. Whereas in the Circular Method, both the legs move circularly: first the hind leg is removed circularly backwards, and then the right; taking care at the same time to keep the body as thin, or little exposed, as possible; and observing the same direction for the use of the left hand, and thrusting upon the Riposte or Back of the Parade, as in the former method upon the Streight Line. But by approving and recommending this Circular Breaking of Measure, it must not be thereby understood as if I in the least approved of that most dangerous, and uncertain circular kind of play at Sharps, called *Dequarteing*, or *Quarteing* and *Volting*. You may see my sentiment of these under their proper title, Article 16. So that by a Circular Line or motion in this place, I only mean that whereby a man may, by taking up less space, and by making a shorter retreat, Break his adversary's Measure with a great deal of more ease, less confusion, and without the least appearance of a mean and cowardly retreat.

I have been the more particular upon these two last *Terms of Art*, the *Judging of Distance* and the *Breaking of Measure*, because in the whole *Art of Defence* there is not any thing which discovers more skill and judgement; nor from which a true Sword-Man reaps more benefit and advantage, whether against a skillful or unskillful adversary, especially at Sharps; than he does from the right performance of what is comprehended under them. Which, because of their mutual dependence upon each other, I thought fit to explain immediately after other, that so my directions for both might be the better understood, and retained by the reader.

XX
Of Redoubling.

This *Term of Art* comes most seasonably to be considered after the Breaking of Measure, and almost explains it self. For it is only the *Redoubling* or reiterating of a thrust. Either when a man, being within distance, hath misplanted it, and that he finds he hath a sufficient Open discovered to him yet to thrust at; or when his adversary Breaks his Measure, so that when he is at his *Elonge* or stretch, he is necessitate to gather, as we say, or bring up his left foot towards his right, and then renew his thrust by *Elongeing*, that so it may reach his adversary.

However, it is a great deal more proper in this last case, against a man's adversary's Breaking of his Measure, than when a man is sufficiently within Distance. Because when a man frequently Redoubles his thrust, being within Distance, altho' it is true that he disorders his adversary by it, yet he also very much exposes himself, and runs the hazard of being catched upon Time, or by a *Contre-temps*. Whereas when it is performed only as a Contrary to the Breaking of Measure, a man does not so much run that risk.

This Redoubling is indeed the true Contrary to a small or moderate Breaking of Measure. For when a man's adversary goes only a little out of his Distance to evite a thrust, what more proper method can he take to bring himself within it again, than to approach him with this gathering up of his left foot, and keeping the right fixed, until by alwise either thrusting and *Elongeing*, or by approaching, he come within Measure of his adversary to reach him.

'Tis true when one's adversary skips or jumps far out of Measure, then a man may advance upon him with the artificial step, as descrived in the Article of Approaching. But if his adversary Break Measure, only just so much as to frustrate his thrust, and make him deliver it in vain, then the only method is to recover the lost Measure by thus gathering up of the left foot, and then Redoubling the thrust with *Elongeing*. And this may be done twice or thrice. Nay, oftener if he find it convenient, and a proper ground. That is, not too uneven and rough to perform it in.

For there are two things chiefly to be observed in Redoubling. The *First* is that when you are engaged in bad and unequal ground, you prosecute it as little as possible. Because of the advantage it may give your adversary over you, by renewing his pursuit, should you make a wrong or false step, besides the hazard you may run by falling in such an unconvenient ground. The *Second* is to take great care when you are to Redouble, upon you adversary's Breaking of your Measure but a very little, that he either take not Time, or endeavour to *Contre-temps* you. And therefore, in this case, be sure to have alwise your left hand in readiness to prevent both.

This last caution is not less to be observed in Redoubling of a thrust when a man is within Distance of his adversary, and hath consequently no need of gathering up his left foot. Because, in this case, his adversary will be as apt to endeavour to *Contre-temps* him as in the former. And that by reason that his great nearness encourages him to it. Therefore great care ought to be taken, especially in an Occasion with Sharps, to prevent such *Contre-temps*. Which can only best be done by either opposing the left hand in time of Redoubling, or otherwise by playing only from the Riposte.

XXI
Of the True Pass, and Half-Pass.

The English Masters give the term *Pass* indifferently to every thrust that a man makes against his adversary. So that whatever kind of thrust a man makes, they then say he has made such and such a Pass upon, or against him. Which is not at all conform to the strict signification of this *Term of Art*. Because there is a very great difference betwixt a true Pass and a thrust, as I shall immediately make appear.

According to the rules, a true Pass is a running motion which a man makes bye his adversary's right side, in the Time he is performing his thrust against him. Whereas a thrust is commonly delivered with a close and fixed left foot. 'Tis true, both of them terminate in a thrust. But there is this difference, that in all thrusts wherein the different Lesson*s* terminate, the left foot is generally kept fixed; whereas Passing is performed, as I said, by a running motion, the body stooping forewards, and the thrust delivered just as a man is Passing bye his adversary's right side.

There is also another very material difference betwixt them. Which is that at Sharps, or in an Occasion, which are all one, a man cannot well offend his adversary without making thrusts at him. Whereas true Passes are indeed only for variety and diversion in School-Play, and scarcely practicable at Sharps. Because of necessity, and almost whether a man will or not, they convert themselves into that which is called the Half-Pass. And the reason for it is that a man, in making of a true Pass, must either design to give his adversary a thrust in Passing or not. If not, then his Pass is of no effect nor use to him. And in that case it is the same as if there were no such Lesson in the Art. And if he do, then by the violence of the running motion, he will certainly sheath, or run his sword into his adversary's body up to the very hilt (for when once a sword enters, especially upon so violent a motion as that of a true Pass, it is not possible either to stop or to retract it, as a man can do a blunt *Fleuret*, in making a true Pass in School-Play). So consequently if a man should attempt it at Sharps, he must either halt when he comes the length of his adversary's body, which alters the nature of the true Pass designed, and converts it into a half one; or otherwise must quite with his sword, which is fixt in it; and which I fancy no man upon Life and Death will venture; that it may be only said, he hath made with his body a true Pass bye or beyond his adversary. By all which it is evident that there is no such thing at Sharps as what in School-Play goes under the name of a true Pass.

However, to render that running motion performed in making the true Pass with blunts also useful at Sharps, Masters have fallen upon that Lesson which, in the *Scots Fencing Master*, I call the Half-Pass, because it is performed both upon the very same Time*s* and Opens, besides a great many others, with the former, and also with the same running motion of the body. Only in place of Passing beyond a man's adversary, a man runs only close to him, executing his designed thrust in the time of his running, and then immediately stopping upon the finding of his sword fixed. For indeed, should he misplant and quite miss his adversary, I see then no reason why in that case he might not convert his Half-Pass into a full or true one by running quite beyond his adversary until out of his Measure, and then recover himself to his defensive posture again.

But this gross misplanting very rarely happening upon a Half-Pass, by reason of this kind of murthering [murdering] Lesson being never almost attempted at Sharps (in respect of the violent motion wherewith it is performed, and disorder it puts a man into when he misplants), but when a man is in a manner certain to effectuate it. Therefore it is, as I said, that at Sharps we have nothing of the true Pass, but only in its place the Half-Pass. Which, if rightly performed, I cannot but acknowledge to be a most firm, sure, and bloody Lesson: the thrust, if rightly planted, rarely failing to be very dangerous, if not mortal. Besides, altho' the true Pass were useful at Sharps, yet a man can only make use of it without and above, or without and below his adversary's sword, by reason of his being obliged alwise to pass upon his adversary's right side. Whereas the Half-Pass may be performed from most Lesson*s*, both without, within, and below the sword, to either side of a man's adversary. And therefore is much the better, as well as safer, Lesson of the two.

By what is said, I think it very clear that unless a man design wholly to misplant his thrust, he cannot possibly make at Sharps what is truely a Pass. Neither, in Fencing, is a true Pass and a thrust all one, as some English Masters would make us believe. And therefore they ought hereafter to rectify that mistake in the signification of this term, and not let the termination of most Lessons go under the name of a Pass, when they are really thrusts.

XXII
Of Enclosing and Commanding.

Many people, and those none of the most ignorant, take *Enclosing* and *Commanding* for one and the same thing. Wherein they are mightily mistaken. For there is as great a difference betwixt them as almost betwixt any two *Terms of Art*, as I shall immediately make appear by the following example.

If *A* should quarrel with *B*, whereupon an Occasion in the Field or rencounter follows; and if *A* should Enclose upon *B*; then according to the common acceptation of Enclosing, the report would run that upon such a day and in such a place, *A* and *B* had an Occasion together, and *A* had the advantage of *B* because he Enclosed upon him. Whereas it is as probable it may have been quite otherwise, and that upon the Enclosing, *B* did Command *A*.

For the better and truer understanding of which, you are to know that a man may Enclose upon another upon two very different designs: either when he finds himself strong enof to grapple with his adversary, and upon the Enclosing really intends to Command him; or when he finds himself too weak for his adversary, and therefore for his own safety Enclosed upon him, that his adversary may have the opportunity of Commanding him. For it is a great escape, not to say folly, in any man, really to attempt a Commanding of the adversary's sword, unless he look upon himself to be above, at least equal to his adversary in strength. Because he being weak, and his adversary vigorous and strong, it is ten to one but after he hath really make a fair attempt to Command, and has actually taken hold of his adversary's sword near to the hilt (which is the most proper part to catch hold of it, the better to prevent the cutting of his hand or fingers), but his adversary may turn the chase upon him by reason of his weakness, and in place of allowing himself to be Commanded, Command and master him. Whereby it is clear that *A*'s Enclosing upon *B* is no argument of his having the better of him. And that therefore in such a case, people should suspend their judgements until they know which of the two not only Enclosed upon other, but Commanded the other's sword. For it is in the securing and Commanding of the adversary's sword, and not in the Enclosing, that the true advantage lyes.

By all which it appears that Enclosing and Commanding are not at all reciprocal terms, but that there are many times Enclosings where there is not the least design to Command, as in the former case of a man's Enclosing for his better preservation; and also frequently Commandings where the person Commanding did not at all Enclose, but took the opportunity for it, upon his adversary's attempting to Enclose upon him.

This false judgement, which people make upon a man's Enclosing upon his adversary, is of a piece with what many people make upon a man's Breaking of Measure. For no sooner do bystanders observe a man in a rencounter to give a little back, but immediately they conclude that he is at a disadvantage by it. Whereas if it be any ways voluntary, it is commonly quite otherwise, and the person who Breaks Measure, if an Artist, by giving a little ground gains the opportunity of not only letting pass his adversary's sudden and violent passion, but also of procuring to himself a more effectual pursuit against him, either from the Riposte, or by making a real attack when the other's furious pursuit is somewhat abated. Therefore in both these cases, as well in Breaking of Measure as in Enclosing upon one's adversary, a man ought not to be too ready in giving his judgement, or determining who hath had the better on't. But if he be a witness to the Engagement, ought to suspend his sentence until he see the consequence and event of either. And according as he finds a man come off, either upon his Breaking of Measure or Enclosing, so he is to pass his verdict. But not sooner, unless he is resolved to give it at random. Which no man of judgement and prudence will desire to be thought guilty of.

Enclosing also resembles so very much the Half-Pass, that many persons likewise make no distinction betwixt these Lessons. Therefore it will not be a-miss that I also clear a little this matter.

It is certainly so far true that Enclosing and the Half-Pass resemble other, as both of them may be performed upon the same occasions and Opens which any one of them can be. But then the great difference lyes in their termination, which wholly depends upon the design of the performer.

For when a man designs a true Half-Pass, it terminates almost alwise in a wound, unless the misplanting, or the adversary's Parade prevent it. Whereas in Enclosing, a man's design being, as I said, one of two: either to terminate it in a Commanding of his adversary's sword, if he be strong enof to grapple with and master him; or only in a forcing of himself close upon his adversary for his own security, that his adversary may have the opportunity to Command his sword. A man, I say, in both these cases, makes but a delusory or seeming motion with his sword, as if he designed to adjust and carry home the thrust to the body, but does really not design it, as in the Half-Pass, but voluntarily suffers it to go aside, that his adversary, humoring and following that squint motion of his with his sword, he may thereby have the better opportunity either to Enclose upon him or Command him.

Whereby it is very evident that altho' and Enclosing and a Half-Pass resemble other much, both as to their motions, and the opportunities and Opens whereupon they may be both performed, yet they differ widely as to their termination or Design. The *First* being only designed either for a man's own security, or to Command and master his adversary, if strong enof for him. But the *Later*, with a real intention to do execution, by wounding, if possible, his adversary.

It is also from the great ease and readiness a man finds to Enclose, or even Command, if he designs it, that I draw one of the great advantages this *Hanging Guard in Seconde* hath over other Guards. But seeing I intend to make as few repetitions as possible, I remit you to the perusal of the Sixth Advantage, where that is sufficiently made appear.

I shall make only one observation more upon one of these two terms: which is Commanding. That as no man who is very weak and feeble ought to attempt to Command an adversary's sword, who is very robust, strong, and vigorous, but rather endeavour to win at and master him with his Art some other way; so it is as great rashness and folly in any man, unless he be most vigorous, active, and nimble, to offer to make opposition and struggle when once his sword is really Commanded. For as it is a dishonour for no man to be mastered by another man of Honour in an Honourable Quarrel (all that is required of a man to save his Honour, being but couragiously to venture his person, not alwise to master and overcome his adversary), so all the benefit that a man can reasonably expect from such an unreasonable opposition and struggling is that he draws more suddenly down his own destruction upon himself by obliging his adversary, who is Master of his sword, to make himself also Master of his Life by dispatching him. Because no good Sword-Man, who understands to make use of the benefit of his Art, will stand dallying and communing with his adversary after he hath once catched hold of his sword; but will immediately, with the same very breath, oblige him also either to yield to him by quitting of his sword, or receiving perhaps a mortal wound. And therefore when a man's sword is once Commanded, he ought (unless some very extraordinary opportunity encourage him to the contrary) to yield it, and submit himself to his adversary's generosity; who if a man of Honour, will certainly treat him as one Gentleman ought to treat another in such a juncture.

Thus have I gone gradually through the whole material *Terms of Art* belonging to Fencing, as I would have done had I been to explain them to the greatest novice; beginning with a Guard, which is that wherewith a man upon all Occasions ought to begin; and ending with Enclosing and Commanding, which many times also puts a conclusion to the Quarrel. And altho' I make no doubt, but several things which I have advanced in explaining them will surprise a great many Masters, as well as others, who pretend to a considerable knowledge in the theory of this Art, yet I make no scruple not only to assert them, but even to maintain them for Truths, notwithstanding of many of them being so opposite, and in a manner contradictory, to the Common Method. For experience perswades me that I am in the right. And Truth founded upon Reason and Experience will alwise hold foot, and I hope convince every impartial and unprejudg'd reader of the great benefit that will redound to the Art, by the discoveries I have made of many very material errors which have, from time to time, crept into it. And which I heartily wish may be hereafter rectified by the more knowing and judicious Masters.

If my explications be likewise seriously considered, they will be found to contain not only the Grounds of a great many Lessons, but even the nicest, as well as most useful, theory relating to the whole Art, most of which was never before made publick. So that should some persons, through mere obstinacy or ill nature, wholly disapprove of and reject this Essay with respect to the *New Method of Defence* I am so earnestly endeavouring to establish by it, yet it cannot but prove of singular use to them, even for their better understanding the theory of the Grounds and Principles whereupon the Lessons of the Common Method ought to be founded. And which are alwise very well worth understanding by every one who designs to become a good Sword-Man, whichever of the methods he most approves of, and takes himself to. So that with whatever design this piece be perused, whether for the establishing of this *New Method*, or for the better understanding the theory of the Old, it must still prove most useful. Which sufficiently answers my design, in being so very full upon all the *Terms of Art*, many of which, as I have said, are also Lessons in the Common Method. Whereas had I only designed to discourse of such of them as are absolutely necessary and useful in this *New One*, their number would have been but small: the simplicity and plainness of it (which is indeed its excellency) requiring but a very few for its being fully understood.

But the theory and judgement of the whole Art being so interwoven with its terms, I made it my choice rather to bring into this Essay the exact explication of the most useful *Terms of Art* (altho' this *New Method* might have been very well described without them), that so I might the more regularly and orderly discover the theory and judgement of the whole Art, kept alwise hitherto, in a manner, as a Secret, than to make this piece so much the shorter by wholly omitting them. And the rather, because it is alwise in the option of the reader to pass them over at pleasure, and only peruse what really belongs to the perfecting of him in the practice of this *New Method*. All which is briefly contained in the First, Fifth, and Sixth Chapters. The rest being more for the explication of the theory and judgement of the Common Method than for the illustration of this New One.

CHAPTER V
How a Man is to Parie or Defend Himself,
from either Blow or Thrust,
upon the Hanging Guard in Seconde.

Being to preceed to my directions as well for the defence, as offence, flowing from this excellent *Hanging Guard*. The explication of it would appear to come in very properly in the beginning of the Chapter where I am to treat of the Parade, or defence, that may be drawn from it. But having done it exactly already in the First Chapter, to which I remit the reader, I intend at this time to save myself that trouble, especially seeing such a repetition would be altogether superfluous. And therefore I shall in place of it offer to him a very necessary advice or precaution, particularly if he be altogether a novice and has never been at Fencing School. Because if he be already well grounded in the Art, and consequently a piece of a Sword-Man, he will not stand so much in need of it.

The difference between a speculative Science and a practical Art does, no doubt, chiefly consist in this: that the former may be acquired by mere theory or meditation, whereas the latter requires both. That is, a man must not only understand the theory pretty exactly, but he must also by practice acquire such an easy habit of performing such and such actions and motions which a complete and useful dexterity requires in that Art, as that it may appear to be almost natural to him. So that at this rate I account it is generally more easy for any man to become absolutely Master of a Science, than it is for him to become perfectly adroit, and an exquisite Master of any practical Art. Because to the first, there is only required an exact speculation; but to the later, not only speculation, but an habitual and consummate practice.

Now of the nature of this last, is the *Art of Fencing*. For altho' its speculation be diverting and necessary, yet its great use is practical. And therefore, altho' the theory of it may be by reading acquired to such a degree by any person of quick apprehension and good judgement, as that he can not only express himself easily, according to the nicest *Terms of Art*, but also converse readily and easily upon all its different heads; yet that knowledge and glibness of tongue will signify little or nothing to him when he shall have an Occasion with Sharps, or be engaged in a skirmish where, perhaps, he may have to deal with more persons than one. It is only a dexterous practice that must then carry him through and save him. It is not his words, but the warding of the thrusts and blows discharged against him that will in such a case make him be reputed a true and great Artist.

As therefore the practical part of Fencing is absolutely the most useful, let no man be so far mistaken as to imagine he can become wholly Master of it by reading. Books, as I have said elsewhere, are useful, necessary, and instructive, and will certainly do a great deal of good to a man who hath been grounded in the Schools. But it is the thrusting, first upon a Master's breast-plate, and next, thrusting frequently upon another at the wall, and defending himself from his comrade's thrusts in School Assaults, that must bring a man to be perfectly dexterous, either in the offensive or defensive parts.

Therefore I would advise all such in whose hands this piece may fall, and who are altogether ignorant of the first principles of Fencing, to apply themselves for two or three months (for I desire no more of them) to some judicious Master. Who at their desire will no doubt comply with them, and instruct them in this *New Method*, altho' very much differing from what is commonly taught. And which none who pretends to be a Master, but in twice reading over, will understand to teach. And when they are thus grounded, they need then no more of them, but only to practice with their comrades and fellow Scholars in Assault.

And in all Assaults let this be their chief aim: to acquire a firm and sure Parade, or defence, which is the only true *Art of the Sword*; the offensive part having by degrees crept into the Art, more for diversion and the gratifying of people's passions when in an Occasion, than for any absolute use in the Art. For this Art was at first never intended to kill or destroy, but to defend and preserve. And therefore it always was, and will be called (when rightly named) the *Art of Defence*. Besides, the offensive part will intrude itself upon a man whether he will or not, so very prompt is mankind to be revengeful and do mischief.

But for such as cannot have the opportunity of a Fencing Master, by reason of their living either in the country, or in some city or town where such Masters are not to be had; and yet who being of a quick and smart apprehension, and desirous to improve themselves, would gladly be instructed without the assistance of a Master; in such a case, they are to make choice of some judicious comrade. And then reading over attentively the instructions in this book, endeavour first to follow them himself by practicing them upon his comrade. And next cause his comrade to play them upon him. But still to ply more the defensive part as the offensive. And by thus mutually assisting one another, they will by daily practice make in a short time such a considerable advance in the Art, as can in reason be expected from any, who wanting the benefit and advice of a Master, are necessitate to become as dexterous as book learning can make them. Which, altho' it cannot be thought that it can reach to such a degree of dexterity as that acquired from a Master, yet will be a great deal better than none. And considering the easiness of this *New Method*, succeed even to a surprizal, and beyond what can possibly be expected from the Common Method. But to proceed to my directions.

A man's only true defence consisting, as I formerly said (see Advantage 2nd), in the cross that his weapon makes upon his adversary's; it follows, of consequence, that the more exact and dexterous he is in crossing his adversary's weapon, the more firm and certain will his defence prove. And he is to chiefly observe this one direction, that he alwise apply such a force in crossing, let the position of his sword-hand be what it will (for it is the cross which makes the defence, not the position of the sword-hand; a formal nicety but too much observed heretofore amongst Fencing Masters), that whatever part of his adversary's weapon he meets with, whether Fort or Foible, he may alwise master its motion. Because the Fort of a sword, as I have elsewhere observed (in the Article 3rd of *Fort* and *Foible*, page 119), may be mastered and overpowered as well as its Foible. And that sometimes even with that part of a man's sword which in other respects may be accounted the Foible, according to the strength communicated to it by the sword-hand. This direction is of great consequence. Therefore punctually to be observed: a man's certain defence flowing from it.

But as a man's adversary can present his sword in several positions, that is, in a manner either level, or with the point of it high or low, so a man is to consider by what method he is to form the greatest or most securing cross against any of these positions. For as was also formerly told in Advantage 2nd, the greater the cross is, and the nearer it approach to a right angle, the longer time must a man's adversary take to Disengage. And consequently the longer will his thrust be in coming home, and so the slower. Whereby a man can more easily defend himself: one of the great advantages redounding to a man from his keeping this *Hanging Guard*, and forming the crosses aright from it.

If your adversary then shall present his sword either near upon a level, or with the point any ways sloping towards the ground, the very ordinary position of your sword upon this *Hanging Guard* will sufficiently cross and oppose it (see Figures 5 & 6 [p.100]). Only observe this, which is also very material, that whatever side you cross him upon, you alwise press his sword so far out of the line of your body upon that side, as that thereby

it be secured from a plain Thrust upon the same without Disengaging, unless he wholly force your sword. Which indeed you are chiefly to guard against, especially when your opponent presents towards your right side, that being the greatest hazard to which, in such a position of your sword, you will be most exposed. For if your adversary, upon this position of your sword, neither attempt to force an Enclosing or plain Thrust upon the same side without Disengaging, but shall attack you by Disengaging, then you will find his motions so very slow, by reason of the great tour he has to make, that you will easily meet with his sword, and cross or oppose it.

But if your adversary present his sword with the point of it high, which he may do to what side he pleases, then there are two ways of crossing it. If his sword be presented with a high point, and towards your left side, the very position of this *Hanging Guard* will also form a sufficient cross against it, by only turning you swords point towards his right side. But if his sword be presented with a high point, either directly towards you, or inclining towards your right side, then the ordinary position of this *Hanging Guard* will not make so good a cross, nor so easily meet with or oppose it. And it is only in this case, and scarcely any other that I know of, where you are to alter the position of your sword and hand, and form a cross with it against your adversary's, by raising of your sword's point towards your left side a-squint from you, tuning at the same time the nails of your sword-hand upward and from you, sheering outwards to the right side, as we commonly say, and your head and shoulders inclining much forwards for your better defence. So that by this alteration of your Guard, you will form an excellent cross against his sword (see Figures 2 & 3 [p. 96, 100]). But still with this precaution: that so soon as ever your adversary strikes or thrusts upon you, or alters the position of his sword, that then immediately you cross him by falling into your ordinary Guard or posture again.

Having shown how you are to cross or oppose your adversary's sword, which upon this Guard is equivalent to what, upon the ordinary *Quarte* and *Tierce* Guards, we call securing or Engaging the sword; which a man ought alwise to do, whatever Guard he takes himself to at the first presenting of his sword, for greater security; I shall next let you see how you are to perform exactly the two Parades or defences naturally flowing from this Guard, and which are abundantly sufficient for the defence of all attacks that can be formed against it, whether by blow or thrust.

It is one of the great advantages of this *Hanging Guard*, that a man's adversary can only attack him upon it in two different parts, *viz.* without and below his sword, and without and above it. Whereas upon the ordinary *Quarte* and *Tierce* Guards, a man can be attackt in four: to wit, without and above, and within and below his sword; and within and above, and within and below it.

There being then only two parts in which your adversary can attack you upon this Guard, that is, either without and above your sword, or without and below it, if he offer to give in a thrust or discharge a blow upon you without and above your sword, as you perceive them coming home upon you, immediately, without altering in the least the position of your sword-hand upon this Guard, Parie or turn off his thrust or blow by moving your sword-hand and arm towards your left side and a little upwards. And for the better gaining of the Foible of his sword, you are also, by bending your sword arm a little, make the motion incline towards your body or left shoulder. By this squint inclination of the motion of your Parade towards your left shoulder, you will better gain the Foible or weak of his sword, and consequently prevent your adversary's forcing home (especially) his thrust upon you. For the blow is not so easily forced upon this Guard as the thrust is. And after you find that you have Paried him, then you may attack him from your Parade from the Riposte, as you please, and as shall be hereafter taught. See Figures 9 & 10 [p. 109].

But if it be a streight and downright blow at your head that your adversary designs against you, and not towards your left side, then you are to Parie it with your sword quite across your face, the nails of your hand turn'd a little upwards from you. And be sure to meet his stroak with the Fort of your sword, by carrying of your shoulders upwards and level, bringing down your head and shoulders a little at the very instant you raise your sword. By all which, you will not only form an excellent cross, the only true defence against blows as well as thrusts, but also, by this little motion of your head and shoulders downwards, answering the motion of your sword-hand upwards, make your design the so much more quick, and consequently the more certain. Because your sword-hand has only the one half of the way to go to meet with the adversary's sword (your head and shoulders performing the other half), which otherwise it would have, did you keep your head and shoulders fixt and unmoveable. See Figures 15 & 16 [p. 173].

Again, if he attack you with a plain Thrust or blow without and below your sword, you are to carry your sword-hand and arm as before directed in the preceeding paragraph save one. But it must be to the other side, and to put by his thrust or blow towards your right side, as before you did it to your left. Only, that bending of the sword arm, and sloping or squint motion towards your body, which I recommended in the former Parade, towards your left side, is much more to be observed upon the thrust given in upon this. Because if there be any weakness at all upon this Guard, it is when a man is attacked upon the right side and below his sword. The position of this Guard making it most easy for a man's adversary to force home a thrust, or procure an Enclosing upon this side. Which last, altho' in some respect a considerable advantage, in my opinion, to both parties, as I have declared in Advantage 6th; yet when a man is upon the defensive part, he ought to take great care to prevent. And therefore it is to be observed, that in Parieing a thrust given in without and below the sword upon the right side, it requires a great deal more strength, as well as quickness, to perform it dexterously, than the Parade upon the left side doth. And that because of the great opportunity a man's adversary hath in engaging the Foible of his sword, and so by a sudden pressure of it, forcing either a thrust or Enclosing.

Now, altho' the strength of a man's Parade should be alwise, as near as possible, proportioned to the strength and swiftness of the motion of his adversary's weapon, yet this being very nice and difficult to be observed but by such as have made a considerable advance in the Art. Therefore, it is much safer to err upon the sure side, and alwise to perform one's Parade with that degree of strength as that it may be sufficient, whether it meet with either the adversary's Fort or Foible, to turn aside any thrust or blow whatsoever. For that strength which can master and Parie a strong thrust, will alwise ward or defend a weak one. And this direction holds likewise as well for the swiftness of a man's Parade, as for the firmness and strength with which he ought to perform it. That is, after a man's adversary's sword is once in motion, and the thrust or blow coming home.

For if a man should begin the first motion of his Parade before his adversary's sword were in motion towards his body, he might come to miss his adversary's weapon. And so, because of his anticipating, in a manner, his adversary's motion, come to receive a thrust or wound. Of which I have had several times the experience myself in School-Assaults, when I have judg'd my adversary, with whom I was not accustomed to Assault, to have a swifter hand than really he had. So that in this case the quickness of my Parade proved a disadvantage to me. But I must confess, only by my own fault in going too soon to the Parade, by reason of my wrong judging (thro' my great earnestness to Parie) the swiftness of the thrust (to be dexterous and adroit at which is a very great nicety and perfection in Fencing, and requires not only a great presence of mind, but also a considerable as well as frequent practice). Whereas if a man were to meet with his adversary's sword, it is impossible for him to be too quick in the motion of his Parade. But as this, of being too quickly upon the Parade, very rarely falls out, I think I may safely recommend you to this direction: of being at least as quick and sudden, but as much stronger than your adversary in the motion of your Parade, as the strength and vigour of your nerves will with easiness, and without any unbecoming constraint, allow of.

Besides, this fault of being sometimes too quick in the Parade cannot, except by mere chance, be committed by any but good

Sword-Men who, having acquired a great dexterity and swiftness in the Parade, are too forward and eager upon it, whereby they precipitate their defence and lose the benefit of it. And therefore it is a great happiness, upon an Occasion, to have that sedateness and presence of mind, as that by too great eagerness to meet with the adversary's sword, a man do not precipitate or over-hasten his Parade, whereby he may render his Art and dexterity in the Parade rather a disadvantage than a benefit to him. And altho' I cannot but acknowledge that it is very difficult to observe this direction, especially at Sharps, by reason that in such a juncture, a man's blood and spirits are raised, and that a man of mettle and vigour, especially if of a sanguine and passionate temper, cannot possibly, in such a case, restrain himself from being too forward; yet it is what all men should endeavour to practice: especially those who have a greater share of Art or skill than others. Otherwise their Art, which ought, and would certainly be, in such an Occasion, a great benefit and advantage to them, will become as it were a snare, and draw more quickly their ruin and destruction upon them than if they had been a little more cool and judiciously slow in performing their artificial motions, especially defensive.

Which brings to my memory a passage in Sir Roger L'Estrange's abstract of Seneca, Chapter 5, where discoursing of anger, he says, *That the huntsman is not angry with the wild boar, when he either pursues or receives him. A good Sword-Man watches his opportunity and keeps himself upon his Guard, whereas passion lays a man open. Nay, it is one of the prime Lessons in a Fencing School to learn not to be angry.*

And in the preceeding Chapter he compares anger to a short madness, and says, *There is so wonderful a resemblance between the transports of choler and those of frenzie, that 'tis a hard matter to know the one from the other, it being commonly accompanied with a bold, fierce, and threatening countenance, as pale as ashes, and in the same moment as red as blood; a glaring eye, stamping with the feet, the hair staring, lips trembling, with a forc'd and squeaking voice.*

And in that same Chapter he calls it, *A wild tempestuous blast, and empty tumor, the very infirmity of women and children; and a brawling, clamorous evil.*

So very strange and unaccountably masterful a passion it is. And therefore so much the more to be restrained and mastered, if possible, by all men of sound judgement and sense, especially Sword-Men who design really to reap benefit by their Art.

But in this case I look upon the nice and excellent directions given to Sword-Men in Fencing, to have much the same influence upon them as the good and wholesome admonitions delivered from the pulpit for the better regulation of our Lives, with respect to morals, have upon most Christians. We hear them, approve of them, and sometimes resolve to put them into practice. But GOD knows with how little exactness and sincerity it is done by the very best of us. Our passions and corrupt inclinations master us, whether we will or not, and we are overcome by them with, I may say, a kind of unvoluntary willingness or compliance. However as in this, it is even a degree of virtue to have good inclinations and resolutions, notwithstanding our being overpowered by our infirmities, so it is no less commendable in Sword-Men to put on the strongest resolutions they possibly can to restrain their forwardness and master their passions when in an engagement, altho' the motion and heat of their blood should wholly, but indeed contrary to their strictest resolutions, master and overcome them. For in such a juncture there is a kind of conflict betwixt nature and reason or Art. And we find by experience, to our great disadvantage, that for the most part, nill we, will we, the former hath the better on't.

Nay, so very great influence and power hath heat and passion over us that there are, I believe, few who have come any length in the world, but who may sometimes have found the strange effects of it in themselves. For to such a degree does it move the vital spirits when we are seized by it, that they rarifie the blood to that height, that it not only swells, but is even like to break and burst through our very veins. Whereby when we are in action, our lungs and other vessels and passages for respiration are so filled, or rather obstructed or choked, that we lose immediately our wind and become quite out of breath, until we be allowed a little respite to recover it again. Which is the true ground of those reasonable *Lists*, or intervals for breathing we observe allowed by people to other between Bouts, as they are commonly termed, when either fighting for a Prize,[13] or engaged for the Life (altho' in this last case, I think it very consistent with Honour, unless there be some previous capitulation to the contrary, for a man to take the benefit of his wind, if he thinks he can thereby master his adversary). For predominant is this unreasonable, though very natural passion, ANGER, over the strictest resolutions we can put on against it. For NATURE! ALMIGHTY and prevalent NATURE! Who, without somewhat more of a natural aid and assistance can possibly, with ease, resist and overcome her? But to our defence again.

In Parieing of the blow, you are also to take care that you Parie always with the blade of your sword, by forming a good cross upon your adversary's weapon. And never suffer your shell, or rather back-ward of the hilt, to receive the stroak. Because this is not only a false Parade, but might also endanger the loss of your fingers, if not the whole hand. By reason that such defence can only safely be made use of against the blow when a man has a Back Sword with a close-hilt or guard, and that now a-days

---

[13] See note 19 below.

there are few such swords made use of, except amongst the High-landers in Scotland, and Back Sword Masters or Gladiators in England.[14] Altho' I cannot but acknowledge that such close-hilts are most safe and useful for both Horse and Foot, when they come to a close fight. Because they are mighty preservers of the sword-hand from any unexpected stroak, when a man is engaged against more than a single man, and consequently cannot form two different crosses and one and the same time, so that his close-hilt supplies the place of one cross, while his sword's blade a-performing the other. And therefore I earnestly recommend the use of them in the Army for both Foot and Horse.

If I mistake it not, the Royal Regiment of Scots Dragoons[15] are furnished with such close-hilted swords, whereof they have no doubt found the benefit, in the several engagements they had in these two or three last campaigns, in which they acquired more than a proportionable share in the glory of the great and surprizing victories obtained over the French. And I doubt not but as the benefit and security of such hilts in a close engagement, for the preservation of one's sword-hand, where perhaps two or three are engaged against one, are more known, the government will hereafter order the Army to be better provided of them. Because for a general and close engagement, better swords there cannot possibly be than those kind of stiff, well-edged Sheering Swords, of a moderate length, and with good, close, or as they are more commonly termed by the vulgar, Shell or Sheep-head hilts.

I shall therefore once again repeat it: that I wish the great benefit of so general and safe a defence, flowing from this Parade, in a close engagement, where people come alwise to sabreing, and sharp blows and thrusts, may be a sufficient recommendation of this *Hanging Guard*; and consequently to all persons, but especially to such as serve in the Army, who it is very probable may be more frequently so circumstantiate, as I have been showing, than other Gentlemen whose chief concern is only for their defence in private quarrels, not in publick engagements (altho' such persons may come sometimes to be surrounded with a mob), where this general defence will prove as serviceable to

them for their preservation as it can be to those who carry Her Majesty's commission. And therefore it ought to be neglected by neither: the one perhaps having his Life to defend in the midst of a rabble, as well as the other has his to preserve in the face of a close, pitched battle.

But perhaps some Hotspur of an officer may say, *To what purpose is this advice to us officers of the Army, who are mostly amongst bullets? Will this Parade ward and defend a pistol or a musquet bullet? If it could, then indeed Fencing were an useful Art, and this a most excellent book. But seeing it cannot do that, what signifies it to us in the Army?*

In answer to which (for I have sometimes to my surprise heard such weak discourse, which makes me gave an answer to it; otherwise it were not worth my while), I say that altho' with this Parade he can neither parry cannon nor musquet bullet; because for these I remit him to his trenches and back-and-breast, or perhaps sometimes heels, when he has not the courage to stand it. Yet seeing an officer, whether of Horse or Foot, is many times tristed [involved] with a close engagement where they come to sabreing; this excellent Parade, though it can Parie neither cannon nor musquet (though it can do that also as much as any other whatsomever, which is NOT AT ALL), yet it will save a man a great deal better, if dexterously made use of, from many a slap and wound he would otherwise receive, than any other Parade of the sword he could possibly make use of. If this Gentleman will not believe me, I allow him to go on in his old Method. And I doubt not, by the end of the next campaign he will be the first that repent it. So leaving it to be perfectly practised by him, if he pleases (for he can never choose nor make use of a better), I shall proceed to the offensive part, or pursuit, most naturally flowing from this *Hanging Guard*.

---

[14] Before pugilism became a popular spectator sport, prize fighters engaged in combat with sharp broad swords, back swords, swords and daggers, and falchions, for purses and the pleasure of the paying public. "...a set of men, brave certainly, and skilful without doubt, who fought for prizes – not such as those of Elizabeth's time, which were played for promotion and good fame, but for a mere pecuniary stake, and, in addition, whatever coins might be thrown on to the stage to them by the public." Hutton, 286. McBane was an accomplished prize fighter.

[15] Known as the Grey Dragoons, or the Scots Greys (for the grey horses they rode), the Royal Regiment of Scots Dragoons was formed in 1681 and fought under Marlborough in the War of the Spanish Succession. Henderson, 37.

CHAPTER VI
Of the Pursuit, as well Blows as Thrusts, Wherewith a Man is to Attack his Adversary from this Hanging Guard.

As the improvement of this *Hanging Guard* gave me a great deal of satisfaction when I first fell upon it, because I thought it might prove a mean to advance the practice of general defence, whereby many a good and brave man's Life may be saved; and that I have all along with a great deal of pleasure described its chief advantages; as also the true and universal defence it gives against all weapons, as well edged as pointed; so it is with a kind of regret and reluctancy that I now engage myself to discover that part of it which, in place of preserving, is wholly intended for the ruin and destruction of our adversaries.

Certainly the true design at first of this useful Art was to teach us chiefly how we might defend ourselves from the barbarous and inhumane assaults of ill-natured and quarrelsome neighbours. For so the true meaning of the word or term *Fencing*, as I have formerly said, imports. So that the offensive part is in a manner forced in upon the Art. Would to GOD, the general pravity of human nature did not give so much occasion for it. For to that degree of bad nature and wickedness is mankind long ago arrived, that they in a manner lay it down as a general maxim that no man can well protect and defend himself, if at the same time he attempt not with all his might to offend and destroy his adversary, altho' never so dear to him before the happening of the perhaps but pitiful and trifling quarrel. And which is yet more surprising, and most of all to be regretted, this spirit of persecution and revenge stops not at the resentment by private quarrels, wherein satisfaction is given betwixt man and man, but even extends itself to the engaging of whole communities.

For we daily see that arbitrary and ambitious princes, through, I may say, an ambitious but perverse mistake, endeavour to perswade their subjects that it is not possible for them to preserve and defend their own dominions, if at the same time they make not inroads and incursions upon their neighbouring territories, whereby they are necessitate not only to engage most of their own people, who otherwise might live most peaceably and plentifully at home (the two greatest of Earthly blessings), but also a considerable number of their allies (who are perhaps very little further concerned in the pretended, and many times groundless quarrel, than only out of complaisance, to humour or gratify their ambition and covetous itch of conquest), in a perpetual Scene of Blood. For,

With no less Eager Zeal is Honour sought;
Honour! that gilded Idol of the Great;
For which, how do th' Ambitious toil and sweat,
And think't, with any Peril cheaply bought?
Hurry'd with strong Desire, brook no Delay,
By what e'er Obstacles withstood;
But with impetuous Fury force their Way,
And to the Gaudy Trifle wade thro'
Seas of Blood.

And that they may the more easily prevail with and engage indifferent, tho' well meaning and valorous, persons to assist them in their unneighbourly and many times un-Christian wars, they bait their hooks with money, and guild them over with the promise and vain expectation of gaining Honour. Which, altho' for the most part false and counterfeit, as commonly acquired and pretended to, and at bottom but a chimera and empty sound which quickly vanishes; or as one very well expresses it, *A glittering Star of Folly, to influence and captivate vain Minds, and to make the Ignorant gaze, as it were upon a blazing and fiery Comet;* yet has such an alluring and prevailing quality over most persons, as that few can resist, being enchanted and caught by it. But true magnanimity, and real and generous Honour consists not in the oppressing and conquering of our neighbours, nor in the defending of mean and pitiful drunken quarrels, for the most part not to be owned by men of sense without blushing; far less worth the while of resenting by men of true Honour. But in defending our Religion, Liberty, and Lives, when encroacht upon and unjustly attack'd. And wherein all brave men and good patriots are concerned and obliged, both by the laws of GOD and nature as well as of man, to engage for their relief. And when it exceeds these limits, it is so far from being true magnanimity and virtue, or deserving the noble, heroick, and just character of Honour, that whoever are abettors of it, except out of mere necessity and pinch, deserve truely rather the epithet of men-killers, as of men of valour and true, heroick Honour. For let the ambitious assert what they will, it is not power and oppression, nay, nor victories and conquest obtained by the greatest conduct and valour, but real virtue that is the only source and true foundation of solid and permanent Honour.

So matters being thus managed by the ambitious, this being indeed the true, but deplorable, state of affairs at present betwixt most princes in Europe, it cannot be expected but the contagion hath in a manner overspread the entire body, but that the particular members must be very much tainted and infected with it. And this perverse and malicious temper being nourished, as well by the pravity of our corrupt nature, as by publick example, prompts and encourages private persons still more and more to imitate this cruel, as well as un-Christian, spirit of revenge.

This vitious and bloody temper then, being, I am afraid, rather to be regretted than rectified; and that it is to be feared people will, notwithstanding of the strongest arguments can be offered against it, still persist in the gratifying of this revengeful and offending disposition; I shall, altho', I must say, very far contrary to my inclinations, discover to them those methods of offending which most naturally flow from this *Hanging Guard*. Declaring alwise that I do it not to encourage them in the least to make use of it merely for the ruin and destruction of their adversaries, but only as a supplement and addition to the former defensive part, for their more general and certain defence. For as true men of Honour, as well as good Christians, we ought by all means possible to endeavour to preserve, not to destroy, our fellow subjects. And this being my design, as I hope it shall be also the resolution of my generous reader (and sure I am it will, if he be a man of true magnanimity and Honour), I frankly proceed to it as follows.

As all Guards, or postures of defence, are generally pursued by either smart and swift plain Thrusts, Feints, Beating, Binding, or Crossing the adversary's sword with a spring from the wrist, Passing, Enclosing, and Commanding, so may this Guard be also attacked by all those different methods, altho' much more naturally by some of them than by others. Therefore, that I may burthen my reader's memory as little as possible, I shall only pick out those Lessons which will, in my opinion, have the greatest success against this *Hanging Guard*, and explain them to him as distinctly and briefly as possible. For as to the pursuit from this *Hanging Guard* against any of the other Guards that a man's adversary may take himself to in opposition to it, seeing as I have already shown in the defensive part the method a man is to take to oppose them with this *Hanging Guard*, and for which he may consult the Plate, Figures 3 & 6, for his better conception of it.

So for the general pursuit of them all, as well as of this, I shall only give him this general rule: that he shall make a thrust or blow as he shall judge it most proper, wherever his adversary gives him an open. And when his adversary does not give him one, then he must make one to himself, either by a Feint, or a springing Cross or Beat. Remembering alwise, after the discharging of his thrust or blow, to return to the posture of this crossing Guard again for his defence. For if he should recover himself to any other posture, he would then quite go from this Guard, and so lose the benefit of its secure and general defence, for which I so much recommend it.

Let this suffice in short for the general pursuit (from this Guard) of other postures of defence, or Guards, seeing it will be a sufficient instruction to any intelligent reader, after I have once fully explained the pursuits most naturally flowing from this Guard against any adversary who shall oppose it with the same posture. For were I to go through all the other Guards in the same manner as I intend to go through this, it would swell this small Essay to a considerable volume, which is not at all my design. And the rather, because if the reader be curious to know more of the pursuits from and against the ordinary Guards, he may consult either the *Scots Fencing Master* (where he will meet with full satisfaction, if variety can please him), or Monsieur de Liancour's book in French, entitled *Le Maitre d'Armes*, or *The Fencing Master*, one of the best books I know in its kind for the Ordinary Method of practice as commonly taught in the Schools. Altho' there are a great many things in it which ought to be rectified, and which I have also attempted to do in some measure all along in explaining the *Terms of Art*, which indeed chiefly belong to the Common Method. This new one, as I have frequently said, standing in need but of a very few.

Now to begin with the offensive part, which relates more especially to this *Hanging Guard*. You are to know that when your adversary presents his sword from it, and that you oppose it with yours, there are chiefly four different positions in which your sword may be placed with respect to his, either at first presenting, or in the time of your engagement. And that is, either beneath or above it towards his left side, or beneath or above it towards his right. But because the most ordinary position of your sword at first presenting will be without and beneath your adversary's sword, the point inclining a little towards the left side (at least you are to endeavour to make it so if possible, for your greater security at first engaging); the other positions proceeding rather from the method of Parieing when engaged, than from the ordinary posture of the Guard. Therefore I shall draw the Lessons, as well blows as thrusts, which I intend to explain from this position of the sword. For when once the Lessons that may be played from this position of your sword are exactly understood, the Lessons from any of the other three positions will be very easily discovered by your own reflection and judgement, if you but apply what I am to say upon this position of your sword, being without and beneath your adversary's, to any of the other three. See Figures 1 & 2 [p. 96].

The adversary's sword then being kept upon this Guard in a sloping position, the point inclining towards the ground (and yours without and beneath it, the point a little to his left side, for your greater security, as I said, at first engaging), makes that there are only two parts whereat most naturally and with greatest ease you may attack him. To wit, without and beneath the sword, and without and above it. It also gives but rarely an opportunity of either Beating or Binding. So that the most proper pursuits against this Guard are a smart plain Thrust, a single or double Feint, Half-passes, Enclosing, and Commanding· of all which in order as I explain the following Lessons.

If your adversary therefore take himself to this Guard, and you upon the same Guard, present your sword without and a little beneath it. Then (supposing alwise that you are within measure and reach of him, for if you are without distance, you must either first approach before you begin your Lesson, or otherwise approach with the first motion of your Lesson, when it will admit of it, and that you can thereby reach your adversary, which by a little practice you will quickly discover) I say, when you have thus presented your sword, you may pursue your adversary, upon these two parts I before mentioned, with six different Lessons or thrusts, and consequently with as many Half-passes and Enclosings. Because against all Guards, a man may for the most part, when he pleases, finish and terminate any thrust with an Enclosing, and his Enclosing with an attempt to Command the sword. But against this Guard especially, nothing can be more easy. And these six Lessons are two plain Thrusts, two single Feints, and two double Feints.

The *First Lesson* is a plain Thrust in *Seconde* upon the same side you are lying with your sword, or without Disengaging; carrying sometimes your sword-hand low, and sometimes in *Tierce* for the better eviting of your adversary's Parade; and the point towards the upper part of his belly only. For I am altogether (as I before said in the Article anent Thrusting, Error 2, p.129) against planting or thrusting too high, the common direction in Schools, where a man must of necessity pierce either bones or very hard cartilages before he can dangerously wound his adversary. Whereas when a man thrusts about the belly, he is not only with more difficulty Paried, but also his sword penetrates with a great deal more ease, and with less force and constraint to his own body. You may also, if you please, very safely convert this thrust into a Half-pass, either for Enclosing or Commanding. Or you may, if you can catch the opportunity, and that your adversary's sword comes to be beneath yours and but a little towards your left side, form a kind of *Flanconade* thrust upon him by directing the point towards the left side of his belly, your sword-hand in *Quarte*, opposing at the same time his sword with your left hand to prevent a *Contre-temps* or Exchanged Thrust as you are giving home the thrust. And if in place of a thrust, you intend

a blow, then you may make a jerk or stroak upwards at the wrist or lower part of your adversary's sword-hand; taking alwise care to edge your blow right, if it be with a Sheering Sword. That is, that you do not strike with the flat side of your sword. A direction to be observed with the delivering of every other blow, as well as this. Altho' this kind of upward jerking blow be indeed more difficult to edge than any other.

But I must here advertise you once for all, that all jerking stroaks upwards from this Guard, such as this I have been describing, altho' they may sometimes happen to disable, yet they are for the most part very weak and do but little predjudice. Therefore I much rather recommend to you those blows which are perform'd by bringing down the sword-hand or blow, as by either carrying of it up or side-wise. And therefore in place of this jerking stroak upwards, you may make a very good blow downwards, either towards his head; or out-side of his wrist, or advanced thigh, leg, or foot; or even upon the inside, if you time it right, and with a slope motion from right to left beneath his sword. For such a down-right blow, if performed seasonably and with vigour, will not only many times disable, but may come to take away the Life when directed towards the head and neck. Whereas the blow upwards with a jerk, being weak, is a great deal more proper for making an open. And therefore may be made use of very conveniently, as well with a Small Sword as with a Sheering, in place of a Feint. For you are sure of one of two by it, that if you hit, you may disable by it, and if you do not hit, yet it will certainly oblige your adversary to discover an open to you without and above the sword (for let some nice Sword-Men fancy what they will, and notwithstanding all their direct injunctions to the contrary, it is scarcely possible for any man to refrain altogether from answering a brisk and lively-made motion of Feint, let him put on the strongest resolutions imaginable to the contrary), whereby you will have an excellent and full down-right stroak at his head or shoulders: the only stroak indeed that I value, and would advise every man to aim at, who really designs to good execution against his adversary with blows. Because the most part of other kinds of blows are, as I said, rather for discovering and gaining an open, though sometimes they may also come to disable. Whereas this kind of downright blow is for real execution, yea even to take away the Life, if vigorously delivered by you and fully received by your adversary.

Altho' after all, when there is a real design against the Life, there is nothing comparable to the thrust, because of its being, when right planted, so much more dangerous and frequently more mortal than the blow.[16] Therefore in this case I would never attempt either a real or feigned blow unless it were to obtain a

---

[16] See p. 60, note 4.

better open to thrust at, or when I could not possibly thrust, which can but very rarely fall out. These three last directions - of making as much use of the down-right or sloping blow downwards as possible; and edging it right when a man does strike in good earnest; and of alwise making most use of the point, especially when there is real and bloody execution intended, even to the taking away of the Life - are of such consequence in an earnest and revengeful engagement with Sharps, that I cannot but advise the reader to mark them.

The *Second Lesson* is a plain Thrust without and above your adversary's sword, by Disengaging and planting it as low (your sword-hand in *Tierce* or *Quarte*, which you please) as you can conveniently force it upon his sword. For in this thrust I find it alwise convenient to take a little more of the adversary's body by pressing of his sword than is necessary upon most other thrusts, by reason of the Parade of this thrust being so very easy to him. This is what I call *Forcing of his Sword*. And indeed without it, or having an exceedingly swift method of thrusting, a man shall scarcely wound his adversary with this plain Thrust without and above the sword, if he has anything of a quick Parade, unless he first cause him to discover an open by making a Feint without and below his sword, which is the next Lesson I am going to describe.

This plain Thrust without and above the sword may be also turn'd, if you please, into a Half-pass and Enclosing or Commanding; and is, in my opinion, a far safer one than that in the preceeding Lesson, without and below your adversary's sword. Because in this, your sword-hand, if you fail in your Commanding, is more disengaged and at liberty to make sure your defence, when you have thus put yourself out of order, than it is in the former. And you can also more readily Command and catch hold of your adversary's sword with your left hand, than you can possibly do in the preceeding Lesson (unless you can in it have the conveniency of Enclosing and Commanding quite beneath his sword, which resembles much the Lesson called in the Schools *Under-Counter*). Altho' either of the opportunities in both Lessons are very good, as a man shall in practice accustom himself to them. These two *Terms of Art*, or rather Lessons, *Flanconade* and *Under-Counter*, were not forgot, but purposely omitted by me in discoursing of the *Terms of Art* because a man cannot play them exactly against this Guard, but only from two thrusts which resemble them a little. And therefore they belong chiefly to the Common Method. And even in it, the opportunity very rarely to be got of playing them, especially at Sharps, I did not think it worth my while to discourse of them. Altho' I now thought it convenient just but to name them, that the reader may know there are two such Lessons taught in the Schools.

As for a blow, the converting of this thrust without and above the sword to it is the most natural that can be formed against this Guard. Because here a man has a plain and full down-right blow at the upper parts of his adversary, either head or shoulders, although the head should alwise be the most aimed at. And albeit this blow be indeed easie enof to defend by the adversary, yet if he fail in it, he may come to be not only disabled, but even to lose his Life by it. Especially if delivered with a good Back Sword or Sabre, rightly edged, and by a strong and vigorous man.

This is one of those down-right stroaks I so much recommended the practice of in the preceeding Lesson. And if a single one take not effect, then it is to be redoubled, not once, but several times, according to the strength of the pursuer. But still with this caution, to take care to defend himself well from his adversary's Riposte thrust or blows. And this is the only true Method of engaging for the preservation of one's Life, either in a single engagement, or amongst a crowd in a battle. For it is nothing but such re-iterated down-right blows accompanied sometimes with a smart plain Thrust, that in such junctures a man is either to expect and fear himself, or to make his adversary apprehensive of. The other subtile, nice, and diverting play with Feints, Crossings, Binding, Beating, and Enclosing, altho' useful in a Single Combat, being but of very little use to a man, either in a battle when he comes to close fight, or when he happens to be accidentally engaged in any rabble where he is environed with a crowd. Therefore I recommend much the practice both of the quick delivery, and defence of this kind of down-right or sloping blow downwards, to all who are concerned in the Army, or who intend to be truely Masters of an useful *Battle with Blows*, whether offensive or defensive.

The *Third Lesson*, as I said, is a single Feint without and below the sword. And because it is made upon the same side that your sword is presented, the motion of the Feint is therefore made without Disengaging, by only making a lively motion with the sword-hand, as if you intended to give home a plain Thrust upon the same side. And immediately afterwards Disengaging, and giving the thrust without and above the sword by a little pressing upon and forcing your adversary's sword, if needful, as in the second Lesson, to make your thrust the more effectual.

For the blow, this thrust may be yet more conveniently, and with greater ease and force, converted into a down-right stroak than that in the preceeding Lesson. Because the motion of the Feint upon the same side your sword is presented adds more life and vigour to it than if the blow were to be delivered simply without it. For here, I may say, the blow, as water does in a strong current, gathers strength in its motion, *vim acquirit eundo*. The motion of the Feint sets the blow first a-going, whereby it is discharged with more violence and force than if it were delivered simply without any antecedent motion, such as that of the lively Feint, made without and beneath the sword before Disengaging.

So that I look upon this Lesson from a single Feint without and below the sword to be absolutely the best a man can make use of upon this *Hanging Guard*: whichever of the two offences he designs, either blow or thrust. Only he is to take special care that in the time he is making his Feint, his adversary take not time upon him by thrusting or striking at the same time he is a-forming of his Feint. Which is the greatest hazard a man is expos'd to, not only in this Lesson, but in all others which are preceeded by a Feint. Therefore let this caution serve once and for all, where any kind of Feints are designed.

And seeing I am upon Feints, there is also another very good kind of blow which may be performed thus: make a slow feigned blow from right to left beneath your adversary's sword, towards his legs. This slow motion of a blow will readily draw out and encourage your adversary to strike out upon that time (and if he do it not the first time, give him a second and even third opportunity). Which so soon as ever you perceive he takes, you are instantly to Parie with the Cross Parade above your sword, as in Figure 16 [p. 173], and give him a Riposted blow either upon the out or in-side of his thigh, leg, or foot, which you please. This is a most useful kind of stroak for disabling the advanced leg, and very often takes, if cunningly gone about. As for the Half-pass, Enclosing, and Commanding upon this Lesson, they are to be performed as in the second Lesson.

The *Fourth Lesson* is a single Feint without and above the sword by Disengaging; and then giving the thrust below the sword at the upper part of the belly, the sword-hand in *Seconde*. And sometimes also with the point low and the hilt high, the better to resist your adversary's Parade. This thrust may also be converted into a Half-pass, an Enclosing, or a Commanding, as in the first Lesson.

As for the blow from this Lesson, the Feint being made above the sword, the blow must be delivered towards the right thigh, leg, or foot, upon the out-side. Being performed after the same manner as in the first Lesson, or as that immediately described in the last paragraph of the third.

The *Fifth Lesson* is a double Feint. The first motion being made without and beneath the sword, or upon the same side your sword is presented. The second, without and above the sword, at the head or breast. And the third, which is the thrust, must be delivered without and below the sword, as in Lesson first. And so are also the Half-pass, Enclosing, and Commanding, if a man shall resolve to make use of any of them from this Lesson, to be performed as in the first.

For the blow, this Lesson being a double Feint, and the first motion being below the sword, makes that the blow also falls to be given beneath, as the thrust was, or at least upon the outside of the sword, whereby it will be but very weak. And therefore I do not so much value it from this Lesson as from the next. And by the way, you are to remember that the thrusts or blows of all double Feints terminate alwise upon the same side of the sword upon which the first motion of the Feint was made. Whereas the blows or thrusts of all single Feints terminate upon the opposite side to that whereupon the first motion of the Feint was made; unless you finish your thrust or blow upon the same side you made your single Feint, which altho' not an ordinary Lesson taught in the Schools, yet is very surprising, and many times takes effect beyond expectation. This I judged fit to advertise you of, that thereby you may dispose of and manage your Feints to your greater advantage when you resolve to follow that method of pursuit.

The *Sixth and last Lesson* I shall at present trouble you with is another double Feint. The first motion being made without and above the sword; the second, without and below the sword; and the thrust, which is the third motion, given in above and without the sword, by forcing or pressing a little upon the adversary's sword, as in the second and third Lessons, that it may take the more upon his body. This double Feint is by far the best of the two double Feints from this Guard. And therefore when a man designs a double Feint he should make much more frequently use of this than of the preceeding, whose thrust terminates beneath the sword. The Half-pass, Enclosing, and Commanding may most safely be performed from this Lesson. And are to be executed exactly as in the second or third Lessons, to which, that I may prevent repetitions, I remit the reader.

As for the blow, there may be a very good and smart one drawn from it above the sword and the upper parts of the body, and altho' it be not quite as strong as those from the second or third Lessons, because it proceeds from a double Feint, yet if smartly and vigorously delivered, it will not only disable, but may, if rightly edged and well planted or directed, especially to the head or neck, and also redoubled if need be, prove mortal.

Thus I have finished the few Lessons I consider most proper for the pursuit against any person who might take himself to this Guard for his defence, wherein I have endeavoured for the reader's greater ease to be as short as possible. And if he understands these six Lessons or thrusts, together with the blows, Half-passes, Enclosings, and Commandings that are most readily drawn from them exactly in execution, upon this position of his sword from whence I have descrived them: to wit, when his sword is presented without and beneath his adversary's, and a little towards the adversary's left side, I say if he be absolutely Master of them from this position of the sword, he will by a little reflection easily apply them to any of the other three positions I before named, *viz.* when his sword is either above the sword towards his adversary's left side, of above and beneath it towards his adversary's right. Those positions of his sword being drawn, as I have said, rather from the different ways he forms his Parade when engaged than from the natural posture of this Guard upon first presenting his sword.

But altho' a man may by frequent practice come to play the above-mentioned Lessons very exactly, either upon a Master's breast-plate, or upon a comrade; yet if he be not accustomed to Assault, where he will meet with opposition and consequently have occasion to make use of his judgement, as well as of the practical part of his Lessons, he may find himself difficulted, by reason of his not being instructed in the fundamentals and chief circumstances which may occur to him, not only in Assaulting for his diversion, but especially when engaged in an Occasion for his Life. Therefore it will not be amiss, before I put a close to this Chapter, to inform him a little as to this matter. And seeing the engaging in good earnest with Sharps is the chief circumstance wherein a man can be concerned, and that if he knows how to acquit himself dexterously in it, he will easily do it for his diversion with blunts, therefore I shall tye myself only to this circumstance of being engaged with Sharps for the Life, and shall give no directions but what I judge absolutely necessary for it. Because in such a case, multiplicity of rules, as well as of Lessons, do for the most part, in place of giving relief and assistance to one's judgement, rather embarrass and confound it.

When a man comes to engage for his Life, it must be either in a crowd, where he is surrounded with two, three, or more; or in a Single Combat. If it be in a crowd or close fight in a battle, either a-foot or on horseback, then he is to defend himself with the Cross Parade, as in Figure 16; returning alwise from the Riposte for his offence either smart blows or plain Thrusts; and going still after every thrust or stroak to the Parade, if they continue to attack him. And these he is to redouble and continue at, so long as his strength will allow him, until he either make way for himself, or get relief from those of his party who are to second him. Any other Lessons belonging to the sword, and which might be of great use in a Single Combat, such as Feints, Beating, Securing of the sword, Half-passes, Enclosing, and Commanding, being of little or no use at all in such close engagements amongst a crowd. Because when a vigorous and brisk officer hath perhaps disabled or run one enemy through, and is actually Commanding of another, there steps in a third, who endeavours to knock him on the head, or cleave him down. For, *Ne Hercules quidem contra multos.* Therefore in such an unequal engagement there is no other course to be taken by a brave man who is resolved to stand to it to the very last, but to discharge incessantly plain Thrusts or blows as smartly and quickly as he can. Taking care

at the same time to receive or defend his adversary's stroaks, as much as he possibly can, upon the blade of his sword, with the above-mentioned Cross Parade.

And seeing armour is now a-days much out of fashion amongst officers as well as soldiers, it were in this case most reasonable, as well as it would be advantageous and convenient, that officers at least should be alwise provided with good long gauntlets, sword-proof, for their left hands, which would not in the least embarrass or incommode them when engaged. But upon the contrary, prove a great relief and assistance to them, for their better defence. For with a good Sheering Sword or Sabre, with a close-hilt, in one hand, and a long gauntlet, sword-proof, upon the other, which will reach near to the elbow, an agile and sharp or quick-sighted, vigorous man may come to defend two or three blows at one and the very same time. That is, at least one upon his gauntlet or armed left hand or arm, by throwing it up to receive the blow, and another with the sword, if not two, *viz.* one upon its blade, and the other upon its close or shell hilt (the only proper hilts for swords of battle). And which defence will be, as I said, a very great advantage to any man, as well soldier as officer, when he shall be in a close engagement, where they frequently come to sharp and bloody stroaks. Therefore I cannot but recommend it, and wish that this providing of officers and soldiers, both Horse and Foot, with good long gauntlets, sword-proof, for their left hands (and which, except in time of action, ought to be hung at their sword belts, for the less incommoding them when marching), may be taken into consideration by such of the government as are more nearly concerned, not only in the providing of the Army with what is needful for offending, but also with what is necessary, as well for the defence and preservation of their Lives, as for the support and subsistence of their persons. For indeed the dexterous use of the left hand is of such use, not only in a crowd, but even in a Single Combat, notwithstanding of the gross and unaccountable neglect of it of late amongst the generality of the professors of the *Art of Defence*, that I cannot enof recommend it. So much, in short, for the behaviour of any man upon this *Hanging Guard in Seconde*, when he shall come to be engaged either in a close fight in a Field Battle in time of war, or amongst a crowd in a town rabble in time of peace.

But if a man shall be so misfortunate as to be engaged in a Single Combat a-foot (because for his behaviour a-horseback, I refer him to what I have said upon that head in Article 19, page 140), then it must be with either an Artist or an Ignorant. But with which of them soever he be to engage, he will find their constitution or temper, in the time of their first engagement, to prove one of the four following.

First, they will either advance and come on precipitantly, with an irregular, violent, and furious pursuit.

Or, *Secondly*, keep themselves almost fixt in one place, without either much advancing or retiring.

Or, *Thirdly*, constantly retire, and give much back.

Or, *Fourthly*, have a mixture of all three. That is, sometimes stand fixt, and at other times advance and retire. And this last and mixt method of play or temper is what I have added myself; the three first being indeed mentioned by Monsieur de Liancour in his French book of Fencing, page 36. But this last by no author that I know of, altho' to my own knowledge it be a humour which a man will more frequently meet with in an earnest engagement, than with any of the other three. And therefore I cannot comprehend why so great a Master should have quite omitted it, for it is certain he could not be ignorant of it. However, whatever might have been his reasons for omitting it, he conceals them, because he speaks not one syllable of it in his entire book. Altho' it be, as I said, a temper whereof there are a great many more persons to be found than of any of the other three. I shall therefore give a very few, but good, instructions for a man's better behaving of himself against each of these four different tempers. That so my reader may not be too much difficulted when he shall be so unhappy as to be engaged in earnest against any of them.

When a man then shall be engaged against any of these four different tempers I have named, he must certainly become one of two. That is, either the defender or the pursuer.

If he become the defender, then I need only remit him to the preceeding Chapter, where I have fully discoursed, not only of the different methods of opposing the adversary's sword at first engaging, but also of the defences belonging to this Guard when it shall be attacked, either from the same posture, or from any of the common Guards in *Quarte* or *Tierce*. Because all that I could here further add would prove in a manner but a repetition of what I have distinctly and fully set down there.

However by a man's taking himself to the defensive part and becoming wholly the defender, I do not here mean that he should wholly, or altogether tye himself up to it. For that were a ready way to encourage his adversary to pursue him the more furiously. And therefore what I am to advise him, and which is indeed the only true play at Sharps, is a middle play betwixt the two extremes. That is, betwixt the tying or binding up of himself only to the Parade and thrusts from the Riposte, and the wholly abandoning himself to looseness of a violent and inconsiderate pursuit, without in the least offering any defence at all. This last being only to be made use of by hardy and forward Ignorants,

who, being destitute of Art, are in a manner necessitate to it because they can do no better. And the former not to be ventur'd upon but by the greatest, most expert, and dexterous Sword-Men.

And this middle kind of play is the lively counterfeiting of a true pursuit by making brisk and lively offensive motions upon his adversary, as if he really intended to thrust at and wound him. And then either converting this half-pursuit into a true one by really giving home the thrusts or blows, and otherwise attacking him according to the particular offensive Lessons before set down. Or otherwise, when he finds that his adversary will force home a pursuit against him, actually to endeavour to Parie him, assisting his Parade at the same time with the help of the left hand and a moderate Breaking of Measure, until the flash of his adversary's pursuit be over, and then take him from the Riposte. Whereby he will himself become the pursuer off the back of his own defence, which will discover him to be a great Master of the Art. This being indeed the only true play, sword-in-hand, for any man who hath come such a length in the Art, as that he can with a good deal of assurance make use of it. This is all that is needful for any man to observe, when he shall take himself mostly to the defensive part against any adversary whatsoever. But especially against those of the first, or rambling temper. For which, to prevent repetitions, it shall at present serve (together with what I have said in page 123) for sufficient instruction or direction against them. Therefore the reader is entreated to mark it, there being indeed contained here a great deal of Art and judgement in what we call sure and wary Fencing, in a very few lines.

And I cannot but in this place take notice how inconsistent the above-mentioned Monsieur de Liancour is with himself when he is giving directions anent a man's behaviour against this rash, and precipitantly forward temper, which alwise advances. For there, page 41 of the Amsterdam Edition, *anno* 1692, he advises a man to thrust for the most part, alwise *out at a venture*, upon such an adversary's pursuit, without so much as ever offering first to go to the sword, or to Parie. Which is a very strange advice for so great a Master. And much the same as if he should have said, *Whenever any man pursues you violently and irregularly, abandon quite your Art, and relying merely upon chance, thrust smartly out upon him*. Which is a ventorious, and I may say, so foolhardy a practice, that notwithstanding of its sometimes succeeding, I altogether condemn in any Artist, unless, as I have said elsewhere (page 137 to which I refer the reader), he be driven beyond the bounds and limits of all Art, so that it can be no more serviceable to him, which is what can scarcely fall out. And if Monsieur de Liancour had confined this direction of alwise thrusting out, only to this difficult juncture I have named, then I should willingly have agreed with him. But seeing he makes this thrusting out (and which is indeed a kind of *thrusting upon Time*) his chief, and I may say only, contrary to this forward and rambling temper, I cannot but dissent from him by disapproving of it. And the rather because in the very same book, Chapter 6, when he is discoursing of Time and the method of seasonably taking it, he wholly disapproves of the practice of it, especially at Sharps; and advises, in place of it, a good firm Parade, accompanied with a dry Beat, or *Batement sec* as he calls it, which is indeed spoke like a true Sword-Man and a judicious Master, and wherein I heartily go along and concur with him. But not at all in this ventorious thrusting out at random, which is not only contrary to all true Art, but even against all sound reason.

I could not well forbear making this observation, lest this imperfect or by-direction, if I may so term it, of M. de Liancour, should have greater influence upon some young persons who may peruse his book than really it ought. For that I may endeavour to reconcile a little these two so opposite directions, he, in my opinion, certainly gives his own true sentiment on the matter, in the above cited Sixth Chapter, where he discourses of Time. And his only omission and escape lyes in the not applying this direction of thrusting out at random against this forward temper to the true circumstance wherein it ought only to be ventured upon. Which is when a man's adversary is only advancing, but not redoubling of his thrusts at the very same time he is advancing. Or, as I said, when a man is reduced to the last extremity and can do no better, and is therefore resolved to hazard all upon a fortuitous thrust. Because it is not probable that so great a Master, and so judicious in many other points, could commit such a blunder as generally to advise a ventorious thrusting out at random, which is so contrary to the fundamentals of all true and solid Art, unless it had been with respect to the extraordinary circumstance I have named. And especially when he so much condemns it in the middle of his book, where he seriously discoursed of the dangerous nature and method of taking Time. Besides that there is a very great difference betwixt a man's thrusting out upon one who is advancing briskly upon him, without thrusting at the same time; and upon another, who in the time of his brisk advancing is alwise redoubling of thrusts. A good Sword-Man may sometimes venture upon the first, because it is a good Time (which is all M. de Liancour certainly meant). But this last is not to be ventured upon, but, as I said, in the very last extremity. And even then it ought to be accompanied, as well as the former, with the help of the left hand. May this serve then at present for M. de Liancour's vindication, and to remove that seeming contradiction or inconsistency which at first view he appears to be guilty of in his above-mentioned book, which for instructing a man in the Common Method of Fencing is indeed a very good one.

And seeing I have been giving directions against this first or forward humour, wherein the use of the left hand is of singular use, as well as Breaking of Measure; I find myself in a manner obliged to obviate an objection, which is of so much the greater consequence as it is leveled against the whole Art. And it is this:

Of what avail or use is your glorious and noble Art of Defence, say some, *when we see by your own confession that all Art with the sword alone, without the assistance of your left hand, is not capable to defend you. So that remove but that, and we shall very quickly make you sensible that in a sudden and earnest attack, a vigorous Ignorant of this first constitution, with his violent and furious pursuit, will render your Art so insignificant and ineffectual that any bystander shall have difficulty to determine which of the two, Art or Ignorance, have the advantage, and are most, in such a juncture, to be valued and esteemed.*

To which I briefly answer, in vindication of the true *Art of Defence*, that if a good and dexterous Sword-Man have no other design but the defence of his own person, and not the destruction of his adversary's also, that then his sword alone, assisted by a judicious Breaking of Measure, is (I will not say infallibly, because there is no such thing to be found in any practice amongst us poor mortals, but so far only as human nature is capable of) sufficient to defend him. But again if he desire to offend as well as defend, then there is an absolute necessity to make use of his left hand for his assistance. Otherwise his adversary, continually redoubling his thrusts irregularly and with vigour upon him, he shall almost never have the opportunity of thrusting, his sword being in a manner wholly taken up with the Parade, by endeavouring to make good his defence. For it very rarely falls out, except when humour'd by a Master in taking a School Lesson, that a sword can both Parie and thrust at one and the same time. Altho' it may sometimes. Tho' then mostly also by chance.

So that it is plain and obvious to every considering person that it is not so much for an absolute necessary assistance to the sword in a man's own defence that the use of the left hand is so much recommended by me, as to put a check and stop to the furious pursuit of the Ignorant; who is very sensible that so long as he redoubles swiftly, it is not almost in the power of his adversary to thrust safely; nay, not even from the Riposte, without running the hazard of receiving either a *Contre-temps* thrust, or perhaps one before he can recover from his Riposted thrust. And it is upon this account that the Breaking of Measure against such rude and irregular ramblers has alwise been esteemed, when the left hand was not to be used. A most reasonable, as well as most artificial and judicious Contrary. And which is still more &

more strengthened by a dexterous use of the left hand, especially in all engagements wherein a man's Life is at stake. Of which Breaking of Measure see what I have said under its proper Article page 140.

Let this serve at present as a sufficient answer to this seemingly great, but indeed very common and trifling, objection against the *Art of Defence*: its being unsufficient with the sword alone to furnish a compleat Sword-Man with a reasonably perfect defence against the furiously quick and irregular pursuits of the most head-strong and desperate ramblers; I say, when the Sword-Man designs only his own defence, and not the death of his adversary. For here lyes the distinction and strength of my answer.

And indeed were I not fully convinced that, in this case, the Art is abundantly sufficient to furnish a man with a certain defence for his person with the sword alone (that is, such certainty as we frail creatures are capable of), I should be much in the wrong. Not only to have spent so much time, I may say, in vain and idly writing of it, but to recommend the practice of so useless an exercise with so much zeal and earnestness to my fellow countrymen as I have all along done. And therefore I hope and expect that this will encourage them, that as I doubt it not in the least myself, so I dare promise that if they punctually follow the directions I have given them in this *New Method*, they shall by their experience confirm my sentiment if ever they shall have to do in good earnest with any of this forward, or rather furious and desperate temper.

Neither will it be amiss that I take notice by the way, and here acquaint my reader, if an Artist, that as Ignorants rack their invention to make objections against the Art, whereby they may, if possible, render it contemptible to such who, being as ignorant as themselves, can therefore know nothing of the matter; so the most part of Artists, and even very good Sword-Men, start difficulties to themselves when they come to engage against such Ignorants, and fancy that they can do far greater feats against them by their rambling than really they can. Which is the chief reason of their often succeeding so ill against them. Whereas if they look'd upon them as really such, that is, as wholly Ignorants in the Art, and with a little more disdain and contempt than commonly they do, and did not also expect something more of a judicious opposition and pursuit from them than it is possible for such maladroits to put in execution; they would find their Art answer better than their expectation; Ignorants oftener and more frequently baffled by them; and consequently the true *Art of Defence* had in that esteem by all Honourable and judicious persons as it most justly ought, and even to a very kind of demonstration deserves. But if this advice be neglected, or no better observed, than, I am afraid, a great many other very good ones I have given all along in this treatise shall be, then it is to be feared, neither will it be any great wonder, if many Sword-Men have not

only the like bad success against such rude and forward ignorant ramblers as formerly. But also that they be disregarded, and had in no esteem by the generality of people as to their skill. And the Art itself likewise, as much undervalued and contemned as ever.

But if a man be necessitate to become the pursuer, then he will certainly find his adversary of one of the other three remaining constitutions or tempers I before named. If of the second, fixt or slothful temper, then he will have little else to do, but in a manner to divert himself, and by making his adversary feel some of his gentlest thrusts, as described in the foregoing Lessons, make him sensible of how much he is Master of him. Taking alwise care however, as he is giving home of his thrusts, to prevent the being catcht upon Time, or receiving a thrust from the Riposte, or an Exchanged one before the recovery of his own body. Against all which, the dexterous use of the left hand will not be a small preventative.

Again if it be against the third, or timorous, temper, which for the most part retires and gives back; then as his adversary retires, he is still to advance upon him with the single step until within distance, and then to make use of any of the preceeding Lessons as he shall judge fit. Not neglecting to redouble them by gathering up his left foot, if his adversary shall break his Measure a little as he is thrusting. And if his adversary still give more ground, and confusedly, then he is to renew his advancing again upon him until within distance for thrusting, and thus to continue it so long as he judges it convenient and safe for him to prosecute his pursuit. But then the former direction to prevent either the being surprised upon Time, an Exchanged Thrust, or one from the Riposte, is no less to be observed against the Retireing or cowardly temper, than against the immovable one.

But lastly, if it shall be against a person of the fourth humour or temper that you shall be engaged, that is, who makes use of a mixt play, by sometimes advancing or taking the pursuit, and immediately again either keeping himself firm in one place, or otherwise giving a little way by a moderate Breaking of Measure, then it is very probable that such an adversary is no Ignorant, but understands a little by Art what he is going about. Upon which account you are to look upon him as such, and be a little more circumspect than against any of the other three. Because here you are to expect more cunning than from any of the other, and that he will answer you according to the rules of Art. Therefore you are to play upon him what of the foregoing offensive Lessons you shall judge will take most effect; performing them alwise calmly and with judgement. And indeed this humour I look upon to be the most dangerous, tho' not the most troublesome or rambling of the four, because it is commonly accompanied by Art. Whereas the other three are not. And therefore I will give two or three very good general directions against it.

The *First* respects a man's adversary, and it is this: that, if possible, before engaging, you look him boldly and steadfastly in the face to observe what kind of frame he is in at that time. A man who is little accustomed to it will draw indifferent sure observations from his adversary's countenance and deportment when he is first going to engage, as whether his pursuit will be violent or slack. For as one very well says, *Profecto in oculis animus habitat*; the eyes are certainly the mirrors or looking-glasses of the mind. And a great deal of a man's inward disposition may, by a judicious observation, be drawn from them, to a Sword-Man's great advantage. Not only before, but when a man can do no better, even at first engaging, as well as in the very time of it.

The *Second* respects a man's self. Which is that in every engagement, whether he resolve to be pursuer or defender, particularly the pursuer, he not only put on a boldness or briskness in his looks, whereby he may in some measure quell or temper his adversary's forwardness; but also whatever Lesson or pursuit he is once resolved to make use of, he go cleverly through with it, without the least hankering or hesitation. Whereby it will commonly be accompanied with a greater success than if he should perform it with a kind of lashness and faintly. For according to the proverb, as *Faint Heart never gained Fair Lady*; so a faint-hearted Sword-Man will never make a good one. Besides that, it is frequently observable that there is a kind of success or good luck which attends magnanimity and a courageous boldness.

So that in this case a stout Sword-Man who is resolved upon the pursuit should act as a good General who is to give battle: who before he engages, endeavours to foresee all difficulties and dangers; but in fighting oversees them, that by his good and brave example he may the more encourage and embolden his soldiers to do the like. Even so a judicious and skillful Sword-Man ought to endeavour, before he begin his pursuit, to foresee what contraries his adversary may probably use against it. But when once he is engaged in it, he should oversee them. That is, not in the least hesitate or be discouraged by them, but go boldly through with it, as if there were no such difficulties or hazards in his way to oppose him. These two general directions being of such great use to Sword-Men when in an Occasion, especially when engaged against others who are as great Artists as themselves, I could not well pass them over. I shall therefore conclude them with my Three Great Fundamentals, whereupon I erected *The Sword-Man's Vade-Mecum*, which are CALMNESS, VIGOUR, and JUDGEMENT. And shall give you in a few lines the abstract of it, which, as a precious and useful preservative against a sudden attack with Sharps, you are alwise to carry about with you in your memory, that so it may constantly be in a readiness to assist you upon a pinch, when perhaps your Honour or Life is at stake.

Therefore, *with CALMNESS, VIGOUR and JUDGMENT...Use...*

1. The *Guard in Seconde* with a sloping point.
2. A good *Crossing Parade* assisted with the left hand.
3. A brisk *Half-Pursuit*, until you make a true & full one.
4. Plain & easy *Offensive Lessons*, briskly performed; and alwise opposing the left hand, to prevent a *Contre-temps*, an *Exchanged Thrust*, or one from the *Riposte*.
5. A moderate and judicious *Breaking of Measure*, until the violence and fury of your adversary's pursuit be over; when you find that he will force a pursuit upon you.

With *CALMNESS, VIGOUR* and *JUDGMENT...Prevent...*

1. Being *Decoy'd* or Deceived by Feints, as much as possible.
2. Being *Catcht upon Time*, when advancing to Thrust.
3. Being without *Distance* when Thrusting.
4. Resting upon a *Thrust* after it is delivered.
5. A *Contre-temps, Exchanged Thrust*, or one from the *Riposte*, by making seasonably use of the left hand, as either you your self, or your adversary, shall Thrust.

These few lines, I do confidently affirm, contain the very marrow and substance of the whole *Art of the Sword*; and are the ABSTRACT of a little book I formerly writ, entitled *The Sword-Man's Vade-Mecum*. A very just and apposite title indeed! For it is such an excellent *Vade-mecum*,[17] that no man who pretends to be anything of a true Sword-Man but ought to have its abstract so fixt in his memory, and so ready upon the drawing of his sword, that the practice of the few excellent directions contained in it should flow from him not only readily and with the least difficulty and constraint, but also with that unaffected (or rather, if I may so word it) *A la Negligence Grace*, and ease, as if they were wholly natural to him.

May therefore the reader fix it well in his memory. And let him depend upon my word for it, that the closer he keep to it upon an Occasion, the more it will conduce to his preservation and safety. And the oftener he practices it, the more & more he will still discover of its worth and excellency, and be sensible and acknowledge that all I have said in its behalf and commendation, with respect to its usefulness and security, falls very short of what it really deserves.

---

[17] A useful thing; a guidebook.

O useful ABSTRACT! who possesses Thee;
And thy Just Precepts practise with these Three;
Needs no Man's Point, or Edged Sabre fear;
Since by Thee, from all Danger he's secure.
Weigh well this Chapter then, who wou'd have Art;
It, and Preceeding, ought to get by Heart.
For in them Two, is compendized All
A Sword-Man needs to know, of Broad or Small.

However, that I may somewhat gratify my young curious reader, and remove a little of that itch which is commonly excited by a kind of curiosity that attends almost all young people when they incline to improve themselves in the *Art of the Sword*, and who are many times surprisingly taken with the seeming great names given frequently by Masters to some of the Lessons in the Ordinary Method, whereby they imagine that there is somewhat of a secret mystery in the Art, more than really there is, I shall here, although it be altogether beyond what I at first intended, make a kind of abstract of the common Lessons of the Ordinary Method, that young Gentlemen may not be hereafter imposed upon or amused by outlandish and apparently great names, to make them imagine that there is something more mysterious in the Lessons of the Art than really there is. And which I am hopeful will render this Essay so much the more compleat, that it contains not only my *New Method of Fencing*, but, in a manner, the substance of what I writ of the Common Method in the other three pieces I formerly published upon the same subject. To wit, the *Scots Fencing Master, The Sword-Man's Vade-Mecum* and *The Fencing Master's Advice to His Scholar*. So that without being at the trouble of enquiring after any of these, to be informed in the Ordinary Method, he needs only peruse this, where in the foregoing explications of the *Terms of Art*, Chapter 4, and particularly in this and the preceeding Chapter, he will find all that is material in them, or needful for him to know, with relation to both this *New Method* and the Old.

When a young country Gentleman comes to town, and steps into a Fencing School, and hears a Master desire his Scholar to play *Feint a la Teste, Botte Coupé, Flanconade, Under-Counter*, or to *Dequarte and Volt*, he is amazed at these terms, and is persuaded that there is a kind of conjuring magick in the Art; and that the understanding but only to play these Lessons upon the Master's breast-plate is enof, in all conscience, to make him a good Sword-Man; and by a kind of enchantment cause him to overcome and master all persons he shall thereafter engage with. When at the same time the Lessons to which such specious and seeming hard names are given, are nothing else but the directing of the Feint or Thrust, to such and such a particular part of the body. For example,

A Thrust or Feint *en dedans*, is nothing but a plain Thrust or Feint within the sword; as *en dehors* is without the sword.

Feint *a la teste*, is only when the Feint is made at the head. And when it is made more directly to the eyes, it is called *aux yeux*; but when made towards the lower parts of the body, is termed by the French, *Feinte basse*. And so are all other Feints denominate, according to the parts of the body towards which they are directed: as to the shoulders, sides, thighs, legs, feet, &c.

For all Feints must be made either upon the length or breadth of the body. And as I before said, page 132, a man may form as many different kinds of them as there are particular members in the body. But because that would make but confusion, therefore Masters have thought fit, and with a great deal of reason, to reduce them to a competent number which may answer the chief parts of the body, either from head to foot upon its length, or from right to left upon its breadth. A list of which I have set down in Chapter 4, Article 13.

Botte coupé, is a Feint again upon the breadth of the body towards the left side, as the former are upon the length of it. See the above-mentioned Article. This much for Feints, which are performed without in the least offering to engage or secure the adversary's sword before making them.

Again there are other Feints which are preceeded by a kind of securing of the sword, such as that from Batterie, see page 138; and from Binding, see page ibid., which is the most secure of any.

Next to Feints, there are Lessons in which a man engages, and in some measure, secures his adversary's sword before performing them, such as *Flanconade*. Wherein, after crossing or overlapping the adversary's sword, the thrust is directed towards his right flank, from whence it hath its name; and *Under-Counter*, which is also an overlapping and raising of the adversary's sword, the hand meantime turning to *Seconde*, until you make an open beneath the sword, whereat you may give in the thrust at the slot of his breast, or a little below it, whence it is called *Under-Counter*. And likewise also all the other thrusts preceeded by a dry Beat or Binding of the adversary's sword with a kind of springing cross, and which is indeed, as I have often said, the only play at Sharps for a man's Life. See Chapter 4, Article 17.

Again there are Lessons which are chiefly for diversion in School Play, and to show a man's address and agility of body, such as Taking of Time, *Dequarteing*, or *Dequarteing and Volting* immediately after other. See pages 134, 136 .

Lastly there are Passes for School Play, Half-passes, Enclosings, and Commandings, which are not only useful for diversion, but also at Sharps; especially from this new Guard in *Seconde*. For all which, to avoid repetitions, see Chapter 4, under their respective Articles. This much for the Lessons offensive.

Again for the defensive part, there are the Parades in *Tierce*, *Quarte*, and *Seconde*, which are nothing else but the position of the sword-hand in one of the four quarters of circle when it is Parieing (see page 118), and signifies not a farthing for the rendering of a man's Parade more certain. That consisting wholly in the good cross he makes upon his adversary's sword (whatever position his sword-hand is in), and not in the particular positions of *Tierce*, *Quarte*, or *Seconde*. Altho' I do not deny, but in some singular cases, a certain position of the hand in *Tierce* may be more proper than if it were in *Quarte* or *Seconde*; as at another time that of a *Quarte* may be more proper than those of the other two; which by a little practice a man will quickly discover of himself. And likewise the *Contre-caveating* Parade is so denominate by me because it is the only true Contrary to Caveating, Slipping, or Disengaging; and consequently admirable against all kind of Feints whatsoever.

This is a short abbreviate of those Lesson in the Common Method which appear so mysterious to young Gentlemen when they first set about Fencing. And which I have in a manner but just named, that when other novices shall hereafter hear them mentioned, they may not be likewise amused or surprised with them, as if there were no such Lessons in this *New Method* like unto these. Because I only name and denominate them according to the part of the body upon which they ought to be played, and not according to the nice or outlandish terms, whether French or Italian, whose sound alone is enof to make them pass with some people for something mysterious, and even so charming and magical as not to be refuted or defended when they come in good earnest to make use of them.

For in two words, and without derogating the foregoing excellent abstract, the whole useful *Art of the Sword*, without making any mystery of it or giving particular names to Parades, Lessons, or Thrusts, consists in this:

First, to make or form alwise a good cross upon your adversary's sword for your defence, whether he be either thrusting or striking.

And *Secondly*, never to thrust or strike yourself, but when you are within distance of your adversary; and when you have a view, sight, or Open for it. And when you have none, then you are either to procure one yourself by Feints, or compel and force him to make one by Beating, Binding, or pressing his sword so out of the line of the secured part as that you have the opportunity by a good Open either to thrust or strike at him as you please.

When you can perform these, that is PARIE and THRUST dexterously and judiciously, and with a kind of assurance and courage (for this is the life and soul of all Fencing), then you will really deserve the name of a *True and Compleat Sword-Man*, altho' you should not know the proper name of any one Parade or Lesson contained in the whole Common School Method.

Thus I have put a close to this Chapter, which, with the First and Fifth, contain the whole of this *New Method of Fencing*, and also a great deal of the practice from the Common. So that if a man fix them well in his memory, and understand my directions, that is, not only with his judgement, but also by frequently practicing them, I dare venture to promise him a more than ordinary success in his defence against all single weapons whatsoever, however way he may be engaged: whether in a Single Combat or in a close engaged battle. So that for both the needful theory and practice of the whole Art, he needs not, except out of mere curiosity, trouble himself with any other book upon this subject; but only endeavour to put its directions exactly in execution, when he shall be necessitate to use them. I shall now proceed to those Principles relating to the Art which I at first promised, and whereupon, in my opinion, all true Art with respect to secure Fencing ought to be founded.

CHAPTER VII
Of some Chief and Undeniable Principles,
Whereupon the Art of the Sword Ought to be Founded.

The following Principles, whereupon I intend to found the whole *Art of the Sword*, being chiefly designed for those who profess the teaching of it: there appears to be no need of my endeavouring to press their usefulness upon them, seeing they make the communicating of the *Art of the Sword* to others their daily employment. And if they make conscience to do it faithfully and judiciously as they ought, they will be so far from being dissatisfied with and disapproving such Principles, that upon the contrary, they will not only approve of them, but even walk by them. Because it will be a great ease and satisfaction to them that I have laid them before them. Not as if there were nothing to be either rectified or added to them, for I am far from having so vain an opinion of my performance, but only as a true model whereby the more ordinary Masters may regulate their teaching, and the more judicious be assisted to invent and contrive of themselves others which may prove, if possible, more solid and useful.

It being then acknowledged by all judicious persons that all Arts whatsoever are only designed to assist and perfect nature and not to cross her, it must certainly follow that that method of teaching the *Art of the Sword*, together with its practice, which is founded upon those Principles that are most consonant and agreeable to nature and the solid dictates of reason and experience, must be the only truest, and that which all men of judgement will acknowledge should be chiefly made use of by all who design to improve themselves, whether it be but to such a degree in the Art as may be only serviceable to them for a defence when they shall be attacked; or whether they intend to push their knowledge so great a length as that they may be in a capacity, when occasion offereth, not only to reason neatly upon the Art, as well as to practice it indifferently, but also to communicate it to others, according to the most exact and judicious, as well as practical rules imaginable.

Having therefore of a long time seriously, and with a great deal of deliberation and attentiveness, thought upon and considered what Principles might, according to strictest reason, be relied upon as a most solid foundation whereupon to establish the *Art of the Sword*, that thereby I might make way for promoting a general and universal method of teaching amongst the Fencing Masters of these Islands; which is so much wished for by many who are encouragers of the Art, and who, observing the many animosities and divisions which arise daily amongst them, but chiefly in appearance, upon the account of the different methods they make use of in teaching, would have them, if possible, removed by such an expedient as this; I found none to answer my expectation and design so well in every particular as these following, which for method's sake I divide into

THREE CLASSES.
The FIRST whereof respecteth the Art;
The SECOND, the Master who is to Teach it; and
The THIRD, the Scholar who is to be Taught.

FIRST,
Of the Principles which respect the Art, or First Class; and they again may very justly have their division.

For, *First*, some relate to the Weapon or Sword that is to be made use of.

Secondly, others to the particular Motions, whether defensive or offensive, which may be performed with that Weapon, and by the assistance of some particular members of the body, such as feet, legs, thighs, trunk of the body, arms, wrists, hands, &c. Therefore,

First,
Of those Principles which relate to the Weapon or Sword.

A sword is a weapon so well known and acknowledged by all to be of such general use for the defence of a man's person that I need but say little of it. Only that as it is a Gentleman's companion, so it ought to be a part of every Gentleman's business to endeavour not only to understand how to make use of it dexterously, but also to know how to make choice of a such a one as may prove most serviceable to him, either in a Single Combat or in a Field Battle, as he shall have occasion.

There are several kinds of sword blades, some whereof are only for thrusting, such as the Rapier; Koningsberg; and narrow three-cornered blade, which is the most proper walking-sword of the three, being by far the lightest. Others again are chiefly for the blow, or striking, such as the symiter [scimitar], sabre, and double-edged Highland Broad Sword. And there is a third sort, which is both for striking & thrusting, such as the broad three-cornered blade; the Sheering Sword with two edges, but not quite so broad as the aforementioned Highland Broad Sword; and the English Back Sword, with a thick back & only one good, sharp edge, & which, with a good point & close-hilt, is in my opinion the most proper sword of them all for the Wars, either a-foot or on horseback. That therefore a man may the more easily know what are the best qualifications belonging to a good and useful sword, he needs only consider a little the following principles which relate to it.

1 That kind or fashion of sword which can offend maniest ways is to be esteemed the best and most useful. *Therefore a good light Sheering Sword is to be preferr'd to any other because it is useful as well in Single Combat as in a Field Battle.*

2 A blade of that mettal which will endure the greatest stress is to be accounted by far the most fit for service. *Therefore 'tis better to have a poor man's blade (as we commonly call it) that stands in the bend, than one of a harder mettal, but brittle as glass.*

3 A blade should be of that stiffness by which all methods of play can be best performed. *Therefore an indifferent stiff blade is much to be preferr'd to one that is very limber; because this will pierce and go through, when that will yield and snap.*

4 The broadness of a blade does noways contribute to the swiftness and certainty of a true Parade. *Because it is a well fram'd cross upon the adversary's sword that gives a true defence, not the breadth of the blade, nor largeness of the hilt-shell.* See page 125.

5 No blade can have too fine an edge, or too sharp a point. *Because the finer the edge and the sharper the point, the better it will cut and pierce; which, next to defending, are the only uses of a sword.*

6 The lighter a sword is before the hand, so much the better is it mounted. *Because the weight lying next to the hand, which is as the centre, the weight of it is less perceptible to the person who is to wield or use it.* See page 120.

7 The weight and length of every sword ought to be propor tioned to the strength and stature of the person who is to make use of it, but the length and largeness of the handle according to every man's fancy. *Because a big or small handle can never endanger a man's Life, when he chooses that which is most agreeable to his hand; but if he have too great a weight to manage, occasioned by the length of his sword, his defensive motions are thereby retarded and rendered more slow, and consequently the person more exposed to the quick blows and thrusts of his adversary.*

Secondly,
Of those Principles which relate to the particular motions, whether defensive or offensive, which may be performed with the Sword, and by the assistance of the several members of the body: as legs, arms, &c. And for regularity and order's sake, they must have also their division, as follows, viz.

First, some should relate to the Guard, or posture of body, wherein a man should generally put himself when going to perform these actions.

Secondly, some relate to the Parade or defensive part.

Thirdly, some again relate to thrusting, or the offensive part. And in all these, each particular member of the body must act its part to the very Life; otherwise nothing will be done with either that vigour, justness, or agility wherewith indispensibly everything in this Art ought to be performed, and without which, all the pains and trouble any man takes to acquire it is but lost and to no purpose. Now of these three in order. And…

First,

Of Principles relating to a Good and Sufficient Guard.

Before I proceed to the Principles relating to a good and sufficient Guard, I think it proper to inform my reader (which I confess had been more properly done in the Article of a Guard in the *Terms of Art*, page 117, had it not then escaped my memory) that I find, by an old Italian book of Fencing postures which I have by me, that some Fencing Masters of old did not denominate their Guards by *Prime*, *Seconde*, *Tierce* &c, with respect to the different positions of the sword-hand, as the greatest Masters have since done, and indeed with a great deal of reason and judgement, whose example I have also followed in discoursing of a Guard, page 117, and of the different positions of the hand, Article 2, page 118 and following; but according to the different situations they gave to their swords when the pitched themselves to such and such a Guard. So that their *Prime*, *Seconde*, and *Tierce* Guards (for I don't find that in those days they had a *Quarte* Guard) signified nothing but to distinguish their Guards into a First, Second, and Third *Guard*. A First Guard, which was kept with the hand very high, and even above their head, with the sword-point a little sloping; and into a Second, wherein the hand was kept about the height of the shoulder, with the hilt and point level; and lastly a Third Guard, wherein the hilt and point were kept also in a manner level, but the sword-hand low, and only about the upper part of the right thigh. Now this being premised, which may very properly be added to the Article of a Guard, page 117, I say:

1 That in a good and sufficient Guard, the trunk of the body should be for the most part in an æquilibre betwixt the two legs, and so equally supported by them and the two thighs; that it rest almost no more upon one leg and thigh than upon the other. *Because in this posture, a man is certainly more firm and ready either to advance or retire, than when he reposeth amost the whole weight of his body upon any one of his legs and thighs; be it either the Right, or which is most ususal (especially amongst the French), the left: but every whit as bad a custom as the other, and in my opinion the worst of the two. For when a man inclines his body a little forwards, he stands more firm and is more earnest upon, and ready to perform his defence. Whereas when he declines backwards, he is unfixt and weak, and may be easily pressed, not only from his more formal defensive posture, but even to be in hazard of falling backwards upon any unexpected or vigorous Enclosing of his adversary upon him.*

2 The body should for the most part, by its situation, be made both pretty narrow or thin, which is done by keeping easily back the left shoulder; and short, which is done by bending the two knees, and sinking low upon them. *Because in this situation, a man's adversary hath the less of it discovered, both as to its breadth from right to left, and length from head to foot, to thrust at. One of the chief qualifications of a good and secure Guard.*

3 The feet should be at such a due distance, and such a situation, as they may most readily move as a man would have them. *Because if they were otherwise placed, that is, either too near or at too great a distance, it might both retard a man's motion in advancing to offend, and in Breaking of Measure to defend; which would be a great disadvantage to him, especially in an Occasion. This Principle co-incides with the First.*

4 The sword should be kept in the hand with that degree of firmness as neither to be a hindrance to the quick performance of any motion with it, which it is when it is kept too fast; nor to suffer it to be beat out of it by any small unexpected jerk or stroak, to which it is most subject when it is kept too slack and loose, and which is the worst method and most dangerous of the two. *Therefore it is by far safest to err upon the fixt and sure side.*

5 The situation of the sword-arm should be such *as that a man may with greatest ease, in an instant, change the position of his sword, either for his defence or offence, as he shall judge it most convenient.*

6 The position of the sword-hand as to *Prime*, *Seconde*, *Tierce*, or *Quarte*, and of the sword as to High or Low, should be such as, with respect to the particular Guard a man is to make use of, *he may, as much as possible, be ready to perform either a good cross or Parade for defending, or a thrust for offending, as he shall have occasion for them.*

7 The left hand should be so placed as to be alwise most ready either to assist a man in his defence, see page 101, or to catch hold of his adversary's sword, or any part of his body whenever he shall design it. *And therefore it is most convenient to keep it advanced towards the right arm pitt.* See Article 10, page 129.

8 In short, in a good Guard, the whole body should be easy and as much unconstrain'd as possible. And there should be a graceful and unaffected carriage in all the members of the body. *That so one's motions may appear to be done, rather with a kind of pleasure and satisfaction, and altogether a la negligence, as we say, than with any kind or constraint or violence to any part of the body.* And thus much of a good and perfect Guard, or posture of defence, which is the very basis and ground work of all true Fencing.

Secondly,
Of Principles relating to the Parade, or Defensive Part.

1 A good Parade ought to be, as much as possible, universal or general. That is, the motion of it ought to cross or oppose all Lessons or thrusts that can be given in upon any part of the body. *And therefore, as against all Small Sword Lessons or thrusts whatsoever, the Circlular or Contre-caveating Parade is absolutely the safest; except when a man is too near his adversary, see page 126. So against all blows, as well as most thrusts, there cannot be better Parades than those drawn from the Hanging Guard in Seconde, as they are represented in Figures 7, 10 & 16, because of their forming such great and admirable Crosses.*

2 A Parade ought to be so timed, as in the twinkle of an eye, to meet with and turn off the adversary's sword, before the blow or thrust hath reached the body, even though they may have been delivered at a pretty near distance. *Because let the motion of a Parade be never so quick, if it meet not with the adversary's sword, it signifies nothing. Upon which account it hath been found, as I observed, page 150, that a good Sword-Man, altho' he can never be Master of too quick a hand, yet may be at a disadvantage by making the motion of his Parade sometimes too quick.*

3 The strength and smartness of a Parade ought to be such as to be strong enof, when it hath met with the adversary's sword, to put it aside, let the thrust be coming home with never so much force. *Because should it be weak, the thrust might be forced home; and that strength which parries a strong thrust, will always Parie a weak one.*

4 A Parade ought to be alwise performed, if possible, with the Fort of the sword, or as near to it as can be. *Because then the adversary's sword cannot so easily force your sword to effectuate his design in thrusting.*

5 As a Parade ought to be performed with the Fort of the sword, when time will allow it (for sometimes a man may be so press'd as to be necessitate to form his cross with the Foible of his sword); *so it must be also taken, or the cross for the most part formed, upon the weak or Foible of the adversary's sword; unless, as I said, a man be so pressed as that he is glad to endeavour to make his Parade good at any rate, whether upon the Fort or Foible of his adversary's sword, as many times it falls out in a brisk and passionate engagement. In which case, the direction of the Third Principle will be of great use to him.*

6 As a good Parade ought to be, for the most part, performed with the Fort of the sword upon the Foible of the adversary's; so there is sometimes an absolute necessity that it meet with the adversary's sword and form the cross, close almost to a man's own body. Otherwise it will not be possible for him to gain the Foible of his adversary's sword, whereby he may make good his Parade. *This Principle is chiefly useful when a man's adversary is very near to him, and that it is scarcely possible for him to gain the weak of his sword unless he make the crossing motion almost close to his own body (when he makes use of the ordinary Beating Parade in Tierce or Quarte), or towards either of his sides, when he is a framing the cross of his Parade from this new Hanging Guard in Seconde.* In this Principle there is contained a nicety in Parieing, which many good Sword-Men, nay, even great Masters, are ignorant and know nothing of. However such a secret as it is amongst some few Masters who really understand the great use and benefit of it, I have freely and candidly reveal'd, not only in this Principle, but also in Article 7, page 124. For whatever some precise people may pretend to, I own that I neither know myself any secrets in Fencing, nor even knew any that did. Neither, if I did, would I keep them up undiscovered, if I judg'd that they might but in the least tend to the benefit and safety of my country-men, when misfortunately engaged in any Occasion.

Having done with the Principles relating to a good and sufficient Guard, and perfect Parade, which are indeed the two things chiefly requisite for a man's true defence; let us next see what can be said upon the *Third Division* of this *First Class*, which is Offending, or Thrusting.

Thirdly,
Of Principles relating to Thrusting, or the Offensive Part.

1 That method of thrusting, or playing any Lesson, is certainly best, which is most easie, and least disorders the body in the time of performing it; provided that method do not discover too much of the body, and consequently too freely expose it to the *Contre-temps* or Riposte thrusts of the adversary. Which if it should, then another method of playing that Lesson is rather to be preferred, in which the body is a little more close and secure, even altho' it should prove a little more constrained, and not so easie for the body as the former. *Because the security of a man's person, and not the ease of his limbs, being that which the practice of this Art chiefly aimeth at. No man can doubt, when these two, with equal arguments, present themselves to receive a decision of precendency, but that which is for the security of the body, and consequently for the preservation of a man's Life, ought, without any difficulty, to carry it.*

2 In the performing of any thrust or blow wherein there is required an *Elonge*, the trunk of the body, upon the *Elonge*, should be so well supported, and so judiciously balanced upon the legs, especially the advanced, that it may be most readily recovered to perform its defensive motions, as occasion shall require. *Therefore moderate Elonges or stretches, especially at Sharps, are to be preferred to those which, being strained, make it very difficult for a man to recover his body quickly after the delivery of either blow or thrust.*

3 In the delivering of every thrust or blow wherein an *Elonge* or stretch is required, especially after a Feint, the sword-hand ought alwise to be the first mover. *Because, the swiftness of the thrust depending upon the motion of the advanced leg, if the hand should be behind the motion of the leg, the thrust would be so much longer a-coming home to the body, and consequently so much the slower.* Therefore, according to this principle, a man can only be said to have a swift hand with respect chiefly to his Disengaging, or to his defence, or Parade, and not with respect to his offending or thrusting. For in this case, he can only be said to deliver his thrust quickly, but not to have a swift hand; which is an improper expression for it, and which hath been all along a general mistake amongst Masters; and a faculty attributed to the wrist of the sword-hand, which at bottom belongs chiefly to the arm, body, or legs. And that I may clear this a little (which will be thought pretty odd after such a long mistake, occasioned by the general use of an improper expression), you are to know that:

When a man is within distance of his adversary, there are chiefly *Three* different degrees of it, wherein he may be placed with respect to him.

The *First* is when, without moving the trunk of his body, he can reach his adversary with the spring or motion which comes from his shoulder and elbow joints. So that at this distance, the thrust does not depend upon the quickness of the wrist or sword-hand, but upon the quick motion of the whole arm, derived from the shoulder and elbow joints. And all the swiftness the hand is concerned with, in this distance, is only to Disengage if there be need for it; the swiftness of which does indeed depend upon the wrist; but the swiftness of the motion of the thrust, wholly upon the motion of the two joints of the arm: that is, shoulder and elbow. This is absolutely the distance at which a thrust can be delivered with the greatest celerity and swiftness which a man is capable of, and in which people very seldom or never find themselves placed, especially in an Occasion; it being so very near, and consequently most dangerous.

The *Second Distance* is when, without *Elongeing*, a man can, with the spring of the trunk of his body and the motion of the above-mentioned two joints, reach his adversary. In which case, the swiftness of the thrust depends chiefly upon the quick motion of the trunk of the body, and next upon the motion of the two joints co-operating with it. So that in this distance, as well as the preceeding, the wrist is but very little concerned, unless, as I said, when a man is to Disengage before he thrust. For if he be to thrust upon the same side he lieth with his sword, it is the trunk of the body and arm that are chiefly concerned in the swiftness of the thrust, and not the hand or wrist, as is generally, but most erroneously, believed. This distance is also very dangerous, being but too near to one's adversary.

The *Third and last Distance* is when a man is necessitate to make a full *Elonge*, or step out with his advanced leg so far as possibly he can, before he can reach his adversary. And in this distance it is chiefly the quick motion of the advanced leg, accompanied with the spring of the trunk of the body, and the motion of the above-mention'd two joints of the arm, whereupon the swiftness of the thrust does depend; for at this distance, neither the extending of his sword arm, nor bending forward of his body, being capable to make him reach his designed mark, without the assistance of his full *Elonge* or stretch. It is evident that the swiftness of his thrust does chiefly depend upon his quick stepping out, and so is owing to the quick motion of his advanced leg; altho' indeed, both his body and sword arm must concur with it. So that in this *Third Distance* (which is that we commonly call *Playing at Half-Sword*, and which is the safest of all the *Three*, when a man is once Master of a good and sure Parade), as well as in the two former, the hand or wrist, you see, is but little, if at all, concerned in the quick delivery or swiftness of the thrust; except when there is occasion, as I said, for Disengaging or making of a Feint.

Indeed, when a man is so near to his adversary as that he can reach him with a quarter, half, or even three-quarter *Elonge*, then the swiftness of the thrust depends much more upon the quick motion or bending forwards of the trunk of the body, than on the stepping out fully with the advanced foot. Because, it being possible to execute the thrust with the motion of the body assisted by the sword arm before the advanced leg is at its full *Elonge*, the thrust will many times be home before the advanced foot not only touches the ground, but be at its full stretch from the other. In which circumstance alone, and no other that I know, it can be justly and properly said (tho' most Masters lay it down as a general rule, albeit a very false one for right thrusting) that a thrust resembles somewhat the shot of a pistol; and that as the bullet is commonly home before the wounded person hears the report of the pistol, so that thrust should be home, and the adversary wounded, before the pursuer's right foot touch the ground.

And the reason for it is evident, because in the two *First Degrees of Distance*, there is no need of moving at all the advanced foot out of its place: the thrust in the *First Degree of Distance* above mentioned, depending only upon the quick motion of the arm; and in the *Second*, upon the quick motion of the trunk of the body, the sword-arm concurring with it; the moving of the right foot in either not being in the least needful. And in the *Third Degree* also, you see it depends mostly upon the quick motion or bending forward of the trunk of the body, except when the thrust cannot be performed without a full *Elonge*, the outmost extent whereof can only carry home the thrust.

But even in this *Third Degree of Distance*, and which is pretty nice, altho', as I have said, the swiftness of the thrust does for the most part depend upon the quick motion of the advanced foot in elonging. Yet in some cases the advanced foot is necessitate to attend, or wait upon, if I may so express it, the motion of the hand before the thrust be finished, even altho' that hand has been (as indeed it ought alwise to be, to prevent confusion) the first mover. And these cases are: when there are great Disengagements or large tours to be made before a thrust can be performed, such as those which must of necessity be per-

formed against this new *Hanging Guard in Seconde*. Whereby the pursuit against it is more slow than against most of the other Guards, and wherein I pretend one of its great advantages does consist, as may be observed in Advantage Second and by the Scheme in the middle of the Plate.

These observations are so much the more curious, as I dare without vanity affirm they were never made known by any author. And it is but of late that I discovered the impropriety of that term or expression, of *Having a Swift Hand*; which, strictly speaking, should be attributed only to it, or the wrist, in Disengaging, making of a Feint, or in forming the Parade. And the swiftness or quick delivery of a thrust, either only to the motion of the joints of the sword arm, as in the *First Distance*; or to the quick spring or bending forwards of the trunk of the body, as in the *Second*; or to the swift motion of the advanced leg, as in the *Third*; the joints of the sword-arm co-operating with the bending forwards or spring of the body in the *Second*; and both the trunk of the body and foresaid joints accompanying the motion of the advanced leg in the *Third Distance*. Which *Third Distance* (so long as a man is within his adversary's Measure) is that wherein a thrust is longest coming home to do execution. Altho' I cannot but own that, albeit it be the slowest, yet it produces the strongest thrust of the *Three*; as the thrust from the *Second Distance* is the next weaker, tho' swifter; and that from the *First* the weakest, tho' indeed the swiftest thrust of all the *Three*.

Thus I have made it appear how improperly the common expression of *Having a Swift Hand* is attributed to such persons as deliver their thrusts smartly, and in a manner in the twinkle of an eye, whether they be at the *First*, *Second*, or even *Third Distance*. And that that expression is only proper either to describe a man's quick Disengagement, sudden Feinting, or extraordinary swift motion in his Parade. Altho' indeed in the Parade, albeit the wrist have the greatest share of it, yet the joints of the arm, particularly that of the elbow, give a mighty assistance to it; whereby the Parade, especially if performed with a good jerk or Beat, is rendered the more firm, strong, and secure. This observation coincides so with the Fifth Article of Measure or Distance, page 130, that it might have been very well brought in there, had I not forgot it. But I judged it better to bring it in here amongst the Principles, altho' not so properly relating to them, as wholly to omit so necessary and curious an observation. Therefore the reader may either consider it separately and apart here, or as if it were joined to the above-mentioned Fifth Article, which of the two he pleases. I shall also, if I have occasion hereafter to speak of a *Swift Hand*, forbear that term, and give it, according to this observation, its proper one, of *Swift Thrusting*.

4 No particular position whatsoever of the sword-hand, in delivering a thrust from one's Guard, can be capable (without the assistance of the other hand, by opposing the adversary's sword with it) to secure the whole body at one and the same time. *Therefore if a thrust be right timed, and smartly and vigorously delivered, there is not such great need of thrusting alwise close by the adversary's sword; nor that niceness to be observed in the position of the sword-hand in Quarte, Tierce, Seconde &c.; or of throwing the head and shoulders this way or that way off the straight line, for the security of them from a Contre-temps, as many Masters do but too critically and peremptorily enjoin.* See Article Tenth, page 130 [and McBane, 2nd paragraph of "Directions."].

5 Therefore when a thrust can be as safely delivered with the hand in that position wherein the sword is kept as if it were altered to any of the other positions, of *Tierce, Quarte* &c., it is altogether of no purpose to change the position of it in thrusting from that, to any of these, and that for the very immediate preceeding reason.

6 In performing any thrust, the more near the point and hilt are to the height and level of the shoulder of the person who is to deliver it (which is the center from which its motion proceeds), so much the further will it reach, provided the rest of the body be equally stretched in it, as in any other thrust given with another position of the arm, and point higher or lower. *Because when the shoulder, sword-hand, and sword point are exactly level, they make a straight line; and a straight line reaches alwise further than another of the same length, which hath one or more angles made in it.*

7 According to the preceeding Principle, in the delivery of every thrust, the point of the sword ought to be carried alwise as level to its hilt, as the nature of the designed Lesson or thrust will allow it; *and that for the very same reason.*

8 To perform any Lesson or thrust perfectly well, there is required in the whole members of the body that vigour, activity, and quickness which can be acquired by no other means imaginable, but by a frequent exercising of those members in the respective actions peculiar to each, which will at last convert all into a habit to, as we commonly term it, a second nature. *So that what a man at first performed, after a little pause or consideration, and with somewhat of difficulty, will be at last so readily put in execution as that his actions will appear to be done rather by a kind of rote, than after a considerate deliberation and judgement. So much doth custom and a habitual practice influence, not only our heads and brains, but even the particular members of every man's body.*

And seeing that there is no Method under heaven so proper for the acquiring of this ease and natural habit in Fencing, as the frequent practicing to Parie and thrust upon a comrade at a wall; I fancy it will not be judged improper if, before I proceed to the second class of Principles, which relate to the Master, I make a short digression and give some few, but most exact directions for Parieing and thrusting a plain Thrust at a wall; and which will prove of singular use in case of any bet or wager betwixt young Gentlemen, either when they are at the Fencing School or otherwise.

FIG. 13

One upon Horseback discharging a blow without and above his Adversaries Sword from the hanging Guard.

FIG. 14.

One upon Horseback defending a blow without and above his Sword, upon the Hanging Guard.

*Directions according to the nicest Rules for the more
Orderly and Regular Parieing and Thrusting of a Plain Thrust,
especially upon a Bet or Wager.*

The Parieing and thrusting of a plain Thrust, dexterously and swiftly, is of so great use in Fencing, and conduces so very much to the rendering a man perfect in both his defence and pursuit, whereby he may really deserve the name of a compleat Sword-Man, that I have thought fit to set down the following Directions amongst my Principles of the Art. That so young beginners may not only be convinced of the great benefit which will redound to them from the frequent practice of them, but that they may also know how they ought to be regularly performed, according to the strictest Rules. And I also do it the rather because I am persuaded the exact observation of the following Directions will prevent a great deal of debate, which would otherwise fall out when Scholars are about to perform them, especially if there be any thing of a competition of skill, or bet, betwixt them; and which it is very convenient sometimes to make, to excite Scholars to the more frequent and assiduous practice of them.

Altho' it hath been a very old, but bad, custom in the Fencing Schools to fix, in a manner, the person who is to Parie with his back, at least left shoulder, near to a wall, that he may not absolutely break his adversary's Measure by the too much bending back of his body; yet I altogether disapprove of it, for these reasons: that not only it many times occasions a contortion of the body which, besides its undecency, may also be the cause of the Scholar's contracting a bad habit; but also that no person in either Parieing or thrusting ought to be in the lease constrained as to the posture of his body, but should have all the liberty imaginable allowed to him (for his greater celerity in the Parade) of an easie Guard, or posture of defence, which it is impossible for any man to have when he is in a manner pinn'd up, and as it were fixt close to a wall.

1 Therefore I shall begin my *First Rule* with this general one, wherein both defender and offender are equally concern'd. And it is, that in either Parieing or thrusting of a plain Thrust, both the defender and the thruster be placed free of any wall or other kind of stay or support. And consequently the middle of the room, or thereabouts, is the most equal or convenient place for both.

2 The place in the room or School being condescended upon and judges named, the defender is to pitch himself to his Guard, or posture of defence, with all possible ease. And the floor or pavement is to be chalked, or otherwise marked at the toe of his right, or advanced foot, and at the side of his hinder foot; that so he may not without being observed move them out of their places in Parieing, whereby he may break his adversary's Measure in time of thrusting; and thereby, in place of fairly Parieing, cunningly evite the thrust.

3 He is to give a sufficient open to the pursuer to thrust at, not only upon the opposite side to that wherein his adversary's sword is engaged, but also beneath the sword, when his adversary is to thrust upon the in-side. Especially if he himself stand to a low and sinking Guard, and make also use of the true Parade with a dry Beat, and near to his body. Because being upon the low Guard, and making use of this Parade, it is impossible for his adversary to hit him where he hath no open, and where he is already defended; which he certainly is within the sword, when he takes himself not only to a low and sinking Guard (the securest of all postures, in my opinion, against the Ordinary

Method), but also makes use of his Beating Parade. And therefore, to remove all debates, his vest should have two marks or lines drawn upon it (if black, with chalk; if of another colour, with red or black, for their being better perceived by the judges). The one of which lines may be drawn straight down, from the outside of his right breast to the head-band of his breeches; and within which line he is not to bring his sword-hand until he be forming his Parade against his adversary's thrust within the sword. The second line, or chalk, is to be made across his body, a little lower than the middle of the trunk, or at his short ribs; and it is above this line that he must keep his sword-hand when he engages his adversary's sword, especially, as I said, when his adversary is to thrust within the sword, and himself to make use of the low Guard and Beating Parade. For the better observing whereof, one of the judges is to be placed opposite to him behind the thruster, and to challenge him if before he be to Parie he exceed those lines: as well the perpendicular line within his sword upon the length, as this last across his body. Because altho' upon the common *Quarte* Guard & common Parade in *Quarte* & *Tierce*, this open below the sword is not so needful; that given within the sword being sufficient, by reason of those Parades being performed only by a simple turning of the wrist or sword-hand (without the least spring or Beat downwards, and forming a good cross near to the body, for the better gaining of the Foible of the adversary's sword when thrusting), which is the reason that they are so uncertain, and of so little use in an Occasion. Yet this open below the sword is absolutely necessary to be given to a man in thrusting a plain Thrust against one who stands to a low and sinking posture & also makes use of the Beating Parade; because if he had it not given to him, he would have, I may say, no open at all to thrust at, that given within the sword now being sufficient enof, when the defender of a plain Thrust takes himself to a low Guard, and cross and Beating Parade.

What I have said of a man's giving his adversary a sufficient open to thrust at upon the inside, and likewise beneath the sword, must be also so understood that he is to do the equivalent without his sword, when his adversary comes to thrust at him without and above it.

4 The defender being thus placed and the lines drawn upon his vest, and floor or pavement of the School, that so he may stand the more fixt, and also thereby give his adversary sufficient open, both within and below his sword, to thrust at, he is next to endeavour to Parie dexterously and firmly, and with as little motion or inclining back with his shoulders, as possible, the thrusts of his adversary, delivered either within and above or below, or without and above the sword. For the performing of which with

the more certainty, it will not be amiss that he exactly peruse what I have said, both upon the *Term of Art*, PARIEING, page 124, and in the Fifth Chapter, anent the Method of opposing his adversary's sword with his, at first presenting and Parieing from this *New Guard*. In which two places he will find all that it is needful for him to know in relation to the theory of the Parade, from any Guard or posture of defence whatsoever. As for the execution of it, it is only an assiduous and frequent practice, and constant habit that must bring him to it, and not the bare reading of those Directions.

The very same Directions or Rules, except as to the giving an open below the sword, that I have set down to be observed by the Parier, or defender, of a plain Thrust, from the ordinary *Tierce* and *Quarte* Guards (that is, as to the situation of the person to Parie, not the Parade) will also serve when a man is to defend a plain Thrust from the *Hanging Guard in Seconde* in this *New Method*. I shall therefore proceed to the Rules to be observed by the pursuer in thrusting of a plain Thrust.

FIG. 15.
One discharging a full blow with a Halbard or Lochabar Ax, without and above the Sword against the hanging Guard.

FIG. 16.
One defending a full blow of a Halbard or Lochabar Ax, without and above his Sword upon the hanging Guard.

As I have put restrictions upon the defender, so the offender or thruster must be likewise limited. Not as to his posture, for that, as I formerly said, must be alwise easie, free and unconstrained, but as to a few other particulars.

1 Whereof the *First* is that (the defender having been placed and bounded according to the directions above) the thruster makes a full *Elonge* or stretch at him from the Guard he designs to thrust from; so that his thrust being planted just above the defender's right breast, his *Fleuret* may bend a little in its Foible next to the point. And then there is to be a chalk made upon the floor, at the inside of his hinder or left foot, that so he may not shorten his Measure by slipping insensibly nearer the defender. And the reason why I order his thrust to be high planted at the taking of his just distance is that he may have as much benefit, when he shall come home to thrust in earnest, by his thrust coming home level to his adversary's body, which is the longest line he can possibly make upon his stretch, as his adversary shall have by his declining or bending any way back his body in Parieing. Which, notwithstanding of the strictest directions, and most positive restrictions that can be laid upon him, a man will always incline to do for his more certain defence, especially upon a bet or wager. Therefore it is but just that the thruster should have this little allowance to balance it, besides what otherways may be conceded to him by Paction:[18] as 4, 6, or 8 inches within his full stretch, according to his dexterity and swiftness in thrusting.

2 Altho' some persons may perhaps give credit to the pursuer, and take his word for it, when he takes his distance for thrusting, that he is at his full or outmost stretch, yet many will not rely upon his ingenuity as to this point. And therefore to be assured that he is at his full stretch or *Elonge*, observe that if his left ham and sword-arm be fully stretched, and his right leg in a perpendicular situation betwixt its ankle and knee, his *Elonge* cannot be complained of. For altho' a man may (by laying on his body, especially of his left thigh and leg, very low upon his *Elonge*) exceed this stretch a little (which I call a full one); yet if his legs and sword-hand be in the positions I have named, his *Elonge* is sufficiently fair, and he may be very justly said to have taken his distance at a full stretch.

3 After whatever fashion the thruster holds his *Fleuret* when he takes his outmost distance or Measure; after the very same fashion must he hold it when he comes to deliver his thrusts in earnest. Otherwise he may deceive the defender by holding his foil short in the handle, and, in a manner, beyond the cross-bars towards the shell, when he is a taking of his distance; and afterwards taking the pommel into the middle of his hand, and stretching his forefinger along the handle, when he comes to thrust. Whereby he will gain near to three inches of distance upon the defender: a piece of subtiltie and cunning not easily first discovered by those such as are novices in the Art.

---

[18] An agreement, a compact, a bargain. *Webster's Revised Unabridged Dictionary*, 1913.

4 It is not enof that the offender have the floor at the inside of his left or hind foot chalked before he offer to thrust. He must also pitch himself to his Guard, and have the floor likewise marked at the toe of his right, and then deliver his thrusts (the button of his *Fleuret* being chalked or coloured with red, for the better discovering of the thrust when he hits) distinctly and swiftly, alternatively upon each side of his adversary's sword. That is, first within and above or below, then without and above it, recovering his body after each thrust to its Guard posture. For the better and more swift performing whereof, let him peruse seriously what I have said upon the term THRUSTING, page 129. For if the thruster should only have his left foot chalked, and liberty to place his right at as great a distance from it as he pleases, this would be a great disadvantage to the defender. Because the swiftness of the motion of the sword-hand depending, as I have made appear, page 169, upon the motion of the advanced foot, the thruster's stretch cannot be computed to be greater or farther than the distance betwixt where his right foot was placed before *Elongeing*, and where it is when at his full stretch. So that in place of making a full *Elonge* upon the defender, which he ought to do, he only performs, in a manner, half, nay, sometimes but a quarter of his full *Elonge*, from the position of his body upon the Guard posture. And consequently his thrust is so much the shorter and sooner home, as his right foot is placed nearer than its due distance to his adversary, before his *Elongeing*. So that at this rate, a man shall even take his distance with a full stretch. And yet if he set himself at his full *Elonge* from the ordinary posture of his Guard before thrusting, shall hit his adversary almost as soon as if he were much more near to him, and, in a manner, only to thrust at him by the advancing motion of the trunk of the body, and spring of his sword arm. Therefore in thrusting a fair and regular plain Thrust, great regard is to be had by the judges to the offender's or thruster's recovering himself, after every given-in thrust, to his ordinary Guard posture and distance betwixt his feet, as at first marked upon the floor, that so the defender may not be thus imposed upon and deceived by him. And here I must tell you, by the way, that nothing prevents the slipping of a man's feet better, when he is to thrust at his full stretch, and that perhaps the floor of the School or his shoes are slippery, than the chalking the soles of them well with a piece of good chalk. This will assist him to stand firm, not only before he offer to thrust, but also when he is making of his full *Elonge*.

5 The thruster is not, before really Disengaging and thrusting, to make the least deceiving motion whereby he may allarum the defender to offer his Parade, before there is just ground for it. For this being a deceiving motion, is equivalent to a Feint, and therefore is not at all fair in this juncture upon the thruster's part. For which reason he is obliged to forbear it, and never to make an offer of thrusting until he really Disengage and launch home his thrust.

6 The thruster is not only to recover himself to his Guard after every thrust, and to Disengage and thrust them distinctly one after another, there being a little interval betwixt each thrust, for the defender's better putting himself again upon his defence; but he is also to plant and lodge all his thrusts in the defender's body: that is, above his two haunch bones. And therefore there ought to be a line drawn level across the defender's belly upon his vest, from one haunch to the other; and no thrust is to be allowed, which is not given above this line. And if any fall either below it, in the thighs or legs, or in the sword arm, they are not at all to be sustained in thrusting a plain Thrust; especially if there be a bet or money upon it, however effectual and dangerous such thrusts would prove in an Occasion, and upon that account to be valued.

Having finished the Rules to be observed by both offender and defender in Parieing and thrusting of a plain Thrust, I think it will not be amiss, before I leave this point, to show after what manner the frequent practicing the Parieing of a plain Thrust is an advantage to the defender, and the thrusting of it none to the pursuer; and upon the contrary, the frequent practicing the thrusting, an advantage to the pursuer, and the Parieing of it none at all to the defender.

When, then, a Scholar thrusts at a very near distance, he gets little or no good by it himself, because being so very near to his adversary, he hath not the opportunity of stretching, and consequently not of acquiring a swift thrust. Whereas in this case the defender reaps a great benefit by reason of the nearness of the thruster, and consequently, difficulty in Parieing; whereby he acquires a good and firm defence. But when a Scholar thrusts at his outmost stretch against his adversary, then upon the contrary, he reaps the benefit by it himself because it accustoms him to stretch well; and so gives him the habit of fully and readily *Elongeing*, and consequently, of swift thrusting. But then his adversary or defender reaps little or no benefit by his offering to Parie, because the thruster being at so very great a distance, it requires no great dexterity nor swiftness of hand to defend him.

Therefore my advice to all who would reap benefit by the frequent Parieing or thrusting of a plain Thrust in the Schools is that if they intend to acquire a swiftness and dexterity in thrusting, that then they alwise thrust at such a great distance or stretch as possible; and if they resolve to become Masters of a quick and firm Parade, whereby they may dexterously defend themselves, then let them allow their adversaries to thrust at as near a distance as they please, or they themselves can possibly Parie.

That is, that their adversaries be so placed as to need to make but a very short *Elonge*, nay, even to thrust sometimes with only the motion of the trunk of the body and spring of the sword arm, without in the least stepping out or *Elongeing*. And this much for the benefit in practicing, as well as orderly and regular Parieing and thrusting of a plain Thrust; which I look upon to be so much the more curious, as it was never heretofore so narrowly canvassed, nor made publick for the benefit of Scholars, altho' most necessary and useful for the more readily breaking their bodies, whereby they may become dexterous in a swift and subtile pursuit, by a plain Thrust and firm and sure Parade against it, which are the two chief pillars, or rather the only sure foundation, of all true Art.

But me thinks I hear some censorious and stingy pretender to Art, with a disdainful and supercilious smile, say, *Here is indeed a great deal of clutter and doe about the thrusting of a plain Thrust, hundreds of which a man may see every day performed in the Schools, without all this formal nicety of measuring the distance, chalking the ground and clothes, and I know not what.*

I acknowledge all this. But then I would gladly know if those plain Thrusts, to which this Spark was so frequently witness, were either delivered according to the strict rules of Art; or if there was any bet or wager upon them. If the former, then I do affirm that they observed the preceeding directions (which are the only fundamental rules of all regular thrusting). Otherwise they could not be but most un-artificially and irregularly performed. And if there was money laid upon it, then there would be a necessity for the parties either to be regulate by such-like rules as I have here set down, or to continue debating and jangling a very considerable time before they could accommodate all the differences and difficulties that would be started upon both sides. All which, if they had knowledge enof to decide it, would certainly terminate in the observing the foregoing rules, or others of the very same nature.

So that when young Gentlemen have a mind to divert themselves by trying their dexterity in thrusting plain Thrusts upon one another, which is indeed so very commendable (and perhaps for a glass of wine or so), then there can never any difficulty in the performing them occur, but what are, in a manner, obviate, and removed by the foregoing directions, the necessity and usefulness whereof will alwise more and more appear when any such bet or trial of skill shall be, by some curious and adroit young Sword-Men, resolved upon. Which I think a sufficient answer to my critical, but I must say, unexperienced objector.

SECONDLY,

Of Principles which respect the Second Class, or Master.

Were it not for the regularity of discoursing a little upon each of the classes I at first named, I might very well forbear saying any thing of either this class of Principles, relating to the Master, or the next, which respects the Scholar. Because when a man designs to improve himself in the *Art of Defence*, he may perhaps not have the opportunity of making choice of such a sufficient instructor as he could wish for, but be necessitate to make use of such as live in the place where he resides, let them never be so unsufficient: for in this case, as in all others, necessity hath no law.

Besides, there are so very many good qualifications required in a compleat Master of Defence, that I doubt much if ever they were all found in any competent degree of perfection in any one man. Therefore when a man can do no better, he must (neither can he be blamed for it) employ such as the place will afford. But if he is living in a country or city where there are greater plenty of Masters, and so make a judicious choice, I think they ought to be Masters, if not of all, yet at least of the most material qualifications following.

I shall not here insist upon those qualifications which Fencing Masters ought to be possessed of, in common with other men. As they are MEN, and a part of the community where they live, they ought to improve and habituate themselves to all those Christian and moral virtues which are required of other good men. Therefore I shall in this place only consider them as PERSONS, who chiefly lay themselves out for the improving of youth in the dexterous handling of their weapons, whereby they may become Masters of a sure and general defence against all kind of weapons, for the safety and preservation of either Life or Honour.

And in this acceptation, not only they, but all other Masters who take upon them the instructing of youth in their more heroick, Gentlemanly, or even diverting, exercises (such as the Mathematicks, Art of War or Evolutions, Fencing, Riding, Dancing and Musick), ought to be imbued with such particular good qualifications as more immediately relate to that Science or Art whereof they are Professors.

Next to the Mathematicks, no doubt, the *Art of Defence* hath the preeminence, because of the great benefit which flows from it to all men for the safety and preservation of their Honour and Lives. And seeing this Art hath been the subject of the foregoing sheets, I judge it will not be amiss that I here discover to the more unexperienced readers a few of the chief qualifications which, in my opinion, an expert and truely great Master of Defence ought to be imbued with; that so young Gentlemen may hereby be the more capable to make a judicious choice (when they shall have variety to pick and choose upon) of a sufficiently qualified Master to instruct them in the most useful *Art of Defence* against the attack of all kinds of weapons, as well edged as pointed.

1 He ought to be a person of civil and obliging deportment, because, having to deal for the most part with young people, and may times of the greatest quality, they ought to be induced to follow the advices and directions which he shall give them relating to his Art by the reasonableness of his arguments, and not compelled to them by the harshness or surliness of his temper. For young people, about that age when they are commonly taught their exercises, are to be judiciously persuaded, not violently forced, to the performing of them. And the weaker and more uncapable some of his Scholars are, the more he ought to encourage them, that they may the more earnestly set about and endeavour to improve themselves. For nothing more discourages and rebutes a young Gentleman at any exercise, than to be alwise finding fault with, and rebuking him for, his perhaps unvoluntary neglects and omissions.

2 He ought to be a Master of a general defence and pursuit, both as to blow and thrust, that so he may communicate the Art of both weapons, Back Sword and Small, to his Scholars. For no Master can pretend to be a compleat Professor of the whole *Art of Defence*, unless he be thus qualified as to both weapons. Because, altho' a man's skill and dexterity, either in the Art of the Broad Sword alone, or in the Art of the Small by itself, may be sufficient to procure him the character of either a dexterous Back Sword Master, or of an exact teacher of the Art of the Small Sword or Rapier. Yet unless he possess the knowledge of both Arts, whereby he can communicate to his Scholars the true defence and pursuit of both weapons, and by joining them in a manner together, procure to his Scholars a general and sure defence against all kind of weapons, as well edged as pointed, he can never deserve the name of a truely compleat Master of Defence, but only of a good Back Sword Master, or of a dexterous teacher of the Art of the Rapier.

And this qualification of joining the practice of both Arts in one is so much the more needful to make a compleat Master of Defence, as it saves a great deal of time to Scholars who, in place of spending a great deal of time to acquire the Art of both weapons separately, save more than the one-half or two-thirds of it by being taught both at one and the same time, as if they were joined together, and one and the very same Art. And indeed they have so much dependance the one upon the other for the procuring of any man a general and true defence against the attack of all weapons, that they ought alwise to be joined together, as in this *New Method*, and rendered inseperable by all who seriously resolve to become dexterous and truely compleat Sword-Men.

3 As he is to be Master himself of a general defence and pursuit, that is, absolutely Master of all belonging to both Arts of Back Sword and Small, so he ought to have that ease and readiness in communicating all the Lessons, both defensive and offensive, to his Scholars; and also endeavour to support and defend them with such convincing reasons, that his Scholars may be fully satisfied that what he teaches them is founded entirely upon good and solid reasons, and not upon a customary and ill-grounded rote, handed down from Master to Provo, without being able to give any other reason for what he teaches, than, *Thus I order you to do*, *and you are not to ask questions*. An evasion and general answer below any man of judgment, particularly a Master who takes upon him to instruct youth in the more regular and certain defence of their Lives, when in an Occasion, or otherwise accidentally attacked.

And indeed for my own part, were I to make choice of one of two: either of a Master who is most dexterous in his own practice, but cannot speak a mouthful of sense upon the grounds of it; or of another whose limbs are somewhat more *Gourdie*, but what he performs, grounded upon most convincing arguments and undeniable reason; I should much rather make choice of this last than the former. Because it is not by my Master's practice that I become a good Sword-Man. And if my Master can but demonstrate the Lessons to me, tho' never so slowly, and give me good reasons for them; an assiduous appreciation and frequent custom of performing them will certainly bring me to that useful practice, which will be a great deal better sounded, and more serviceable to me than a customary rote. For which I can give no other reason than the old Aristotelian argument, *Ipse dixit præceptor*. Thus said my Master. I do not however pretend that theory alone, without a competent degree of practice, no more than a great deal of practice without theory, is sufficient to qualify any man to take upon him the title of a Master of Defence. I only assert that of the two, I had rather my Master were but an ordinary practitioner, and much Master of the theory, than that he should be a most dexterous and adroit practitioner, and could not give the least convincing reason for what he does. Theory indeed and solid reasoning being, in my opinion, more required and useful in a Master, for the greater improvement of his Scholars, than a bare practical rote, founded upon nothing

but a glib and ready motion of some of the members of his body, without the least assistance of the head or judgement.

4 He ought to observe order and decency in his School, as well by ordering his servant to keep it neat and clean, and the Scholars' shoes and *Fleurets* in their particular places, for the more ready delivering them to the Scholars when called for, as by exactly attending the Scholars himself. Not only upon the days when he is to teach, but also upon the days of the week set apart for Assaulting, which ought to be two at least: suppose Tuesdays and Fridays. For Saturday being commonly a day for other diversions, it were a loss to the Scholars to forbear teaching also upon the Monday. Likewise one day in the week for Assaulting is too little; Scholars in the seven days interval being apt to go a little out of practice: the only support and preserver, I may say, as well as improver of this chiefly practical Art. And therefore two days in the week are absolutely necessary for Assaulting; as well for the Master's own ease, as for the greater benefit and improvement of his Scholars in their practice. Without which, their Lesson-labour will avail them but very little when in an Occasion.

5 That those Assaults may be the more decently and regularly performed, he ought to have established laws for them, which should be printed in large characters, and affixt to some place in the School, whereby they may be exposed to all who come into the School; that before Assaulting they may take a view of them, to prevent debates which would otherwise certainly fall out were there no such regulations. A draught of which, for his greater ease, and according to my own judgement, I have given in the annexed sheet which folds out. [p. 96]

6 He should have also once a year a Prize to be Played for,[19] to which his Scholars ought to contribute. And should likewise have printed laws for that effect, to prevent all confusion and debates which would otherwise, upon such an occasion, inevitable fall out. A specimen whereof I have also given in the above-mention'd folding out sheet; no-ways pretending that either these, or the former for Assaulting, should be the only ones to which a Master ought to tye himself; but only as a draft whereby he may the more easily frame others for his School as he shall have need for them. Altho', in my opinion, there will be but very little material to alter in them, having omitted nothing relating to common Assaulting, or Playing for a Prize, which I judged absolutely

---

[19] This is not the prize fighting of the Bear Garden and McBane. Rather, it is an ancient ritual of passage in arms. "Prizing was English martial art's equivalent of the gradings of Asian martial arts systems…Those bold, rumbustious, and, dare one say, contentious people saw such events not merely as proof of knowledge but as contexts to be fought and won, contexts in which a brave performance would win them the prize of promotion and the respect of their peers." Brown, 39.

necessary. Now altho' the contents of these two last paragraphs are not so properly Principles relating to the qualifications required in a good Master, as regulations for his Scholars' more regular Assaulting (as well in the ordinary Diets appointed for that purpose, as in the more extraordinary ones set apart for Playing for Prizes), yet I have placed them amongst the Principles relating to a Master because they have a great dependence upon his being a well qualified one.

I shall not also here enlarge upon several other particulars which are very material. Such as, that he ought to keep an order and decency in his School; begin his Scholars with light *Fleurets*, and accustom them by degrees to weightier, which will strengthen their arms and wrists; make them Assault sometimes in their walking-shoes and ordinary wearing-clothes; as also sometimes in the open fields, when the weather is good, the better to accustom them to the judging of Measure (a most useful thing when a man comes to be engaged for his Life!); together with several other very necessary things which I willingly omit, because, as I said, they are not so properly Principles respecting his personal qualifications, as consequences of them.

These are the chief and most necessary qualifications required in a compleat Master of Defence, where (in great cities especially) a man hath variety at his command. And when a young Gentleman has the good fortune to meet with such a one, he may very safely commit himself to his conduct in instructing him in the true *Art of Defence*. But, as I said, when a man is living in a place where he hath not that variety to pick and choose upon, he must even make the best he can of a bad bargain, and supply, by his own judgement and assiduity of practice, what is wanting in his, perhaps, very well meaning, but otherwise very ignorant country Master. For he must indeed be a great ignoramus in the profession, from whom a well body'd, sprightly, and judicious young Gentleman cannot, by his own diligence and application, draw some benefit, for at least a moderate improvement in the defence of his person upon an Occasion. Which, how indifferent soever, must be acknowledged (when once a man is come the length to be capable to put it, altho' not with the greatest judgement, yet but readily and briskly in practice) to be alwise better than none at all. I shall therefore proceed to the *Third and last Class of Principles*, which relate to the Scholar.

THIRDLY,
Of Principles relating to the Third Class, or Scholar.

As the Principles, or qualifications, which relate to a Master have been few in number, so these belonging to a Scholar will be yet fewer. For as the scarcity of Masters may, as I said, sometimes oblige a young Gentleman to employ one who is none of the best, and to be satisfied with his qualifications, let them never be so indifferent, which is the reason that he must dispense with them, such as they are; even so a Master who takes upon him the instruction of young Gentlemen in their weapons, being obliged to accept of any Scholars who shall address themselves to him, renders the qualifications in a Scholar the less to be regarded, and consequently the Principles relating to them the fewer, because he is to make the best Sword-Men he can of his Scholars, without having regard to their perhaps not being the best natur'd, or best shap't young men in the world. Yet notwithstanding of this, there are some qualifications that are indispensably required in all Scholars who resolve really to profit by their Master's instruction in this Art; of which I shall name only two or three of the chief.

1 All Scholars, of what texture or disposition soever, ought as much as in them lyes, not only to have a kind of liking to, and respect for their Master's person; but also to comply with his directions; and endeavour to put them in practice, altho' they appear to them at first ordering to be never so difficult, and, according to their own judgement, even almost impracticable. Because it is to be supposed that a Master is always more competent in matters relating to his Art than his Scholar. Upon which account he ought, until he come to acquire more judgement and practice in it, to submit to, and even have a kind of implicit faith for the truth of all his Master shall require of him. Besides, when a Scholar has either a dislike to his Master's person, or condemns and undervalues his judgement, it is in such a case almost impossible for him to profit by him. And therefore where it is not natural, he ought to force upon himself a kind of love and respect for his Master, even altho' his natural parts should not much deserve them.

2 A Scholar ought punctually to attend, as well in the days appointed for Assaulting, as in those for teaching; because practice is the life and soul, if I may express it, or all true Fencing. Therefore whenever a Scholar begins to become careless and remiss, and inclines to JACQUE, and pass away that time wherein he ought either to receive his Lesson or Assault with other less useful divertisements, it is a shrewd token that he will never make a very extraordinary Sword-Man. And that because he has no great liking to it. Nay, of so great consequence is a man's natural inclination, and particular disposition and genius, for his greater success in the Art, that it hath been frequently observed, and I have been also witness to it myself, that one of such a natural and clever disposition will, by his natural address and agility, not only keep his own, as we commonly say, but even many times have the better, in Assault, of those who, altho' they have been a long time at the School, yet being slow and lash in their temper, reap not that benefit by their Art which otherwise

they would, did their natural genius and inclination excite them more to it. And which, by the way, ought not to be objected as a reflection upon the usefulness of this Art, but upon the natural disposition and genius of the person which has almost no liking nor tendency this way, but only as it is, in a manner, prest and forc't upon it.

'Tis true that education and custom have not only a great influence, but many times even force upon people's employments, quite contrary to their natural inclinations; as great and frequent practice in Assault, will also a little Fencing upon young Gentlemen who have naturally no great liking for it. But, for the most part, it is the energetical power and efficacy of a natural genius and disposition which inclines and determines most people to that particular kind of employment which they resolve chiefly to follow while in this world, and which is the cause of one man's excelling in one thing, and another man in another. For example, of one man being only a knowing philosopher and great Scholar, in place of being a wise and prudent politician; of another being a great mathematician, in place of being a good mechanick; and of a third being a skillful statuary, painter, or limner, in place of being only an expert taylor or shoemaker; and so of all the other Sciences, Arts and Handicrafts. And last of all, of some persons being great and dexterous Sword-Men, while others are but only pretenders to it, and mere bunglers.

So very efficacious and prevalent is a natural genius and apt disposition in any man, to make him succeed and improve, after more than an ordinary manner, in whatever Science or Art he shall take himself to, that he may be justly said to excel in it. And in Fencing especially, which depends so much upon agility, as well as judgement and practice, it is no doubt a great satisfaction and ease to a Master, when he meets with a vigorous and well-made body, accompany'd with a ready apprehension and good judgement. But such extraordinary qualifications being very rare, he is to rectify the defects of nature, as much as possible he can, by the rules of Art, and to make, as I said, the best Sword-Man he can of his Scholar, let his genius and other personal qualifications for the Art be what they will.

There are a great many more Principles, or rather qualifications, required of both Master and Scholar, were I to enter into a particular detail of the matter by enumerating all that in a larger sense may be said to belong to each. But seeing as I intend brevity upon this head, and that those I have mentioned are indeed the most material, I shall put to a close my Principles relating to the *Art of the Sword*; which I judge so much the more necessary, as I am fully persuaded no directions for any Art can be trusted to, or relyed upon, which are not grounded upon a good and solid foundation of Principles, supported not only by experience, but by the convincing arguments and dictates of unerring reason.

I am also very hopeful that the publishing of these Principles, which I have, in a manner, but only named, and glanced at the reasons for them (for to discourse on each of them fully would alone make up a little volume), may be a means to encourage a general and universal Method of teaching the true *Art of Defence* in these Islands. And so remove the trifling animosities that have been but too long kept up betwixt many very good Masters, which I have the charity to believe did proceed more from the want of such an easie and rational directory as this to reconcile them, than from any private pique or malice.

I should now, according to the method I at first laid down, come to the conclusion of this Essay, wherein I am to answer some objections which are commonly made against this Art by those who, not for lack of ignorance I must say, are no great well-wishers to it. But this being the last time that I intend to put pen to paper upon this most useful and Gentlemanly subject; for I believe that I have said almost all relating to it, that either I can, or is material for any Gentleman (if I had said *Master*, I should not have said much amiss) to understand; I judge it will not be altogether out of the way, nor unacceptable to my reader, especially if a well-wisher to the Art, if, before I proceed to it, I give him a short account of the encouragement which the *Art of the Sword* hath met with of late in this Kingdom. That so the Methods taken for it being made publick, they may (now after the, I hope, happy union of the two Nations[20]) excite some of the more curious and skillful, as well as generous, British Nobility and Gentry, who may be Members of Parliament, to stand up for it, and make such rational overtures and proposals for its improvement and encouragement to the next or some other ensuing British Parliament, as it in its wisdom shall judge most proper and expedient to condescend to.

In the year 1692 several Noblemen and Gentlemen, whereof I was one, entered by contract into a Society for the greater encouragement of this Art, wherein, besides the regulations laid down by us for our more ordinary meetings, wherein we were to take trial of, and admit into the Society such Honourable persons as should apply to us to be admitted into it, we had also our more solemn anniversary, or yearly meetings appointed, upon which days we were to wear a certain Badge, which, amongst other devices, carried the designation of the person to whom it belonged, as well as that of the Society, which we named The Society of Sword-Men in Scotland. But this Society being only erected by ourselves as private persons, we were of opinion that

---

[20] The Treaty of Union between England and Scotland, creating Great Britain, 1707; effectually depriving Scotland of her sovereignty, while linking her economically to wealthy England. The treaty fertilized the seeds of Jacobitism, and would lead to forty years of revolt, and ultimately, disaster for the Highlands.

it would be of far greater esteem, and serve better the ends for which we chiefly designed it (and which I shall immediately give an account of), if we could procure the civil sanction to it, and have it erected into a Royal Society of Sword-Men. For which end, about four years thereafter we made application to the then Secretary of State, who assured us that he would use his endeavours with King William (of glorious memory) to grant us a *Signator* under the Great Seal for it. But the Parliament being about that time to meet, which was in *anno* 1696, to which the Earl of Tullibardin (now Duke of Athol) was Commissioner, we judged that it would be still more Honourable for our Society, and give it greater weight and force, if we could procure an Act of Parliament for it in our favours.

Accordingly, upon the 16th September in the above-mentioned year, there was a draught of an Act offered by one of our Society, who was then a member of Parliament; which after first reading was remitted to the then Committee for Contraverted Elections; and upon the 28th of the same month approved of by them. But the Parliament being very shortly thereafter adjourned, it was not reported that session. And so from that time it lay over till this last session of the Duke of Queensberry's Parliament, *Anno* 1707, when at one of our meetings it was proposed that the design should again be insisted upon, and another new overture or Act, with some few alterations and amendments, offer'd; which was agreed to by the Society. And accordingly there was one drawn, whereof, for the reader's greater satisfaction, and that he may the more readily understand our most generous and Gentlemanly design in it, the tenor follows.

Draught of an ACT, Anno 1707, for Erecting a Royal Society of Sword-Men in Scotland.

"Our Sovereign Lady, with the advice and consent of the Estates of Parliament, considering, that the Science and Art of Defence is reputed over all Europe, an useful and necessary accomplishment for all Gentlemen; and seeing it is of late improved by certain of Her Majesty's good subjects within this her ancient Kingdom of Scotland to that height of perfection, as that the rules and principles thereof, which were formerly looked upon as precarious and uncertain, are now rendered clear and evident: And also considering, that the right teaching and improving the said Art of the Sword, doth very much tend to the education of youth in general, and especially for the accomplishment of such as shall be employed to serve in Her Majesty's Army; and that many persons have and do take upon them to teach the said Art, who are altogether unqualified and ignorant, or at least cannot teach it so exactly as is required, to render a man perfectly dexterous, which may be prevented if there were a Society of Skillful and Experienced Sword-Men erected and constitute for taking tryal of all persons who shall take upon them to teach the said Art. And being informed of the qualifications of Her Majesty's Lovits, who all or most of them have by a sedulous application and long practice attained to a more than ordinary knowledge of, and dexterity in the Art of the Sword; and being resolved to give all due encouragement for promoting thereof: Therefore Her Majesty with advice and consent from the Estates of Parliament, does hereby create, erect and incorporate the forenamed persons, and such persons as shall by them, or any quorum of them be hereafter admitted and received in manner underwritten into a free Society, to be called now and in all time coming, The Royal Society of Sword-Men in Scotland, with power to them, or any quorum of them, to make, create and elect a Clerk and all other necessary Members of Court, and with full power to said Society, or any five of them, with their Clerk, which is hereby declared to be their quorum, to have a yearly general meeting within the Burgh of Edinburgh upon the second Tuesday of each January, beginning their first general meeting upon the second Tuesday of January next to come, and so forth yearly thereafter the said time and place for ever, and with power to them to carry at their said general meetings, or any other time they shall think fit, the Badge following, which is hereby granted them as a distinction for, and sign of their said Society, *viz.* a piece of gold or silver enamuled, or embroidery of gold or silver upon cloth or silk as they please, in form of a double star, having a circle within it, and a cloud in each side of the circle; out of which clouds there shall proceed from the dexter, an arm holding a sword pointing upwards; and from the sinister, another arm holding a *Fleuret* likewise pointing upwards, which crossing the sword about the middle, shall form a Saint Andrew's Cross, above which there shall be a scroll with this inscription, *Recreat & Propugnat*; and upon the outer verge of the circle there shall be another inscription in larger characters, thus: *Gladiatorum Scoticorum Societatis Regalis symbolum*; as also, with full power to them, or quorum of them foresaid at their general meeting, to elect a Preses, Treasurer, Officers, and what other Members they shall think necessary for the right government of the said Society; which Members are hereby declared to continue for an year only, unless again elected at their next general meeting, and ordains annual elections to be then for that effect, and with power to the said Preses, or and two of the said Members with their Clerk, to meet at any time they shall think fit immediately after the date hereof, before the foresaid first general meeting, and from time to time betwixt their said general meetings as they shall see cause; and in case of the absence of their Preses or Clerk, with power to them or any three of them, to elect them for that time allenarly; which Preses, Clerk, and any two of the Members of the Society are hereby declared a quorum in these ordinary meetings, and with power to the forenamed persons, or respective quorums of them above-mentioned, either at the said general or particular meetings, to receive and admit into their said Society, such persons as after trial they shall find qualified, who when admitted, are hereby declared to have and enjoy the same privileges with the above-named Members; and also with power to them at their said meetings, to project, reason, conclude upon, and enact such methods and regulations alwise consisting with our Laws and Acts of Parliament, as they shall find convenient for promoting the Art of the Sword, and supporting of the said Society; and particularly, with full power to them to cognoice upon, and determine all differences betwixt parties upon points of Honour, for the more effectual preventing of Duels. And in regard, several persons within this Kingdom do, or may hereafter usurp to teach the said Art of the Sword albeit nowise qualified, to the great prejudice of our subjects; Therefore, Her Majesty with consent foresaid, grants full power to said Society, or any quorum of them, to call before them all Professors or teachers of the said Art of the Sword within the said Kingdom, and to examine them, and take trial of their qualifications, and to admit or reject them as they shall see cause; and if admitted, they shall be thereafter repute as qualified Masters of that Art, and be licensed to teach in such places of the said Kingdom where the said Society shall think fit; and also with power to the said Society or any quorum of them foresaid, to cause seize upon and imprison any persons whatsomever, Professing or teaching the said Art within the said Kingdom, who shall refuse to submit themselves to the foresaid trial; and hereby grants Warrant to the Judge Ordinary to whom such persons shall be delivered prisoners, to secure them in their prisons ay and while they find sufficient caution, that they shall subject themselves to the trial of the said Society within such a time as the said Society shall think fit; and also, that they shall not Profess nor teach the said Art in all time hereafter within the said Kingdom, without the special License of the said Society, under penalty of the sum of _____ Scots money, to be paid by ilk one of the contraveeners to the said Society *toties quoties*. And moreover, Her Majesty with consent foresaid, gives and disposes to the said Society, all and sundry rights, liberties, privileges, freedoms and immunities, which are known, or competent to belong to that or any such like Societies within the said Kingdom, alse fully and freely, as if these privileges were specially insert thereuntil, and that the said Society have a common Seal to be appended by their Clerk to all Admissions, Warrants, Licenses, and other Writs to be granted by them concerning their said Society, bearing the impression of the forementioned Badge, and grants Warrant to the Lion King at Arms, and his Clerk and Deputies, and all others concerned, to allow and matriculate the samen."

This draught, together with the former Act, which had been approved of in the Committee, *Anno* 1696, was delivered to a Member of Parliament, who was not only to present it, but also to give a short narrative of the progress had been made in it, especially by the approbation of the Committee to which it was remitted in the before-mention'd session of Parliament. But as all sublunary designs, as well as things, have their settled and appointed periods for being accomplished, so it seems this was not the time when this most Gentlemanly and Honourable project should receive its finishing stroke. For the Parliament being taken up by affairs of the greatest consequence, particularly that of the Union of the two Kingdoms, was the reason of this design being only proposed toward the end of the session. So that there being, at that time, and as it is alwise usual toward the rising of a Parliament, a kind of hurry in business, the Act could not be conveniently brought in, nor moved, altho' the Gentleman to whom it was recommended, and who, as I said, was a Member of Parliament, did what he could in discretion for it.

Here is, you see, a most Honourable, Gentlemanly, and useful publick project of several worthy and dexterous Noblemen and Gentlemen, for the encouragement of the *Art of the Sword*. And not a private design, or, as some no well-wishers to the Art would have clandestinely and underhand insinuate, a monopoly to gratify some particular private persons: a most mean and ungentlemanly thought, and unworthy of any to propagate, who carries a sword by his side, far less the Honourable persons already engaged in this most useful project. And which I am persuaded could never be contrived or asserted by any, but such who, being sensible of their gross ignorance in the Art, did therefore despair of ever having the Honour of being admitted into the Society.

For to give in a few words a short view of the great benefit and advantage which would redound to the subjects, particularly the Gentry, of these Islands, by such a Royal Society of brave and dexterous Sword-Men, were it once by law established.

First, it would give great encouragement to the Art, whereby a great many Gentlemen, who are now-a-days, notwithstanding of its real use, somewhat averse to and careless about it, would be excited to follow it. And consequently be in a better capacity to defend their Lives, either in a battle or private quarrel, especially if they follow this *New Method of Fencing* I have here discovered to them, than they could possibly formerly, either wholly without any Art, or I may freely say, even with the Common Method. Which will be a means to save many a brave man's Life, and consequently many good subjects. For let some people banter Fencing as much as they please, not only as to its being no use in a battle, but even in a single engagement betwixt man and man; yet I do affirm and maintain, that the *Art of Defence*, as now rectified in this *New Method*, will not only be most useful to prevent the bad consequences which commonly attend private quarrels by Duelling, but also a great means to save many an officer or single soldier's Life, when they come to a close engagement in a battle, sword in hand. And which in all probability they would have lost, had they not made use of the secure and excellent defence it furnishes them with, when performed with judgement, and especially if assisted by the dexterous use of the left hand, and secured by a good sword-proof gauntlet, as I proposed on page 158. Than which, if the great benefit of them were once by a little use come to be known, nothing would be esteemed comparable to them for a ready defence in a close engagement. But to bring so good and useful a defence into the Army, must be the approbation and authority of a General, and not the advice of a private person; altho' I have judged it my duty to discover and propose it.

Secondly, such a Society would prevent the Lieges being hereafter imposed upon by weak and ignorant Professors and teachers of the Art; seeing all such persons will, by the Act establishing the Society, fall under their jurisdiction. And they will certainly take care that none be admitted as Masters to teach the Art within these Islands, but such as shall be found duly qualified by them; and for which there will be, no doubt, alwise in the Society a competent number sufficiently capable to make such Masters undergo the tryal which shall be required by the Society of them, whether by examination, practice, or both.

I am fully persuaded, and dare confidently assert, that bad and ignorant teachers, with which these Islands are but too well stor'd at present, have done more real prejudice to the true *Art of Defence* than all the pretended objections against it could ever possibly have done, had not such objections been seconded, and, in a manner, made good by the ill consequences of the bad teaching of some, and, if I may so word it, too artificially nice instruction of others. Which, when put in practice, were found by the more judicious to be a great deal more proper for diversion in a School Assault, than for security and safety, either in a single Occasion, or when sabreing in a close field battle. So that it is no great wonder if this most useful Art hath been of a long time discountenanced and condemned by many, and under, as it were, a kind of eclipse. But which will, I hope, be now retrieved, and by the assistance of this new, secure and excellent easie *Method of Defence* I have here published, return to its ancient reputation and lustre, especially when encouraged by such a Royal Society.

Thirdly (and which is indeed the most glorious, because the most Christian design of all), this Royal Society of Sword-Men, if once established by law, and according to the terms of the preceeding Act, will serve in place of a Court of Honour, wherein all points of Honour, with relation to private quarrels between Gentlemen, will be impartially determined, and the parties reconciled. Which will, if not wholly, yet in a great measure, prevent Duelling; wherein, god knows, how many brave young Gentlemen lose their Lives in taking satisfaction, for many times pitiful and trifling quarrels not worthy of a just and Honourable resentment. And that merely upon the account of no such court of Honour being established by authority to determine in matters betwixt disagreeing and quarreling persons; and who, were it once brought into fashion, would never decline either its authority or decision, but most calmly and willingly (without thinking it the least tash upon their Honour) succumb and comply with it. For the Members of such a Royal Society of Sword-Men being authorized by law, would lay down such methods, not only for taking up and removing, but also preventing all kinds of quarrels, that there would be scarcely any fall-out within these Islands, but what would be immediately taken up and agreed by the mediators appointed in all parts, but especially in the great cities and towns, who would have their particular commissions from the Society for that effect. Together also with a recommendation from the government to the Justices of Peace, and Magistrates of the counties and towns, where such quarrels might happen, to concur with, and assist them, to secure the parties until they were reconciled, or a particular account of it sent to the Society, in case of an obstinate refusal.

If such a noble and useful design now as this should be brought about by the establishing of a Royal Society of Sword-Men, what a great Honour it would be to those worth Noblemen and Gentlemen who were the first contrivers of it and promoters of it in this Kingdom? It would certainly be most Honourable and glorious. For to be a merciful peace-maker, and to save, are heavenly and divine attributes, and can never be quarrell'd or condemned by any who are convinced they have a soul to be saved, and which may come to perish by being sent suddenly and unexpectedly into another world by an un-Christian as well as unlawful Duel. And that only for lack of such an excellent preserver and protector of all true valour and Honour, as this Royal Society would infallibly prove to be, were it once established by an Act of Parliament, and effectually put into execution.

And yet this project, how Gentlemanly and useful so ever it might prove, had its enemies. But what man or design ever yet was there, who wanted a set of such ill-wishing people to traduce and discourage them? However I have indeed the charity to believe that this proceeded more from their being out of humour, and dissatisfied that they were not amongst the first encouragers of it, than out of any malicious design to obstruct or frustrate its succeeding or taking effect, had it been fully projected in plain Parliament. Which, as I said, could not possible be got done, because of the hurry and crowd of business which was brought in towards the close of it.

This is a true, impartial, and short account of the first erection and design of our present Society of Sword-Men in Scotland, together with the methods have been taken from time to time to promote it. And I can say this with more confidence and certainty, being myself the first contriver, and one of the chief promoters of it all along, so far as it has yet advanced. And seeing as I have, as a private Gentleman, contributed what lay in my power, as well for the improvement of the Art by writing, and giving instructions for it in several former pieces as well as this, as for promoting this most useful and Honourable design of getting our Society authorized by law; of all which I do not in the least repent me (for it is below no Gentleman who carries a sword to endeavour to propagate, according to his power, the knowledge and Art of it). So I cannot but wish and expect that now, after the Union of the two Nations, some of our British Nobility and Gentry who are well-wishers to the Art, and who may lie nearer to the fountain of Honour, as well as of justice, than it is probable WE may hereafter do, will generously take it off our hands, and cordially join in prosecuting this most useful design by laying it before Her Majesty and the British Parliament.

Neither is it to be doubted but Her Majesty, and the representatives of these Nations, which have acquired so much renown and glory of late by the sword, will Honour it by public Act, and do some thing for the greater encouragement and promoting the most Gentlemanly and useful Art of it. Which they can never do better, nor more effectually, than by establishing by law such a Royal Society of Sword-Men as is here proposed; and which, in place of being called, as was formerly intended, The Royal Society of Sword-Men in Scotland, ought then to be named that of Great Britain. That as our hearts and interests are now by law, and I hope also cordially and sincerely, united; so our swords may also be effectually joined, as well for the disappointment and terror of our enemies, as for the mutual support and defence of one another, so long as Sun and Moon shall endure.

I shall now come to the Conclusion of this Essay, wherein I shall endeavour to obviate, or rather resolve and answer, some strong and plausible objections in appearance (tho' indeed at bottom, but very frivolous) against this most Gentlemanly and useful Art. And which shall at present serve as a kind of encomium upon it, to excite young Gentlemen not only to a more frequent practice of it, but also to a more careful and assiduous application of the excellent rules and instructions which are here and there dispersed through this whole book; but more particularly collected and contain'd in that admirable abstract of *The Sword-Man's Vade-Mecum* set down in the Sixth Chapter, page 162, and that other in page 164. Both of which I cannot too much recommend to the reader's making himself absolutely Master of, by wholly relying upon them for his securest practice, as well as fixing them in his memory and judgement for his more readily and easily making use of them upon an Occasion: with which, the gentlest, best natur'd, and most calm and temperate man alive knows not how soon he may be misfortunately trysted.

The CONCLUSION,

By way of Encomium upon the Art of Fencing;
wherein the Chief Objections against it,
are fairly Proposed and Answered.

There are two sorts of people who are the chief objectors against the usefulness of Fencing. The *First* are those who have, I may say, a kind of natural aversion to it, and who are but very few in number. Neither can there be any reason given for it. So that the prejudices they have entertained against it, in a manner, from their infancy, have to them all the force of a demonstration. These are a sort of men who, never troubling themselves to argue on any matter, go *through stitch*, as we say, in all their opinions; and never take them up but with a secret resolution never to quit them, tho' for others infinitely better. There is no informing nor enlightening of them; and when one has reason'd with them never so justly, all the answer you are to expect is that of the country fellow to his priest, *You may silence me, but you shall never convert me.* Now were it only for such persons that I intended the arguments here set down to prove the usefulness of this Art, I might very well have spared my pains. For, as I said, such persons are obstinately resolved to be proof against the strongest arguments can be offered to them in its favours. So that there being no possibility of perswading them, I must even leave them where I found them. And since I cannot convince them of their unreasonable prejudices against it, I will, I hope, at least be allowed to regret them.

But there are a *Second* sort of enemies, or rather objectors, against the usefulness of Fencing, who are only enemies to it at the second hand, if I may so express it. That is, not out of any natural predjudice or aversion of their own, but from what they hear from the above-mentioned, or such other inveterate enemies to it; and therefore are not so obstinate as they, but of a great deal more convinceable temper. So that it is chiefly upon such plausible and tractable persons' account (who ought rather to be pitied as condemned, seeing the aversion they have to the Art is not so much natural and voluntary, as with an insinuating kind of subtilty and cunning carried home and enforced upon them); I say, it is chiefly upon such persons' account that I have undertaken to draw together in this Conclusion, some of those objections which appear to be of greatest weight against the usefulness of the Art, together with my answers to them.

And indeed it is somewhat unaccountable and surprising that an Art, by which men may reap benefit and advantage, but never prejudice, should have any enemies or objectors at all against it; especially any who pretend to the priviledge of carrying a sword by their side. But 'tis very probable it may be with such persons as it is with the condemners of divinity, and even of providence itself. For to make the allusion in the words of a very excellent author, and with all due regard and deference to so noble and sublime a subject: as it is impossible for any man of sense who considers the fabrick of the whole, nay, the smallest and most unconsiderable part of the universe, to doubt a First or Supreme Being, until, from the consciousness of his sins and provocations, it become his interest there should be none; so, I may say, it is impossible for any reasonable man who seriously reflects upon and considers the excellencies and advantages of Fencing to doubt or question the usefulness of it, until, from a sense of *his* own ignorance in it, and the advantages he is sensible, Artists will, in all probability, in an Occasion, have over him by it, it does become his interest that there should be no such thing as Art; or at least that what is called the *Art of the Sword* should be of no use. However that I may be as good as my promise, and prosecute my design as I first proposed, I say;

As the *Art of Fencing* is chiefly designed for the defence and preservation, not for the ruin and destruction, of mankind; so certainly is it a great accomplishment, and does mightily heighten and increase people's esteem for it, where it is possessed by one of a sedate, calm, and peaceable disposition. Whereas, on the other hand, it tends much to its prejudice and contempt when it is at the disposal and command of any hot, surly, and ill-natur'd or quarrelsome person. For as such persons take only the benefit of it for the better assisting and carrying them through in their more unmannerly and impertinent insults, which disturb the peace and tranquility of the society wherein they live, and company they converse with, for which they ought to be discountenanced by all good men; so the other make only use of it for their just defence, in any Occasion wherein they may be unhappily engaged. So that such persons being necessitate sometimes to make use of their Art in good earnest, is so far from yielding any satisfaction or pleasure to them, that they are rather obliged to show their skill and dexterity in it with a kind of regret and reluctancy.

For I have many times observed that neither the bravest and most courageous men of Honour, nor greatest Sword-Men, are the most given to quarrels. And that because neither of them like to suffer what they so much esteem, namely their valour, to be exposed either too frequently, or at too cheap a rate. But then it is generally as true that when such persons do engage in an Honourable Occasion, they do it indeed with a witness. They neither go into the fields, nor draw in the streets to raise a noise and a hubbub by discharging a few blows or thrusts; and then all is immediately husht and over, by reason of a patcht-up reconciliation, which noways deserved the name of a real satisfaction. But upon the contrary, when such persons engage, they do it out of a true point of Honour, and merely to demand a just satisfaction for a really received injury. And this, I confess, is seldom done by the most expert Sword-Men, but at the expence of some blood. Whereas, according to the common method of picking petty quarrels, and resenting them (for indeed they do not deserve the name of injuries or real affronts), a man shall hear of several rencounters, and not so much as a drop of blood drawn on either side. Which is, however, a thing, in my opinion, very rare to be expected from the Common Method of practice; and where there is given a just Occasion for resentment, and the parties offending, obliged in point of Honour to give a just satisfaction. So that the matter standing thus with valorous and expert Artists, Fencing, or the true *Art of Defence*, gives indisputably to such persons the two following advantages.

FIRST, it creates a respect to them from many who, did they judge them to be as mal-adroit as themselves, would perhaps, when in company, venture to pass a jest or banter upon them; who, knowing their valour and adroitness, will judge it more safe for them to forbear it, knowing certainly that they will not easily be let pass without being demanded satisfaction for it. Also in any little difference which may arise amongst the company, such persons who are known to be not only judicious and men of Honour, but likewise skillful and adroit at their weapons, will in all probability be the persons to whom such differences are referred. And for whose decision the whole company will, no doubt, have the greater regard, in respect of their knowing nicely the punctilios of Honour, which all good sword men are presumed and ought to understand. And that they certainly know they will not smooth over any affront wherein a man's reputation or Honour are really concerned, without advising them to demand such satisfaction as, by the rules of Honour, the nature of the offence requires.

SECONDLY, the true *Art of Defence* gives any man who is absolutely Master of it (even altho' endued but with a very moderate natural forwardness or boldness) a certain kind of assurance, I had almost said courage, upon an Occasion, which no unskillful person can have. And that in so far as the Artist not only certainly knows all the opens by which his adversary can attack him, but also the probable means, not only to prevent them, and to defend himself, but also offend his adversary; so that if he come to fail in either, he knows that he hath himself only to blame for it, not the unsufficiency of the Art. Whereas an unskillful person is, in such a case, discouraged and rendered in a manner desper-

ate; which obliges the most part of them, out of mere necessity, to take themselves to a most violent and irregular pursuit (which I have elsewhere very justly called *Temeritatis vel Ignorantiæ audacia*, or the *temerity and fool hardiness of ignorance*), whereby they endeavour, if possible, to force the Artist from his Measures. And so they are conscious to themselves that, upon such an Occasion, they can perform nothing with any kind of design, judgement, or certainty, because of their being altogether ignorant of the rules of Art. But which being all exactly understood by the Artist, are an encouragement and support to him, by not only increasing his courage, as it were, but even giving him a kind of assurance while in the heat of his engagement. So that, in this case, it may be most justly asserted that an expert Artist supports and fortifies himself by his Art, while an Ignorant is necessitate to do it, if possible, by temerity and despair. And indeed it is pretty odd to see such a kind of co-incidence betwixt two so very opposites as Art and Ignorance; and that they should both tend to the producing of that boldness and forwardness which is to be found in some men, especially Ignorants, who, being quite destitute of Art, cannot pretend to the least support and assurance they might in reason expect from it. But the great difference, as I have been observing, lyes in this: that the courageous forwardness and assurance possessed by the Artist proceeds from a reasonable and well-grounded confidence which he reposes in his Art; and which will rarely fail a man of judgement, if performed by that sedateness and presence of mind with which it requires to be execute. Whereas the Ignorant's ventorious forwardness, or rather temerity, flows from his being most sensible of his great want of Art and skill; and in place of being so well grounded in the former, is only the result of despair, which is the spur that sharpens him up to it. So that the temerity and affected assurance which is, I may say, screwed and forc'd from it, can but very rarely (and even then but by mere chance) produce those good consequences which a true, sure, or solid Art can. This is the distinction I thought fit to make betwixt the ventorious hardiness or temerity of a forward Ignorant, and the well-grounded confidence and assurance of a brisk, skillful, and judicious Artist or Sword-Man.

I remember that I have many times heard Artists reproach'd and upbraided with such expressions as these: *To what purpose is all your Art and regular Lessons, as well defensive as offensive, when it is frequently observed that a vigorous and stout Ignorant or Naturalist, with a swinging irregular pursuit, will put any of you off from all your orderly postures of defence, so that you shall be in such a condition as not to be in a capacity to make use of your Art; nor in a manner know to what hand to turn you; of so very little use and advantage is Art, many times, to those who pretend a great deal of knowledge and dexterity in it, especially when vigorously attacked.*

In answer to which, I must in the *First* place ask such persons who make this objection, whether or not they are really persuaded that a man's Art diminishes his natural courage? I cannot believe they will answer in the affirmative, there is so very little shadow of reason for it. Because this were a strange virtue in it indeed: that Art, according to some peoples' wild fancies and assertion, should render a man who is naturally brave and cou- -rageous, upon his obtaining of it, an arrant coward; by (as it were a most unreasonable kind of transmigration) infusing a mean and timorous soul into a body formerly possessed by a brave one, whereby it is wholly divested of that heroick virtue wherewith nature had endued it from its infancy. No, no, this were to make a too rash as well as false conclusion, and to encroach a little too much upon the just dictates of reason and sound sense.

If then Art does not abate courage (for I do not deny but it many times makes a man more cautious in an engagement than perhaps otherwise he would be; this being indeed *Peritiæ & experientiæ cauleta*, or the *circumspectness and wariness of Art*, which, however, has not the least tendency to cowardice, and is much rather to be approved of, as condemned), then certainly an Artist hath this advantage by his Art: that altho' he should be sometimes beat out of, or driven from, his postures of defence, and put from making use of his artificial Lessons of offence; yet he still knows when and where opens are given to thrust at, and so can take the opportunity of them, which no man altogether ignorant of the Art can do. So this, not to mention the benefit he hath in knowing how to thrust swiftly, and also to plant and adjust his thrusts well, is one considerable advantage he hath by his Art; altho' he had no more, but even did wholly abandon the defensive part, and should answer the Ignorant in his own coin as to the offensive.

But *Secondly*, it is a most gross mistake to fancy that a truely expert and compleat Artist can thus be beat from either his posture of defence, or measures of pursuit, by any Ignorant or rambler whatsoever. A novice or half-skilled person may indeed be driven into confusion, by reason that he is but just, in a manner, grounded in the Art. But one truely expert and by practice consummate in the Art never can; because his defence and pursuit are founded upon, and proceed from, true and solid principles, and not from an ill-grounded rote. So that forming a true cross upon his adversary's weapon, when upon his defence; and launching alwise home a thrust vigorously, upon an open, either offered by his adversary, or forced by himself when offending; he can never be said either to defend or pursue irregularly or in confusion; by reason that the forming of a good cross upon the defensive, and the thrusting always at an open upon the offensive part, being the two chief principles upon which this Art is founded, and he acting consequentially to these Principles can therefore never be said to act in confusion, let the posture of his

Guard be never so awkward or disorderly in appearance, or the position of his sword-hand, perhaps in *Quarte* when it ought to be in *Tierce* or *Seconde*, upon his offence. And which are at bottom but trifles with respect to true Fencing, when a man comes to an earnest engagement with Sharps.

THIRDLY, seeing it is clear that, according to reason, Art can never diminish, but that it ought rather to produce and increase courage; then certainly an Artist can never be at any loss or disadvantage by being a professor of it. Because when he pleases he can make use of it. And since it impairs not, nor diminishes, his natural valour and boldness, he may also, when he has a mind for it, *Un-Art* himself, if I may so say, or lay it, as it were, aside for that occasion, and answer the Ignorant's forwardness by his own natural courage, as if he had no Art (which, by the way, is no bad method for young sword men, when they shall be engaged in an Occasion before they are well confirmed in their Art). Whereby he is still in equal circumstances with his adversary, and in the same condition; if it can be supposed that a compleat Artist can so much divest himself of his skill, as if he had no Art at all.

So that it is evident that any man who has truely Art is so far from being at a disadvantage by it any manner of way, that he hath also this following undeniable advantage; which alone is sufficient, were there no other at all, not only to make all men of good sense and judgement to value and esteem it, but also to silence entirely all its enemies whatsoever, who are not, out of mere caprice, resolved to continue obstinate. Which is that *whereas his adversary can only appear in the field in one capacity to defend his Life and Honour (to wit, as a mal-adroit and Ignorant, and as one relying merely upon a fortuitous chance for his preservation or victory); the ARTIST can appear, sword in hand, in a twofold capacity. That is, either as an Artist, to defend himself by his address and skill, or, if he please, as altogether as very arrant an Ignorant, and inconsiderately forward a mal-adroit, as his adversary.*

From all which I draw this undeniable conclusion: that true Art and a skillful address in the Gentlemanly and most useful *Science of Defence* must be, for the most part, of singular use and advantage; but that it is next to impossible it can ever be prejudicial to any man, if he but act, I shall not say exactly (for that, I dare affirm, never any man did, nor do I really believe can), but even indifferently, and in a good measure according to its most rational, as well as exact, Rules and Directions.

All which I think sufficiently answers the above-mentioned common, tho' weak, objection. Which, however, is rarely made by any who have but the least tincture of Art; but only by such as are wholly ignorant of it. And who, therefore, according to a natural, and I may say innate, pride and vanity, but too common to our whole race, cannot endure to be thought ignorant of any useful exercise, for the understanding whereof they hear other persons applauded. And amongst other Gentlemanly exercises, hearing this of Fencing commended by the most judicious, and the persons who are dexterous at it had in esteem and respected for it; and knowing themselves to be, by their laziness and neglect, altogether ignorant of it; they therefore look upon themselves as obliged, out of a vain, self-conceited, and false point of Honour (if it can deserve that Gentlemanly word), to vindicate their own ignorance by railing at and undervaluing the Art, and all who possess it.

And I dare appeal to all such enemies of it, if they will but deal candidly and be ingenuous, if what I have said be not the chief, if not the only, reason for their pretended dislike to this Art. And if, in their judgement and conscience, they are not really convinced of its use and excellency; notwithstanding of their dissembling so far as to deny it with their words. For let some morose people pretend to never such an unaffected indifference for the practical knowledge of this Art; yet I am fully persuaded there never was any man who, being altogether ignorant of it, was necessitate to appear in good earnest, with sword in hand, but would with all his soul have wished himself to be amongst the number of the most skillful and expert in Fencing.

I know it is also commonly objected that however dexterous a man may be, yet he can never pretend to an absolute certainly or infallibility by his Art. And therefore seeing it is possible that his Art may fail him, all things being subject to a kind of chance, it is as good for a man to take his venture; and rather than consume a great deal of time in acquiring an uncertain Art, even resolve to hazard all at one home-push. Or as the late Mr. Lock[21] in his *Education of Youth*, Sect. 187, was pleased to word it, *Put all upon one thrust, and not stand Parieing*. Whereby it hath been often seen, that *Bold and forward Ignorants have not only preserved their own Lives, but have also mastered and overcome their adversaries, altho' reputed very dexterous Sword-Men.*

To which I answer, that altho' what is said seems at first view to carry somewhat of reason with it, especially when affirmed and backed by the authority of so great a man as the late Mr. Lock; yet I am hopeful when it is considered a little more narrowly and distinctly it shall not have such influence & weight with any considering person as to make him in the least forbear, far less wholly neglect, the improving himself in the most Gentlemanly and useful of Arts, especially after the serious perusal of the following answer.

I have all the deference imaginable for Mr. Lock's writings, and esteem them as I do those of other learned men. But however I may be obliged by his strong and convincing reasons to go along with, and yield very much to him as a philosopher, yet I must beg pardon to dissent from him as a Sword-Man. For his advising to put all upon one thrust and not stand Parieing shews his skill in Fencing to be as bad and little to be regarded as his knowledge in philosophy, by reason of his great learning, is to be valued and admired. And I think it but a very weak argument to insinuate that because we poor mortals are in a manner subject in all our actions to an inevitable destiny, that therefore we ought not to use the most rational means for our preservation. For as Mr. Dryden[22] says:

> If Fate be not, then what can we foresee?
> Or how can we avoid it, if it be?
> If by Free Will, in our own Paths we move,
> How are we bounded by Decrees above?

Which he answers very well by the following two lines:

> Whether we Drive, or whether we are Driven,
> If Ill, 'tis ours; if Good, th' Effect of Heaven.

I say it is but bad arguing from the uncertain events of our best performances, that therefore we ought not to improve ourselves in those Arts whereby we may prevent a great many accidents which would otherwise certainly befall us. It is much the same as if I should affirm that because of my learning to walk, I am not infallibly certain never to dislocate any of my joints when I am walking abroad; therefore I ought not to stir out of doors at all, but to keep close at home; where I am no more infallibly certain neither, but that the very same misfortune may befall me even in walking about my room, or stepping in to my bed. Therefore I conclude that as it would be folly in any man never to walk or stir abroad because he is not infallibly certain but that he may dislocate his ankle, or break a leg, nay, even be knock'd on the head by an accidental blow of a stone or tile blown from a house-top, whereof we have had several instances; so would it be no less ridiculous for any man to neglect the improvement of himself in the *Art of Defence* because he is not infallibly certain, or that it is not impossible, but that his adversary, whether Artist or Ignorant, may, when engaged against him, either wound or kill him.

For what man is there, of what employment soever, that dares pretend to an absolute certainty in it? Don't we daily see Godly Divines draw erroneous doctrines from good and orthodox texts? Great lawyers, false practicks from good institutions; Skillful

---

[21] John Locke, *Some thoughts concerning education*, 1693.

[22] John Dryden (d. 1700), English poet, dramatist and critic.

physicians, dangerous administrations from safe and excellent aphorisms? And even learned philosophers and mathematicians to build false hypotheses upon pretended mathematical demonstrations? The only Science from whence unerring truth can certainly flow. Nay, the most skillful gamesters come some times off with loss. And the greatest warriors and most renown'd and cautious Generals are sometimes beat and entirely routed, of which we have had fresh and happy instances for these nations in the late campaigns. Since then all these professions are thus by turns fallible, must it be only Sword-Men who ought to be infallible in the practice of their Art? No! There is not the least reason for it, and indeed it were a kind of folly to expect it.

Such weak arguments as these cannot be of force to influence even the most shallow persons we can think of, so as to cause them to neglect their most useful exercises; far less prevail with men of any understanding and judgement to undervalue the true *Art of Defence*, which is of so great benefit and use for the preservation of both Life and Honour. For laying wholly aside such whimsical arguments, we ought (as true Christians) to use the lawful means, let the event prove what it will. And I must also take the freedom to inform those who are of Mr. Lock's perswasion in this point, that if they should have to deal with a true and compleat Artist, he would not give them the opportunity of putting all upon one thrust. *For the Artist would so attack them with a brisk half-pursuit; and still cross their swords, if they were to make use of this New Method; or accompany his pursuit with such a continual Beating and Binding of their swords, if they inclined to make use of the Common; that they would hardly have the opportunity of Disengaging their swords; nay, scarcely of recovering or raising their points, so closely would their skillful adversary keep them engaged and under a continual kind of twist or circular motion. Or otherwise, he would answer them smartly from the Riposte, his Parade being assisted by the left hand for his more certain defence.* Than which there is not, as I have many times said, and cannot repeat it too often, a better Method in the whole Art to put a stop to and Master an irregular and furious pursuit.

Thus ought, and certainly would, a true Artist engage upon an Occasion. And if he do, what, pray, comes of his adversary's attempting to put all upon one thrust (unless it were to run himself head-long upon the Artist's sword's point), when himself is allowed so very little time to thrust, especially if altogether an Ignorant, that he can scarcely know what position his own sword is in?

But I take the true reason of the mistake to have proceeded from hence: that there are but very few truely great Artists; the most part of people who have that character bestowed upon them,

not in the least deserving it. So matters standing thus, and such half-skilled persons being frequently baffled by Naturalists of a brisk and forward temper, Mr. Lock's meaning has been misunderstood: as if thereby he had concluded that such forward persons would have the same success against the greatest and most skillful Artists, as they sometimes have against such half Sword-Men, whose number is indeed but too great. For these are his very words in the fore-cited place: *And certainly a man of courage, who cannot fence at all, and therefore will put all upon one thrust, and not stand Parieing, has the odds against a Moderate Fencer*; which two last words I desire may be taken notice of and remarked, in which I most heartily concur with him. For indeed I am almost of opinion that a man had better have no Art at all, than have but so very little a smack of Fencing as not to be capable to put it into practice. Or to use Mr. Lock's own words, be only a *Moderate Fencer*. Whereby I understand a certain kind of pretenders, who have more theory, or rather prattle, than true practice; and which upon an Occasion will many times prove of less use to them than a brisk and hardy natural pursuit, such as I immediately recommend to young Sword-Men, page 186. But then there is a vast distinction to be made betwixt such a moderate, or rather bungling, Artist, and a person truely Master of the *Art of Defence*. The most forward naturalist that is, would but pass his time very sorely, if engaged against such a Sword-Man.

Let then all Gentlemen endeavour not to become *Moderate Fencers* (as Mr. Lock very justly terms such half-skilled persons), but really expert and dexterous Sword-Men. And my life for it, their *Art of Defence* shall prove of singular benefit and use to them at Sharps, especially if the Occasion be Honourable. For it is but just, that a man's Art should fail him when he offers to draw his sword either in a mean quarrel, or for a bad or unjust cause.

Therefore to vindicate the late Mr. Lock (who deserved a great deal of applause, as for that excellent little piece of the *Education of Youth*, so still more for his incomparable Essay upon *Human Understanding*), I am fully persuaded that had he understood as much of Fencing as he did of philosophy, he would never have given so dangerous an advice. For alwise to pursue and thrust, without being in the least ready or offering to go to the Parade if a man's adversary should offer to thrust out upon him, or to take him from the Riposte after he hath thrust, is what ought not to be so much as named by any who pretend to the least Art. Except in the extraordinary circumstances I have named, pages 137, and 159, where it ought also to be accompanied with the help of the left hand, the better to produce a *Contre-temps* or an Exchanged Thrust. But this being an old received maxim amongst Ignorants: to always pursue most furiously, especially when engaged against one who has the reputation of an Artist, half-skilled persons; Mr. Lock did take it upon trust, and so set it down as a general rule, for which he ought to be excused. The giving just and true directions for this Art being (as he was a divine and a philosopher, but not a good Sword-Man) altogether out of his sphere.

I have insisted the longer upon this, lest so vulgar an error of advising alwise to thrust without in the least being ready or attempting to Parie when needful, maintain'd by many persons (who, altho'' very judicious in other matters, yet being no Sword-Men, ought not to be look'd upon as competent judges in this point), and also backed with the authority and advice of so great and learned a person as the late Mr. Lock, might have perhaps too strong an influence upon many young Gentlemen who have not as yet come so great a length in the Art as to be capable of themselves to discover the uncertainty and weakness of it. But I am very hopeful what I have said will undeceive them, and that they will be so kind to themselves as to rely rather upon my judgement as upon Mr. Lock's in this determination, until they be Masters of so much Art as to be competent judges of it themselves. And the rather, because it is only a point in Fencing, not a decision in philosophy; to whom, in such a case, I should be very ready to yield.

In fine, Fencing, or the true *Art of the Sword*, is both DIVERTING and USEFUL. DIVERTING in so far as, by School Play, a young Gentleman may pass away some idle hours he perhaps knows not well how to dispose of otherwise (for I am far from advising any Gentleman to make it his whole and only business), whereby he will render his body more agile and nimble; and also, by a moderate exercise, discuss and expel many of those gross and superfluous humours which, if nourished and increased by too sedentary a life, or too much ease, might prove prejudicial to his health. And USEFUL in respect of the assurance and safety it fur-

nishes every man with, who is perfectly Master of it. For altho'' there be no absolute certainty or infallibility in almost any thing this side of Time, save in a mathematical scheme or demonstration; yet the true *Art of Defence* furnishing a man with a rational Method of securing and defending himself against the attacks of his adversary with any kind of weapon, whether edged or pointed, whereby his adversary may discharge either blow or thrust against him; it cannot be denied but with respect to THIS, the *Art of Fencing* is singularly advantageous and useful.

Altho' after all, and to be ingenuous, it cannot be denied but that the best of Sword-Men have their good and bad days, as every one must acknowledge who has been accustomed to such kind of exercises. And happy is it for a man when a lucky and fortunate day concurs with a just and Honourable Occasion. So that, in my opinion, I cannot make a better simile than to compare an adroit and knowing Sword-Man to a very good and skillful gamester, who even against a very great bungler may have now and then a bad run, as we say. But still it is acknowledg'd that, upon the main, the skillful gamester hath great odds against the bungler, and will at last certainly carry off the ready. Even so in Fencing, a good Sword-Man may by misfortune, or by failing in his Art, come to be worsted by an Ignorant or mal-adroit (for as I said, Sword-Men are no more infallible than other men). But still this is no reflection upon the Art; and good Sword-Men will, upon the main, have a singular and evident advantage over all unskillful persons whatsoever: it is alwise to be supposed singly and one after another, and that the Artist be sober and free from the effects of wine or other strong liquor, whereby he may be frustrate of any benefit he might reap from his Art. For to drunken or very passionate people this Art can be but of little or no use, whatever some persons who are addicted to these vices may fancy or assert to the contrary.

Therefore the uncertainty above-mentioned, notwithstanding of their greatest Art, ought to humble Sword-Men, and prevent their being too confident, or relying too much upon their skill; seeing it is thereby most palpable and evident that there is a just and invisible, as well as inevitable, destiny, or rather providence, which attends and over rules every man's actions. Let all then who have acquired Art, notwithstanding of their greatest knowledge and dexterity in it, carry themselves humbly and modestly, and without being the least puff'd up by it. And when they shall be necessitate to make use of it in good earnest, for the preservation of their Lives or Honour, let them boldly and, as I advised in page 161 (for the less people apprehend or dread their adversaries, so much the better), make use of the ordinary means and talents Art hath bestowed upon them for their just defence, resigning themselves in the mean time, with all submission and humility, to the unerring conduct of that OVERRULING POWER, which being TRUTH itself, hath declared, *That the Race is not to the Swift, nor the Battle to the Strong, but that Time and Chance happeneth to all.*

THE END

A Scheme of LAWS
(according to the Author's own Sentiment)

To be observed in all *Fencing Schools*, wherein the Master desires a Decency and Order to be kept by his Scholars, especially upon the Ordinary Days for *Publick Assaulting*, or when there is a *Prize* to be Play'd for; and which ought to be Printed in large Characters, and placed in the most conspicuous Part of the School, that none who are to be concerned, may pretend Ignorance.

I shall not here say any thing of the Fencing School, *or* Room *where a* Prize *is to be Played for, because, commonly people provide themselves of the most convenient Rooms can be had for these Purposes, in the Places where they are to be Established; only there is this one General Direction, that I would have observed in making Choice of One, That as a* Fencing School *ought to be a large and well-lighted Room, so it ought to have a little* With-drawing Room *to enter from it, for the more Conveniency of the Scholars shifting themselves; or for any other Persons who are to Play for the* Prize, *retiring themselves to, until they put themselves in Order for it; which would not be very decent to be done before the whole Company, who are only to be Spectators. This being premised for the Conveniency of the Scholars, or other Players; I say, that in my humble Opinion, they ought to observe the following, or some other such like Laws; both upon their* Weekly Assaulting Days, *or when they are to*

Play for a Prize. *And*

FIRST.
LAWS to be observed
upon the Weekly Assaulting Days.

I.

The days of the week appointed for Assaulting ought to be Tuesdays and Fridays, for the Reasons mentioned page 177.

II.

All Cursing and Swearing, and obscene Language, should be discharged as much as possible; because, a Fencing School being a Place to which Persons of the best Quality do frequently resort, for their Exercise and Divertisement, all such Ungentlemanly, as well as Immoral Habits ought to be discountenanced; and that Decorum and Civility observed and paid by the Scholars to one another, as it becomes Gentlemen, not only as they are Christians, but even as they pretend to be Men of True Generosity and Honour.

III.

All Persons, as well those who are only Spectators, as Scholars, should be obliged to Silence; at least, to Discourse within their Voices; because, thereby the Assaulters will be less disturbed, and the Master's Advices and Reproofs, when they commit any Escapes, better adverted to and observed.

IV.

No Scholar or other Person, should offer to Assault, or present a *Fleuret* to any, without having the Master's Consent; because, it would be not only Indiscretion to do it without first having acquainted the Master of it; but it would be a ready Means to occa-

sion a continual Hurry and Confusion in the School, while the Scholars are either Assaulting, or the Master a-giving of a Lesson.

V.

No Scholar nor Spectator, without a License from the Master, should offer to Direct or give Advice, to any who are either taking a Lesson or Assaulting; because, *First*, it is Unmannerly, without Permission or being desired, to take upon them to Play the Master. *Secondly*, Censurers frequently reprove their Comrades, for the very same Escapes they themselves are most guilty of; which is the Reason that they are many times laught at by the Company for their impertinent Officiousness, which they might have prevented, had they been a little more Silent and Reserved.

VI.

No Scholar under two Months Teaching in this *New Method of Fencing*, or three at least in the Ordinary One, should be allowed to Assault in Publick; because, until they be a little confirmed in their Art by their Private Assaults, they can do nothing in their Publick, but Misbehave or Ramble; whereby the Art is undervalued by such Spectators as know not the Reason for their thus Failing, and who are also perhaps glad of such a pretence, to ridicule it.

VII.

No Scholar under three Months Teaching in this *New Method*, or five or six in the Ordinary One, should be suffered to take their Lessons, or Assault in their Ordinary wearing Clothes or Shoes; because, until a Man be pretty well confirmed in his Lessons, and his Body and Limbs accustomed thereby to good

Stretches, his Play would be but very slow and unfirm, should he so soon quit with his Fencing Shoes and Vest.

VIII.

None should be allowed to Play, above five or six fair Given or Received Thrusts; because, if people Play as briskly as they ought, their Vigour will be spent in that time; and what they do afterwards, is but slow and without Life, and so unpleasant to the Spectators; therefore they had better give place to others, in which time they may take their Wind, and fall to it again if they please.

IX.

Although at Sharps Thrusting at the Face be very disabling, yet it is not to be allowed in School assaults; because, of the Predjudice and Hurt People may receive by it in their Eyes; but *Popping out* (as we term it) at the Wrists, Arms, Thighs, Legs or Feet ought to be allowed, although not reckoned as Thrusts; because, thereby a Man accustoms himself to be dexterous at it at Sharps, where it is most useful for Disabling; and if he do not practice it in School Assaults, he shall never have the Opportunity to become dexterous at it at all; besides, that the *Popping out* upon these Parts can do a Man's Adversary no Predjudice with a *Fleuret*, as it would do at his Face or Eyes, which is the Reason that I would have it discharged at these parts.

X.

The use of the Left-hand ought to be allowed in School Assaults as well against Artists as Ignorants, that thereby a Man may become dexterous, at both Opposing and Parieing his Adversary's Sword with it; which it is impossible he can ever be, unless by frequently making use of it, both when taking a Lesson and Assaulting: And indeed it is too good and useful an assistance for a Man's Defence, to be wholly laid aside or neglected.

XI.

The better to prevent *Contre-temps* in Assaulting, although a Man give his Adversary a *Contre-temps*, or even an Exchanged Thrust, before the recovery of his Adversary's body from his Thrust; yet if he himself did not offer to go to the Parade, but did designedly receive the Thrust, that he might the more easily give the *Contre-temps* or Exchanged Thrust to his Adversary; the Thrust his Adversary gave him should be charged upon him; that thereby he may be discouraged from the Practice of such a false and Murdering kind of Play, which is the loss of Many Brave Men at Sharps, where commonly in such a case, both go to the Pot together. *Nota*: No people are more guilty of this than the French, by reason of their imperfect *Quarte* and *Tierce* Parades, and upon than account, their too frequently Catching at Time; whereby in Duels or Rencounters, both Parties are for the most part either Kill'd or Wounded.

XII.

Two Commands are to be reckoned equal to a Thrust; because, although they are not so dangerous, yet seeing it is a bad habit that a Man accustoms himself to, to suffer his Sword at every Bout, as we say, to be Commanded; it is but just, that for every two he should be charged with a Thrust, that so he may the better guard against them; as also the more to encourage his Adversary to Command him, because of its great Use and Safety at Sharps.

XIII.

Upon Commanding no Struggling is to be allowed to the person Commanded, after his *Fleuret* is once catcht hold of, nor Tripping to the person Commanding, after he is Master of it; because, however allowable such active and nimble Defences may be upon a pinch at Sharps, yet in a School Assault, all such kind of struggling betwixt Scholars is Rude and Undecent.

XIV.

When a *Fleuret* is broken in an Assault, the Person in whose hand it is, ought alwise to pay it; because, if it be by a Thrust upon his Adversary, his Adversary has loss enough, by being at the Disadvantage of receiving a Thrust, although he pay not the *Fleuret* also; and if it be broken by a Blow, whether it be by his own Beat or his Adversary's, he ought to have taken care to prevent either; upon all which Accounts, I think it most reasonable, that the Person in whose hand the *Fleuret* was broke, should alwise pay it: Which Decision will be found to remove a great deal of Debate, that arises many times upon this Point.

XV.

Lastly, all these Laws should be observed, under such a Penalty as the Master shall judge fit to impose, for the Breach of Each: And that Mulct [much] ought also to be exactly Collected; Otherwise, the having such Laws in the School will turn to no effect; and the Scholars will have no more Regard for them, than if there were no such Laws at all to be Observed by them.

SECONDLY,
LAWS to be observed upon a Bet, *or when a* Prize *is to be Play'd for.*
All the preceeding Laws for Assaulting, in so far as they are not contradictory to these following, are to be observed as well in Playing for a Prize, as upon the Weekly Assaulting Days; but where they differ, then observe the following, I say when a Prize is to be Played for.

I.
There should be Printed Advertisements, to acquaint People both of the kind of Prize that is to be Play'd for, as also of the Day that is appointed for it; together with the Place and Persons Names, to whom those who intend to Play should give up their Names, and their Contribution for it, unless it be a Prize given *gratis*.

II.
The Day whereupon the Prize is to be Played for Approaching, there ought to be a sufficient guard provided by the Overseers or Judges, from the Magistrates of the Town, or Commanding Officer of the Place, that so any kind of Rabble or Confusion may thereby be better prevented. For which Reason also,

III.
None should be admitted to be Spectators, but such as shall have Tickets given to them, which they are to deliver to the Door-keeper as they enter.

IV.
None should be allowed to Play for the Prize, but such as have duly given up their Names at the Time and Places appointed.

V.
For the greater Order and Regularity in Playing for a Prize, the Number of Players ought to be Even, that so they be the more easily Paired, and those who Beat their Adversaries, also marked with the less difficulty; Therefore if there be an Odd Player, they should all draw Lots who is to forbear Playing for that Prize, and the Person upon whom the Lot falleth, should have the Money he contributed for the Prize returned to him, and shall forbear Playing for that time.

VI.
None should be allowed to Play but in such a Garb or Habit as this one following (and which is a most decent one for Assaulting in) *viz.* a black Velvet Cap, and white Waistcoat, Drawers and Stockins; the Waistcoat and Drawers of what kind of Stuff every Man will be at the Charges of, whether Holland, Taffaty, Sattin, *&c*. But in the time they are Playing, the Skirts of their Waistcoats ought alwise to be put beneath the Head-band of their Drawers, that so it may be the better perceived where the Thrusts are given: For which End also,

VII.
The *Fleurets* they Play with, should be of equal Length, and their Buttons dipt in a little Vermillion and Water, that so the Thrusts after they are given may be the more easily discovered, and Booked without any Debate, and which ought alwise to be done by the Judges after every Thrust; neither should any be allowed to Play against any more than One in a Day; because after the first Assault a Man's Vigour is spent, and being to Play for a Prize, it were most unreasonable, to oblige him to Play against any other Fresh Person that Day: As for the Number of Thrusts to be Play'd for, see the Eighth Law for Weekly Assaulting.

VIII.
No Thrusts should be allowed nor accounted as fair, which are not given in the Trunk of the Body; that is, Betwixt the Neck and Headband of the Drawers as to its Length, and betwixt the two Shoulders as to its Breadth.

IX.
All Enclosing and Commanding ought to be discharged in Playing for either a Bet or a Prize; because, however, useful they may be at Sharps, yet upon this Occasion, the frequent use of them, would take away the whole Grace, Neatness, and Pleasure of the Play: But the use of the Left-hand is to be allowed, because it may so fall out, that some forward Ignorants, or Ramblers, may Lift themselves to Play for the Prize, out of no other Design, but to bring a Slurr upon the Art, by endeavouring if possible, to Baffle any of the Artists, upon which very Account, were there no other, the Parieing with the Left-hand is to be allowed. And in case of *Contre-temps* or Exchanged Thrusts, the Eleventh Law for Weekly Assaulting, is to be observed.

X.
Each Person being to Play against every one, it will take as many Days for Playing for the Prize, and before the Victory can be Decided in any one's Favours, as there are Persons Listed, save one; because each being to make but one Assault in a day, according to the Seventh Law, it will take so much time before it go through them all; And whoever after the Last days Assaulting shall be found by the Account in the Book, to have Beat maniest, shall be declared by the Judges to have gain'd the Prize, to whom it is to be Delivered by them, passing what Compliment upon him they shall think fit.

I have only given this Scheme of Laws to be observed in Fencing Schools as a Model, whereby Masters may more easily regulate themselves in their Weekly Assaulting Days, or when a Prize is to be Played for; and not as an Unalterable Form, wherein no Rectifications can or ought to be made. Therefore, notwithstanding of what I have here offered, it is left to every Master to Rescind or Add, as he shall judge it most proper and convenient; although I must say, that I have endeavoured to set down none, but what I thought most Material, and in a Manner absolutely Needful.

POSTSCRIPT.

*T*he following letter being transmitted to me, upon printing this last sheet of the contents, from a Professor of the Art, who hath a very good taste and judgement in matters relating to *True Fencing*; and who had perused the single sheets as they were printed; I judged that I could not better supply this vacancy in the end of it, than by publishing in it his letter, and consequently his sentiment of this *New Method of Fencing*; and which I own I did the more willingly, because it is so apposite to the subject matter and design of my book, and also ingeniously enough pen'd.

If any shall fancy, that I have caused to print this letter, as well as those few verses that are at the beginning of this piece, out of mere ostentation and vanity; I shall only say, that such persons are very little acquainted with either my inclinations or temper: However, seeing I have been long ago sensible, that it is as impossible for any author to stop all people's mouths, as it is for him to satisfy and convince all men's judgments; so since ever I attempted to offer my service to the publick in this manner, I have firmly resolved (especially being conscious of my own sincerity and innocence) to stand proof, against all such censorious and cavilling assaults whatsoever: Besides, I am of opinion, that *Honoris argumentum, non Levitate & Blandiloquentia, sed Opere & Labore acquirendum est.* Follows the letter.

To the much Honoured,
Sir William Hope of Balcomie, *Baronet.*

SIR,

As he who commends what is but poorly done upon any subject, ranks his own judgement with the author's. But, when he sincerely approves, of what must inevitably gain the esteem and applause of all wise men, proclaims, in a manner, not only his own skill, but pays also a just compliment to the performer; so it is to be supposed he must understand good reasoning, and the Sword too, who is not only charmed with so great a performance, but is also capable of giving his opinion to the purpose, of your *New and Easy Method of Fencing from the Hanging Guard in Seconde.*

For my own part, tho' by what I have said, I seem to flatter my self when I justly commend my best friend, I dare confidently affirm, that he who seriously reads this book, and is not in love with the Art, as you have improv'd it, hath something so very heavy and dull in his temper, that (like the fellow in the *Turkish Spy*, who had never been in love) he deserves to be delivered by the ears, to any man who has lost his ass.

I have long taught the Science of Defence; and I may justly term it so, for your labours prove it really such: The close practice if it hath been chiefly my part; its nicest theory and that too your's; and if at any time during my leisure hours, I studied improvements, for the credit and reputation of my employment, and the benefit of my Scholars; yet by having the honour to reason with you upon the matter, my coarser notions were still refin'd, and I came away, determined to follow those rules I had propos'd to myself confirm'd more by your solid arguments and approbation, than by the chain of conveniencies and inconveniencies, which I had believed I had forseen.

There have been but few pieces of any note publish'd, for near two hundred years, upon the Art of Fencing, but what I have read; most books of that kind, and which are in any repute, being either written or translated into English, some of them at my own charges, and for my own use: But if all of them were rob'd of their particular beauties, and they crowded into one piece, it would be found to fall so far short of what you now impart to the world, as the ordinary homilies of a weak country vicar, compared with the most elaborate discourses of the greatest English divine.

The Small Sword or Rapier, was formerly confin'd to too narrow bounds; 'twas judged only proper to engage a weapon of its own size and strength; but you have after a most convincing manner undeceived the world, and turn'd it loose, to stand and maintain its ground, both a-foot and on horseback, against the strongest and most bloody weapons, such as Sheering Sword, Sabre, Battel-Ax, &c. Arms it durst never encounter with until now, without a too visible disadvantage; all which is wholly removed, by this *New and Excellent Method* of yours; for which, everyone who reads it, and is a lover of the Art, will pay everlasting respect to your memory.

And in a more particular manner, all Fencing Masters are your debtors: You have, Sir, left us little or nothing to find out: Practice for the future will be our only task; nor can we possibly miscarry in that, when the rules and method of it, are so distinctly and pointedly express'd, that the meanest capacity (allowing him a little knowledge in the Art before) cannot fail of understanding to defend by it, at once, what is dearest to mankind; LIFE and HONOUR. If my letter be too long, impute it to gratitude, (which when real is not ty'd to common forms) not only for your New and Great Discoveries in the Art of the Sword, but also for the many favours conferred upon,

Sir,

Your most obliged and most humble servant,
WILL MACHRIE.[23]

Edinburgh, 28. August 1707.

---

[23] William Machrie, Fencing Master, Judge and Arbitrator of all who make any publick Trial of Skill in the Noble Art of the SWORD, within the Kindom [sic] of SCOTLAND. Hope, William, *The Sword-Man's Vade-Mecum*, Edinburgh, 1691, p. 8.

Glossary

Assault	To engage in a fencing bout in the salle d'armes.
Avolt	Volte. "An action that carries the body to the right or left by pivoting on the right foot." Gaugler, 58.
Back Sword	A stout, single-edged sword with a basket or cage hilt.
Batter	To strike with the edge and foible of one's sword upon the foible and edge of the opponent's sword.
Blunts	Dull practice swords; foils.
Boar, Boer, Boor, Bouer	A Dutch peasant.
Broad Sword	A stout, two-edged sword with a basket or cage hilt.
Buckler	A small round shield, held in the left hand.
Caveating	Disengaging.
Change	Disengage. "…which is Changing his point from one side of your blade to the other, and under your blade…" McBane, General Directions.
Contre-caveating	Counter-disengaging.
Contre-temps	A thrust that counters an attack; a double or exchanged thrust.
Descrive	Describe.
Dragoon	"European mounted soldier of the 16th and 17th centuries who could fight as a light cavalryman or as an infantryman. Named after the muzzle-loading carbine called the dragoon that they carried, they were originally used as an arm of the infantry, being organized in companies, and their officers bore infantry titles. By the 18th century most light cavalrymen were called dragoons (or carabiniers)." *The Macmillan Encyclopedia*, 2000.
Elonge	Lunge.
Evite	Shun.
Falchion	A short, curved, single-edged sword with a clipped point. Used by British prize fighters.
Fascines	Bundles of branches used to fill in ditches, so soldiers may pass over them.
Field	The field of battle or combat; the duelling ground.
Fleuret	Literally, *little flower*. The French word for a foil, the practice weapon for the Small Sword.
Foil	The blunt practice weapon for the Small Sword.
Grenade	A pomegranate-sized (hence the name) cast-iron ball filled with gunpowder and metal shrapnel, ignited with a fuse, and thrown at the enemy.
Grenadeer, grenadier	Elite assault soldier, armed with a slung musket, sword, and grenades. The grenadier was a fearsome component of 17th, 18th, and early 19th century armies.
Halberd	A polearm with a large ax head, and spikes on the top and rear.
Hanging Guard	A sword guard formed by carrying the hand above the head, with the blade sloping downwards.
Ignorants	People with no knowledge of the art of fencing.
Jacque	Jack. To Play the knave, to do a mean trick.
Lesson	"This word is often applied to a definite attack, or botte." Castle, 273, n. 2.
Lochaber Ax	A Highland polearm with a large, long ax-head.
Master	An expert who trains men in the use of the sword.
Occasion	An affair of honour; a duel.
Open	An opening, or exposed target, on one's person or the person of one's adversary.
Parade	The French word for *parry*, a defensive, deflecting action of the sword.

Pike	A heavy wooden spear, about fifteen to eighteen feet long, with a sharp metal head. Used in bristling formations of organized pikemen.
Pistole	A French coin, worth 16 shillings, or 4/5 of a Louis d'Or.
Pole-ax, pollaxe	A pole-arm of approximately six feet in length, with an axe or hammer head, often with sharp spikes on top and rear.
Pursuit	An attack
Push	To thrust.
Push at the wall	"After having lunged for some days on the cushion, to fix the wrist and body a little, you must push at a Scholar, who being placed at the wall will parry your thrusts…" L'Abbat/Mahon, 111.
Push on the floor	To practice fencing on the floor of the fencing salle, having license to move forward and back.
Quarter	Mercy. Exemption from being immediately put to death, granted to a vanquished opponent by the victor in a battle or fight; clemency or mercy shown in sparing the life of one who surrenders.
Quarter Staff	A staff, typically seven to nine feet in length.
Rencounter	A hostile meeting or encounter between two adversaries; a duel; sometimes distinguished from a regular duel by being unpremeditated.
Renverse	To overturn or overthrow; to bring to confusion.
Round Parade	The circular parry.
Scholar	A student studying under a fencing Master.
Sharps	Real, sharp swords.
Shearing or Sheering Sword	The Spadroon. "Because for a general and close engagement, better swords there cannot possibly be than those kind of stiff, well-edged Sheering Swords, of a moderate length, and with good, close, or as they are more commonly termed by the vulgar, Shell or Sheep-head hilts." Hope, Chapter V.
Shell	Descriptive of the guard of a Small Sword or Fleuret, and of some Rapiers and Spadroons.
Slip	To evade or escape an attack.
Small Sword	The dress sword worn by European gentlemen of the late 17th, 18th, and early 19th centuries. The hilt typically consisted of a knucklebow, short quillons, small annelets (the vestigial finger rings of the rapier) and a small double shell guard. The blade was typically of a hollow-ground triangular profile, with a wickedly sharp needle point.
Spadroon	A two-edged military sword, lighter than a broad sword, made to both cut and thrust. A spadroon may have a simple cross hilt, or a shell-guard and knuckle-bow, like a small sword or rapier.
St. George Guard	A high guard, in which the sword arm is held above the head, and the blade angles slightly forward. It arises naturally from the hanging guard. It takes its name from the depictions of St. George slaying the dragon. St. George is, of course, the patron Saint of England.
Targe	The round Highland shield, made of layers of wood, and covered with hide and brass studs. Many targes also had a protruding central spike.
Throng	Crowded; busy.
Traverse	A step to either side. McBane may use "traverse" to mean a diagonal step, as well.
Tristed	An obsolete spelling for "trysted;" to be involved or engaged with.
Ventorious	Characterized by venturesomeness.
Within the sword	The area, opening, or target presented to the left of the sword arm.
Without the sword	The area, opening, or target presented to the right of the sword arm.

Bibliography

& Recommended Reading

Arnold, Thomas, *The Renaissance at War*. Cassell & Co., London, 2001.

Brown, Terry, *English Martial Arts*. Anglo-Saxon Books, Hockwold-cum-Wilton, 1997.

Castle, Egerton, *Schools and Masters of Fence*. George Bell & Sons, London, 1892.

Chandler, David, *Military Memoires of Marlborough's Campaigns*. Greenhill Books, London, 1998. [The first-hand accounts of McBane contemporaries Capt. Robert Parker, Royal Irish, and Comte de Mèrode-Waterloo.]

Churchill, Winston, *Marlborough, His Life and Times*. 6 v. Charles Scribner's Sons, New York, 1935.

Conrad, Barnaby, *The Martini*. Chronicle Books, San Francisco, 1995.

Daiches, David, *The Last Stuart*. G.P. Putnam's Sons, New York, 1973.

Duffy, Christopher, *Siege Warfare: The Fortress in the Early Modern World, 1494-1660*. Barnes and Noble, New York, 1996.

Durant, Will and Ariel, *The Story of Civilization: The Age of Louis XIV*. Simon and Schuster, New York, 1963.

Eyre-Todd, George, *The Highland Clans of Scotland*. D. Appleton & Company, New York, 1923.

Gaugler, William, *A Dictionary of Universally used Fencing Terminology*. Laureate Press, Bangor, 1997.

Grimble, Ian, *Clans & Chiefs*. Birlinn Limited, Edinburgh, 2000.

Henderson, Diana, *The Scottish Regiments*. Harper Collins, Glasgow, 1996.

Hogg, Ian, *The History of Fortification*. St. Martin's Press, New York, 1981.

Hope, William, *A Vindication of the True Art of Self-Defence*. William Brown and Company, Edinburgh, 1724.

Hope, William, *Scots Fencing Master*. John Reid, Edinburgh, 1687.

Hope, William, *The Fencing Master's Advice to his Scholar*. John Reid, Edinburgh, 1692.

Hope, William, *The Sword-Man's Vade-Mecum*. John Reid, Edinburgh, 1691.

Hutton, Alfred, *The Sword and the Centuries*. Barnes & Noble Books, New York, 1995.

Innes of Learney, Sir Thomas, *The Tartans of the Clans and Families of Scotland*. Johnston and Bacon, Edinburgh, 1975.

L'Abbat (translated by Andrew Mahon), *The Art of Fencing*. James Hoey, Dublin, 1734.

Lang, Andrew, *A History of Scotland*, v. 3. Dodd, Mead, and Co., New York, 1904.

Maclean, Fitzroy, *Scotland, a Concise History*. Thames and Hudson Limited, London, 1993.

McIan, R.R., *The Clans of the Scottish Highlands*. Alfred A. Knopf, New York, 1980 (originally published in 1845).

Pepys, Samuel, *The Diary of Samuel Pepys*. University of California Press, Berkeley, 1974.

Petrie, Sir Charles, *The Jacobite Movement*. Eyre and Spottiswode, London, 1959.

Reid, Stuart, *1745 A Military History of the Last Jacobite Rising*. Sarpedon, New York, 1996.

Chivalry Bookshelf

Medieval History - Reenactment - Western Martial Arts - Arms & Armour

Over the last ten years there has been a resurgence of interest in Western heritage as expressed through medieval culture and "chivalric" martial arts.

Chivalry Bookshelf has been established to serve this vibrant community, working both to disseminate quality information and to increase community membership by producing works that serve the interested novice as well as the expert.

Comprised of individuals who have been instrumental in building the resurgence and featuring the authors who continue to grow interest based on their scholarship, practical experience and passion, we hope to produce works of enduring quality.

Consisting both of reprinted works of import and new translations, studies and instructional manuals, books are selected on the basis of their importance both in history and to the study of European martial culture.

For students of the European or Western Martial Arts, Chivalry Bookshelf has lined up an impressive array of primary translations and reprints backed up by interpretations from today's most influential teachers. Hardcover editions of such puissant masters as Sigmund Ringeck, Fillipo Vadi, and Fiore de Liberi are supported by "how to" study guides from Bob Charron, Saint Martins Academy; Greg Mele of the Chicago Swordplay Guild; William Wilson of the Tattershall School of Defence.

For students of Arms & Armour, we have several exciting projects in the works; our quality reprint of Bengt Thordeman's Armour from the Battle of Wisby is but the first of several important titles.

Whatever your interest in Western martial culture, we cordially invite you to peruse our titles through the website and to take the first step into a rich world of swordsmanship, tournaments and Medieval - Renaissance history.

Secrets of German Medieval Swordsmanship: *Sigmund Ringeck's Commentaries on Johannes Liechtenauer's Verse*
Christian Henry Tobler
ISBN: 1-891448-07-2
400pp., 700+ photographs, hardcover
$49.95 (January, 2002)

Armour from the Battle of Wisby
Two volumes in One
Bengt Thordeman
ISBN: 1-891448-05-6
654pp, 1052 photographs
$99.95

ARTE GLADIATORIA: *15th century Swordsmanship of the Italian Master Fillipo Vadi*
Translated by Luca Porzio
ISBN: 1-891448-16-1
166pp., 78 full color plates, hardcover

Chivalrous Conqueror
Biography of the Black Prince by Chandos Herald
ISBN: 1-891448-04-8
(forthcoming, Spring 2002)

Arte of Defence:
A Practical Guide to the Study of the Rapier
William Wilson
~248pp, illustrated. (forthcoming, Summer 2002)
ISBN: 1-891448-18-8

Italian Medieval Swordsmanship:
Fiore de Liberi's Flos Duellatorum
In Two Volumes, Translated & Interpreted by Bob Charron
ISBN: (Vol. 1): 1-891448-06-4
ISBN: (Vol. 1I): 1-891448-13-7

Available through Fine Booksellers or on the Web

http://www.chivalrybookshelf.com
Toll Free (866)-268-1495

Highland Broadsword

Mark Rector
Paul Wagner

Scots wae hae wi Wallace bled,
Scots wham Bruce has aften led,
Welcome tae yer gory bed
or tae victorie!

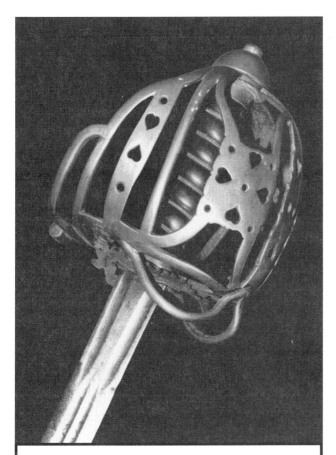

While the use of the broadsword, shield, and longsword died out as lighter weapons were introduced, the Highland Scot continued to practice the use of the Highland Claymore, Dirk & Targe into the early 19th century.

In this follow-on work to *Highland Swordsmanship*, authors Mark Rector and Paul Wagner have collaborated to present four fascinating manuals.

Lay the proud usurpers low!
Tyrants fall in every foe!
Liberty's in every blow!
Let us do, or die!

Lunge from the hanging Guard, the Parry with the left hand